How Chiefs Became Kings

Feathered image *(kiʻi hulu manu)* of the war god Kū, collected during the third voyage of Captain James Cook, and now in the Institut für Ethnologie der Georg-August-Universität. (Credit: Eigenes Werk, Creative Commons license CC-BY-AA.)

How Chiefs Became Kings

Divine Kingship and the Rise of Archaic States in Ancient Hawai'i

Patrick Vinton Kirch

UNIVERSITY OF CALIFORNIA PRESS

University of California Press, one of the most distinguished university presses in the United States, enriches lives around the world by advancing scholarship in the humanities, social sciences, and natural sciences. Its activities are supported by the UC Press Foundation and by philanthropic contributions from individuals and institutions. For more information, visit www.ucpress.edu.

University of California Press
Oakland, California

© 2010 by Patrick Vinton Kirch

First paperback printing 2019

Library of Congress Cataloging-in-Publication Data

Kirch, Patrick Vinton.
  How chiefs became kings : divine kingship and the rise of archaic states in ancient Hawai'i / Patrick Vinton Kirch.
    p. cm.
  Includes bibliographical references and index.
  ISBN 978-0-520-26725-1 (cloth : alk. paper);
978-0-520-30339-3 (pbk. : alk. paper)
  1. Chiefdoms--Hawaii—History. 2. Hawaiians—Kings and rulers. 3. First contact of aboriginal peoples with Westerners—Hawaii. 4. Hawaiians—Politics and government. I. Title.

GN671.H3K57 2010
320.4969—DC22
                        2010006346

Cover illustration: A Hawaiian chief, tattooed and wearing a feathered cloak and helmet. Drawn by artist Jacques Arago during the 1819 visit to Hawai'i of Louis de Freycinet on the *Uranie*. Courtesy of the Bancroft Library, University of California, Berkeley.

*Dedicated to the Legacy of
Three Unrivaled Nineteenth Century
Native Hawaiian Scholars:
John Papa ʻĪʻī
Samuel Mānaiakalani Kamakau
David Malo*

Contents

Preface ix

1. From Chiefdom to Archaic State: Hawai'i in
   Comparative and Historical Context 1
   What Are Archaic States?
   Theories of Primary State Formation
   Hawai'i as a Model System for State Emergence
   Marshall Sahlins's Challenge
   A Phylogenetic Model for Polynesian
   Cultural Evolution
   The Nature of Ancestral Polynesian Society
   How Did Contact-Era Hawai'i Differ from
   Ancestral Polynesia?
   Was Hawai'i Unique in Polynesia?

2. Hawaiian Archaic States on the Eve of
   European Contact 29
   Sources for Reconstructing Contact-Era Hawai'i
   Hawaiian Polities: Size and Scale
   Class Stratification and Divine Kingship
   Elite Art, Craft Specialization, and Wealth Finance
   Political, Administrative, and Settlement Hierarchies
   Systems of Production
   The Hierarchy of Priests and Temples

The State Cults and the Ritual Cycle
Land and Labor
War
Summary

3. Native Hawaiian Political History — 77
   Genealogies of Renown, Traditions of Power
   Founding Traditions of Settlement and Voyaging
   Political Developments of the Fifteenth to Mid-sixteenth Centuries
   Usurpation and Political Consolidation in the Hawai'i and Maui Kingdoms
   Dynastic Histories of the Seventeenth to Eighteenth Centuries
   Political Developments of the Contact Era
   Agency in History: *Ali'i* Routes to Power

4. Tracking the Transformations: Population, Intensification, and Monumentality — 125
   The Hawaiian Cultural Sequence
   Population and Demographic Trends
   Contrastive Agroecosystems
   Temporal Pathways of Intensification
   Marine Resources and Aquaculture
   Monumentality and the Temple System
   Royal Centers and Elite Residence Patterns
   When Did the Hawaiian Archaic States Emerge?

5. The Challenge of Explanation — 177
   Previous Explanations for Hawaiian Cultural Change
   Ultimate Causation: Population, Intensification, and Surplus
   Proximate Causation: Status Rivalry, Alliance, and Conquest
   Why Did Archaic States Emerge First on Hawai'i and Maui?
   Hawai'i and Archaic State Emergence

Notes — 223

Glossary of Hawaiian Terms — 239

References — 243

Index — 267

Preface

Four decades of field research, thinking, and writing about the Hawaiian Islands and their unique variant of Polynesian culture lie behind this book. When I first entered the field of Hawaiian archaeology, in the late 1960s, Hawai'i was regarded as the most complex of the Polynesian chiefdoms; indeed, ethnohistoric accounts of Hawai'i influenced thinking within the New Archaeology about the very nature of chiefdom societies. Everyone who has tackled the Hawaiian case—whether from ethnographic or archaeological perspectives—recognizes that Hawai'i stands apart in certain respects from its Polynesian sister societies. Nonetheless, I only gradually came to the conclusion that these differences were not merely *quantitative*, in the sense of more intensive production, greater stratification, or more elaboration of material symbols of elite status, along a Polynesian continuum. In addition, Hawaiian society at the moment of contact with the West was *qualitatively* distinctive from other Polynesian groups. The very structure and fabric of society had diverged significantly from that typical elsewhere in Polynesia, most especially in the ways that the control over land and production had been divorced from the kinship system. Thus, instead of sitting at the apex of a "conical clan," which ramified downward to incorporate the entire society, the hereditary *ali'i* (elites) of Hawai'i had become a separate, endogamous class. The highest *ali'i* claimed descent from the gods; indeed, they claimed to be *ali'i akua*, "god-kings." As in other parts of the ancient world, the Hawaiians had invented divine kingship, a hallmark of archaic states.

In the nineteenth century, Hawaiian elites took on the trappings of European monarchy, and Hawai'i remained an independent Kingdom until the last queen, Lili'uokalani, was overthrown by a mob of pro-American businessmen in 1893. But as I shall argue in this book, Hawai'i knew kingship well enough long before hearing of King George (whom the famous Kamehameha I regarded as his "brother") and other European rulers. How, when, and why did this particular Polynesian society transform itself from a classic chiefship—in which society is fundamentally organized by principles of kinship, the so-called "conical clan"—to a society with endogamous classes, in which the ruling elites claimed kinship with the gods, and forbade those they ruled over from even keeping genealogies? These are questions that go to the core of comparative cultural evolution, and answering them requires a broad-based research strategy, capable of integrating multiple lines of evidence. Such a research strategy was outlined nearly a century ago by one of the pioneers of the Americanist school of holistic anthropology, Edward Sapir, who, along with Alfred Kroeber, realized the analytical power of combining the methods and data of linguistics, archaeology, ethnohistory, and comparative ethnography. The late Roger Green and I have similarly argued that *historical anthropology* should renew its commitment to Sapir's multidisciplinary strategy (Kirch and Green 2001:1–9). Elsewhere, we have endeavored to show how multipronged research that does not hesitate to join archaeology to linguistics, and which draws on the advantages of the "direct historical approach," can open up the world of Ancestral Polynesia in ways not accessible to a single discipline. This book continues the application of a Sapirian historical anthropology, applied here to the late precontact Hawaiian archaic states.

This book began, in a concrete sense, with an invitation to deliver a keynote address to the Association for Social Anthropology in Oceania (ASAO), in Vancouver, B.C., in February 2000. By then I had begun to crystallize my thoughts about Hawaiian archaic states, and used the opportunity to address what I call "Marshall Sahlins's Challenge" (see Chapter 1). Among those attending the Vancouver conference was Professor Maurice Godelier, who invited me to visit his seminar at the École des Hautes Études en Sciences Sociales in Paris as a Professor Invité. In May 2002, I presented a revised version of my Hawaiian thesis, both to Godelier's seminar, and later to the CREDO research group based in Marseille. The lively intellectual feedback I received in Paris and Marseille, from Maurice Godelier, Jonathan Friedman, Pierre Lemonnier,

Serge Tcherkézoff, and others helped me to work through some of the critical issues in my arguments.

Around the same time, I launched a major new field project, the Hawai'i Biocomplexity Project, with a multidisciplinary team involving ecologists, soil scientists, and demographic modelers (Kirch et al. 2007). As the stimulating results of this project began to accumulate, I received in 2005 an invitation from Joel Janetski of Brigham Young University, to deliver the endowed Grace Elizabeth Shallit Memorial Lecture. The Shallit Lecture offered an opportunity to synthesize my rapidly evolving ideas on the emergence of Hawaiian divine kingship and archaic states, and resulted in a short published paper (Kirch 2005), which in turn became the basis for this book.

Drawing on more than four decades of research—and the myriad and often complex collegial relationships such work entails—it is difficult to single out just a few colleagues and collaborators for acknowledgment. Many, many people have aided me over this long period, whether by sharing original data, through lively discussion of ideas, by working together on field teams, or in other ways. But I would like to thank in particular a few key individuals whose influence has been especially profound. I begin with Douglas Yen and Roger Green, who in the late 1960s were both staff members of the Bernice P. Bishop Museum in Honolulu, and who took this young student into their confidence and gave me incredible opportunities for research both in Hawai'i and elsewhere in the Pacific. Both continued over the years as close friends and mentors; I deeply regret that Roger passed away as this book was in final draft, and that I will not benefit from his reactions to my arguments. Second, I thank Marshall Sahlins, who invited me to collaborate in his Hawaiian ethnohistoric research in 1974, leading to our joint project in the Anahulu Valley in the early 1980s. Marshall's encyclopedic knowledge of Hawaiian ethnohistory—gained in part from his deep knowledge of the Kingdom's archives—has been an endless inspiration. Third, the late Charles Pili Keau, a *kupuna* and *kupa o ka 'āina* of Wailuku, Maui, was a friend and a colleague for many years, and shared with me his profound knowledge of Hawaiian cultural traditions.

I would also like to thank a number of colleagues and collaborators who have worked with me, or in parallel with me, over the years in the field of Hawaiian archaeology. Robert Hommon, Ross Cordy, Jeff Clark, Tom Dye, Eric Komori, Paul Cleghorn, Holly McEldowney, Toni Han, Elaine Jourdane, Martha Yent, Steve Athens, Paul Rosendahl, Marshall Weisler, Jane Allen, Matt Spriggs, Tim Earle, Alan Carpenter,

Boyd Dixon, Michael Kolb, Peter Mills, Melinda Allen, Mark McCoy and others have collectively made huge contributions to our knowledge of the Hawaiian precontact past. That I am able to write this book at all is in large part a testament to the collective accomplishments of this generation of archaeologists. I would also like to single out my collaborators on the Hawai'i Biocomplexity Project, which has been ongoing since 2001: Peter Vitousek, Oliver Chadwick, Shripad Tuljapurkar, Michael Graves, Thegn Ladefoged, Charlotte Lee, Tony Hartshorn, Julie Field, and Sara Hotchkiss. They have taught me more about soil nutrient capacities and demographic modeling (among other things) than I ever thought I would care to know, but in the process have reaffirmed for me the incredible power of multidisciplinary research.

I would be remiss not to acknowledge the tangible monetary support of my major research sponsor over the years, the U. S. National Science Foundation. A succession of grants from the NSF Archaeology, Biocomplexity, and Human Social Dynamics programs has enabled my field and laboratory investigations of Hawaiian precontact history and ecodynamics. I especially thank Archaeology Program Director John Yellen for his advice and efficient administration of my grants over the years. In Hawai'i, I have also been aided by professionals of the State Historic Preservation Division, the Department of Hawaiian Home Lands, and the Department of Land and Natural Resources, all of whom assisted with permissions and access to research sites. To all of these individuals and agencies, *mahalo nui loa*.

Finally, I would like to thank those colleagues and friends who have directly assisted in the editing and production of this book. Blake Edgar, my editor at the University of California Press has been an enthusiastic supporter of the project and has patiently kept me on track. Matthew Spriggs and David Burley provided positively critical reviews of the manuscript. I am especially grateful to Marshall Sahlins for carefully reading the draft and for making extensive comments, especially on the ethnographic portions. My wife, Thérèse Babineau, has been a constant source of support and encouragement, and also provided several of the photographs of archaeological sites in this book. David Cohen made the maps of O'ahu, Maui, and Hawai'i Islands.

Quinta Pacifica
November 2009

CHAPTER I

From Chiefdom to Archaic State: Hawai'i in Comparative and Historical Context

Polynesian social evolution reached its greatest development in the Hawaiian Islands, where all changes in direction or further elaborations of traditional forms under way elsewhere finally came to fruition.

Goldman (1970:200)

Kingship implies that politics is a cosmological affair as much as cosmology is a political reality.

Valeri (1985b:92)

For more than nine-tenths of our history as a distinct species, we humans organized ourselves exclusively in small social units, in which social distinctions were dictated largely—if not indeed exclusively—by age and gender. Then, during the early Holocene, with the domestication of plants and animals, and the creation of agriculturally based economies and the population growth this spurred, we embarked on a series of experiments in social organization, with new kinds of status positions, including heritable rank. By around five thousand years ago in Mesopotamia and Egypt, slightly later in China and the New World (specifically in Mesoamerica and the Andes), these experiments in large-scale social organization led to the emergence of what have been called "archaic states." Such sociopolitical structures took slightly different forms in different places, but they all shared several criterial characteristics, including class-endogamous social strata, typically organized into at least three and often four administrative levels, with divine kings at their apices (Feinman and Marcus 1998). Just how such archaic states developed, and the causal factors and dynamics responsible for these changes, continue to pose major research issues for anthropological archaeology.

Isolated in the central North Pacific, thousands of kilometers from any other land or peoples, and discovered and settled by humans only very late on the stage of world history, the Hawaiian Islands might seem to have little relevance to this major anthropological problem. Indeed, while Hawai'i has contributed its share to anthropological theory, its indigenous society has most often been classified as a chiefdom—perhaps the most complex chiefdom ever documented (Earle 1997:34; Johnson and Earle 2000)—but not as a state. One aim of this book is to overturn such received anthropological wisdom. The thesis I advance here is that at the time of its fateful encounter with the West, late in the eighteenth century, Hawai'i consisted of three to four competing archaic states, each headed by a divine king. These unique economic, social, and political structures emerged out of an earlier, more typical Polynesian chiefdom society within the previous two to three centuries.

Nearly everywhere else in the world, archaic states first emerged long before there were detailed historical records. They were not observed in the process of formation; their existence can only be inferred from the archaeological record. But if my argument is correct, in Hawai'i we have a unique case of several emergent states that arose so late on the stage of world history that they were indeed historically observed and recorded—in the annals of Captain James Cook (AD 1778–79) and other European voyagers at the close of the eighteenth century. In fact, Hawai'i's own rich political history—encapsulated in indigenous oral traditions—offers an account of this critical period in distinctly Hawaiian cultural terms. Moreover, precisely because Hawai'i was so thoroughly isolated from the rest of the world prior to European contact, its transformation from chiefdom to archaic state cannot have been influenced by external forces. This is not a case of "secondary" state formation, but truly one in which the processes of change were wholly endogenous. Thus in Hawai'i we have an especially good opportunity to understand the conditions—whether environmental, demographic, economic, social, ideological, or, most likely, some combination of all these—that led to the emergence of primary states, along with their most salient feature, divine kingship.

I am not the first to suggest that prior to contact with Europeans, Hawai'i crossed the threshold between societies based on an ideology of kinship (chiefdoms) and societies incorporating qualitative class distinctions, the latter organized around the concept of divine kingship. Robert Hommon (1976) advanced just such an argument, while Allen (1991) did not hesitate to classify Hawaiian political organizations as archaic states. Van Bakel (1991, 1996) likewise treats contact-period Hawaiian society as a state (see also Seaton 1978). Spriggs (1988:71), pointing to the extreme isolation within which Hawaiian social change occurred, ventures that "Hawaii perhaps represents a unique ideal type, a real *'isolierte Staat.'*" Most scholars, however, taking their lead from Service (1967) who regarded Polynesia as the type region for chiefdoms in general, have preferred to place Hawai'i at the pinnacle of the "chiefdom" category (e.g., Cordy 1981; Johnson and Earle 2000; Kirch 1984; Earle 1997). Timothy Earle, for example, regards contact-period Hawai'i as "the most complex of any Polynesian chiefdoms and probably of any chiefdoms known elsewhere in the world" (1997:34). To some, the question may simply be a pointless diversion into semantics or—heaven forbid—neoevolutionary typologizing (Yoffee 2005). I take the view that if Hawaiian society did indeed change in fundamental ways late in its precontact history—so that it no longer fits comfortably within the range of sociopolitical variation evidenced elsewhere among Polynesian chiefdoms—then it offers a special historical case that may lend understanding to more general processes of social change and transformation.

Fortunately, we do not need to rely exclusively on archaeological evidence in attempting to discern whether the term "archaic state" should apply to those Hawaiian polities in existence at the moment of contact with the West, in AD 1778 to 1779. The documentary sources of Hawaiian ethnohistory are exceedingly rich, and include not only the extensive accounts of Western explorers and observers beginning with Cook, but also an array of indigenous Hawaiian oral traditions and historical narratives, many written down by Hawaiian elites in the early to late nineteenth century (e.g., Malo 1951; Kamakau 1961, 1964; see Valeri [1985a:xvii–xxviii] for an excellent discussion of these sources). Drawing on this wealth of anthropological material, in Chapter 2 I critically evaluate how Hawaiian polities compare with a set of key criteria widely regarded to be indicative of archaic states (for these, see Feinman and Marcus 1998).

In short, I will argue that Hawai'i on the eve of European contact, having crossed the qualitative divide separating one fundamental kind of human sociopolitical organization, the chiefdom, from another, the archaic state, encapsulates a history that—despite its isolation and recent time scale—has a significance larger than itself. Hawai'i offers a "model system" for how differences in rank originally dictated by kinship gave way to a durable inequality legitimated in new cosmogonic and religious ideologies, how control over the means of production passed from the domestic to political economies, and, ultimately, how chiefs became kings.

WHAT ARE ARCHAIC STATES?

Before going further, it is probably a good idea to set out what is meant by the term "archaic state." What are the criterial features of an archaic state, and how do these differ from the classic characteristics of chiefdoms? First, I must stress that the particular definition of "archaic state" used here refers to *primary* states that emerged directly out of less complex social formations. By "primary" state we mean a political formation that developed through endogenous processes, and not in response to interactions with an external state or states; these latter are referred to as *secondary* states. There are numerous historically and ethnographically described secondary states (one thinks, for example, of the Buganda and other Nilotic kingdoms, or of the Shan states of highland Burma), but these do not meet the definition of an archaic state as used here. Indeed, because the term *archaic state* as I use it refers exclusively to primary states, it is an archaeological construct. Archaic states have never been studied by ethnographers; they are known only from the archaeological record—except, as I argue in this book, for the case of Hawai'i at the moment of European contact.

Definitions of the "state" in general have a long and tortuous history, tracing back to the classical philosophers and continuing with social theorists such as Hobbes, Rousseau, Morgan, Marx, and Spencer. Morgan (1877) may have been the first to consider the state in a "modern" social science context. Service's influential book (1975; see also Haas 1982; Wright 1977) pointed to the difficulty that archaeologists frequently face in deciding whether a particular phase in a prehistoric sequence should be classified as a "chiefdom" or a "state" (1975:304). Indeed, since early states are regarded as having frequently developed out of "ranked societies" (Fried 1967) or "chiefdoms" (Carneiro 1981), the very fact that we are dealing with continual processes of change, with an evolutionary continuum, makes such broad unilineal classifications problematic (Crumley 1987; Yoffee 2005). And yet, at the same time, most archaeologists would tacitly acknowledge that states were in certain fundamental ways different from chiefdoms or ranked societies.

In this book, I follow the position outlined by Marcus and Feinman (1998) in their important edited volume *Archaic States*. They note that all of the participants in their advanced seminar did not agree on a uniform definition, but that there was general consensus on a few key criteria. To quote them:

> [I]n contrast to modern nation states, archaic states were societies with (minimally) two class-endogamous strata (a professional ruling class and a commoner class) and a government that was both highly centralized and internally specialized. Ancient states were regarded as having more power than the rank societies that preceded them, particularly in the areas of waging war, exacting tribute, controlling information, drafting soldiers, and regulating manpower and labor. . . . For some well-known states where texts are available, one could add to this stipulation that archaic states were ruled by kings rather than chiefs, had standardized temples implying a state religion, had full-time priests rather than shamans or part-time priests, and could hold on to conquered territory in ways no rank society could. (Marcus and Feinman 1998:4–5)

As I demonstrate in Chapter 2, this definition could have been written explicitly for contact-era Hawai'i. While some scholars (e.g., Service 1967, 1975) have emphasized the importance of a monopoly of force in defining state power, it seems to me that the emergence of *divine kingship* is equally critical, as suggested by Marcus and Feinman. While chiefs may enjoy a special relationship with the gods, they are not descended from gods. Early kings, on the other hand, were "often deified, or allowed to flirt with notions of human deification" (Possehl 1998:264). Possehl goes on to elaborate:

> The political form we have come to call the archaic state has a strong focus on kingship, or centralized leadership, that is in all likelihood given to the aggrandizement of the individuals who rise to this office. The economies of states tend to be centralized, heavily (not exclusively) controlled from the office of the king, so that it can effectively serve the diplomatic and military needs of the political apparatus. This implies a staff of functionaries (a bureaucracy) to implement and monitor the economic decision making, as well as to collect revenue and produce for the use of the center. (1998:264)

In addition to such important qualitative characteristics of states, the latter are also generally regarded as having important quantitative differences that set them apart from chiefdoms, especially with respect to the sizes of governed populations, and to territorial scale. Feinman

(1998) discusses these matters, noting disagreements among scholars. For example, some have suggested that the upper population limit for chiefdoms is around 10,000 (Sanders and Price 1968:85; Upham 1987:355–56), whereas others put that bound closer to 50,000 (Baker and Sanders 1972:163). Feinman draws attention to research showing that when societies reach and surpass the "magic number" of 2,500, it is no longer possible for information to be shared by all members of the society (1998:108). As a consequence, "all societies with communities greater than that size had at least two levels of decision making." Renfrew (1986) proposed that early state modules typically controlled about 1,500 km^2 of territory, although we also know that many archaic states controlled substantially larger areas.

In this book I take the following to be essential characteristics of archaic states: (1) they exhibit well-developed class endogamy; (2) they were ruled by kings who typically traced their origins directly to the gods, and who were often regarded as instantiations of deities on Earth; (3) their political economies were to a large degree centrally controlled by the king's bureaucracy; (4) the king's status and power were legitimated by state cults involving a formalized temple system, overseen by full-time priests; (5) the king's power was maintained by a monopoly of force, involving a full-time warrior cadre or standing army; and (6) the king and his court occupied special residential quarters (palaces), and enjoyed various privileges and material luxuries supplied by a cadre of full-time specialists and craftspersons. As I demonstrate in Chapter 2, all of these criteria are amply fulfilled by the Hawaiian polities ethnohistorically known at the moment of first contact with Captain Cook's 1778 to 1779 expedition, and on into the early decades of interaction with the West.

THEORIES OF PRIMARY STATE FORMATION

It is not my aim to criticize or evaluate prior theories of primary state formation, which now constitute a considerable body of literature; such a task would be well beyond my present scope. Haas (1982) reviewed many of the early formulations, beginning with Plato, and continuing with Hobbes, Rousseau, Morgan, Marx, and Spencer. He finds that virtually all theories, including those of more recent times, can be grouped into either "integration" or "conflict" schools of thought, depending on the author's view of the role of the state (see also Cohen 1978). By the mid-twentieth century, philosophical speculation about the role of the state, and its origins, began to be replaced by anthropological theories that were grounded in comparative ethnographic data derived from a variety of state and nonstate societies in different parts of the world. An important work that drew on comparative data from various Old World societies was Wittfogel (1957), who saw the key to state origins in the control and management of large scale irrigation works. Among the most influential of the comparative anthropologists, however, were Morton Fried (1967) and Elman Service (1967, 1975; see also Cohen and Service 1978). Haas (1982) regards Fried as a proponent of the conflict school, and Service as a champion of the integrationist position. Both anthropologists drew attention to the likely role of *chiefdoms* as the stage of stratified or ranked society from which the first primary states emerged. (For both Fried and Service, the Polynesian ethnographic literature provided the type examples for chiefdoms.) Of course, their theories were grounded in comparative ethnography, and therefore lacked any direct historical evidence for the transformation of chiefdoms into states. Another highly influential ethnographer of this time period is Carneiro (1970, 1981), who advanced a "circumscription" theory of state origins. In Carneiro's model, chiefdoms became states through conquest warfare and expansion, after reaching conditions of environmental circumscription when agricultural land became limiting.

Archaeological efforts to understand the mechanisms of state origin can be traced back to Gordon Childe (1936, 1942), who synthesized archaeological data from the Near East using a Marxian framework. But with the development of "processual" archaeology in the 1960s and 70s, the rise of sociopolitical complexity, and in particular the origins of the state, became major research themes. Heavily influenced by the writings of Fried and Service, archaeologists began to seek empirical evidence for the transformation of chiefdoms into states, especially in the Near East, the Aegean, and Mesoamerica (e.g., Adams 1966; Parsons 1974; Peebles and Kus 1977; Renfrew 1982; Sanders 1974; Sanders and Price 1968; Wright and Johnson 1975). Various causal factors began to be debated as new streams of archaeological data were generated; these included population pressure and circumscription (Carneiro 1970), warfare (Webster 1975), trade (Rathje 1972; Wright and Johnson 1975; Wright 1977), and peer-polity interaction (Renfrew 1986). One result was that unicausal or "prime mover" explanations favoring a single variable were seen to be overly simplistic, not meshing with the complexities of the archaeological record (Wright 1977). Processual archaeology thus advanced the case for evolutionary processes involving the interaction of multiple factors, often conveyed graphically in terms of systems diagrams. A classic example of the processual mode of explanation of state origins is Flannery's (1972) paper on the cultural evolution of civilizations, which applied evolutionary principles such as "promotion," "linearization," and "hypercoherence."

Inevitably, the emphasis on macroscale process led to a critique that processual archaeology had distanced itself from the real nexus of social change—the repetitive interaction between individual agents of change and the structures of everyday life. With the integration of practice theory and concepts of agency into anthropology (e.g., Bourdieu 1977; Giddens 1979; Ortner 1984), archaeological discussions of sociopolitical complexity including the origins of the state have broadened the frame of discourse (Pauketat 2001). Marcus and Flannery (1996) were among the first to meld together evolutionary ("processual") theory with what they called "action theory" (e.g., agency), in their archaeologically well-documented study of the rise of urban society in the Oaxaca Valley of Mexico (see also Flannery 1999). Recent research on the origins of states in the New World has continued to advance a productive integration of process and agency, for example in the work of Spencer (1990, 1998; Spencer and Redmond 2001, 2004) and Stanish (2001). It is within such an integrated "process-practice" theory of sociopolitical evolution that I situate my own attempt to understand the long-term evolution of Hawaiian society.

HAWAI'I AS A MODEL SYSTEM FOR STATE EMERGENCE

The value of Hawai'i for understanding fundamental processes of sociopolitical evolution stems from more than just its isolation and late timing on the stage of world history. It owes as much to the now well-established knowledge that the Polynesian societies—of which Hawai'i is just one out of 30 ethnographically attested groups—form a historically cohesive unit of cultural evolution, making them ideally suited to the anthropological tradition of "controlled comparison" (e.g., Goodenough 1957, 1997). Sahlins (1958), Goldman (1970), and other pioneers in the Polynesian field recognized that these societies were all, as Sahlins put it, "members of a single cultural genus that has filled in and adapted to a variety of local habitats" (1958:ix). More recently, application of a rigorous phylogenetic approach in historical anthropology, which combines the methods and independent data sets of historical linguistics, comparative ethnography, and archaeology, has refined our understanding of the historical relationships among the various Polynesian descendant societies (Kirch and Green 1987, 2001). This allows us not only to understand better Hawai'i's place in the broader spectrum of Polynesian societies, but to trace in quite specific ways how Hawaiian society diverged from an earlier Ancestral Polynesian society antecedent to all of the ethnographically known Polynesian groups.

In biology, as in anthropology, much analytical power comes not only from the application of controlled comparison (Kirch 2010a), but from choosing certain special cases as "model systems." Krogh (1929) proposed that for many problems in science, there is some particular species of choice on which the problem may best be studied, with the results nonetheless applying generally (see Krebs 1975). For example, the *Drosophilia* fruit flies have proved to be the animal of choice for many problems in genetics. Recently, ecologist Peter Vitousek has argued that oceanic islands—and the Hawaiian archipelago in particular—offer ideal model systems for understanding both natural ecosystem processes and human-environment interactions (Vitousek 2004). Our own joint Hawaiian Biocomplexity Project, focused on dynamically coupled natural and human systems (Vitousek et al. 2004; Kirch et al. 2004; Kirch 2007a), seeks to employ this model system concept to address the problem of how island societies "faced the challenge of making a transition from intensive, exploitative use of their island's obviously limited resources, to more sustainable use of those resources" (Vitousek 2004:23).

Hawai'i, in my view, also offers a model system for understanding a particular stage in the evolution of sociopolitical formations, the transition from chiefdoms to archaic states. Precisely because Hawaiian society crossed this critical threshold so late in world history, because it was observed and described in considerable detail, and because its archaeological record is particularly rich and increasingly well understood, Hawai'i offers an unusually clear window on the processes whereby chiefs became kings.

My argument progresses through several discrete analytical stages and, in keeping with my commitment to a holistic historical anthropology, integrates multiple lines of inquiry and independent data sets. My analytical strategy begins with comparative ethnography and linguistics, moves to ethnohistory, then to indigenous oral histories, and finally to archaeology. This kind of historical anthropology and the specific theory and methodologies that it entails have been discussed at length by Kirch and Green (2001).

I begin, in this introductory chapter, by applying a comparative ethnographic and linguistic approach to situate Hawai'i within its broader Polynesian context. A phylogenetic model is required, as well as the use of controlled linguistic analysis for key Polynesian concepts and their Hawaiian semantic values. Such analysis will show that Hawai'i does not conform to the patterns typical of other Polynesian chiefdoms, that it had been transformed into something qualitatively different by the time of contact with the West.

In Chapter 2 I turn to a rich corpus of ethnohistoric and ethnographic sources to trace the contours of the Hawaiian archaic states that were functioning at the time of first contact with the West. These sources include both Western accounts of Hawai'i at the close of the eighteenth century, and extensive Native Hawaiian writings compiled by an indigenous intelligentsia in the mid-nineteenth century. My discussion follows the major categories held to be criterial for archaic states, and tests the hypothesis that the contact-era Hawaiian polities are properly conceived of as states, rather than as chiefdoms.

Chapter 3 is the first of a pair of chapters concerned with properly historical analysis. Taking advantage of a rich corpus of indigenous Hawaiian oral traditions, set in a genealogical framework of the principal ruling dynasties, I trace the rise of the Hawaiian polities through an "insider" or emic perspective. These historical accounts provide important clues into the power strategies employed by the Hawaiian elites, including usurpation, incestuous marriage and other alliances, and conquest warfare. And, most important, situated as they are in the actions of individual persons, the traditional histories offer a perspective that privileges *agency* over long-term process.

My second historical data set, presented in Chapter 4, counterposes the emic with an etic methodology, based on archaeology. Drawing on the rich record of archaeological surveys and excavations accumulated over the past half century, I query this material evidence for major trends in demography, settlement, economic intensification, specialization, monumental architecture, and other material correlates of sociopolitical transformation. Just as the Hawaiian traditions evoke personal agency, the archaeological data sets allow one to privilege *process*, the longer-term contexts within which individual actions were situated. Extensive radiocarbon dating lends these archaeological data an "absolute" chronology of change that can be compared with the relative dating provided by the traditional genealogies.

Finally, Chapter 5 strives to meld emic and etic—and agency and process—in an explanatory model of cultural change in Hawai'i. Anthropologists realized some time ago that single "prime mover" causes (warfare, trade, or population pressure) while often important factors in the emergence of sociopolitical complexity, in and of themselves do not offer satisfactory explanations. I will argue that to understand such a complex process as the emergence of divine kingship and an archaic state mode of social formation necessitates disentangling *proximate* from *ultimate* causations. Not only were multiple causal factors at work, they operated at different spatial and temporal scales. This is the route I shall follow in attempting to understand, not merely describe, archaic state emergence in precontact Hawai'i.

MARSHALL SAHLINS'S CHALLENGE

In a classic refutation of diffusionism, Edwin G. Burrows (1938) first demonstrated that the cultural diversity exhibited within Polynesia did not require multiple migrations, but could be accounted for through endogenous processes of change. Subsequently, anthropologists came to appreciate Polynesia as a true *cultural region* (Sahlins 1958; Goldman 1970; Kirch and Green 2001). To borrow Kim Romney's phrase (1957:36), the Polynesian cultures collectively constitute a "segment of cultural history." They share a common genesis, having diverged and differentiated over time from a common ancestral culture. Most of the similarities among Polynesian cultures thus are the result of *homology*, or shared inheritance. By the same reckoning, the 30 or so ethnographically documented Polynesian cultures diverged over two and a half millennia, and cultural innovations including adaptation to differing island ecosystems have led to a fascinating range of variation within this segment of cultural history (Kirch 1984, 2000).

From this vantage point of controlled comparison, Hawai'i has always stood out as somehow special, apart, from its sibling Polynesian cultures. Sahlins (1958) enumerated many of the traits that characterized—and often uniquely distinguished—Hawaiian culture as recorded in the early decades of encounter with Europeans. Indeed, Hawai'i has been taken to represent a historical working out of the inherent possibilities of the "chiefdom type" of social formation (Service 1967). In *Stone Age Economics*, for example, Sahlins wrote that "a few of the Polynesian societies, *Hawaii particularly*, take the primitive contradiction between the domestic and public economies to an *ultimate crisis*—revealatory [sic] it seems not only of this disconformity but of the economic and political limits of kinship society" (1972:141, emphasis added). Later, in *Islands of History* (1985a), Sahlins identified a key aspect of what sets Hawai'i apart, something of the greatest possible import for understanding how a chiefdom might be transformed into an archaic state. This is the apparent sundering of the classic Polynesian structure of land-holding descent (or more properly, "ascent") groups and its replacement with a system of territorial land control.

> Hawaii is missing the segmentary polity of descent groups known to cognate Polynesian peoples: organization of the land as a pyramid of embedded lineages, with a corresponding hierarchy of ancestral cults, property rights, and chiefly titles, all based on genealogical priority within the group of common descent. Not that these concepts have left no historic traces, or even systematic functions. (Sahlins 1985a:20)

Controlled comparison allowed Sahlins to recognize just how significant this absence of the classic "segmentary polity" is for ancient Hawai'i. Yet while he alludes to "historic traces," as a comparative ethnographer dependent largely on historical and ethnographic texts it was not the *longue durée* of Hawaiian history that engaged Sahlins, but rather the "structure of the conjuncture" that was played out in the first contact between Hawai'i and the West (Sahlins 1981, 1985a). Yet the deep-time historical question of when, and how, Hawai'i became *qualitatively* distinctive among the array of Polynesian sociopolitical formations continues to lurk in the wings. For example, we cannot understand what happened in Hawaiian postcontact history without appreciating that it was the preexisting distinctiveness of Hawaiian cultural structures that "gave capitalism powers and effects unparalleled even in other Pacific societies" (Sahlins 1992:216). Thus in Volume I of *Anahulu*, Sahlins returns to the same question:

> Everything looks as if Hawaiian society had been through a history in which the concepts of lineage—of a classic Polynesian sort, organizing the relations of persons and tenure of land by seniority of descent—had latterly been eroded by the development of the chiefship. Intruding on the land and people from outside, like a foreign element, the chiefship usurps the collective rights of land control and in the process reduces the lineage order in scale, function, and coherence. *Of course, no one knows when, how, or if such a thing ever happened.* (Sahlins 1992:192, emphasis added)

That final phrase, "no one knows when, how, or if such a thing ever happened," is tempting bait to attract the archaeologist and historical anthropologist! Contrary to the view of Ohnuki-Tierney (1990:3, fn. 2), that "the *longue durée* is not easily accessible for histories of nonliterate peoples," I beg to dissent. Historical anthropology does possess the tools to trace historical transformations such as those that led to a radical transformation of the Polynesian lineage system in Hawai'i. Accessing the *longue durée* of the "peoples without history" is difficult, but not intractable. Let me briefly review how we might proceed.

If the deep-time history of Hawai'i is to be historically unraveled and dynamically understood, at least two things will be required. First, we must know—with some degree of empirical certainty—what came before. Second, we must be able to trace, with rigorous chronological controls, changes in Hawaiian sociopolitical structures. Since these "structures" are themselves ephemeral (i.e., not "material"), their transformation cannot be tracked directly, but only by means of "proxy" signals or indicators that have left material traces, sedimented in and on the Hawaiian landscape. Alternatively, we may attempt to read such structures from the indigenous Hawaiian accounts of their kings, warriors, and priests. Better yet, both kinds of proxy data on historical structures can be compared and contrasted, using one to cross-check the other.

In the remainder of this chapter, my task is to situate Hawai'i within the broader spectrum of Polynesian societies. I will do this with reference to a specific *phylogenetic model* of Polynesian cultural and social differentiation (Kirch and Green 2001). Using such a model allows the historical anthropologist to achieve two important goals: first, we can define with some precision the contours of the ancestral culture and society that were antecedent to the later, descendant cultures and societies known to us through ethnohistorical and ethnographic sources. Second, by comparing certain key characteristics of contact-era Hawaiian society (especially as these are lexically marked by distinctive terms) with the ancestral forms of those characteristics, we can gain some notion of just how far Hawai'i had diverged over the course of a thousand years of independent history.

A PHYLOGENETIC MODEL FOR POLYNESIAN CULTURAL EVOLUTION

A holistic anthropological approach to cultural history, adducing independent lines of evidence from linguistics, ethnography, human biology, and archaeology, can be traced back to Sapir (1916). But the modern formulation of a phylogenetic model for cultural evolution is owed to Romney (1957). Observing that there is no necessary correspondence among language, biology, and culture, Romney noted that when "a group of tribes" shared "a common physical type, possess[ed] common systemic patterns, and [spoke] genetically related languages" this was powerful evidence that these tribes shared "a common historical tradition at some time in the past" (1957:36). Romney called this a "segment of cultural history," and pointed out that "it includes the ancestral group and all intermediate groups, as well as the tribes in the ethnographic present." This idea of a group of historically related cultures, along with their antecedents, was taken up by Vogt (1964, 1994) who applied it to the Maya. Vogt laid out a detailed methodology for establishing such "segments of cultural history." Vogt's research strategy was later applied by Flannery and Marcus (1983) to investigate cultural divergence among the Zapotec and Mixtec populations of Mesoamerica.

Realizing the potential of this approach, Kirch and Green (1987) took up the phylogenetic model in order to trace the historical diversification of the Polynesian cultures. One of the strong advantages of Polynesia for applying a phylogenetic model lay in the significant advances that historical linguists had made in unraveling the genetic relationships among the Polynesian languages. Biggs (1967, 1971, 1998) and Pawley (1966, 1967) had used the classic "genetic comparative method" of linguistics, thereby establishing through exclusively shared patterns of phonological, lexical, and grammatical innovations, the specific branching pattern of the Polynesian linguistic tree.[1] This allowed us to construct a Polynesian phylogenetic model on a robust linguistic framework, one that did not depend on dubious lexicostatistical similarity matrices.

Following our initial articulation of a phylogenetic model for Polynesia (Kirch and Green 1987), we tackled the detailed reconstruction of Ancestral Polynesian culture, culminating in our 2001 monograph.[2] This required a refinement of the theoretical apparatus for historical anthropology, including a "triangulation method" for reconstruction (Kirch and Green 1987, 2001).[3] Polynesia proved to be admirably suited for such a phylogenetic approach, both because multiple lines of evidence confirm that the 30-plus ethnographically documented Polynesian cultures share a common ancestor, and because the cultural phylogeny, or branching pattern of cultural diversification, can be quite precisely defined thanks to the linguistic framework. Moreover, the branching pattern indicated by the linguistic phylogeny is independently confirmed by archaeological evidence for sequences of dispersal and island settlement, by human population relationships (both somatic and genetic, i.e., mtDNA), and most recently by proxy indicators of mtDNA lineages of Pacific rats (*Rattus exulans*) spread by the Polynesians during their voyages (Matisoo-Smith et al., 1998). Ultimately, the value of this Polynesian phylogenetic model lies in the power it lends to assess whether a particular cultural trait is (1) *homologous*, a shared retention of the ancestral culture, (2) a shared innovation of one cultural subgroup, (3) a *synology*, or borrowing, or (4) the result of parallel convergence. The details of applying a phylogenetic model are, of course, complicated and are addressed at length in Kirch and Green (2001).

How does the application of this phylogenetic model to historical reconstruction in Polynesia help us to understand the emergence of "archaic states" in Hawai'i? The critical point is that by establishing a precise phylogenetic model for the divergence of the varied Polynesian cultures, and by reconstructing the ancestral form of Polynesian culture that existed prior to that divergence, the historical anthropologist can assess in just what ways later Hawaiian society and culture changed from the common, ancestral condition. In any study of evolutionary change—biological or cultural—establishing the ancestral state is essential. Only by knowing this original baseline can we accurately determine what has later been innovated, and distinguish innovations from retentions of the ancestral condition.

It is now well established that Polynesia constitutes a *monophyletic* group of cultures, which had its origins in a branch of the more widespread Lapita Cultural Complex around 900 BC (Kirch 1997; Green 1979, 1997). The Far Eastern Lapita subgroup rapidly established itself in the Fiji-Tonga-Samoa region of the central tropical Pacific. By around 500 BC distinct subpopulations and speech communities had differentiated between those occupying the Fijian islands and those who had claimed the Tonga-Samoa archipelagoes (along with smaller Futuna and 'Uvea). It was in this Tonga-Samoa region that the distinctive Ancestral Polynesian culture, and its Proto Polynesian language, emerged out of the founding Lapita antecedent. Proto Polynesian, as a language interstage, is robustly marked by approximately 1,400 lexical innovations (Marck 1996b, 2000). Archaeologically, this early stage in the development of a distinct Polynesian culture is attested by more than 30 excavated sites containing Polynesian Plainware ceramics along with other artifacts (Kirch and Green 2001: Table 3.2).

After something like a millennium in their ancestral Polynesian homeland, internal cultural and linguistic differentiation had already begun to develop. This was marked by a split between the southern Tongic languages and the northern Nuclear Polynesian languages, suggesting a breakdown of the original widespread Proto Polynesian dialect chain at its longest and hence weakest link, between the archipelagoes of Tonga and Samoa. Around the middle of the first millennium AD or slightly later, the ancestral Polynesian populations of the homeland region began to expand eastward, into seas and islands that had remained up to this time unexplored and unsettled by humans. The central Eastern Polynesian archipelagoes of the Cooks, Societies, Marquesas, Australs, and Mangareva were settled first, between circa AD 600 and 900. This eastward expansion was associated with a number of cultural and linguistic innovations that were shared among the newly founded Eastern Polynesian communities who maintained contact through frequent long-distance voyaging (Green and Kirch 1997). Finally, from the tropical core of central Eastern Polynesia even longer voyages of exploration led Polynesian groups to the most remote of Pacific islands: Easter Island, the New Zealand temperate islands (named Aotearoa by the Polynesians), and in the North Pacific, Hawai'i.

In the remainder of this chapter, I outline the essential features of what has been reconstructed for the social and political world of the Ancestral Polynesians, those predecessors of the first Hawaiians who occupied the "homeland" islands of Western Polynesia from about 500 BC until the great diaspora into Eastern Polynesia that seems to have begun sometime after AD 600 to 800. This is an essential first step in our primary goal of understanding how in the later stages of Hawaiian history, an archaic state form of society emerged. What were the essential characteristics of the earlier, underlying form of society? We must know the answer to this question if we are to account for the process that resulted in the late precontact Hawaiian leaders becoming kings, rather than chiefs.

THE NATURE OF ANCESTRAL POLYNESIAN SOCIETY

In our 2001 book, Green and I present exhaustive evidence for the reconstruction of six major "domains" of Ancestral Polynesian life: the environment and how it was cognized and classified; subsistence including horticulture and fishing; patterns of food preparation and cuisine; material culture; social and political organization; and the realm of gods and ancestors, and how these were worshipped and invoked in a yearly ritual cycle. For each of these domains, we began with the extensive lexical reconstructions of Proto Polynesian (PPN) vocabulary, augmenting these with semantic history hypotheses derived from close comparison of ethnographic texts, and wherever possible cross-checked with the material evidence of archaeology.[4] Here, I limit myself to a brief summary of the last two domains, those pertaining to sociopolitical organization and to ritual. In seeking to understand the emergence of archaic states in late precontact Hawai'i, it is essential that we have a clear perspective on the social and ideological contours of the antecedent culture, in this case Ancestral Polynesia. For only then can we be sure that we are correctly identifying those *innovations* that were essential to change, distinguishing them from features of Polynesian culture that are widely shared and hence are retentions from the ancestral condition.

Social Groups

Claude Lévi-Strauss's notion of the *sociétés à maison*, or "house society" has significantly informed anthropological analysis of Austronesian social organization. First brought to the attention of anglophone anthropology in *The Way of the Masks* (Lévi-Strauss 1982:172–87; see also Lévi-Strauss 1971), the house society was succinctly described by Lévi-Strauss as "a corporate body holding an estate made up of both material and immaterial wealth, which perpetuates itself through the transmission of its name, its goods, and its titles down a real or imaginary line, considered legitimate as long as this continuity can express itself in the language of kinship or affinity and, most often, of both" (1982:174). Ethnographers of Austronesian-speaking cultures distributed throughout Oceania and island Southeast Asia quickly recognized the relevance of the house society concept for understanding traditional social organization (e.g., Carsten and Hugh-Jones 1995; Fox 1993b; McKinnon 1991, 1995; Waterson 1990). The relevance of the house society concept has likewise caught the attention of Polynesian archaeologists (e.g., Kahn and Kirch 2004; Kirch 1996; Green 1998).

As Kirch and Green argue (2001:201–7), early Polynesian societies are best understood as house societies. The two most important, lexically marked social groups were the PPN *kainanga and the *kaainga.[5] The former we reconstruct as a land-holding or controlling group, exogamous, probably unilineal, tracing "ascent" from a founding ancestor.[6] The latter was a more restricted social group controlling rights to an estate, along with the principal dwelling or house site of that estate; a residential group. The *kainanga was the larger and more extensive kind of social group, incorporating all of the descendants of a common ancestor or ancestral pair. Its leader was the *qariki, a senior ranked male who served as the group's secular and ritual leader. Rights to land, as well as other privileges, were determined by membership in a specific *kainanga. However, as Goodenough (1955, 1961) recognized long ago, in most Oceanic societies there are two distinct types of kin group associated with land rights, with the second kind of group being residential; in Ancestral Polynesian society this was the *kaainga. Residential affiliation with a particular *kaainga gave one access to a named house site and its estate, with garden lands, access to adjacent reef or other resources, and other privileges. Thus the larger and more inclusive *kainanga would be made up of a number of smaller *kaainga, each constituting a residential group and indeed constituting the domestic units of production and consumption. These individual *kaainga, as is typical in house societies, were ranked relative to one another, in terms of their relationship to the founding ancestor of the larger *kainanga. Such internal ranking is likely to have promoted a degree of "heterarchy" (Ehrenreich et al. 1995), with competition between individual *kaainga for access to resources and for prestige.

These Ancestral Polynesian social groups, and their PPN terms, were so fundamental to Polynesian social organization that they have persisted over more than 2,000 years, and have been carried forward into almost every ethnographically attested Polynesian society. Variants of PPN *kainanga are widely described for Western Polynesian and Polynesian Outlier societies, while in Eastern Polynesia a lexical innovation at the Proto Central-Eastern Polynesian (PCEP) language interstage prefixed *mata to *kainanga, to form the compound PCEP word *mata-kainanga.[7] In most Eastern Polynesian societies, reflexes of PCEP *mata-kainanga reference the largest kind of social group, as in the Marquesan mataʻeinaʻa ("tribe"; Handy 1923) or Society Islands mataeinaʻa ("tribe or clan"; Oliver 1974). Only in Hawaiʻi was the meaning of *mata-kainanga radically transformed with major consequences for social organization, as I shall demonstrate shortly. Similarly, PPN *kaainga also has widespread persistence throughout Western, Outlier, and Eastern Polynesia. In most cases, the descendant terms reference a homesite, place of residence, and often also lands associated with the group of kin occupying such a residence (Kirch and

Green 2001: Table 8.4). The Hawaiians would later radically alter the meaning of this word as well.

Rank, Status, and Leadership

No word may be as widely recognizable or as important to scholars of Polynesian chiefship as *ariki*, the virtually pan-Polynesian term for "chief." Cognates are found in no fewer than 32 Polynesian languages (Kirch and Green 2001: Table 8.9), allowing a robust PPN reconstruction of **qariki*. In my early synthetic work on Polynesian chiefdoms (Kirch 1984:64), I assumed that such a pervasive term indexed the existence, in Ancestral Polynesian society, of "the institution of hereditary chieftainship." This claim led some critics, including Sutton (1990:669), to point out that an uncritical projection of ethnographic period semantic values for *ariki* back 2,000 years into the past was not justifiable. This prompted Green and me to construct a far more rigorous semantic history hypothesis for the original meaning of **qariki*. Based on a core set of denotata that reflexes of this term share across multiple descendant societies, we proposed a more nuanced semantic reconstruction, as follows: the senior, male, titled leader of the **kainanga* social group, who inherited his position patrilineally within the senior ranked line of this group, and who acted as the group's secular as well as ritual leader. This combination of both secular and sacred functions within the single person of the ancestral **qariki* is important, because certain later Polynesian societies—Hawai'i in particular—deviated considerably from this ancestral model. This reconstruction of the function and role of PPN **qariki* matches well with the conclusions of Koskinen, who carried out a detailed comparative ethnographic study of *ariki*ship. To quote him:

> Probably the term *ariki* was used as a chiefly title throughout Polynesia from the earliest times. The character of the oldest form of the Polynesian *ariki* chieftainship was perhaps more clearly sacerdotal. When the same term was later applied to a chief in the sense of a ruler, it marked a change. In time, a new type of *ariki*ship evolved. (Koskinen 1960:148)

The late-eighteenth-century Hawaiian variant of **qariki*, *ali'i*, was indeed a very different kind of *ariki*ship from that which we reconstruct for Ancestral Polynesia.

If the **qariki* was the leader of the Ancestral Polynesian **kainanga* groups, did the smaller **kaainga* residential associations also have formal leadership positions? We believe that they did, and we reconstruct

TABLE 1.1. SOCIAL GROUPS AND LEADERSHIP ROLES IN ANCESTRAL POLYNESIAN SOCIETIES

	Formal	←	Power	→	Instrumental
Position, Status	*sau*, high chief	*qariki*, chief	*fatu-qariki*, chiefly elder	*fatu*, family heads
Function	Societal, political, and ceremonial roles	Priestly functions	Priestly functions	Decision-making controllers of resources
Social Group	*mata*	*kainanga*	Highest-ranked *kaainga*	*kaainga*
	Sacred	←	Sanctity	→	Secular

NOTE: After Kirch and Green (2001, Fig. 8.1).

the PPN term *fatu* for this category (Kirch and Green 2001:231–34, Table 8.10). *Fatu* were probably senior males of their respective *kaainga*, who exercised control or authority over the land and resources of the residential group.

A final term of considerable importance is PPN *tufunga*, reflected in many later Eastern Polynesian languages as "priest," but in Western Polynesian or Outlier languages meaning an "expert," "craftsman," or "skilled person." Our phylogenetically constrained reconstruction suggests that in Ancestral Polynesia *tufunga* were secular specialists, and that the meaning "priest" was a semantic innovation at the PCEP interstage, after the breakup of the original Proto Polynesian speech community. This Eastern Polynesian innovation has important implications, for it indicates that at this same time there was a critical change in the role of the *qariki*, who it will be remembered originally incorporated both secular and ritual functions in his role as the head of the *kainanga*. With Eastern Polynesian *tufunga* taking on a ritual role, we see the first steps in the development of distinct secular and sacred status positions. This, again, would become highly elaborated in Hawai'i, as will be shown later.

Table 1.1 summarizes our reconstruction of certain key components of Ancestral Polynesian social organization, as reflected through Proto Polynesian terms for four lexically indexed statuses, and three discrete kinds of social group. It was from this structural base that the later Polynesian societies developed their unique social variations, and the historical path taken by Hawaiian society led to the greatest elaborations and divergence from the ancestral pattern.

Gods, Spirits, and Ancestors

Absolutely fundamental to all Polynesian religions—and permeating their social systems as well—are the entwined concepts of *mana* and *tapu* (as well as *noa*, the antithesis of *tapu*) (Handy 1927; Shore 1989). Reflexes of these three words are found in virtually all Polynesian languages (Kirch and Green 2001: Table 9.1), so we can be certain that **mana*, **tapu*, and **noa* were also part of the PPN vocabulary. *Mana* "manifests the power of the gods in the human world" (Shore 1989:164). It flows from the supernatural world of gods and ancestors, but must be mediated through various kinds of ritual activities, which in Ancestral Polynesia would have been the purview of the **qariki* leaders. These rituals, and those who performed them, were made *tapu* to protect them (i.e., keep them from being polluted), especially through certain rites that involved various forms of binding and tying. As Shore writes, "such rites channeled divine potency for human ends and rendered phenomena intelligible by providing an encompassing and transcendent form, but also were acts of human submission to the divine" (1989:164). More important, for understanding the origins of divine kingship in later Hawaiian society, **mana* and **tapu* provided the critical basis for distinctions between those who were more closely related to (ascended from) the ancestors, and who enjoyed both the privileges and responsibilities of controlling *mana*, and those who did not. The Hawaiians in particular elaborated **tapu* to a high degree, transforming it into the well-known *kapu* system with its distinctive protocols and prohibitions (see Chapter 2).

As to the deities and ancestors who populated the spirit world of Ancestral Polynesia, the PPN word **qatua* can be reconstructed from reflexes in a large number of Polynesian languages, and can reasonably be glossed as "deity." Three quite closely related words, **tupuqa*, **tupuna*, and **tupunga*, all based on the root **tupu* meaning "to grow," referenced ghosts, spirits, and deceased ancestors. These ancestors were responsible for channeling *mana* to the living, and to them much ritual supplication and offerings were due. Ancestral Polynesian cosmology is more obscure, but Marck (1996a, 1996c) makes a cogent argument for the importance of a "Primordial Pair" concept, which entailed complementary male (= sky) and female (= earth) elements; such concepts are widespread throughout Polynesia and hence are arguably retentions from an original cosmogonic theory.

Although the Ancestral Polynesians had a term for "deity" (as opposed to ancestor), *qatua, there is no evidence that they had the kind of functionally differentiated pantheon found in the later Eastern Polynesian societies, including Hawai'i. The only deity whose name can be confidently reconstructed is that of *Taangaloa, who may have been the first-born anthropomorphic god of the Primordial Pair. The names of *Taangaloa's siblings, the well-known *Taane, *Tuu, and *Rongo,[8] can be reconstructed only back as far as the PCEP language interstage, after the breakup of Proto Polynesian that followed on the initial movement of people into the islands of central Eastern Polynesia. We must therefore conclude that this functionally differentiated pantheon was an innovation within Eastern Polynesia, probably soon after the diaspora out of the Western Polynesian homeland had begun. Certainly, however, the development of the four first-order anthropomorphic gods occurred prior to the initial settlement of Hawai'i, and would have been a part of Hawaiian theology from the beginning.

Ritual Spaces and the Ritual Cycle

Both Koskinen (1960) and Kirch and Green (2001) agree that one of the principal functions of the Ancestral *qariki was to perform an annual cycle of rituals, effecting the proper flow of *mana from gods and ancestors, and thus ensuring the fertility of the land and sea, and the reproduction of society at large. Based again on comparative evidence (see Kirch and Green 2001:249–56), the architectonic spaces in which such rituals were performed consisted of a sacred house (PPN *fale-qatua), which quite likely was the actual dwelling of the *qariki, or a former dwelling of his ancestors (*tupunga). This was fronted on the seaward side by an open, cleared space (*malaqe). The house itself was situated on a slightly elevated mound or foundation, named the *qafu, which may frequently have contained burials of these ancestors. Following patterns seen elsewhere in the Austronesian world, and thus having considerable antiquity, one or more posts within the *fale-qatua were ritually marked, representing deities and/or ancestors; these posts functioned as "ritual attractors" (Fox 1993a). Some rites would have been performed within the house, while others, including the preparation and ritual consumption of the psychoactive plant *kava (*Piper methysticum*) were probably carried out in the open *malaqe court.

These fundamental elements of ritual space were elaborated in distinctive ways in later Western and Eastern Polynesian societies. In Western Polynesia, the *malae* remained an open ceremonial court, flanked in some cases (such as Tonga) by large burial mounds (an elaborated form of the original sacred house mound). In Eastern Polynesia, the *marae* typically became a formal court, often enclosed by a wall and sometimes elevated on stone platforms; at one end was the *ahu* (from PPN **qafu*) and the ritual posts of the original house were replaced by wooden or stone anthropomorphic images (PCEP **tiki*), of which the Easter Island statues are the most famous. The later Hawaiian temples followed this Eastern Polynesian pathway of architectural development, although the widespread term *marae* was replaced in Hawai'i with an innovated term, *heiau*.

Polynesian systems of timekeeping involve a lunar calendar with 12 or 13 lunations (Makemson 1941), calibrated to the sidereal year by annual observation of the acronitic rising and setting, or heliacal rising, of the star cluster Pleiades (PPN **Mata-liki*). The names of the Proto Polynesian lunar months (Kirch and Green 2001: Table 9.7) relate to a set of natural phenomena including wet-dry seasonality, which was critical to a horticultural cycle based on trophytic yams (*Dioscorea alata* and other species). Shortly following the acronitic rising of Pleiades, an important ritual event was the first fruits offering of the early maturing yams. In the early Eastern Polynesian societies, this ritual time became known by a newly innovated term, PCEP **mata-fiti*, a new year's celebration or harvest period. The Proto Polynesian lunar month names were mostly retained, with transformations, down into later calendar systems throughout Polynesia, including that of contact-era Hawai'i. Observation of the acronitic rising of Pleiades continued to determine the onset of the new year in Hawai'i up until the time of Cook's arrival, marking the onset of the *Makahiki* (from PCEP **mata-fiti*).

In the preceding paragraphs I have now outlined the fundamental, systemic patterns of social organization, leadership, theology, calendrics, and ritual that can be traced back two thousand years to Ancestral Polynesian society. These were the structures that gave meaning to the lives of the early Polynesians, and which would be reworked, reorganized, elaborated, and transformed by the different Polynesian societies which trace their origins back to the ancestral culture. To understand how Hawaiian society changed from a chiefdom to an archaic state mode of organization, a knowledge of this ancestral condition is essential, for it provided the starting point—the structural building blocks—for all that was to come later.

HOW DID CONTACT-ERA HAWAI'I DIFFER FROM ANCESTRAL POLYNESIA?

Knowing the key contours of Ancestral Polynesian society provides a tool for calibrating just how far contact-era Hawai'i had diverged from the original Polynesian mode. We can make an initial assessment by contrasting some of the key Proto Polynesian terms for social groups and statuses with their Hawaiian reflexes and the meanings attached to these in contact-period Hawaiian culture. The relevant terms and glosses are set out in Table 1.2.

If we begin with the *kainanga social group (and its slightly later PCEP form *mata-kainanga), the contrast between Proto Polynesian and Hawaiian is striking, for what was originally a land-holding "ascent" group had, in late precontact Hawai'i, become a very loose notion of "the common people" in general. Clearly, the first Polynesians to voyage to Hawai'i and settle those islands had brought the *mata-kainanga concept with them. But at some point in Hawaiian history the meaning attached to this term was radically changed. Gone from the Hawaiian definition is any hint of association between the maka'āinana and land, in the sense of inherent rights to hold or work land. This lends strong support to the kind of social history alluded to by Sahlins, in which the archaic concepts of lineage had been eroded by the aggrandizement of the chiefship. At European contact, land was divided into territorial units, each under the control of a chief; commoners, the maka'āinana, validated their rights to land by annual payment of tribute to these chiefs (see Chapter 2).

But there is more. Turning to the second kind of social group present in Ancestral Polynesian Society (*kaainga), the local residential group controlling a specific estate and its dwelling site, we find that this word too has undergone a remarkable semantic transformation in Hawai'i. Indeed, the entire notion of a social group has now been lost, with the Hawaiian cognate variant 'āina giving only the sense of *land* in its most generalized form. Moreover, the specific Hawaiian word for a territorial unit (notably controlled by a chief, not by an ascent group) is an innovation, the well-known term *ahupua'a*. The word is an interesting compound formed of the roots *ahu*, "altar," and *pua'a*, "pig," presumably connected with the rise of a territorial system of temples.[9]

TABLE I.2. PROTO POLYNESIAN (PPN) AND
HAWAIIAN (HAW) COGNATE TERMS FOR SOCIAL
GROUPS AND STATUS POSITIONS

Language Stage	Lexeme	Gloss
PPN	*kainanga	A land-holding or controlling group, exogamous, probably unilineal, tracing "ascent" from a founding ancestor
PEP	*mata-kainanga	PPN *mata merged with *kainanga, to indicate the basic land-holding social group
HAW	maka'āinana	Commoner, populace, people in general
PPN	*kaainga	In Ancestral Polynesian society, a social group controlling rights to an estate, along with the principal dwelling or house site of that estate; a residential group
HAW	'āina	Land, the earth in general
PPN	*qariki	In Ancestral Polynesia, the senior, male, titled leader of the *kainanga social group, who inherited his position patrilineally within the senior ranked line of this group, and who acted as the group's secular as well as ritual leader
HAW	ali'i	Chief, chiefess, ruler
HAW	mō'ī	King, sovereign (a lexical innovation)
PPN	*fatu	In Ancestral Polynesia, the leader of a *kaainga group, one who oversaw the use and allocation of the group's land and resources
HAW	haku	Lord, master, overseer, owner, proprietor
PPN	*tufunga	In Ancestral Polynesian society, a specialist of any kind; not specifically a priest
HAW	kahuna	Priest, leader of a cult

What, then, of the corresponding leadership positions for these two kinds of social groups? In Ancestral Polynesia, it is clear that *qariki were leaders of the more inclusive *kainanga ascent group, with their functions encompassing both secular and ritual duties. But in late-eighteenth-century Hawai'i, the cognate word ali'i had come to index a *class of elites*, highly elaborated and internally differentiated, and held to be apart from the common people, the maka'āinana. This class of ali'i was further marked by lexical subdivisions, such as ali'i nui (nui, "big, great"), ali'i 'ai moku (kings or district chiefs), ali'i 'ai ahupua'a (chiefs in charge of a territorial unit) and so on. Moreover, we have in Hawaiian a lexical innovation, mō'ī, not found elsewhere in Polynesia, and properly glossed as "king, sovereign."

All this becomes more interesting with Proto Polynesian *fatu, a term that originally referred to a *kaainga group leader (probably, but not necessarily always, a senior male of that group). Since *kaainga-type residential, land-holding ascent groups had ceased to exist in late prehistoric Hawai'i, there could be no such leadership position. Rather, a semantic shift had again occurred, with Hawaiian haku now carrying the generalized meaning of "lord, master, overseer, owner, or proprietor." In effect, haku had become a kind of synonym for chief, ali'i.

Finally, consider the category of *tufunga, which to the Ancestral Polynesians meant a specialist or expert, but which did not—according to our triangulation analysis—include ritual duties, for these fell within the purview of the *qariki. It is largely in Eastern Polynesia that reflexes of PPN *tufunga take on the meaning of priest or ritual specialist, and Hawai'i carried this semantic shift to its ultimate conclusion, with kahuna becoming a formal class of priests, parallel to and competing with, the class of chiefs. As with the term ali'i, the class of kahuna included a large number of lexically marked distinctions, including the kahuna nui, the "high priest" who officiated at the war temples of the king, and other terms.

To sum up, systematic comparison of a set of terms for social groups and social statuses—all pervasive throughout Polynesia and derived from the Ancestral Polynesian heritage shared by all descendant Polynesian cultures—reveals how thoroughly Hawai'i departs from the general pattern of Polynesian social structure. The core social groups controlling land rights everywhere else were no longer in existence, having been replaced by a territorial system controlled by elites. The terms for group leaders persist, but with new semantic extensions indicating heightened power. And a general category of specialists has morphed into a class of full-time priests. Were it not for the homologous continuity in the lexical roots themselves, the Hawaiian system might not even be recognizable as Polynesian!

WAS HAWAI'I UNIQUE IN POLYNESIA?

My thesis is that Hawai'i, with the development of class stratification, land alienation from commoners and a territorial system of administrative control, a monopoly of force and endemic conquest warfare, and, most important, divine kingship legitimated by state cults with a formal priesthood (including human sacrifice), should be regarded as a set of emergent archaic states at the time of first contact with the West. But was Hawai'i the only late precontact Polynesian society to have undergone such developments? Are any other of the 30-odd Polynesian societies known to ethnohistory potential candidates for a similar reconsideration of their place in a taxonomy of sociopolitical formations? Certainly there was considerable variation in Polynesian societies at the time of first contact with the West, despite the now well-established fact that they can all be traced back to common origins in the Ancestral Polynesian homeland. Two of the classic comparative works on Polynesia, those of Sahlins (1958) and Goldman (1970), offered classifications of Polynesian societies based on the degree of stratification or hierarchy (see Kirch 1984: Table 2). In his Group I societies, those with "structurally complex ranking systems, usually with three status levels," Sahlins (1958:11) placed Hawai'i, Tonga, Samoa, and Tahiti (Society Is.). For his part, Goldman included Tonga, Hawai'i, the Society Islands, and Mangareva in his "Stratified" category. Tonga, the Society Islands, and possibly Samoa are the only other societies in Polynesia in which late precontact sociopolitical evolution might have paralleled the sequence in Hawai'i (see Claessen 1978, 1991). Significantly, these all occupy relatively extensive archipelagos, in the tropical core of Polynesia, where the potential for intensive agriculture and a large population base was good. Indeed, the populations of these islands are thought to have been substantial at the time of initial European contact, as were those of Hawai'i (Kirch and Rallu 2007).

While the Society Islands, Samoa, and Tonga all exhibit certain trends toward increased social stratification and inequality, along with other interesting developments such as large-scale monumentality, in my view only for Tonga might a case also be made for the late emergence of an archaic state. Most compelling is the evidence that Tonga, like Hawai'i, had indigenously innovated the institution of divine kingship (Gifford 1929; Goldman 1970; Kirch 1984:223–26). Indeed, Tonga had evolved a dual paramountship with distinct sacred and secular rulers, the Tu'i Tonga and the Tu'i Kanokupolu. The Tu'i Tonga traced his descent directly from 'Aho'eitu, the progeny of a union of the god Tangaloa 'Eitumatupu'a with a mortal woman. Moreover, the Tongan elite as with their Hawaiian counterparts assumed direct control over the kingdom's lands, instituting a territorial system of land control. Thus, as in Hawai'i, the Tongan reflex of the ancient PPN term for the land-holding group *kainanga, came to mean "people of nonchiefly rank." This book is not the place to explore further the possibility that Tonga constitutes a second case of an emergent archaic state within Polynesia. But that hypothesis will surely provide a fruitful avenue for future investigations.

CHAPTER 2

Hawaiian Archaic States on the Eve of European Contact

The kapu of a god was superior to the kapu of a chief, but the kapus of the *ni'aupi'o* and *pi'o* chiefs were equal to the gods'.

Kamakau (1964:10)

[T]he predicates of the king are identical to the predicates of the divine . . . The king, therefore, can do everything and be everything because each god constitutes the possibility of a different action or form of being. He unifies the divine in relation to the human; he is the perfect human because he instantiates all the properties of the divine.

Valeri (1985a:153)

Through the use of controlled comparison constrained by a phylogenetic model (Chapter 1), we know that in several critical respects contact-era Hawaiian society had departed radically from the structures of economic, social, political, and religious organization typical of most other Polynesian groups. To comprehend the nature of Hawaiian archaic states more fully, however, requires a closer engagement with the ethnohistoric details. I will focus on several criteria that have played a central role in the archaeological literature on archaic states: issues of scale (both demographic and territorial); the existence of class stratification; concepts of divine kingship; elite art and ideology; administrative and temple hierarchies; and other criteria that have frequently been invoked as typical of states (see Chapter 1). This also gives me latitude to define more precisely the contours of the late Hawaiian archaic state, and how these departed from Polynesian norms. My synthesis, however, is presented in synchronic terms, in that it is meant to describe Hawaiian society in the late-eighteenth century, on the eve of Western contact. The properly historical questions of when, how, and why Hawaiian society changed from an older Polynesian chiefdom structure into the archaic states of the mid-eighteenth century, are discussed in Chapters 3 through 5.

SOURCES FOR RECONSTRUCTING CONTACT-ERA HAWAI'I

Various sources are available for a reconstruction of Hawaiian society in the late-eighteenth century.[1] The critical time period is from the moment of Cook's arrival at Kaua'i Island on January 18, 1778, until the death of Kamehameha I in 1819, which effectively marked the end of the *ancien régime*, with the Protestant missionaries arriving in 1820. During these four decades, the traditional *kapu* system remained in effect, even though Kamehameha abandoned the practice of human sacrifice and the war cult of Kū after his successful conquest of O'ahu in 1804. The journals of early European voyagers, beginning with those of Cook's own expedition (including the journals of Cook, Clerke, King, Ledyard, and Samwell; see Beaglehole 1967), chronicle Hawaiian culture at the moment of "first contact." Cook's expedition exemplified the Enlightenment tradition of emerging scientific observation, and incorporated a visual record through John Webber's exquisite sketches and drawings, later engraved for publication (Joppien and Smith 1988). The European voyager accounts continue with such important figures as Vancouver in 1792, the traders Dixon and Portlock in 1789, La Pérouse in 1798, Broughton in 1804, and the Kotzebue expedition in 1816 to 1817.

The second category of sources, one that I privilege in this book, is that of several Native Hawaiian scholars, especially David Malo (1951), John Papa 'Ī'ī (1959), Samuel Kamakau (1961, 1964, 1991), Kepelino (Beckwith 1932), and Kēlou Kamakau (in Fornander 1916–20). During the nineteenth century these scholars wrote down various *moʻoʻōlelo* (or *moʻolelo*), a Hawaiian term that may be broadly glossed as "history" (Pukui and Elbert 1986:254).[2] 'Ī'ī was a chief and retainer in the court of Kamehameha I and Liholiho (Kamehameha II). His *Fragments of Hawaiian History* ('Ī'ī 1959) offers a firsthand account of life in the royal court. Malo, born in 1795, spent part of his youth in the following of the high chief Kuakini, and his father had been a member of Kamehameha's court and army.[3] In 1831, Malo entered the missionary seminary at Lahainaluna, Maui. While enrolled there, encouraged by Sheldon Dibble (who compiled his own *Mooolelo* [Anon. 1838]), Malo made extensive inquiries among the older generation, and between 1836 and 1837 wrote what is probably the single most important account of traditional Hawaiian culture (Malo 1951). Samuel Kamakau, a bit younger than Malo (he was born in 1815), was also a Lahainaluna student and his family traced its descent from the priestly class of Oʻahu and Kauaʻi. He published his *moʻolelo* in a series of Hawaiian language newspaper articles from 1865 to 1871. Kepelino, born around 1830, was not a part of the Lahainaluna group, but his father was a descendant of the famous voyaging priest Pāʻao and his mother was a daughter of Kamehameha; he was thus well schooled in the priestly and noble traditions (Valeri 1985a:xxvi). Finally, Kēlou Kamakau was a lesser *aliʻi* of the Kona District of Hawaiʻi about whom little is known; he seems to have been a contemporary of Malo. Collectively, these authors provide an extraordinary source of material on the traditional Hawaiian archaic state.

A third set of documents comes from the period after the death of King Kamehameha I in 1819, and includes the accounts of missionaries and their wives, of traders and merchants resident in Honolulu and elsewhere in the islands, as well as the archives of the increasingly bureaucratic and record-conscious Hawaiian Kingdom. Especially important are the thousands of pages of testimony deriving from the Mahele, or division of lands among the king, principal chiefs, and common people, which took place between 1846 and 1854 (Chinen 1958; Kirch and Sahlins 1992). Up until the Mahele, the traditional system of land tenure and tributary relations continued more or less intact, and the claims and testimony of chiefs, land managers, and the common people themselves illuminate this system in often exquisite detail.

Finally, a tradition of ethnographic and historical scholarship began in the late-nineteenth century (e.g., Remy 1859; Fornander 1916–20, 1996), and continued in the mid-twentieth century with the work of scholars such as Edward S. C. Handy and his Hawaiian collaborator Mary K. Pukui (Handy 1940; Handy and Handy 1972; Handy and Pukui 1958). More recently, there are the works of Marshall Sahlins (1981, 1985a, 1992, 1995) and his former students (Linnekin 1990; Earle 1978, 1997), of Valerio Valeri (1972, 1985a), and of the Native Hawaiian scholar Lilikalā Kameʻeleihiwa (1992).

HAWAIIAN POLITIES: SIZE AND SCALE

At the close of the eighteenth century, the Hawaiian archipelago was divided into four independent and frequently warring archaic states (Fig. 2.1). Although these polities were independent, their ruling dynastic families were complexly interrelated through marriage. The largest

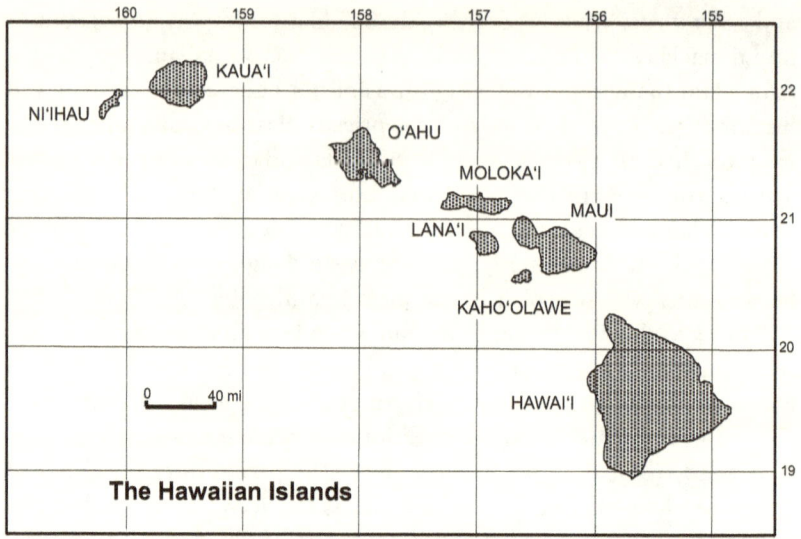

Figure 2.1. Map of the main Hawaiian Islands.

was centered on Hawai'i Island, and prior to Cook's arrival had gained a significant foothold on southeastern Maui. The Maui polity, second largest in area, incorporated the smaller nearby islands of Kaho'olawe and Lāna'i. Moloka'i was under the rule of the O'ahu Island polity, although the former had at times been a part of the Maui dominions, and its place in the political structure changed hands repeatedly. Kaua'i Island, isolated by a 177 km gap of frequently stormy seas, formed an independent polity, and incorporated the smaller island of Ni'ihau.

Table 2.1 shows the geographic scale of each of these polities, as well as low and high estimates of their populations. The size of the Hawaiian population at contact has been a matter of much debate and continuing research (Schmitt 1968, 1973; Stannard 1989), hence the range of values. Recent paleodemographic research in particular regions such as Kahikinui, Maui and Kohala, Hawai'i (Kirch and Rallu 2007), lends support to the higher values given in Table 2.1.

The geographic scale of documented early state societies ranged enormously, with those on the smaller end of the spectrum overlapping with complex chiefdoms (Feinman 1998:103–4). As Feinman's careful consideration of the matter of scale and sociopolitical complexity brings out, there is no clear threshold in either population or territorial size marking the boundary between chiefdoms and archaic states. Nonetheless, the Hawaiian values for both of these are well within the ranges

Archaic States at European Contact 33

TABLE 2.1. SIZE AND SCALE OF HAWAIIAN POLITIES AT CONTACT

Polity	Islands Incorporated	Population		Geographic Scale (km^2)
		Low Estimate[a]	High Estimate[b]	
Hawai'i	Hawai'i, part of East Maui	120,000	150,000	10,658
Maui	Maui, Lāna'i, Kaho'olawe	78,500	85,800	2,164
O'ahu	O'ahu, Moloka'i	70,000	96,200	2,249
Kaua'i	Kaua'i, Ni'ihau	31,500	64,000	1,622

[a]Based on Emory, in Schmitt (1968, Table 6).
[b]Based on estimates of Lt. King on Cook's 1778–79 voyage (Schmitt 1968, Table 6).

given by Feinman (1998: Tables 4.1, 4.2) for late Post-Classic polities in Oaxaca, or by Yoffee (2005: Table 3.1) for early Near Eastern city states. All of the Hawaiian polities had territories larger than the 1,500 km^2 that Renfrew (1986:2) has suggested is typical for "early state modules." Clearly, the contact-era Hawaiian polities exhibited both population sizes and territorial scales consistent with other archaic states elsewhere in the world.

CLASS STRATIFICATION AND DIVINE KINGSHIP

Archaic states are not simply *quantitatively* different from complex chiefdoms—larger in size, geographic extent, or number of administrative levels—but *qualitatively* distinctive in how members of society are assigned to social categories, and in how these categories are ideologically defined and legitimated. In chiefdoms, there is at least the pervasive ideology of kinship as the glue that bonds society together; the "conical clan" may have a clear rank order, but in theory everyone is descended from a common founding ancestor (Sahlins 1958; Kirchhoff 1955). Hence the divergence of Hawai'i from the widespread persistence of some form of lineage or descent/ascent group structure, is especially striking. As we saw in Chapter 1, Hawaiian society retained a cognate form of the generalized Polynesian word for ascent groups (*maka'āinana*), but had radically transformed its meaning to "commoner," someone whose right to work the land was contingent on the regular payment of tribute (*ho'okupu*) to the hierarchy of overlords.

Similarly, the old Polynesian word designating a residential group and its estate (PPN *kaainga) was also retained (HAW 'āina) but had come to signify "land" in the most general sense. Indeed, the alienation of land—the sundering of the ancient and pan-Polynesian system of rights to land by virtue of kinship and residence—had transformed the maka'āinana into a distinct class of persons.

Late Hawaiian society comprised not a continually graded series of persons linked by bounds of kinship but distinct, named, endogamous classes of persons.[4] Kepelino laid this out especially clearly when he wrote that "the Hawaiian nation [ka lahui Hawaii] is divided into three classes [papa]" (Beckwith, ed., 1932:124–25). He names these as (1) ali'i, (2) noa, and (3) kauwā (1932:25), which can be approximately glossed as "elite," "commoner," and "outcast."[5] Kepelino's use of the word papa is noteworthy, for here is another semantic innovation, in this case of the old Proto Polynesian term (PPN *papa) for a flat surface, or rock stratum. While still retaining those original meanings, the Hawaiian word has added the connotations of "rank, grade, order," and the compound term papa ali'i refers expressly to the "chiefly class" (Pukui and Elbert 1986:316). Other Hawaiian authorities including Malo (1951:60–61) and Kamakau (1964:8–9) emphasize the division of society into distinct classes. Kamakau's account first treats the papa ali'i, distinguishing the chiefs (with their several ranks) and priests (whom he notes were part of the ali'i class), then turns to the commoners and outcasts. Kamakau (1964:8) uses papa kanaka (kanaka, "man" or "mankind") for the intermediate class, including within this "the people in general" (maka'āinana). He gives a number of colloquial epithets for commoners, such as "reddened men" (from long work in the sun), "humble commoners," and "kindling wood," all of which speak eloquently to the relative status of the vast majority of the population. The papa kauwā, at the bottom of the social scale, are sometimes translated in Western literature as "slaves," but a better term is probably "outcast." Malo (1951:68–71) explains that kauwā was a general term of degradation that was widely used in a metaphoric sense, such as a younger brother referring to himself as the kauwā of his older (higher ranked) brother, or a retainer calling himself the kauwā of his chief. True kauwā, however, were a special category of persons (often physically marked by special tattoos on their faces) who could be taken for the purpose of human sacrifice at war temples.[6]

In short, late precontact Hawaiian society segmented itself into three lexically marked social classes. These were ranked relative to one another, not only according to a system of hierarchical privileges and access to resources, but in relation to a deeply ingrained ideological system (the *kapu* system) which underpinned the annual cycle of religious practices. In principle, if not wholly in practice, the classes were endogamous; the major exceptions consisted of the appropriation of exceptionally beautiful young women of the commoner class by elite males, but only as secondary wives or concubines. The primary wives of the elites, and especially the royal wives of the king, were carefully chosen from among the *ali'i* class. Royal marriage was highly prescribed. And, the classes were sharply differentiated economically: Elites held title to the land but did not work it; commoners worked the land and supported the elites through obligatory payments of tribute and labor. Thus, contact-era Hawai'i was a true class society, a trait that puts it squarely in the realm of early archaic states, as opposed to chiefdoms.

In Polynesia generally as well as Hawai'i, a distinguished pedigree—a genealogy that could be traced back through an unbroken line of named ancestors—was the hallmark of the chiefly class. A guild of specialists, called *po'e mo'o'ōlelo* (the term might be properly translated as "historian"), had the task of memorizing the genealogies of elite families, along with accounts of their deeds and achievements (Beckwith, ed., 1932:134). Malo (1951:191–92) describes the arduous process of convening the *hale nauā*, a formal court of inquiry into the genealogies of chiefly lines at the time of ascension of a new king. In marked contrast, Hawaiian commoners did not keep genealogies. As Davenport writes: "Although commoners were assumed to have the same [ultimate] genesis as aristocrats, they were descendants through lesser, forgotten filial links, hence they did not have lengthy genealogical proof of their common origins with aristocrats" (1994:2). Instead, *maka'āinana* attached themselves in tributary relations to lesser territorial chiefs (*ali'i 'ai ahupua'a*) and to land managers (*konohiki*), a process known as *kumi haku* (to seek a lord, or overseer). Commoners' rights to work the land, and their access to particular resources, were governed by these tributary relationships, and not (as elsewhere in Polynesia) through membership in genealogically determined ascent groups. In the thousands of pages of native testimony pertaining to *maka'āinana* land claims recorded during the Mahele of 1848 to 1854, almost nowhere are commoner claims justified on the basis of lineage (Sahlins 1992). Rather, time and again the *maka'āinana* supplicant justifies his claim by reference to his regular payment of tribute (*ho'okupu*) and of labor to his *konohiki* and *ali'i* overlords.[7]

The *ali'i* or elite class was internally differentiated, the gradations depending on genealogical status. The main Hawaiian writers differ slightly in their details, but agree with respect to the major ranks of *ali'i* and their relative status. In Table 2.2 I enumerate the main *ali'i* categories, drawing on these sources as well as the careful analyses of Valeri (1972) and Davenport (1994). To understand this complex ranking system, one must delve briefly into two closely related matters: the Hawaiian *kapu* system, and concepts of marriage and blood purity.

TABLE 2.2. THE NAMED CATEGORIES OF *ALI'I*

Rank	Category	Comments	Associated Kapu
HIGHEST ↑	Nī'aupi'o	Offspring of parents both of highest rank	kapu moe
	Pi'o	Offspring of full-sibling marriage of *nī'aupi'o* rank	kapu moe
	Naha	Offspring of half-sibling marriage of *nī'aupi'o* rank	kapu noho
	Wohi	Offspring of *nī'aupi'o*, *pi'o*, or *naha* father with a close female relative	kapu wohi
	Papa	Offspring of *nī'aupi'o*, *pi'o*, or *naha* mother with a lower-ranking male chief	
	Lōkea	Offspring of high-ranked father with mother a relative through younger siblings	
	Lā'au ali'i	Parents are children of high chiefs through secondary matings	
↓	Kaukau ali'i	Flexible term signifying an inferior or dependent status; descendants of high chiefs through collateral branches	
LOWEST	Ali'i noanoa	Literally, "without kapu." Offspring of a high chief and a commoner woman; not recognized as *ali'i* unless special provision made	

As in other early state societies (especially Egypt and Inka Peru [Trigger 2003:163, 184]), high-ranking Hawaiian elites intermarried to concentrate the blood line, and incest prohibitions that pertained to most of society were loosened for those at the top. Hawaiian genealogies and oral traditions speak abundantly to the practice of royal endogamy, with sibling and half-sibling marriages encouraged at the pinnacle of society. Of the various chiefly ranks described by Kamakau (1964:4–6) the most exalted was the nīʻaupiʻo, whose parents were both themselves of this highest rank. When the sibling offspring of a nīʻaupiʻo couple mated, in Kamakau's words "the sister marrying her brother, and the brother his sister, this wondrous marriage (hoʻao) of theirs was called a hoʻao piʻo, an arched marriage. . . . The children born of these two were gods, fire, heat, and raging blazes, and they conversed with chiefs and retainers only at night" (1964:4). Slightly lower in rank were the naha chiefs, who were the offspring of half-brother and half-sister matings.

The principle underlying these close kin matings—which violate the otherwise nearly universal incest taboo between brothers and sisters—is the desire to concentrate the blood lines of the highest ranking elites. As Kameʻeleihiwa points out, in Hawaiian cosmogonic myth ". . . incest is by definition a formula for creating divinity," and indeed, ". . . the very act of incest is proof of divinity" (1992:40). Indeed, such matings underscored the aliʻi's transcendence of rules and norms that governed the ordinary population, putting them above and beyond normal society. It is a feature that distinguishes Hawaiian kingship from other Polynesian chiefship.

Such unions were only permitted to take place among the highest ranks, and were consecrated with great solemnity. "The copulation was completed in a special tent of bark cloth that had been set up in a public place. Before joining his wife inside, the husband placed an image of his personal deity outside the tent, and the assembled priests prayed that the union would be fruitful" (Davenport 1994:18). As Davenport explains, the Hawaiian metaphor is expressed in terms of a coconut midrib, a nīʻau, representing the descent line. "In the Hawaiian language such merging of close collaterals was expressed as the looping back (piʻo), the return (hoʻi), and the curving (naha) of midribs of coconut leaflets (nīʻau) onto each other" (1994:48). Many of these "consanguineal marriages" were between half siblings in which the women were the product of a "secondary" marriage of either the father or mother, and the result was to systematically unite several dominant chiefly lineages (Valeri 1972:40).

The trinity of core cultural concepts of *mana*, *kapu*, and *noa* is pervasive in Polynesian societies, and in Hawaiʻi was hyper-elaborated, corresponding to the promulgation of the concept of divine kingship. These concepts, and especially those of *mana* and *kapu* (or "taboo," as it has come into English as a loanword from Polynesian), are the subject of a vast anthropological literature, canvassed, among others, by Shore, who observes that "without an understanding of *mana* and its related concepts, there is no path into Polynesian worldview" (1989:137). Polynesians located the ultimate source of power and fecundity in the sprit realm, abode of their ancestors and their gods; *mana* was the manifestation of that power in the world of humans. As Handy (1927:26) wrote: "Mana was exhibited in persons, in power, strength, prestige, reputation, skill, dynamic personality, intelligence; in things, in efficacy, in 'luck'; that is[,] in accomplishment." Life literally depended on the continual transmission of *mana* from the gods to humans and earth, for *mana* was "always linked to organic generativity and thus to all forces of growth and vitality" (Shore 1989:164).

But *mana* did not flow equally to all persons; quite the contrary, *mana* followed the pathways of rank and genealogical descent that also ordered Polynesian societies, and the more hierarchical these became, the more differentiated the distribution of *mana* across the social order. In all Polynesian societies, *mana* was concentrated in persons of rank, but in the more highly stratified societies the chiefs came to occupy particular roles as sources or vehicles of *mana* on which the society at large depended for its well-being. Nowhere was this more so than in late Hawaiian society. The Hawaiian divine kings, as gods on earth, were essential for the reproduction of society; they also held the power of life or death over the common people, most often exercised through the rites of human sacrifice. Death, as the polar opposite of life, is another aspect of *mana*.

Kapu is often glossed as either "sacred," or "prohibited," and refers to that state which is necessary for the protection of *mana*. Its opposite is *noa*, "free" from *kapu*, hence sometimes glossed as "profane." These simple glosses mask a tangled set of relationships that bind the three terms into a complex whole. Recall that Kepelino used *noa* as the term for the class of common people; they were *noa* in relation to the *ali'i*, who were *kapu*, because the latter were intermediaries between the gods and the society at large, the all-important transmitters of *mana*. What is sometimes referred to as the "*kapu* system" was in reality a whole series of socially and ritually prescribed practices that controlled the daily lives and bodily practices of all ranks of late Hawaiian society. At its core was the *'ai kapu*, the "eating taboo" that controlled gender relations, and specified that men and women could not eat together, that their foods must be cooked in separate ovens, and that certain foods (pork, in particular, but also certain kinds of bananas, fish, and so on) were prohibited to women. As Kameʻeleihiwa argues, however, the *ʻai kapu* was a metaphor that provided "the underpinning of the entire *kapu* system" (1992:36). "It was the *Aliʻi Nui* [divine kings] who had to follow the dictates of the *ʻAikapu* most closely, because they were the *Akua* [gods] on earth who mediated between ordinary humans and the destructive-reproductive forces of the unseen divinities of the cosmos" (1992:36). Thus the prohibitions regulating the "horizontal" relations between genders become amplified on a "vertical" plane as a parallel set of prohibitions and strictures regulating contact between the *aliʻi* (*kapu*) and the commoners (*noa*). "The *Aliʻi Nui* became fearful *Akua*, and the *makaʻāinana* in their reverence, avoided direct contact with them" (Kameʻeleihiwa 1992:38).

The *kapu* enveloping the most sacred Hawaiian chiefs and kings were elaborated and intensified to a greater degree than elsewhere in Polynesia (except, perhaps, Tonga). Their premises, their clothing, their food, and their bodies were all subject to and regulated by a complex set of prescriptions and prohibitions, designed to protect their *mana* and keep them from contact with polluting influences (*noa*). Thus, for example, Malo tells us that "when a tabu chief ate, the people in his presence must kneel, and if anyone raised his knee from the ground, he was put to death" (1951:57). In part, this reflects the fact that the meals of the king included meat which had been consecrated in the temple rituals (Valeri 1985a:126–27).[8] The eating house of the king was in effect a spatial extension of the temple, a sacred place in its own right. That the *ʻai kapu* underpinned the entire *kapu* system is not an exaggeration, for when, in 1819, following the death of Kamehameha, the young king Liholiho (Kamehameha II) sat and ate with his late father's favorite wife, Kaʻahumanu, and the other chiefly women, this was the symbolic act of abolishing the entire *ancien régime*.

Taking a cue from Norbert Elias (1983, 1994), who has written eloquently on the rise of etiquette and courtly culture in Europe, it is worth observing that the Hawaiian royal courts had undergone a similar "intensification" of courtly behavior, a corollary no doubt of their intense "prestige-fetish" (Elias 1983:134). Kepelino devotes much of his account of chiefship to the various specialized attendants who made up the household of a highly ranked *aliʻi*: the *kahu* or family guardian, the "head executioner" (*ilāmuku*) who was responsible for putting to death anyone who violated the *kapu* of the noble, the bodyguards (*kiaʻipoʻo*) who watched over the sleeping *aliʻi*, the keeper of the royal wardrobe (*mālama-ukana*), the head steward (*ʻāʻī-puʻupuʻu*), the keeper of the royal possessions or "head treasurer" (*puʻukū-nui*), a special attendant to look after the king's private parts when he was ill, and yet other functionaries (Beckwith 1932:122–31). Kepelino writes that "court etiquette" (*ka noho ana nihinihi*), including proper modes of acting, speaking, walking, and sitting, were mandatory in the presence of a high chief or king (1932:140–41). John Papa ʻĪʻī, who from the age of about 10 years served in the royal court of Kamehameha (his functions included carrying the spittoon of the young *nīʻaupiʻo* chief Liholiho), provides many vignettes of courtly life (e.g., 1959:58–61). Among other activities, he describes the time devoted by members of the royal household to such sports as *maika* stone bowling (special *maika* courts were adjacent to the royal compound), surfing, boxing and other martial arts, gambling, and *kōnane* playing (a game similar to checkers) (1959:63–77).

Contact between the highest ranked *aliʻi* (the first four ranks of Table 2.2) and the common people was strictly controlled and restricted. A special symbol, the *pūloʻuloʻu* (a staff tipped with a round ball of white barkcloth), was set up to mark the chiefly enclosure. "Anyone who came in without permission was put to death" (Kepelino, in Beckwith 1932:134). As indicated in Table 2.2, the two highest ranks of *aliʻi*, the *nīʻaupiʻo* and *piʻo*, were due a particular form of deference known as the *kapu moe*, the "prostrating taboo." This required everyone immediately to strip off any upper body garments, and lie prostrate on the ground until the chief had passed out of view.[9] Anyone failing to perform the *kapu moe* was subject to immediate death. The only persons exempt from the *kapu moe* were *aliʻi* of the next two categories (*naha* and *wohi* chiefs), who nonetheless were required to sit in the presence of the *nīʻaupiʻo* and *piʻo aliʻi*. The great ideological significance of the *kapu moe* is that it was also the *kapu* of the *akua*, the gods. Thus gods and the highest *aliʻi* (literally, *aliʻi akua*) shared the same forms of obeisance. Owing to the onerous nature of the *kapu moe*, the highest ranked *aliʻi* rarely ventured out among the commoner folk, and often traveled about at night to avoid being seen.[10] Kepelino offers the following description of a royal entourage:

> As to the prostrating tapu of the chief [i.e., king], when the chief wished to go forth the announcer went ahead proclaiming the tapu of the chief, thus: "Tapu! lie down!" Then everyone prostrated himself on the way by which the chief was passing and the tapu chiefs who followed him, all dressed

with great splendor in feather cloaks and helmets, attended by waving
kahilis and with perfume sprinkled on their garments (Beckwith 1932:138).

Clearly, the highest ranks of *ali'i* shared a number of attributes with
the gods, and indeed were explicitly called *ali'i akua* or "god-kings"
(Valeri 1985a:143; Malo 1951:54; Kamakau 1961:4). Valeri (1985a:
142–53) discusses the ethnographic evidence for divine kingship in late
Hawai'i, and I will reiterate only a few key points. As the ritual leader
of his people, who intercedes with the gods to assure the flow of *mana*,
the king "instantiates different major gods or groups of their particular-
izations according to a precise ritual calendar" (1985a:142). Thus when
he goes to war, the king offers a human sacrifice at the *luakini* temple of
Kū, but at other times he consecrates temples to the agricultural gods
Lono and Kāne. The king shares with these gods the right to the *kapu
moe*, the prostrating *kapu*. Another sign of their divinity is the capacity
of high-ranked *ali'i* to practice incestuous marriage, something that the
gods provide the model for (as in the creation myth of Wākea and Papa,
Beckwith [1940]). Gods and kings share other material insignia as well:
the *pūlo'ulo'u* staff, and the wrapping of their bodies in feathered garments (see below). Holding the power of life or death over ordinary
humans, the king is frequently described as the ultimate devourer, a
shark (in particular, the tiger shark, *Galeocerdo cuvieri*). In the lines of
a chant recorded by Fornander (1916–20, 6:393–94):

> A shark going inland is my chief,
> A very strong shark able to devour all on land;
> A shark of very red gills is the chief,
> He has a throat to swallow the island without choking.

By the time of initial contact with Europeans, Hawaiians had taken the
older Polynesian concepts of chiefship and rank, and subjected them to a
form of hypertrophy, the logical extension of which was that their rulers,
their kings, were now held to be divine. This was not simply a quantitative extension of the Ancestral Polynesian ranking system; it was a truly
qualitative change by which Hawaiian society had entered a new realm.

ELITE ART, CRAFT SPECIALIZATION, AND WEALTH FINANCE

While early civilizations varied greatly in their particular styles of
elite art, in all cases "the upper classes sponsored the creation of elaborate works of art that symbolized their power and social exclusivity"

(Trigger 2003:564). Hawai'i fits this pattern well, with the specialized production of material culture items reserved for exclusive use by the elites; indeed, these items were finely differentiated in scale and stylistic details so as to signify rank gradations. Hawaiian elites supported the production of art objects through the patronage of craft specialists who often resided in, or adjacent to, the royal households. Lacking metallurgy, and with the island's geologic resources restricted to basaltic rocks, Hawaiian craftsmen had a limited range of materials with which to work. Despite these limitations, they produced spectacular objects of great sophistication, most notably in featherwork (Brigham 1899).

The use of bird feathers is widespread in Polynesia (Steadman 1997), both for items of bodily adornment (such as headdresses or breastplates) and as ornamentation on woven mats or other objects. However, cloaks or capes covered in feathers are known from just three Eastern Polynesian societies: New Zealand, the Society Islands, and Hawai'i. Based on careful analysis of the techniques used in production of these capes, Buck concluded that these were independent inventions in each island group, and that "the Hawaiians should be given credit for having invented their own feather capes and cloaks" (1957:216). Moreover, no other Polynesian society elaborated or perfected the art of featherwork to the extent found in late Hawaiian society. Cook's company—who understood innately the ways in which dress defined gradations in both European civil and naval society—was deeply impressed by the feathered cloaks as well as helmets worn by Hawaiian elite men (Fig. 2.2). Samwell wrote that "a more rich or elegant Dress than this, perhaps the Arts of Europe have not yet been able to supply" (Beaglehole 1967:1179). Both Samwell and Lt. James King describe the variation in length and styles of capes and cloaks, noting that these correspond to gradations in chiefly rank (Beaglehole 1967:1179, 1392). Samwell writes:

> Inferior Chiefs have Cloaks made of Cock's Tail feathers with a Collar of red & yellow, others of white bordered with Cocks feathers & a Collar of red & yellow. Some of the first Chiefs have long cloaks made of the fine yellow feathers of the Cocks with a Collar and borders of red and yellow feathers (Beaglehole 1967:1179).

Samwell was mistaken in his assumption that the brilliant yellow and red feathers came from "Cocks" or jungle fowl (*Gallus gallus*). Rather, these were obtained from several species of endemic forest birds, particularly the 'i'iwi (*Vestiaria coccinea*) and 'ō'ō (*Moho nobilis*), which supplied the majority of red and yellow feathers, respectively (Buck

Figure 2.2. Detail of a Hawaiian *ali'i* with feathered helmet and cape as depicted by John Webber, artist on Captain Cook's third voyage. (*Source:* Cook and King, 1784, *A Voyage to the Pacific Ocean*, London, Plate 64.)

1957:217). Obtaining these feathers was the work of bird-hunting specialists who frequented the mountainous interiors of the islands, trapping the birds with sticky lime placed strategically on tree branches, or by netting them. The capes and cloaks, called *'ahu'ula* in Hawaiian,[11] were manufactured exclusively by male craftsmen, "so as to further mark the distinction against women," who were prohibited from wearing these articles (Buck 1957:217). Kaeppler (1997:85) argues that these male craftsmen were also priests.

Chiefs of various ranks wore rectangular or circular capes, but only the highest-ranking elites—in particular the divine king—was permitted to wear a full-length cloak extending from the neck very nearly to the feet. The labor investment in a cloak of this size is staggering. The Kamehameha cloak in the Bishop Museum is comprised of an estimated 450,000 feathers of the rare yellow *mamo* bird (with a few red *'i'iwi* feathers along the neck border), representing approximately 80,000 birds. The taking of so many birds, accumulation of the necessary feathers, production of the fine netting, and tedious work of attaching several hundred thousand feathers by hand with fine threads, represents a labor investment and surplus accumulation of extraordinary proportions. Thus Buck quite correctly concludes that "while the capes remained the insignia of chiefs, the cloaks became the royal robes of kings" (1957:231).

The resplendent feathered finery of Hawaiian elites did not end with capes and cloaks, but was topped off by helmets (*mahiole*), another uniquely Hawaiian innovation within Polynesia. As with the capes, there was variation in style and materials, which to the initiated again provided a visual signal of social position: "The crested helmets covered with colored feathers were the natural complement of the feather cloaks and so completed the regalia of high chiefs and kings. Other helmets, decorated with human hair or mushroomlike ornaments, were the headdresses of warriors and lesser chiefs" (Buck 1957:231). Bird feathers were also used in two other kinds of elite symbols: necklaces (*lei*) and fly whisks or standards (*kāhili*).[12]

To appreciate fully the symbolism of the feathered capes, cloaks, and helmets, one must note that the same red and yellow feathers adorned the surfaces of woven anthropomorphic images, notably of the war god Kū (see Frontispiece). The images were made from the split fibers of *'ie'ie* vine (*Freycinetia arborea*), applying the same weaving technique used in the feathered helmets. Individual images vary, but most have a crest (as in the helmets), inlaid eyes of pearl shell, and an open mouth fringed with dog's teeth. Several such surviving feathered images are illustrated by Kaeppler (1978: Figs. 56–58). The Kū image illustrated in the frontispiece was collected on Cook's third voyage, probably at Hawai'i Island (Kaeppler 1998:242–43); it is covered in red feathers with a crest of yellow feathers. These feathered images accompanied the king on his travels, and into battle.

The iconography of the king wrapped in his feathered cloak, his head protected by a crested, feathered helmet inevitably merges with the image of his personal war god, similarly crested and wrapped in identical red and yellow feathers. But to the Hawaiians, the cultural symbolism was far deeper and complex. As Thomas observes, "the layers of feathers were understood to bear a chief's divinity and genealogies" (1995:161). Valeri (1985a:15: Table 1) enumerates various attributes of the war god Kū, including the sacred color red, the *ōhi'a-lehua* tree (to which the prized *ō'ō* bird was attracted, for its red flowers), and the *'ie'ie* vine (from which the feathered god images were woven), the feather-giving *ō'ō* bird itself. Kū is the deity not only of war, but of mountains and remote high places whence the precious feathers come. The *ōhi'a* forests with their red flowers are themselves like cloaks over Kū's terrain, and they form "a group with the *'ie'ie* and birds with precious plumage" (Valeri 1985a:272). The king and the war god are symbolically joined, equally wrapped in sacred feathers; thus the king is truly, in Kamakau's words, an *ali'i akua*, a "god-king" (1961:61, 71; 1964:5, 10).

Kaeppler (1985:118), based on careful analysis of late-eighteenth- and early-nineteenth-century feathered cloaks in museum collections, suggests that "... status based on prestige and power was in a state of flux" during this period, manifest particularly in changes in the color and design of cloaks. Red is the ancient sacred color of Polynesian chiefs, and the term *'ahu'ula* actually translates "red shoulder garment" as Kaeppler points out. "The red colour gradually diminished and the garments became more and more yellow, marking a change from religious to political symbolism." The feathered god images, however, remained exclusively red. Kaeppler suggests that the yellow feathers were becoming "more scarce and precious" and could only be "commanded in great numbers by powerful personages" such as Kamehameha. Hommon has also suggested that "... a major goal of Hawaiian warfare was the acquisition by warrior chiefs of scarce goods such as pigs and yellow feathers" (2009:14). This is a point I return to in Chapter 5.

Hawaiian elite art was by no means restricted to featherwork, although this clearly constituted the pinnacle of the material arts. Rank and status were indicated as well by other kinds of personal adornment, including necklaces and bracelets of carved tusk, bone, shell, and ivory. Of particular significance was the *lei niho palaoa* neck ornament, a highly stylized, hook-shaped pendant carved from the tooth of a sperm whale, suspended by multiple coils of finely braided human hair (Buck 1957:535–38), which could only be worn by members of the *ali'i* class. The eight-ply square braids of human hair number more than 200 strands in smaller *lei niho palaoa*, but in some of the larger specimens there are more than 1,000 strands (Buck 1957:537).

Polynesian barkcloth manufacture reached its apogee in Hawai'i, with the "greatest varieties of texture and colored designs" (Buck 1957:166), no doubt in large part due to elite patronage of barkcloth (*kapa*) specialists. *Kapa* sheets were decorated by watermarking with incised beaters, as well as by stamping and painting with a variety of dyes, and were scented as well (Kooijman 1972:97–175). Whereas feathers were associated with the war god Kū, *kapa* was closely linked to Lono, god of dryland agriculture and patron of the common people. White *kapa* streamers adorned the *akua loa*, or "long god" during the Makahiki or new year tribute-collecting procession.

Craft specialization extended to other media such as wood carving (elaborate bowls and calabashes were produced for elite households, for holding and serving food, water, and *'awa*), weaving, and the production of weapons and musical instruments. Of special note is the royal patronage of canoe builders, an expert guild known as *kahuna kālai wa'a*, whose tutelary deity was a manifestation of the war god Kū, Kūpulupulu (Buck 1957:254). Double-hulled sailing canoes were especially important to the ruling elites, as their normal mode of transport both between coastal residences and between islands, and for warfare. Both at Kaua'i in 1778 and again off Maui and Hawai'i in 1779, the high chiefs and kings who met Cook invariably traveled on large double canoes, often in groups of three or more canoes. About 15 meters long, with mat sails, platforms, booms, and other attachments, these double canoes were complex constructions requiring skilled carpentry and other crafts (Haddon and Hornell 1936). Hawaiian oral histories (see Chapter 3) recount significant fleets of such double canoes being constructed under the kingly aegis.[13]

Drawing on distinctions made by D'Altroy and Earle (1985; see also Brumfiel and Earle 1987:6; Johnson and Earle 2000:257), the economies of complex societies are sometimes characterized in terms of *staple* finance versus *wealth* finance. The former are based on subsistence goods, which are collected by the state apparatus and used to support the elite classes (and which may be redistributed by the elites). In the latter, the state uses some form of nonfood material wealth as currency. These, of course, are idealized types. Brumfiel and Earle (1987:6) cite "the Hawaiian chiefdoms and Inka empire" as examples of "decentralized staple finance systems." In his later comparative study of chiefdom political economy, Earle (1997) puts great emphasis on Hawai'i as a type case of a staple finance system. In my view this is an oversimplification, for it neglects the fact that the Hawaiian elites collected tribute not exclusively in the form of subsistence products, but also in a range of material goods, notably barkcloth, woven mats, cordage, and especially the highly prized red and yellow birds' feathers necessary for the capes, cloaks, and helmets of the *ali'i*. The king accumulated these manufactured goods in his storehouses, and redistributed them to the elite cadre who supported him. Control over precious feathers—and the highly symbolic cloaks, capes, helmets, and *kāhili* made with them—was an important power strategy to the Hawaiian rulers. Thus the Hawaiian economic system, while founded first and foremost on the staple finance provided by its vast intensive agricultural complexes was not without a significant element of wealth finance as well.

POLITICAL, ADMINISTRATIVE,
AND SETTLEMENT HIERARCHIES

Scholars of archaic states have long stressed that such polities were characterized by administrative hierarchies of at least three and often four levels, typically reflected in their settlement hierarchies. Indeed, the presence of clear settlement hierarchies is often used by archaeologists to infer the administrative structure of ancient states (e.g., Flannery 1972, 1995, 1998; Spencer 1987, 1990; Spencer and Redmond 2001; Wright and Johnson 1975). The complex hierarchy of administrative and territorial divisions into which each Hawaiian island kingdom was subdivided provides a convenient point of entry for understanding the Hawaiian political system. Traditional Hawaiian political and economic life was organized around a formal, nested hierarchy of units (Kirch and Sahlins 1992). Each independent kingdom (tier 1) included an entire island (*mokupuni*), sometimes with smaller subsidiary islands, which in turn was usually subdivided into either six or twelve districts, called *moku* (tier 2). *Moku* in turn were segmented into a large number of smaller territorial units called *ahupua'a* (tier 3 in the land hierarchy). *Ahupua'a* typically ran from the coast to the upland forests, crosscutting the concentrically zonated resources of an island. Although they ranged greatly in size, *ahupua'a* could incorporate as much as 10 km². On the geologically older islands where topography was defined by stream valleys, *ahupua'a* typically corresponded with watersheds, their boundaries running along ridgelines. On younger landforms, boundaries were more arbitrary, with the *ahupua'a* units paralleling each other in narrow strips running from the coast inland. There were no fewer than 600 such *ahupua'a* units in the Hawai'i Island polity at contact (Cordy 2000:31). *Ahupua'a* formed the core of the political and economic system, and in theory each was an economically self-sustaining unit, able to draw on a full range of resources, from ocean and littoral zones, through arable lands for cultivations, and reaching up into the higher elevations for timber and forest resources. Although they were central to Hawaiian economic organization, the *ahupuaʻa* were not the lowest tier in the hierarchy, for *ahupuaʻa* were yet again divided into smaller segments called *ʻili* (tier 4), each of which comprised multiple households and agricultural plots. Moreover, specific *ʻili* called *ʻili kūpono* were reserved for the king. In valleys, *ʻili* often corresponded to irrigable sections on stream terraces (as in the Anahulu Valley; see Kirch and Sahlins 1992), whereas on the volcanic flow slopes of the younger islands *ʻili* comprised narrow strips within the *ahupuaʻa*. These four major tiers in the nested hierarchy of territories each carried proper names, toponyms that precisely labeled and designated a particular terrain (and, by extension, its inhabitants).

This territorial land structure corresponded to an equally precise political and administrative hierarchy of overlords, consisting of *aliʻi* of various grades, but not to be confused with the hierarchical ranking system of chiefs described earlier. At the apex of the polity sat the king, the *aliʻi nui* or "great aliʻi," sometimes also called the *mōʻī*.[14] The *aliʻi nui* ruled over the entire *mokupuni*, assisted by various administrative aides. *Aliʻi nui* were often of the highest ranks, but not necessarily of *nīʻaupiʻo* or *piʻo* rank; indeed, as we see in Chapter 3 there was a tradition of usurpation of the kingship by slightly less highly ranked *aliʻi* (often of *wohi* or *naha* rank), whose *mana* was manifest in their abilities and deeds, rather than in their exalted genealogies. The famous Kamehameha I, who ultimately united the entire archipelago in the early-nineteenth century, was of *wohi* rank (Kamakau 1964:5).

The districts (*moku*) into which the kingdom was divided were each under the control of a major chief of high rank, called the *aliʻi-ʻai-moku*. The operative term *ʻai* in this compound term has the core meaning of both "food" and "eat" but with metaphoric extensions connoting to "consume," "grasp," or "hold onto" (Pukui and Elbert 1986:9). Thus the figurative extension of *ʻai* includes "to rule, reign, or enjoy the privileges and exercise the responsibilities of rule." The term *aliʻi-ʻai-moku* might thus be simply translated "ruler of the *moku*," but as in many Hawaiian expressions there are layers of *kaona*, "hidden meanings", folded in. He is as well the chief who "eats" the district (recall the metaphor of the chief as land shark), and literally "eats from" its productions. In a parallel fashion, the more numerous *ahupuaʻa* territories were apportioned to chiefs who were called the *aliʻi-ʻai-ahupuaʻa*, the chiefs who "ate" the *ahupuaʻa*. Low-ranked chiefs might hold just a single, marginal land unit, but more powerful and higher-ranked *aliʻi* frequently held more than one *ahupuaʻa*.

The three tiered hierarchy of land rulers, beginning with the *ali'i nui* who had the power to reallocate lands to the *ali'i-'ai-moku* and *ali'i-'ai-ahupua'a* under him, did not extend down below the level of the largely self-sufficient *ahupua'a* territories. Rather, the administration of the *ahupua'a*, including its various *'ili* subdivisions, was put into the hands of a *konohiki*, a resident "land manager" who acted on behalf of the *ali'i-'ai-ahupua'a*. Konohiki were, in fact, often lower-ranked members of the *ali'i* class (such as *kaukau ali'i*), frequently junior collaterals of the *ahupua'a* chiefs themselves. For example, in the case of Waialua District, O'ahu Island, an important holding of the high-ranking *ali'i* Ka'ahumanu, the *konohiki* appointed to reside in the district and oversee the interests of the chiefess was La'anui, husband of her sister Pi'ia (Sahlins 1992:31). In the Hawaiian conception, the chief was the *mea hale* ("owner" of the house), while the *konohiki* or land manager was the *noho hale* ("resident" of the house), reflecting the vertical relationship between landlord or *haku'āina* and tenant or *hoa'āina* (1992:32, 46). The same relationship was then further promulgated between the *konohiki* and the various commoners who occupied and worked the *'ili* segments that made up his *ahupua'a*. Often the choicest *'ili* lands went to relatives of the *konohiki*, as with La'anui, who gave control of no less than 12 *'ili* and the large fishpond 'Uko'a to his kinsman Ku'oko'a (1992:141). Thus the hierarchical relations between landlord and tenant extended downward to the local level, that of the *'ili* and even lower, to the individual set of garden plots held by a single household, the *mo'o* (a fifth tier in the settlement hierarchy).

There was a good reason that *ali'i-'ai-ahupua'a* entrusted the management of their *ahupua'a* lands to resident *konohiki*, for the chiefs themselves were expected to be resident for at least much of the time at the royal court. Many of the *ahupua'a* level chiefs held administrative or other functional positions in the court, or were noted warrior chiefs. Moreover, it was not in the interest of the *ali'i nui* to have his chiefs off in the countryside where they might be tempted to make mischief, such as fomenting rebellion among the common people.

As was common in many dynastic states (Elias 1983), the central administration was effectively one and the same as the royal household, an incipient bureaucracy embedded within the king's extended residential group. Malo (1951:187–88) lays out the dualistic structure of this administrative body, referring to the "two strong forces, or parties, in the government": the *kahuna nui* or chief priest on the one hand, and the *kālaimoku*, or chief councilor, on the other.[15] The functions of the *kahuna nui* and other subsidiary priests will be considered in detail later. The *kālaimoku* was charged with advising the king on all secular affairs, including war. Among his chief duties was to oversee the royal storehouses "in which to collect food, fish, *tupa* [barkcloth], *malo* [loincloths], *pa-u* [female skirts], and all sorts of goods" (Malo 1951:195). Only the *kālaimoku* had the regular privilege of holding secret meetings with the king, and he controlled the access of other *ali'i* to royal audiences. As Kepelino makes clear in his own account of "the government," the Hawaiian system was highly decentralized, or distributed.[16] While the king "was the supreme head," whose power was most clearly indicated by his ability to redistribute the *moku* and *ahupua'a* land divisions to the chiefs under his rule, the daily management of these hierarchically nested lands rested largely in the hands of the *konohiki* (Beckwith 1932:146). "The *Konohiki* took charge of farm lands and sought means to benefit their overlords and chiefs."

This highly distributed management system corresponds with an equally dispersed settlement pattern. Hawai'i lacked anything approaching urban centers, and although there were substantial differences in population density corresponding to an uneven topographic distribution of soil and hydrologic resources (see discussion that follows), the general trend was of dispersed households, each occupying and farming its own adjacent plots. Moreover, while the commoners were sedentary on their lands, the *ali'i* were known to move about in relation to available food stocks. This peripatetic pattern of chiefly movement is well described, and underlies the metaphor of the chief as a "shark who travels on the land" (*He manō holo 'āina ke ali'i*; Pukui 1983:87: Proverb 799). Nonetheless, there were distinct chiefly and royal centers, marked by concentrations of larger residences adjacent to temples of the main state cults of Kū and Lono. On Hawai'i Island, one such royal center was in Waipi'o Valley, yet another at Hōnaunau in the leeward Kona District (see Chapter 4). 'Ī'ī (1959:65) provides a description of the physical layout of the royal court of Kamehameha at the mouth of Nu'uanu Stream, at what is now Honolulu, in the early postcontact period. Surrounding the king's own extensive household compound were the residential courts of several principal *ali'i* and advisors, the houses of warriors, and the main Hale o Lono or temple to the god in whose name the annual tribute was collected. While this settlement plan has certain innovations reflecting Western contact (notably the gun drilling field and the shipyard), in most respects it was probably typical of royal courtly centers in the late precontact era.

SYSTEMS OF PRODUCTION

To comprehend further the workings of the contact-era Hawaiian political economy, it is necessary to turn to the main systems of agricultural and aquacultural production. As noted earlier the Hawaiian economic system had elements of both "staple" and "wealth" finance to it. Nonetheless, it is true that intensive agricultural production was essential to the functioning of the Hawaiian archaic state. The primary root, tuber, and tree crops that formed the Hawaiian subsistence base were not generally amenable to storage, limiting the possibility of a magazine economy. Both taro and sweet potato, which dominated Hawaiian farming systems, were consumed relatively soon after harvest. In a subtropical climate, without the means of effective storage and concentration of staples, the dispersed and distributed nature of Hawaiian settlement and administrative control has a compelling logic. One way in which food could be stored, however, was to convert staple starch calories into protein, in the form of domestic pigs and dogs, of which the Hawaiian elites were notably fond (Sahlins 1992:28).[17] Not surprisingly, among the regular tribute items demanded by the *ali'i* were significant quantities of these two animals, especially large hogs, which were also among the obligatory sacrificial offerings at the state temples.[18]

Following a widespread dichotomy in Oceanic agricultural systems (Barrau 1965; Kirch 1994), Hawaiian agricultural production consisted of distinct "wet" and "dry" types. On older land surfaces, where erosion of the volcanic shield surfaces had created stream drainages with permanent water sources, agricultural production was dominated by the irrigated monoculture of taro (*Colocasia esculenta*). Alluvial and gentler colluvial slopes were terraced and divided into sometimes quite extensive arrays of flooded pondfields, fed by stream diversions and irrigation channels (or, on coastal plains, by springs) (Fig. 2.3). These irrigated *lo'i* lands were highly prized, for they could be kept under nearly continuous cultivation, and produced high yields (Handy 1940; Handy and Handy 1972). The steeper slopes above the irrigation canals (referred to as *kula* lands) were devoted to mixed planting of secondary crops with dwelling sites interspersed.

Where permanent streams or springs were lacking, most notably the younger land surfaces of East Maui and Hawai'i Islands, dryland or

Figure 2.3. The alluvial floodplain of the Hanalei Valley, Kaua'i Island is covered in a reticulate grid of irrigated pondfields. Such irrigated field complexes dominated the agricultural landscapes of the older Hawaiian Islands, especially Kaua'i and O'ahu. (Photo by P. V. Kirch.)

rain-fed farming systems dominated the agrarian landscapes. Extensive zones of dryland field systems have been identified on these two islands, including the Kohala, Kona, and Ka'ū field systems on Hawai'i, and the Kaupō and Kahikinui field systems on Maui (Ladefoged et al. 1996, 2003; Allen, M. S. 2001; Coil and Kirch 2005; Kirch et al. in press; Kirch 2010b). In these dryland systems some taro was grown in higher elevation zones with greater rainfall, but sweet potato (*Ipomoea batatas*) was the more important crop, supplemented to a certain degree by yams (*Dioscorea* spp.). These systems were characterized by vast reticulate grids of stone and/or earthen walls or bunds, demarcating individual field plots. The Kona field system was visited by Cook's 1779 expedition, whose members were impressed with the intensity of land use:

> [A]bout two miles without the town [the settlement at Kealakekua Bay] the land was level, and continued of one plain of little enclosures separated from each other by low broad walls . . . Some of these fields were planted,

Archaic States at European Contact

and others by their appearance were left fallow: In some we saw the natives collecting the coarse grass that had grown upon it during the time it had lain unimproved, and burning it in detached heaps. Their sweet potatoes are mostly raised here, and indeed are the principle object of their agriculture, but it requires an infinite deal of toil on account of the quantity of lava that remains on the land notwithstanding what is used about the walls to come at the soil . . . We saw a few patches of sugar cane interspersed in moist places, which were but small: But the cane was the largest and as sweet as any we had ever seen, we also passed several groups of plantain-trees. (Ledyard 1963:118-19).

Menzies (1920:75-76, 154-55), naturalist on the 1793 to 1794 Vancouver expedition, confirms Ledyard's account of intensive cultivation, including the practice of mulching. He adds the observation that in addition to root crops, the fields were also extensively planted in paper mulberry shrubs (*Broussonetia payrifera*) for barkcloth production, an aspect of the wealth finance system.

The observations of Ledyard and Menzies regarding mulching and the high degree of labor input to the dryland field systems resonate with Kamakau's remark that whereas in the older, western islands (where irrigation dominated) agriculture was exclusively a male occupation, in Maui and Hawai'i women joined the men in sharing the burdens of field work (1961:239). As I have argued elsewhere (Kirch 1994:252-68), this is a predictable corollary of critical agronomic differences between the irrigation and dryland production systems. Whereas the former required a substantial labor investment in their initial construction (as "landesque capital" intensive systems, Blaikie and Brookfield 1987), their continued maintenance and operation demanded comparatively low rates of labor input relative to their high yields. In contrast, the dryland systems needed significant continued labor inputs, especially in weeding and mulching of the fields, to produce more modest yields.

More critical to understanding the dynamics of the late Hawaiian economic and political systems is that the archipelago-wide distribution of these two major kinds of agricultural productions systems was highly uneven. The vast zones of dryland production are confined almost entirely to Hawai'i and East Maui, with one other significant area on the Kalaupapa Peninsula of Moloka'i. Conversely, the main zones of irrigation are restricted to the older islands of Kaua'i through Moloka'i, with more limited areas on the intermediate age volcanic cones of West Maui and Kohala on Hawai'i Island. As a consequence, the capacity for surplus production in the O'ahu and Kaua'i polities was considerably greater (at least on a per capita basis) than in the Maui and Hawai'i polities. Moreover, the vulnerability of the dryland systems, especially to drought, and the recurrent possibility of famine, were always lurking in the wings in the case of the latter two islands. These factors played a huge role in the dynamics of Hawaiian sociopolitical transformation, as I argue further in Chapters 4 and 5.

To underscore the resource differences between islands and their polities further, the marine resource base displayed an increasing gradient of productivity from east to west, that is, geologically younger to older. Coral reefs, on which marine biomass production depends, develop gradually along midplate volcanic island coastlines. Reefs are lacking or only minimally developed on Hawai'i and East Maui, and hence the biomass of fish and shellfish along these rocky or cliff-bound shorelines is relatively low. In contrast, the older islands, especially O'ahu and Kaua'i, boast extensive zones of fringing reef with correspondingly rich fishing and gathering potential. The Hawaiians, however, did not limit their exploitation of littoral and inshore resources to capturing the natural fish and shellfish fauna. Unique among Polynesian peoples, they developed true fishpond aquaculture (Summers 1964; Kikuchi 1976). Mostly, the ponds consisted of semicircular arcs of stone walls, constructed with thousands of boulders carried out and piled up on the reef flats, enclosing areas in which mullet and milkfish could be farmed. But these ponds could only be built on the older island shorelines where mature coral reefs had developed. The few ponds on Hawai'i and East Maui were limited to small natural anchialine pools in the lava formations, and had only limited yields. In contrast, the broad reef flats of south Moloka'i, O'ahu, and parts of Kaua'i provided ideal habitats for fishpond construction.

The differences in production zones across the four major polities that controlled the archipelago at the time of contact in 1778 to 1779 are summarized in Table 2.3. Without any doubt, the two largest polities, Hawai'i and Maui, were the most constrained in terms of both agricultural and aquacultural production. The O'ahu and Kaua'i polities enjoyed the greatest extent of both irrigation and aquaculture. The Hawaiian kings were well aware of these unequal resource distributions, and it comes as no surprise that the driving goal of Kamehameha I of Hawai'i Island was to conquer and acquire the rich islands of O'ahu and Kaua'i. He invaded O'ahu in 1795 but could not hold it for long; then he managed to reconquer and occupy it in 1804. Kaua'i eluded Kamehameha longer, his war fleet being twice sundered in the wide,

Archaic States at European Contact 55

TABLE 2.3. GENERAL DISTRIBUTION OF
PRODUCTION ZONES BY POLITY

Polity	Irrigation	Dryland Fieldsystems	Fishponds
Hawai'i	Limited to valleys in Kohala District	Extensive zones in leeward Kohala, Kona, Ka'ū, and Hamakua districts	87 recorded ponds, mostly limited to small anchialine ponds
Maui	Limited to small valleys on parts of East Maui and on West Maui	Extensive zone of dryland production from Kaupō through Kula districts of East Maui	16 recorded fishponds
Moloka'i[a]	Extensive irrigation in the windward valleys of Ko'olau District; some coastal irrigation in Kona District	Formal fieldsystem on the Kalaupapa Peninsula	73 recorded fishponds along southern coast
O'ahu	Extensive irrigation complexes in windward valleys as well as leeward plains	No fieldsystems per se; some dryland cultivation in leeward valleys (e.g., Mākaha)	184 recorded fishponds
Kaua'i	Extensive irrigation in all valley locations	Limited to some colluvial areas in leeward zones	65 recorded fishponds

[a]Moloka'i was no longer an independent polity in late prehistory but was variously under the control of the Maui or O'ahu polities.

rough channel isolating Kaua'i from the rest of the archipelago. In the end, that "separate kingdom" was brought under his control through diplomacy and royal marriage (Kuykendall 1938).

THE HIERARCHY OF PRIESTS AND TEMPLES

A key feature of archaic or dynastic states is their use of religious ideology and ritual practice in the service of the state. Flannery (1998:36) draws attention to the pervasive role of temples and full-time priests in many archaic states, as well as to the presence of priestly residences. Trigger notes the importance of sacrificial cults in early civilizations, especially cults involving human sacrifice (2003:472, 484–85). His comparative study demonstrates that in most early civilizations, the king was the chief intermediary between the gods and the people. Priests, while important and often hierarchically organized, did not rule; these were not theocracies (Trigger 2003:495–521). Nonetheless, a formal state religion that legitimates the political and social order was key to most early states, and Hawai'i is no exception.

The Hawaiians, as with other Eastern Polynesians, were polytheistic, and four major deities dominated: Kū, Lono, Kāne, and Kanaloa (Malo 1951:81; Valeri 1985a: Table 1). Kū, god of war, was perforce the principal god of the king, and his anthropomorphic images, covered in brilliant red feathers, were carried into war as well as displayed at tribute collections of the king. But Kū had other functions, including fishing, canoe building, and sorcery; he was associated with the color red, with high mountains and forests, and it was to him alone that human sacrifices were offered. Lono, who divided the annual ritual calendar with Kū, was the god of dryland agriculture, fertility, and birth; his signs were clouds, thunder, and the rain essential for sweet potato growth. Lono's ritual season was marked by the first visibility of the star cluster Pleiades (in Hawaiian, Makali'i) around November 17 (Valeri 1985a:199), and continued for the next four lunar months. This was the Makahiki, whose significance I will address later. During the Makahiki, the cult of Kū was in abeyance and warfare was forbidden. Kāne represented the male power of procreation, but was also the god of flowing waters, and as such was the patron deity of irrigation and fishponds.[19] The East and the rising sun were especially associated with Kāne (Beckwith 1932:14–16, 80), and the path of the sun across the sky was his road. Finally, Kanaloa was a deity of death, of the subterranean world, and of the sea (Valeri 1985a:15). Each of these major gods had his own cults, his own priests, and his own particular temples and rituals.

The king concerned himself in particular with the annual ritual cycle alternating between Kū and Lono. While the commoners, the *maka'āinana*, also participated in the state rituals, and indeed were required to furnish the substantial quantities of sacrificial offerings (pigs, dogs, coconuts, and other foodstuffs) necessary for major temple rites, these commoners practiced—on a daily basis—an entirely separate, more private religious cult. Commoner religious practice focused on the collective body of ancestors, the *'aumakua*. The word *'aumakua* derives from the prefix *'au,* designating a group, and *makua,* the word for "parent" (Pukui and Elbert 1986:32). *'Aumakua* were literally then the collective body of parents, grandparents, and ancestors of particular

Archaic States at European Contact 57

family groups of *maka'āinana* who—having no proper names because deep genealogies were not kept by the common people—took the form of various natural creatures, such as sharks, owls, octopuses, eels, shellfish, and plants. Prayers were offered to the *'aumakua* in the *mua*, the men's eating house, along with offerings of *'awa* root and taro or other foods placed at a simple shrine.[20] This distinction between the daily worship of the collective, nameless *'aumakua* in the men's houses of the commoners, and the ostentatious public ceremonies carried out with great formality on the temple platforms dedicated to the state gods, is further witness to the strong class distinctions that permeated late precontact Hawaiian society.

Although much of its terminology derives from the older Proto-Polynesian vocabulary, the Hawaiian priesthood was elaborated well beyond anything known elsewhere in Polynesia (Handy 1927). The general term for priest is *kahuna*, a derivation from PPN **tufunga*, "expert" (see Chapter 1). In Hawai'i, *kahuna* were full-time specialists. There were several major classes of *kahuna*, the most important being the *kahuna pule*, *kahuna lapa'au*, and *kahuna 'anā'anā*. The priests who officiated at temples controlled by the king and major chiefs were the *kahuna pule*. These were subdivided into a number of specific orders or cults, especially those pertaining to Kū and Lono (*mo'o Kū* and *mo'o Lono*). These priests were drawn from high-ranking elite families, typically of *papa* rank (in which the person's mother comes from one of the three highest ranks). The most important priest of the order of Kū was the *kahuna nui*, or "high priest" (Valeri [1985a] calls him the "royal chaplain"), who carried the responsibilities for the king's religious duties and looked after his temples and main gods.

Kahuna lapa'au were medicinal priests or curing experts. Kamakau (1964:98) lists eight specific varieties, including those who specialized in diagnosis, others who used sorcery or magic in treatment, and priests who were particularly knowledgeable in the application of herbal medicines. Greatly feared were the *kahuna 'anā'anā*, or sorcerers, who tended to perform their work outside of, and indeed in opposition to the main state cults (Valeri 1985a:138). *Kahuna 'anā'anā* were thus somewhat marginal figures, although they could wield substantial power and influence. Another marginal category is that of the *kāula*, or "prophets," one that can also be traced back to Ancestral Polynesia. These individuals were thought to have direct relationships with particular gods, and would enter into trance states in which they spoke the god's oracle. Although *kāula* did not participate in the state cults, they were frequently sought out by kings for their advice. A famous example from the immediate contact era is that of Kapoukahi, a prophet of Kaua'i who was consulted by the chiefess Ha'alo'u, on behalf of Kamehameha, to ascertain what acts would assure the latter's ascendancy over all of Hawai'i. Kapoukahi said that a great temple must be built on the hill of Pu'ukoholā (Kamakau 1961:149–50). The great temple was duly constructed, and was dedicated with the sacrifice of Kamehameha's archrival, Keōua.[21]

The hierarchy of priests was matched by an equally complex hierarchy of temples and ritual places, collectively known as *heiau*. The word *heiau* is again a Hawaiian innovation, apparently derived from *hai*, "to sacrifice"; elsewhere in Polynesia ritual spaces are generally referred to by some variant of the word *marae* (from PPN *malaqe*; see Chapter 1). In some cases, *heiau* were simply natural places where offerings were left, but more typically they involved some form of built architecture, both a stone foundation and perishable superstructures of wood and thatch. The simplest forms are shrines, sometimes incorporating an upright stone representing the deity (as in the phallic Pōhaku o Kāne shrines dedicated to the procreator god Kāne). But most *heiau* consist of substantial stone enclosures, platforms, terraces, and compound forms, with ground plans in the range of several hundred to 3,000 square meters, and on up to the largest temples with as much as 12,000 square meters in area. In Chapter 4 I review in greater detail the archaeological record for such monumental architecture.

Kamakau (1976:129–47) and Malo (1951:159–87) provide detailed accounts of *heiau* (see also Kepelino [Beckwith 1932:58]). Valeri (1985a:172–88) drew on these sources to work out the indigenous emic classification of temples, a task that is complicated by a rich terminology that appears to reference crosscutting systems of architectural and functional categories. The functional categories indexed *heiau* associated with particular gods of the Hawaiian pantheon. The most fundamental distinction was between war temples (*heiau kaua*, also called *luakini*, or *po'okanaka*) and temples for the promotion of agriculture (*heiau ho'oulu 'ai*, literally, "temple to produce the growth of food").

Among the most important types of *heiau*, following the indigenous Hawaiian terminology, were the following: (1) *Pōhaku o Kāne*, shrines to the creator god, usually simple constructions focused on an upright stone. (2) *Ko'a*, fishing shrines dedicated to Kū'ula, the god of fishing, usually located at points around the coastline. These are small enclosures or platforms, often with an elongated, upright waterworn cobble representing the deity, and abundant offerings of branch coral. (3) *Hale o Lono*, literally, "house of Lono"; these were evidently the most common type of *heiau ho'oulu 'ai* or agricultural temples, at least in the dryland regions of Hawai'i and East Maui. (4) *Luakini*, the main war temples reserved for the king and dedicated to Kū. They are typically the largest constructions in terms of the size and mass of their extant stone foundations (Fig. 2.4). As will be described later, the dedication of a *luakini* temple required multiple human sacrifices. A particular form of *luakini* is the Hale o Kā'ili, dedicated to the king's war god, Kūkā'ilimoku (Valeri 1985a:184); the great temple of Pu'ukoholā, constructed by Kamehameha in 1791, was such a *heiau*.

As Valeri decodes it (1985a:183–88: Table 4), the temple system with these major functional categories was promulgated hierarchically

Figure 2.4. Kāne'aki Heiau in the Makaha Valley, O'ahu. The stone temple foundation was excavated, and the perishable superstructures were restored by E. Ladd. (Photo by T. Babineau.)

throughout the polity, with each category replicated at various levels. Thus, for example, on Hawai'i Island each of the six districts (*moku*) had its own *luakini* ('Ī'ī 1959:160). The king had his proper *hale o Lono*, as did each of the district and *ahupua'a* chiefs. Moreover, *heiau ho'oulu 'ai*, dedicated either to Lono or Kāne, seem to have been present even within individual *'ili* segments of an *ahupua'a*. Likewise, *ko'a* shrines were constructed around the coastal areas by each local community of fishermen.

The spatial pattern of *heiau* distribution, and its correspondence to the territorial pattern of land divisions, can be illustrated with the case of Eastern Moloka'i, based on the *heiau* record obtained by J. F. G. Stokes (MS; Summers 1971) early in the twentieth century. *Luakini* temples were concentrated in the Kona District (rich in fishponds and irrigated taro fields), and to a lesser degree in the windward Ko'olau District, especially Hālawa Valley (a major center of wet taro production; Kirch and Kelly 1975). The largest *luakini* on the island is 'Ili'ili'ōpae, a massive terraced platform with an estimated stone fill volume of 15,750 cubic meters (Kirch 1990b:216). At a lower level within the island's temple hierarchy, Hālawa Valley nicely illustrates the distribution of *heiau* within a single, large *ahupua'a*. Here are found two somewhat smaller *luakini*, Mana and Papa *heiau*, and 12 smaller agricultural temples (in this case probably dedicated mostly to Kāne), corresponding to the major *'ili* land divisions within the valley. On the coast, as well, is an important fishing shrine (*ko'a*). In another Moloka'i *ahupua'a* pattern studied archaeologically by Weisler and Kirch (1985; Kirch 1990b: Fig. 9), Kawela and its adjacent territories of Makakupa'ia and Makakupa'ia Iki on the dry leeward side of the island, *hale o Lono* temples are located immediately inside the eastern boundary of each *ahupua'a*, where they presumably served in the annual tribute collection rites of the Makahiki, described below. A similar spatial patterning of *heiau* in the district of Kahikinui, Maui, is described in Chapter 4.

THE STATE CULTS AND THE RITUAL CYCLE

To understand the role of religion in the emergent Hawaiian states, we may examine more closely the functions of the *kahuna pule* and their principal cults both in legitimating the divine kingship, and in serving the political as well as economic interests of the king and the *ali'i* class. The Hawaiian lunar calendar was divided ritually into two parts: a period of four lunar months collectively called the Makahiki, sacred to

Lono, and a longer period of eight lunar months when the main temple rituals of Kū were practiced (Valeri 1985a:194–99). The closing of one year and signaling that a new one would soon commence began with a rite in which the king placed a rag before the main war temple of Kū (K. Kamakau in Fornander 1919–20:35); after this the king and *kahuna nui* gathered at night in the temple to await the first visibility of Makali'i (literally, "little eyes"), the star cluster Pleiades.[22] When these were visible, the king performed the *kuapola* rite in which he broke open green coconuts, signifying life, purification, and renewal.

The ensuing Makahiki season of four lunar months duration has been called both a "New Year's Festival" (Valeri 1985a) and a "harvest festival" (Handy and Handy 1972) by various scholars. The period was sacred to Lono, god of dryland agriculture, and during this time ritual activity centered on the *hale o Lono* temples, particularly the main *hale o Lono* of the king. Symbolically, Lono returned from Kahiki, the distantly remembered homeland beyond the horizon, to fertilize the land and in particular to bring the rains to the vast dryland field systems.[23] It is no coincidence that the Makahiki corresponds to the *ho'oilo* or "wet" season of winter rains (brought by so-called *kona* storms) that deposit most of the annual quotient of rainfall on the leeward sides of the islands, where the great sweet potato and dryland taro plantations were situated. The planting of sweet potatoes was most likely completed by the time that the Makahiki was declared, and the Makahiki season therefore corresponds closely to the main growing period for the crop. The fact that war was forbidden during this interval, and indeed that the gardens themselves were declared to be *kapu* for a certain period, can be seen as a ritually inscribed means to assure that nothing would adversely affect the new crop.[24]

The Makahiki had its origins in the Proto Central Eastern Polynesian *Mata-fiti*, probably a simpler form of first-fruits prestations to the gods and chiefs (see Kirch and Green 2001:257–60; see Chapter 1). By the time of contact with the West, however, the Makahiki had taken on a much larger function with respect to the emergent Hawaiian state: it was the principal ritualized form of tribute exactation. I can here only give the barest outline of the complex set of rites by which the king and his subsidiary *ali'i* used the Makahiki to collect their respective *ho'okupu* or tribute.[25] Accounts are given by Malo (1951), 'Ī'ī (1959:70–77), and Kamakau (1964:19–21), and discussed in some detail by Handy and Handy (1972:327–71) and Valeri (1985a:200–233). Indeed, some aspects of the Makahiki rites were witnessed and described by the Cook expedition at Kealakekua Bay in 1779. Not the least of these was the ritual feeding of Cook himself, cum Lono, as described and analyzed by Sahlins (1985a), and famously illustrated by the expedition's artist, John Webber.

Two distinct phases of tribute collection occurred during the course of the Makahiki. The first has been much less remarked in the conventional anthropological summaries, but is clearly described by Kēlou Kamakau (Fornander 1916–20, VI:38–41):

> And when seven more nights had come to pass and on the day of *Laau-ku-lua*, the deities of all the lands were turned on this day. They were not to be stood up, as the annual restrictions prevailed, and the collectors of tributes [*na kanaka halihali waiwai*] from all over the land were near, and had brought a great collection of goods for the king's annuity, consisting of dogs, cloths, malos, fish and all other things and placed them before the king, all the districts paying tribute this day. And in the night of *Laau-pau* (the 20th) the collection was displayed and the king's feather deity and the lesser priests came to distribute the offerings this night. This was a very sacred night, no fires burning, and no noise to be heard. They offered prayers this night and then went to sleep. (Fornander 1919–20, VI:38–39)

This passage describes a kingdom-wide collection of prestige foods (dog, in particular) and wealth items (especially barkcloth) brought specifically for the king, and indeed placed in front of the feathered image of his personal god, Kūkāʻilimoku. As Valeri points out, during the process of collection of the tribute (the *waiwai*, literally "wealth"), the "gods of each land (*akua ʻāina*) cannot remain upright but are placed in a horizontal position, doubtless as a sign of homage to the king" (1985a:204). The assembled wealth is then redistributed to the various priests, *aliʻi*, warriors, and other favorites of the king; notably, nothing is given to the *makaʻāinana* who produced the goods (Valeri 1985a:204).[26]

The second phase of tribute collection under the aegis of Lono has been much more widely remarked and described in detail, both by Native Hawaiian writers and ethnographers. This is the famous circuit of the "long god" (*akua loa*) and shorter circuit of the "short god" (*akua poko*) through the territorial units comprising the kingdom. The *akua loa* consisted of a wooden shaft tipped with a carved human head, with a cross-beam attached from which were suspended streamers of white barkcloth and the white pelts of *kaʻupu* birds.[27] The image was brought before the king, "who cried for his love of the deity" (K. Kamakau in Fornander 1916–20, VI:42), placing a *niho palaoa* necklace on the image, and feeding pork, taro, and coconut pudding (*kūlolo*), and ʻawa to the man who carried the image (thus representing its mouth).[28] Properly anointed and supplicated by the king, Lono was sent forth across the land to do his work: "After this the long god was carried forth on a circuit of the land. The different lands paid tribute to the deity in cloth, pigs, feathers, chickens and food" (K. Kamakau in Fornander 1916–20, VI:42). The long god took 23 days to complete his right-handed (clockwise) circuit, whereas the short god took only four days on a left-hand counterclockwise circuit, apparently restricting his visit to the particular lands (*'ili kūpono*) of the king.[29] Kamakau gives a vivid description of the work of the long god as it made its circuit throughout the land:

> Much wealth was acquired by the god during this circuit of the island in the form of tribute (*ho'okupu*) from the *moku'aina, kalana, 'okana,* and *ahupua'a* land sections at certain places and at the boundaries of all the *ahupua'a*. There the wealth was presented—pigs, dogs, fowl, poi, tapa cloth, dress tapas (*'a'ahu*), *'oloa* tapa, *pa'u* (skirts), malos, shoulder capes (*'ahu*), mats, *ninikea* tapa, *olona* fishnets, fishlines, feathers of the *mamo* and the *'o'o* birds, finely designed mats (*'ahu pawehe*), pearls, ivory, iron (*meki*),[30] adzes, and whatever other property had been gathered by the *konohiki*, or land agent, of the *ahupua'a*. If the tribute presented by the *konohiki* to the god was too little, the attendant chiefs of the god (*po'e kahu ali'i akua*) would complain, and not furl up the god nor twist up the emblems and lay him down. The attendants kept the god upright and order the *ahupua'a* to be plundered. Only when the keepers were satisfied with the tribute given did they stop this plundering (*ho'opunipuni*) [in the name] of the god (Kamakau 1964:20–21).

Although perishable foodstuffs such as the *poi* (pounded taro root) were evidently consumed by the crowd accompanying the Makahiki circuit, no doubt the other valuables listed by Kamakau were returned to the king's storehouses. While Hawai'i has generally been characterized as having a "staple finance" form of economy (Earle 1997), most of the goods assembled during the two Makahiki tribute collections consisted of various kinds of material manufactures, some of considerable prestige value (such as the fine barkcloths, mats, birds' feathers, and ivory mentioned by Kamakau). Thus, to reiterate a point made earlier, there was a considerable component of wealth finance underpinning the late Hawaiian economy.

The Makahiki season concluded with a series of rites whereby the king wrested symbolic control of the polity from Lono (Valeri 1985a:210–13). Most dramatic of these was the *kāli'i* rite. By this time the Lono gods had returned to the principal *hale o Lono* temple, and the king set forth in a canoe and landed in front of the temple. A sham battle ensued, with spears thrown at the king and/or his champion (an expert in spear dodging), who was obliged to parry them. Symbolically, the king thus reclaimed his polity. He then went to the *hale o Lono* to see the god images, and sacrificed a pig in honor of Lono, who had done the hard work of visiting the land "that belongs to us both" (Valeri 1985a:212, translating from K. Kamakau). After this the Lono images were taken down, wrapped up, and stored in the *mana* house of the *luakini* heiau until the next year. In the concluding rite of the Makahiki, a "tribute canoe" (*wa'a 'auhau*), filled with foods of various kinds was set to sea and allowed to drift off, carrying Lono back to Kahiki, whence he would return again in eight lunar cycles.

With the Makahiki season ended, the king—following various purification rites and the first open sea trolling for *aku* (bonito) fish—prepared with his high priest to undertake a second and even more complex set of rites dedicated to Kū. In essence, these rites were concerned with various stages of building and dedicating a *luakini heiau*, or temple of human sacrifice, the exclusive prerogative of an *ali'i nui*. In practice, new temples were not constructed every year, but rather from time to time, especially in preparation for an intended war of territorial conquest (as with Kamehameha's construction of the great *luakini* temple of Pu'ukoholā at Kawaihae). On an annual basis, however, the principal *luakini* of the king was refurbished, and some version of these rites performed. Malo (1951:159–87), 'Ī'ī (1959:33–45), and K. Kamakau (Fornander 1916–20:VI:2–45) all give indigenous accounts of the *luakini* temple rites, and Valeri has synthesized and interpreted these and other sources extensively (1985a:234–339). In their full version, the rites began with the *haku 'ōhi'a*, the selecting and carving of a special *'ōhi'a* (*Metrosideros polymorpha*) log into an image of Kū. The *'ōhi'a* tree was a manifestation of Kū, and the nectar of its flowers nourished the forest birds that provided the brilliant red and yellow feathers for the capes, cloaks, and helmets of the *ali'i*, and for the images of Kū. The *haku 'ōhi'a* was the first occasion on which a human sacrifice would be offered, the body buried along with that of a sacrificial pig at the foot of a selected tree.

After the image had been carved and transported to the temple, various houses on the stone foundation had to be constructed, thatched, and consecrated (or refurbished and reconsecrated, as the case may be), coinciding with the *kauila nui* rite. With these preliminaries accomplished, the new image of Kū was brought into the temple to be erected between the *'anu'u* tower and the *lele* altar. Once again a human sacrifice was required for this *'aha hulahula* rite, with the corpse "thrust into the hole where the base of the god's image is to stand" (Valeri 1985a:289).

All of these were preliminaries to what Valeri calls the "final transformation of the god" which was marked by a "great sacrifice" (*ka haina nui*) requiring enormous quantities of pig, bananas, coconut, red fish, special barkcloth, and, once again, human victims. As Malo writes, these offerings were all in specific quantities of 400: "When the chiefs and the people had finished feasting on the pork, the king made an offering to his gods of 400 pigs, 400 bushels of bananas, 400 cocoanuts, 400 red fish, and 400 pieces of *'oloa* cloth; he also offered a sacrifice of human bodies on the *lele*" (Malo 1951:174). In a peculiar rite the following day, the king's ritual double (Kahoʻāliʻi[31]) consumed the eye of one of the human victims.[32] These rites also involved the binding and wrapping of the images, for example in *kapa* loincloths. The concluding rites of the entire sequence took place not at the *luakini* temple, but at the *hale o Papa* temple of the female *aliʻi*, officiated by the priest of Papa (a principal female deity), and involving the participation of the king's wife. Valeri (1985a:330) interprets these final rites as the "desacralization" of the male congregation, allowing them once again to enter into contact with women and the society at large.

The above précis of the Hawaiian state cults should give some sense of how the Hawaiian rulers and their priests used the ritual cycle both to cement their power and to extract surplus from the *makaʻāinana* class. The Makahiki rituals were carried out in Lono's name by his priests, and accompanied by various celebrations and games. The common people were in various ways made to feel that Lono was "their" god, who brought prosperity to the land. But there can be little doubt about who benefited from the tribute collections that swept the lands for the collective *waiwai*, "wealth" that they could yield. And the withholding of wealth was not advisable, as the threat of greater plundering was real. In contrast, the rituals of Kū were carried out by the king and his chief priest, and their goal was to establish the bond between the king and this most fearsome god, to reinforce the divinity of the king. These rites also required large quantities of sacrificial items, such as hogs and other foodstuffs that had to be provided by the common people. But more, they required human sacrifice, either of those who had broken some *kapu*, or at times of war, the body of a vanquished chief or king. Witnessed from special seating places outside of the immediate temple walls by assembled males, these terrifying rites reinforced the power of the king. Any false movement, cough, or noise by one of the participants or observers could bring instant death ('Ī'ī 1959:43–44). The threat of death, and real death (of the sacrificial victims) permeated the *luakini* rites, underscoring the king's power of life and death over the people.

LAND AND LABOR

Having examined the system of tribute collection that was carried out in the name of Lono, the "people's god" (surely, a marvelous case of mystification of the true relations of production!), we need to explore in greater detail the commoners' relationships to land. In the *ahupua'a* system of territorial land divisions that had replaced the ancient Polynesian pattern of land-holding ascent groups, commoners no longer exercised rights to residential and agricultural land by virtue of genealogical connections to a social group. *Maka'āinana* land rights had to be annually renewed through payment of both tribute and labor to the chiefly overlords.[33] All this is especially evident in the archival records of the Mahele, the division of lands among the king, principal chiefs, and commoners between 1846 and 1854 (Chinen 1958).

In 1846 King Kamehameha III was convinced by the Protestant missionaries to end the traditional system of land tenure, and transform it to an allodial system of fee simple land rights. The first step was the appointment of the Board of Commissioners to Quiet Land Titles (usually abbreviated as the Land Commission), consisting of three Native Hawaiians (including John Papa 'Ī'ī) and two foreign residents. Their first task was to adopt a set of "Principles" whereby land claims might be adjudicated, based on a careful examination of the traditional system of land rights. These Principles, established in 1846, were later published (Commissioner of Public Lands 1929:1–7), and provide insights into the complex set of relations that linked land, labor, and tribute up and down the hierarchy. The commissioners recognized that in theory all of the lands belonged to the king, for he alone had the right to allocate them to subservient chiefs, or to dispossess chiefs of land they had formerly held: ". . . the King, representing the government, having formerly been the sole owner of all the soil, . . . must be considered to be so still" (1929:3). The Principles further set out quite explicitly the hierarchical set of relations and obligations that defined rights to land:

> When the islands were conquered by Kamehameha I, he followed the example of his predecessors, and divided out the lands among his principal warrior chiefs, retaining however, a portion in his hands, to be cultivated or managed by his own immediate servants or attendants. Each principal chief

Archaic States at European Contact   67

divided his lands anew, and gave them out to an inferior order of chiefs, or persons of rank, by whom they were subdivided again and again; after passing through the hands of four, five or six persons, from the King down to the lowest class of tenants. All these persons were considered to have rights in the lands, or the productions of them.[34] The proportions of these rights were not very clearly defined, but were nevertheless universally acknowledged. . . .

All persons possessing landed property, whether superior landlords, tenants or sub-tenants, owed and paid to the King not only a land tax, which he assessed at pleasure, but also, service which was called for at discretion, on all the grades from the highest down. They also owed and paid some portion of the productions of the land, in addition to the yearly taxes. They owed obedience at all times (1929:1).

What the commissioners referred to as the king's "land tax" to be assessed at his pleasure was presumably the collections made during the Makahiki. But note in addition the reference to "service" as well as the additional "portion of the productions of the land" which are clearly differentiated from the "yearly taxes." Further details on how these latter assessments were implemented come from the thousands of pages of testimony accumulated by the Land Commission. I will draw on examples from two areas that have been analyzed in considerable depth: the Anahulu Valley on Oʻahu, by Kirch and Sahlins (1992), and the Hālawa Valley on Molokaʻi (Anderson 2001).[35]

As noted earlier, the most important subdivision in the land hierarchy was the *ahupuaʻa*, in theory a self-contained economic territory. This in turn was subdivided into *ʻili*, and these into *moʻo*, the latter consisting of individual farming plots allocated to specific *makaʻāinana* households. But not all cultivation plots were allocated to commoner households. A significant number of fields were designated as *kōʻele* plots, under the direct supervision of the land manager or *konohiki*. The productions of these plots were used for the support of the *konohiki*, his chief, and further on up the hierarchy. The Hālawa Valley case exemplifies this pattern, where a significant number of the irrigated taro pondfields were of this *kōʻele* type.[36] Moreover, most of the largest pondfields situated on the rich alluvial soils were *kōʻele* fields (Anderson 2001:109: Fig. 4.3). The productions of the *kōʻele* plots were not only reserved for the *konohiki* and chiefs, but the labor required to cultivate these plots had to be supplied by the *makaʻāinana*. Indeed, the land claims submitted by the Hālawa commoners make it clear that their rights to work their own *moʻo* plots were validated by the labor they supplied by working in the *konohiki*'s *kōʻele* fields (usually one day in five).

For the Anahulu Valley, a detailed analysis of land claims (Kirch and Sahlins 1992) shows that the *maka'āinana* class was made up of several distinct categories of persons depending on their historical relationships to the land and to their *haku'āina*, or landlords. Families that had been resident on their *mo'o 'āina* plots for two or more generations were regarded as *kama'āina* ("children of the land"). Having worked their fields and provided their expected allocations of labor and tribute for a respectable period, they were usually awarded their claims by the Land Commission (Sahlins 1992:182–91). In contrast, the claims of the *hoa'āina* ("friend of the land") and *'ōhua* (family dependents) categories were more tenuous. These persons had come into the valley only recently, either under the aegis of the *konohiki* (in the case of the *hoa'āina*) or through marriage or some other form of kinship affiliation with a *kama'āina* family (the *'ōhua*). When, in 1848 to 1854 these persons made claims for land, they were very often rebuffed in testimony by the resident *konohiki*, who asserted that it was he, or his chief, who really "owned" the land and that the newcomer merely worked it under his direction. Thus, in the final outcome of the Mahele, the *kama'āina* claimants received on average about 5.9 acres per claim, whereas the *hoa'āina* and *'ōhua* received only about 1.8 acres per claim (Sahlins 1992:187: Table 8.6).

The Anahulu case provides rich details regarding the extraction of surplus from the *maka'āinana* by the stratified hierarchy of *konohiki* and *ali'i*. The valley's capacity for surplus production can be fairly precisely defined, because we have firm quantitative data on both the extent of taro pondfield production and on household demography from the early contact period (Kirch 1992). These data suggest "a surplus production level somewhere around 50 percent (about 70 metric tons/year above subsistence needs)" (Spriggs and Kirch, in Kirch 1992:161). The harsh realities of surplus exaction are documented in a series of manuscript letters written in the 1830s and curated in the Archives of the Hawaiian Kingdom, from Paulo Kānoa, the "secretary" of the ruling high *ali'i* Ka'ahumanu, to the resident *konohiki* La'anui (Sahlins 1992:143–45). On behalf of the chiefess, Kānoa made incessant demands for pigs, taro, *poi* (pounded taro), sweet potatoes, firewood, fish, barkcloth, and other productions of the *ahupua'a*. The *maka'āinana* sometimes resisted, following a tradition of commoner resistance against oppressive *ali'i* that has resonance in precontact traditions (Malo 1951:195). To be sure, these records from the early Hawaiian Kingdom, several decades after initial contact, reflect an intensification of chiefly oppression under the influence of Western capitalism. Nonetheless, the basic structures of hierarchical extraction of the productions of the land can be traced back into the late precontact era.

WAR

Elman Service wrote: "Chiefdoms are chiefdoms and states are states ... A state is unlike a chiefdom because it is integrated by a special mechanism involving legitimized force" (1967:173–74). In contact-era Hawai'i, the legitimate use of force included not only the ability of kings to wage wars of territorial conquest, but also to exercise the right over life or death in the everyday affairs of the common people. This kind of continual threat no doubt was highly effective in maintaining *ali'i* control. The frequent references in the ethnohistoric sources to death as a penalty for breaking some *kapu* are striking. Failure to perform the prostrating *kapu* in the presence of a high-ranking *ali'i*, any number of violations against the person or property of the king of a chief, coughing or uttering any noise during a religious service, and various other infractions were all punishable by death. 'Ī'ī recounts an incident of his youth in the court of Kamehameha, when he lingered to watch an evening ceremony during the nights of Kāne (1959:60–61). "The kapu was imposed with the words: 'Kapu la, make la, a 'apu'e (It is kapu, it is death, a very strict kapu).' All talking and noises of every kind were silenced, under penalty of death" (1959:61). Young 'Ī'ī was seized with a tickling in his throat and could not hold back two or three muffled coughs. Fortunately the priests did not hear him, but "those who were in the house with him were distressed," knowing that it would be death if he were overheard. The power of the king over human life was, of course, ritually evident in the offerings of human sacrifices in the *luakini* temples, described earlier. Sacrificial victims were often taken from the *kauwā* class of "slaves," but could also be anyone who had broken a *kapu*.

The four polities into which the archipelago was segmented at the time of European contact were in an endemic state of warfare; and, such wars continued after contact until AD 1795 when the Hawai'i Island king Kamehameha I succeeded (with the use of Western guns) in conquering the Maui and O'ahu kingdoms. As Kolb and Dixon (2002:517) note in a recent review of Hawaiian warfare, wars were large-scale affairs, with "well-organized groups of combatants numbering up to perhaps 15,000 individuals." The 1795 war fleet of Kamehameha comprised no less than 1,200 canoes. While large armies of invasion doubtless included conscripts from the commoner class, there were also full-time elite corps of warriors (drawn from the lesser chiefly ranks) who had specialized training in marshal arts, called *lua* (Paglinawan et al. 2006). Malo mentions that in the royal court "there were those who were expert in all soldierly accomplishments, and the arts of combat were very much taught" (1951:65). These martial arts included spearthrowing, spear-thrusting, using a spear as a pole vault to pursue the enemy, striking with clubs or sticks, wrestling, and boxing. "In the cool of the afternoon sham fights were frequently indulged in; the party of one chief being pitted against the part of another chief, the chiefs themselves taking part" (1951:65).

Buck (1957:417–64) devotes a chapter of his monograph on Hawaiian material culture to weapons. The considerable catalog of weapons includes spears, both long and short, barbed and nonbarbed; truncheon daggers; bludgeon daggers; long-bladed daggers; curve-bladed daggers; daggers onto which were lashed shark's teeth; wooden and stone clubs in a diversity of styles; clubs tipped with shark's teeth; shark's teeth attached to cords (as "knuckle dusters"); tripping clubs; slings; and strangling cords. A particularly curious aspect of Hawaiian technology is that, although they possessed small bows and arrows (used by the *ali'i* to hunt rats, for sport), these were never adapted for use in war.

Battles were almost always conducted in broad daylight, the armies confronting each other largely through hand-to-hand combat (Emory 1965:234). Although some simple fortifications are known archaeologically (as at Nu'uanu on O'ahu [McAllister 1933a:88, pl. 11A] and Kawela on Moloka'i [Weisler and Kirch 1985]), and referred to in oral traditions (such as the famous fortified hill of Ka'uiki at Hāna, Maui; Kamakau 1961:30, 80), most combat took place without the benefit of forts; often battlefields were open plains. Refuge caves are also known (Kirch 1985:175–76), but were most likely used by commoners who wished to make themselves scarce at times of armed conflict.

Emory, who authored a summary account of Hawaiian contact-era warfare, was impressed by its "high degree of development" (1965:240). He regarded this as "the warfare of feudalism, with its recognized rules and formalities, its prayers, invocations, and ceremonial preparation." As noted earlier, war was prohibited during the Makahiki season, and could only be undertaken after the rites of dedication of the *luakini* temple were completed. If a major interisland war of conquest were contemplated, this would certainly necessitate construction of a major new temple (or extensive renovation of an existing structure), and offering

Archaic States at European Contact

of multiple human sacrifices. Battle tactics varied, and the Hawaiians had specific names for various kinds of formations (e.g., *kahului*, a crescent-shaped formation of men with the leader in the middle; *makawalu*, warriors divided into groups; *kūkulu*, two solid lines advancing against each other; Emory 1965:237–38). Emory describes the battle engagement as follows:

> Skirmishing might be started by a single warrior advancing and challenging someone to meet him. In general, however, it was started by the slingers on each wing harassing the enemy. When the forces were near enough, showers of spears were cast forth. The first person to be killed was called a lehua. If he could be secured by his victors and dragged to sacrifice, it was considered an omen of great favor for that side. The first, ulukoko, the second, makawai, and the third, helu one, victims were offered as sacrifices to the war god (1965:238).

Hawaiian warfare was not limited to land battles, and the traditional accounts describe a number of key naval engagements. Fleets of double-hulled war canoes (*wa'a peleleu*) were essential for transporting armies across the often turbulent ocean channels separating the major islands, such as the 'Aleinuihāhā Channel between Hawai'i and Maui. These canoes were 20 or more meters long and outfitted with platforms between the hulls (Haddon and Hornell 1936:6–19; Buck 1957:268–70). Kamehameha's famous Peleleu fleet is reported to have included some 1,200 canoes.[37]

The indigenous Hawaiian historians, in particular, Kamakau (1961; see also Fornander 1996), provide numerous accounts of wars in the late precontact period. Warfare was common within a short period after the death of a king, when the legitimate heir typically faced challenges from collateral kinsmen wishing to usurp his station. This, of course, was the story of the famous 'Umi who overthrew his half brother Hākau (see Chapter 3), and much later of Kamehameha's rise to power over Kīwala'ō and Keōua. While some wars were undertaken for simple revenge, or to enhance a chief's prestige, most wars had the goal of territorial conquest, the addition of productive lands and commoners to work them (Hommon 1976:153). As Kamakau described it in one case, the king of Maui, Kahekili, "coveted Oahu and Molokai for their rich lands, many walled fish-ponds, springs and water [irrigated] taro patches" (1961:32). Indeed, as I have argued elsewhere (Kirch 1994:266–68), the kings of Maui and Hawai'i, whose economic bases depended on the more risk-prone dryland field systems, were especially covetous of the irrigated valleys and fishponds of the older westerly islands. Earle (1997:142) likewise concurs that in Hawai'i "the goal became conquest of communities and their productive facilities and commoner populations."

SUMMARY

The boundary between a complex chiefdom and an archaic state is blurry, in part because early states often if not always developed out of complex chiefdoms. The emergence of *primary* archaic states was a process, and we need to avoid semantic traps that reduce this process to static categories. Nonetheless, as discussed in Chapter 1, there are certain critical quantitative and especially qualitative characteristics that most scholars agree on as essential to the definition of an archaic state (Marcus and Feinman 1998). I have now reviewed the ethnohistoric and ethnographic evidence for early contact-era Hawai'i, advancing the case that Hawaiian society at the close of the eighteenth century met most if not all of the key definitional criteria for archaic states. While Hawaiian societies were originally organized around Ancestral Polynesian concepts of chiefship, by the time of their initial engagement with the West they had crossed a threshold marked by the emergence of divine kingship, and by the sundering of ancient principles of lineage and land rights based on kinship, and their replacement with a strictly territorial system.

Quantitatively, Hawaiian polities at the time of Cook's 1778 to 1779 expedition incorporated thousands of square kilometers (and sometimes more than a single island) and had populations ranging upward of 100,000 persons. These values are well within the range of archaic state polities documented for other parts of both the New and Old Worlds. But more important are certain qualitative aspects of late Hawaiian society which differentiated it from other Polynesian chiefdoms, and indeed from earlier phases in the evolution of Hawaiian society itself. These qualities have to do with a fundamental shift from a social formation based around kinship bonds, especially eponymous ascent groups which controlled access to land and other resources (the Ancestral East Polynesian *mata-kainanga*), to a formation defined by class stratification and kingship. In contact-era Hawai'i, *nā kanaka*, "the people" were fundamentally in opposition to *nā li'i*, "the chiefs" (Sahlins MS). The people—retaining the word *maka'āinana* as an etymological echo of the past, but now divorced from its former associations to lineage and land—had no genealogies extending farther back than grandparents, indeed were prevented from keeping them. In stark contrast the chiefs elaborated their ancestral connections back to the gods, and retained specialists to recite their name chants. In the new Hawaiian system, the *ali'i* were organized into dynastic "houses", these intermarrying and thus forming reticulate ambilateral networks. In severing the kinship fabric that once bound commoners to chiefs, in creating separate endogamous classes of commoners and elites, Hawaiian social organization exhibits a key axis of the transformation from chiefdom to archaic state.

The sundering of the ancient ascent group ("lineage") system and its replacement with a class of commoners brought with it other fundamental changes, especially the control and distribution of land, and the rights to appropriate the surplus production of territorial estates. As Valeri (1985b) and other scholars have noted, the late Hawaiian land system has strong resemblances to Medieval European feudalism, even though the Hawaiian *maka'āinana* were not serfs. But their rights to work their garden plots, to fish in certain bays, and to collect plants from the forest zone, were all validated not by genealogical connection to lineage groups, but by the regular payment of tribute up through the hierarchy of lords (*konohiki* ω *ali'i* → *ali'i nui*) who controlled the specific *ahupua'a* and *moku* territories into which the kingdoms were subdivided. This relationship was summed up succinctly by Malo: "It was the *ma-ka-aina-na* who did all the work on the land, yet all they produced from the soil belonged to the chiefs; and the power to expel a man from the land and rob him of his possessions lay with the chief" (1951:61). Indeed, failure to work hard enough could result not only in expulsion from the land, but in death.

Archaeologists who study the rise of complex social formations, including states, often put much stock in the number of tiers that can be identified in settlement or administrative hierarchies (e.g., Wright 1977; Spencer and Redmond 2004; Stanish 2001). Two or three tiers are typically regarded as characteristic of chiefdoms, and four tiers of archaic states. Here again the late Hawaiian territorial system with its formal organization into districts (*moku*), *ahupua'a*, and *'ili* segments fits comfortably with the state level criteria. More importantly, perhaps, the formalized and regular collection of tribute (*ho'okupu*) was efficiently organized by means of this land-and-landlord hierarchy. Such tribute, or tax as it might equally be called, included not only large quantities of foodstuffs ("staple finance" in Brumfiel and Earle's terminology), but significant quantities of durable goods such as barkcloth, cordage, and birds' feathers ("wealth finance"). All this is far removed from the "first fruits" prestations of a typical chiefdom, even though the origins of the Hawaiian *hoʻokupu* no doubt can be traced back to ritual harvest offerings in Ancestral Polynesian times (as the etymology of the word, "to cause to grow" implies).

Important as the above criteria are to state formations, in and of themselves they are not sufficient to define an archaic state. To quote Marcus and Feinman, "archaic states were ruled by kings rather than chiefs" (1998:5), and in particular by divine kings who traced their descent from the gods. That contact-era Hawaiʻi had developed a concept of divine kingship is abundantly attested in the ethnohistoric and ethnographic evidence. As Malo put it: ". . . the people held the chiefs in great dread and looked upon them as gods" (1951:61). The elaborate systems of *kapu*, including the prostrating *kapu* for the king and his closest kin, highly developed court etiquette, and special rituals to commemorate the birth and circumcision of royal heirs are all indicators of this. Hawaiian *aliʻi* reserved for themselves the right to practice marriage between siblings or half siblings, royal endogamy, something witnessed as well in the archaic states of Egypt and the Andes. And, the king and highest chiefs literally held the power of life or death over the common people. Human sacrifice was a necessary part of the king's annual temple rites dedicated to his war god Kū. Ritual homicide is a common phenomenon of early state societies and of divine kingship, and here Hawaiʻi fits within expectations.[38]

The ideology of divine kingship needs to be reinforced by a formal ritual apparatus, and hence as Marcus and Feinman also emphasize, archaic states ". . . had standardized temples implying a state religion, [and] had full-time priests rather than shamans or part-time priests" (1998:5). The lives of Hawaiian kings revolved around the seasonally organized state cults of Kū, god of war, and Lono, god of dryland agriculture. Each god had his own distinctive temples, and the rituals were conducted by full-time priests who specialized in the cult of one or other of the deities. Moreover, many of the *luakini* temples dedicated to Kū were massive constructions, their stone foundations incorporating thousands of cubic meters of rock. This kind of monumentality is yet another quantitative expression of the power of kings and a marker of archaic states.

Finally, archaic states carried out wars of territorial conquest, a stage of warfare beyond the raiding typically associated with chiefdoms (e.g., Redmond 1994). At the time of European contact, the Hawaiian polities of Maui under Kahekili and Hawaiʻi under Kalaniʻōpuʻu had for

Archaic States at European Contact

some time been engaged in extensive campaigns of territorial expansion. Hawai'i had annexed part of East Maui, whereas Maui had taken Moloka'i and O'ahu. Both kings maintained large, standing armies. While some authors have stressed the expansion of Hawaiian warfare after European contact, when guns and other armament became available, the basic patterns of conquest warfare were already well established long before Kamehameha I and his consolidation of the archipelago.[39] Oral traditions associated with such wars, describing the expansion of polities from multiple independent chiefdoms on each island to consolidated islandwide states, are presented in detail in Chapter 3.

The combination of quantitative and qualitative criteria summarized above bolster the case that the late Hawaiian polities as encountered by Cook and other early European explorers fit conformably with the pattern of primary archaic states known for other regions of the world. Before closing this account of Hawai'i at the moment of "first contact," however, it is worth pointing to two phenomena sometimes associated with archaic states in which Hawai'i did not participate: urbanism and writing. As I demonstrate in Chapter 4, Hawaiian kings did occupy quite large and elaborate royal centers, but there were no towns or cities. There are probably at least three good reasons for the lack of urban centers: the dispersed settlement pattern of commoner residences tied closely to their intensive irrigated and dryland fields; the lack of animal or wheeled transport; and, the fact that Hawaiian crops were mostly roots or tubers, which could not be stored for long periods. Urban centers need efficient systems of transport to bring staples from the countryside, and these staples need to be of a type that can be stored, as in granaries. Instead of surrounding themselves with dense concentrations of their subjects, the Hawaiian kings and chiefs developed a pattern of peripatetic movement about the countryside, descending on the *maka'āinana* until the local resources were depleted, and then moving on to the next *ahupua'a*. Hawaiian kings went to the people, rather than bringing the people to them. They were, as the Hawaiian proverb says, "sharks who traveled on the land."

The lack of a writing system is also noteworthy, although Hawai'i is not the only archaic state with this deficiency; the Inka similarly lacked written texts. What the Hawaiian kings and their incipient bureaucracy did have was a highly elaborated oral-aural culture, with specialists whose job it was to memorize genealogies, traditions, and important information of all kinds. Whether the Hawaiians would have invented a writing system in due course—had Cook and the West not intruded on their isolated shores—is anybody's guess. Given the lack of a magazine economy—no storehouses full of grain to count and keep track of—I am inclined to think that writing may not have been very useful to the Hawaiians. Nonetheless, when the Protestant missionaries introduced an orthography for the Hawaiian language in the early 1820s, the Hawaiian people—commoners and chiefs alike—took up literacy with a frenzy (Schütz 1994). During the nineteenth century, the literacy rate in Hawai'i far exceeded that in the United States or Europe. Much of the interest in writing had to do with putting the vast oral traditions down on paper, which again speaks to the emphasis on oral–aural transmission in the ancient culture. Anthropologists should be grateful that these traditions were committed to paper and hence to posterity, for they provide an unparalleled window into the functioning of an archaic state society.

CHAPTER 3
Native Hawaiian Political History

> Hawaiian chronology counts by generations, not by reigns nor by years.
>
> Fornander (1996:108)

> As a general rule, the oldest and most senior lines are in the western islands, Kauaʻi and Oʻahu, whence originate also the highest tabus. But then, the historical dynamism of the system is in the east.
>
> Sahlins (1985a:20)

Evidence for the precontact transformation of Hawaiian society over several centuries derives from two distinct sources. One, representing an "insider" or emic perspective, consists of indigenous Hawaiian oral traditions, collected and codified in the nineteenth century by several Hawaiian and Haole (foreign) scholars. An earlier generation of scholars relied heavily on these traditions for its interpretation of Hawaiian history (Fornander 1916–20, 1996). The other represents an "outsider" or etic perspective in the form of archaeological data, accumulated gradually over the past century. Most scholarly writing in the later half of the twentieth century dealing with Hawaiian precontact history and sociopolitical change has tended to privilege archaeology, although lately a renewed interest in incorporating oral traditions into archaeological interpretations has manifested itself (Cordy 2000).

A theoretically sufficient account of the emergence of archaic states in the Hawaiian Islands, out of an earlier form of Ancestral Polynesian chiefdom, requires careful attention to both emic and etic, traditional and archaeological, evidence. Drawing on both sources lends greater analytical clout to the task of understanding historical change in

Hawai'i, for several reasons. First, the two sources are independent: The one consists of indigenous forms of knowledge passed down orally over successive generations, whereas the other—the material, archaeological evidence—has been acquired through the application of scientific methods. As independent sources, they can be used to cross check each other, and when the results are mutually corroborative, lend greater support to the resulting interpretations. Second, these two sources address different aspects of the historical process. The indigenous traditions consist of what the *Annales* historian Fernand Braudel (1980) called *l'histoire événémentielle*, an event-focused history that recounts the births, deaths, wars, conquests, usurpations, marriages, and amorous affairs of the ruling *ali'i* and their kin. The traditions, to the extent that they offer interpretations of the actions of the great chiefs and kings, do so in terms of personal motivations: jealousy, greed, love, the desire for revenge, conquest, and so on. In terms of current social theory, we might say that the traditions offer an account of Hawaiian history grounded in individual human *agency* (Bourdieu 1977; Giddens 1979; Ortner 1984; Dobres and Robb 2000; Sahlins 2004). As such, they tell us what mattered directly to the actors themselves. But not all agency is of the same stripe. When the actions of *ali'i* display repetitive patterns over time, in the context of similar social and economic conditions, one may argue that a kind of structurally prescribed agency is at play. On the other hand, from time to time some *ali'i* broke out of their cultural bonds to innovate entirely new structures. This is contingent, individual agency at work. To understand the dynamic contexts underlying structural agency more fully requires that we apply Braudel's other model, the *longue durée*, the long run of history that is revealed in environmental, demographic, economic, and social structural patterns. For this we must turn to the material evidence of archaeology, which can access the long-term record of contextual change within which the chiefs and kings formulated their strategies and acted out their plans.

A brief comparison with advances in Mesoamerican archaeology and prehistory may be informative, for the Hawaiian oral traditions in many respects parallel the record of Maya rulers encoded in the hieroglyphic texts found on stelae and temple façades. A veritable revolution in the interpretation of Maya prehistory was sparked by the breakthroughs in translation of the hieroglyphic texts (Culbert 1991; Schele and Miller 1986). Whereas older models based exclusively on the material archaeological record saw the Maya as a peace-loving society consumed with a passion for astronomical observation and calendrics, the texts—once they could be read—told an entirely different story. A record of kingly successions, wars, and conquests provides the indigenous agent-based *histoire événémentielle* that was lacking in the archaeological record alone. Although the Hawaiian traditions were not originally set down in written texts, they are intriguingly parallel in form and content to the Maya hieroglyphic texts, and like the latter can be linked to a chronological framework (based on chiefly genealogies, as described later). Just as it would now be unthinkable to write Maya history without drawing on both the evidence of archaeology and of the translated texts, so Hawaiian history needs, in my view, to incorporate both archaeology and the indigenous oral traditions.

GENEALOGIES OF RENOWN, TRADITIONS OF POWER

Hawaiian elites, members of the *ali'i* class, were profoundly interested in their own political histories, and elaborated an oral–aural culture wherein historically based traditions (*mo'olelo*) and genealogies (*mo'okū'ahuhau*) were meticulously preserved and transmitted from one generation to the next. Specialists (*kū'auhau*) within the royal courts were charged with mastering these genealogies and histories (Malo 1951:261). Kamakau, one of the primary sources for *mo'olelo*, describes the importance of genealogists to the chiefs, noting that the *ali'i* "took care of people who knew genealogies—lest they be scorned, *ho'okae 'ia*, or be regarded as 'juniors,' *ho'okaikaina 'ia*; or as the 'youngest,' *ho'opoki'i 'ia*" (1991:80). Kamakau's words reflect a deeply ingrained and widespread Austronesian emphasis on rank, especially as reflected in birth order (Fox 1995). In all Austronesian societies, claims to rank and power depended on being able to demonstrate, through recitation, an unbroken genealogical chain back to high-ranking ancestors. In striking distinction to most Polynesian societies, however, in Hawai'i at the time of European contact, the possession of a genealogy had become an exclusively chiefly prerogative. Commoners were absolutely denied the right to cite a pedigree. As Kamakau writes: "To commoners, genealogies were of no value because their parents forbade them to act like chiefs or to have children born in the back country who would trace their ancestry up to the chiefs (*pi'i aku i na li'i*). So the children of the *maka'āinana* were taught only the names of their fathers, mothers, and grandparents" (1991:80).

The Hawaiian chiefly genealogies provide an internally consistent historical framework that extends back in time approximately 23 generations prior to the rulers encountered by Europeans at the close of the eighteenth century, a period of roughly five centuries. These genealogies codify succession within chiefly lines, as well as details of marriages between chiefly houses. Linked to this genealogical framework are specific *moʻolelo* (histories), which describe the actions of key participants, such as intrigue and plotting, waging war and the outcomes of specific battles, construction of temples and the offering of individuals as sacrifices, the initiation of administrative structures, and economic development through the building of fishponds and irrigation works.

The genealogies and their linked traditions were passed from one generation of *kūʻauhau* (expert) to the next, through oral transmission, the task of memorization often being aided by the frequent coding of the texts in the form of poetic chant (Emerson 1909). This rich body of oral literature might have been lost to us were it not for the efforts of several key individuals in the nineteenth century, who collected, collated, and set to paper the *moʻokūʻauhau* and the *moʻolelo*. Chief among these were David Malo and Samuel Mānaiakalani Kamakau (see Chapter 2), who drew not only on their own training, but on their access (through their rank and family connections) to many other *kūʻauhau* from whom they collected and assembled their compilations. Kamakau was especially prolific in collecting *moʻolelo*, and published these in a large series of articles in Hawaiian language newspapers, later translated by Mary Kawena Pukui and edited by Dorothy Barrère (Kamakau 1961, 1991).

Another major compilation of genealogies and traditions derives from the work of Abraham Fornander, a Swedish immigrant who arrived in Hawaiʻi in 1838, and a decade later married ʻĀlanakapu, a Hawaiian *aliʻi* from Molokaʻi Island (Davis 1979). Fornander learned the Hawaiian language, and perhaps inspired by his own youthful interest in Viking traditions (Davis 1979), became deeply absorbed in Hawaiian traditional history. Holding well-salaried posts with the Hawaiian Government (Inspector of Schools and later a judge of the Circuit Court), "he hired two, and sometimes three, intelligent and educated Hawaiians[1] whom he paid for several years to travel throughout the islands, taking down from the lips of the elders, in their exact words, all they could remember of the past" (Davis 1979:199). Fornander drew on this vast body of Hawaiian language manuscripts for his *Account of the Polynesian Race* (Fornander 1996), of which Volume II focuses on the Hawaiian traditions. While Fornander's account remains a valuable source in its own right, more important perhaps are the three massive volumes titled the

Fornander Collection of Hawaiian Antiquities and Folk-Lore, published by the Bernice P. Bishop Museum in dual Hawaiian and English text, between 1916 and 1920. These consist of Fornander's collection of manuscripts, which were acquired by Charles Reed Bishop after Fornander's death in 1887.

A distinctly secondary source of the late-nineteenth century, but one nonetheless worth consulting, is the account of His Hawaiian Majesty David Kalākaua (1990 [1888]), a high *ali'i* and last King of the independent monarchy from 1874 to 1891. Although the title page credits Kalākaua as author, the text seems to have been in large part ghostwritten by R. M. Daggett, who is credited as the editor. Kalākaua was keenly interested in Hawaiian traditions, and is noted for having assembled a group of traditional experts, the Hale Nauā, to help revitalize Hawaiian culture, including chant and dance. Yet another valuable source on the chiefly genealogies is Edith Kawelohea McKinzie's compilation of genealogies published between 1834 and 1900 in a variety of Hawaiian language newspapers (McKinzie 1983, 1986). Finally, one cannot ignore the work of folklorist Martha Beckwith (1940), born and raised on Maui in the early years of the twentieth century, who dedicated her life to collecting and interpreting Hawaiian mythology and traditions.[2]

The first modern scholar to integrate the corpus of genealogically based oral traditions with archaeology was Robert Hommon (1976) in his unpublished doctoral dissertation on Hawaiian "primitive states." Hommon recognized that the deeper portions of the chiefly genealogies were "cosmogonic in nature," but he argued that the "latter portions and the associated legends are intended to portray the relationships and exploits of mortal men and women" (1976:122). Hommon regarded the last 21 generations of these genealogies as historically accurate. He followed Stokes's lead of using 20 years to a generation (Stokes 1933), which would take Hawaiian political history back to approximately AD 1400, a time just after the so-called "voyaging" or "migratory" period (which I discuss later). Hommon drew principally on Kamakau (1961) and Fornander (1996) to compile chronological listings of the ruling *ali'i* of each of the main islands (Hommon 1976: Appendices A to C), and integrated these into a comprehensive political history. He then incorporated evidence from the archaeological record to outline a model of "state formation" in Hawai'i (see Chapter 5).

Ross Cordy (2000, 2002a, 2002b) has recently drawn on the Hawaiian *mo'olelo* to interpret precontact history. In an extensive treatment of Hawai'i Island and in shorter reviews of O'ahu and its Wai'anae

District, Cordy links the oral traditions to specific archaeological sites, especially for Hawai'i Island after AD 1400.

An issue that has vexed scholars is the average length of the age interval that should be assigned to each generation in the Hawaiian chiefly genealogies. Fornander (1996) used 30 years, while Stokes (1933), based on a consideration of the reproductive ages of known *ali'i*, came to the conclusion that 20 years was most likely. Along with Hommon (1976) and Cordy (2002a), I also favor a 20-year generational interval. I believe that a chronology based on this average generational length provides the best fit with the archaeological evidence. The number of chiefly generations between the time of contact and initial island rulers whom we can regard as real historic actors varies depending on the particular island sequence. Hommon (1976, Appendix C) lists 25 successive rulers for Hawai'i Island, 19 for Maui Island, 18 for O'ahu Island, and 20 for Kaua'i Island. The genealogy of O'ahu given by Cordy (2002a, Table 1) has 23 generations of rulers, beginning with Māweke down to the time of the kings who were ruling when Cook arrived in 1778 to 1779. (If to Hommon's O'ahu list, we add the six additional generations between Lakona and Māweke, the total number of O'ahu rulers is 24.) The chiefly genealogies provided by Hommon (1976: Appendices A–C) and by Cordy (2000: Tables 7.1, 7.2, Figs. 8.1, 10.1; 2002a, Table 1) provide a framework for a relative chronology and sequence for key island rulers. The traditions presented in Fornander (1916–20, 1996), Kamakau (1961, 1991), Malo (1951), and other sources provide cross-references among the rulers of each main island, especially in terms of marriages and wars, so that the principal actors can be temporally correlated. In Table 3.1, I give estimated AD dates for such a relative sequence, using the preferred 20-year interval, counting back from the last generation, which is taken to be AD 1750–1770, just prior to European contact. Table 3.1 also lists some of the principal *ali'i* of O'ahu, Maui, and Hawai'i islands, based on their sequence in Fornander (1996).

FOUNDING TRADITIONS OF SETTLEMENT AND VOYAGING

The *mo'olelo* do not offer historically reliable information regarding initial colonization of the Hawaiian archipelago by Polynesians. There are, to be sure, various fragmentary and often clearly mythological accounts of early arrivals from ancestral lands to the south (lands glossed in Hawaiian as "Kahiki"), including such well-known legendary figures

TABLE 3.1. APPROXIMATE CHRONOLOGY AND SEQUENCE FOR KEY RULERS OF OʻAHU, MAUI, AND HAWAIʻI ISLANDS

Estimated AD Date (20-year Interval)	Some Principal Oʻahu Island Rulers	Some Principal Maui Island Rulers	Some Principal Hawaiʻi Island Rulers
1310	Māweke		
1330	Muliʻelealiʻi		Pilikaʻaiea
1350	Kumuhonua		
1370			
1390			
1410			
1430			Kalaunuiohua
1450			
1470	Haka		
1490	Māʻilikūkahi		
1510		Kakaʻalaneo	
1530			
1550		Kawaokaʻōhele	Līloa
1570		Piʻilani	Hakau, ʻUmi a Līloa
1590		Kiha a Piʻilani	Keawenui a ʻUmi
1610	Kākuhihewa	Kamalālāwalu	Lonoikamakahiki
1630		Kauhi-a-Kama	
1650			
1670		Lonohonuakini	
1690	Kūaliʻi	Kaʻulahea	Keaweikekahialiʻi-okamoku
1710	Peleʻiohōlani	Kekaulike	Alapaʻinui
1730	Kūmahana	Kamehamehanui, Kahekili	Kalaniʻōpuʻu
1750	Kahāhana, Kahekili, Kalanikūpule		Kīwalaʻō, Kamehameha

as Pele and Hawai'i-loa (Fornander 1996). Nānā'ulu, and with his brother 'Ulu, are likewise supposed by the genealogies to have arrived in Hawai'i as many as fifteen generations prior to Māweke in the chronology given in Table 3.1.[3] However, during the first five generations following Māweke, corresponding roughly to AD 1310 to 1390, there are a number of detailed traditions that refer to voyages from and/or to Kahiki, some of them round-trip voyages. There has been much scholarly discussion and debate concerning the historical accuracy of these voyaging traditions, and their significance for Hawaiian cultural history (e.g., Fornander 1996; Beckwith 1940:352–75; Stokes 1933; Cartwright 1929, 1933; Cordy 1974c; Cachola-Abad 1993). Late nineteenth and early-twentieth-century scholars, including the Polynesian anthropologist Peter Buck (Te Rangi Hiroa) (1938), regarded the voyaging traditions of this "Migratory Period" as true historical accounts, although at times embellished by their tellers. Later scholars such as Cordy (1974c) discounted the *mo'olelo* of multiple long-distance voyages as mythological. Recently, the weight of scholarly opinion has shifted toward recognition of the likely historical validity of the traditions. This change is a response both to the demonstration of Polynesian voyaging performance with the experimental double-hulled canoe *Hokule'a* (Finney 1994), and to new archaeological and other empirical evidence of long-distance interactions within Eastern Polynesia (e.g., Collerson and Weisler 2007).

I will not review the voyaging traditions in depth, as the events they recount precede the period in which Hawaiian chiefship and society were radically transformed. Nonetheless, they are important to consider as they mark the end of a period in which Hawai'i was still connected to other Polynesian lands to the south, and the beginning of a 500-year period of total isolation. Two important examples provide some flavor of these accounts and their likely historical significance for Hawaiian cultural history.

One of the greatest voyaging sagas features several generations of one extended family of *ali'i*, descended from Māweke, the nominal ruling chief of O'ahu at the beginning of the sequence (Table 3.1), and a descendant of Nānā'ulu.[4] A 20-year generational interval puts Māweke's reign at the beginning of the fourteenth century AD. In classic Polynesian fashion, Māweke partitioned O'ahu among his three sons: Muli'eleali'i, the first born, Keaunui, and Kalehenui. Mulieleali'i ruled over the Kona District including the famed lands of Waikīkī (which had also been his father's primary seat), Keaunui controlled the districts of 'Ewa, Wai'anae, and Waialua, and Kalehenui received the windward Koʻolau District with its reefs, fishponds, and irrigation lands. This scenario was repeated in the next generation, with Muliʻelealiʻi also having three sons, Kumuhonua, ʻOlopana, and Moʻikeha, in birth order. On Muliʻelealiʻi's death, and following Polynesian rules of patrimonial succession, the oldest son Kumuhonua took over control of the primary Kona estates. ʻOlopana and Moʻikeha received only minor holdings within the Kona District. But now another classic Polynesian pattern asserted itself: the displeasure of younger, junior ranking siblings who only saw their prestige and access to land and resources diminishing with each successive generation. The younger brothers, ʻOlopana and Moʻikeha, plotted against Kumuhonua and organized a sea attack of war canoes against him. ʻOlopana and Moʻikeha were spared, but forced into exile.

ʻOlopana and Moʻikeha took up residence on Hawaiʻi Island, in the great valley of Waipiʻo (later to become the principal seat of the emergent Hawaiʻi Island kings). The *moʻolelo* speak to their development of that valley's irrigation systems, and indeed they may well have brought with them knowledge gained from Oʻahu's irrigation infrastructure, which by the fourteenth century was already advanced (see Chapter 4). ʻOlopana took as his wife Luʻukia, the daughter of the local Kohala chief Hīkapoloa. Then a series of storms and floods wreaked havoc across Waipiʻo's floodplain, destroying the irrigation works. This is entirely plausible, for Waipiʻo is known in historic times for dangerous flooding. ʻOlopana and Luʻukia, along with Moʻikeha, abandoned the valley to undertake a voyage back to the homeland of their ancestors, in Kahiki.

The three *aliʻi* sailed to Kahiki and settled in a land called Moa-ʻula-nui-ākea. Circumstantial evidence suggests that Moa-ʻula-nui-ākea was synonymous with the fertile Punaʻauia District along the southwestern coast of Tahiti in the Society Islands. This district remains the domain of the important ʻOropaʻa line of Tahiti chiefs (*ariʻi*), ʻOropaʻa being the Tahitian spelling of ʻOlopana (Handy 1930:71–72; Henry 1928:79–81). Moreover, in the center of the district lies the great valley of Punaruʻu, which has its equivalent on Oʻahu (Punaluʻu), as well as a once sacred temple Taputapuātea, which is matched by a temple of the same name on northern Oʻahu (Kapukapuākea).

ʻOlopana remained in Moa-ʻula-nui-ākea, but Moʻikeha, after an affair with Luʻukia, decides to return back to Hawaiʻi. Guided by his chief navigator Kamahualele, Moʻikeha's double canoe makes the return voyage and visits each of the main Hawaiian islands from Hawaiʻi to Kauaʻi, where he is greeted by that island's chief Puna. Moʻikeha marries Puna's two daughters, and after Puna's death succeeds to the paramountship of Kaua'i. Late in life, however, he is taken with a desire to see his son La'a (by another mate in Kahiki) who was left behind as an infant when Mo'ikeha left Moa-'ula-nui-ākea. Mo'ikeha's son Kila is chosen to make the long voyage back to Kahiki to fetch La'a. Kila, again guided by Kamahualele, makes the voyage and returns with La'a to see his father Mo'ikeha in Kaua'i. La'a henceforth becomes known as La'a-mai-Kahiki (La'a-from-Tahiti). La'a spends some time in Hawai'i, including in the district of Kahikinui on Maui, but finally departs again for Kahiki, leaving from the southeastern point of Kaho'olawe Island, known as Lae-o-Ke-ala-i-Kahiki ("Cape of the Road-to-Tahiti"). This round trip voyage of La'a from Kahiki to Hawai'i and back is one of the last of such trips referenced in the *mo'olelo*.

The second example of a voyaging tradition is that of Pā'ao, roughly contemporary with Mo'ikeha, in the fourteenth century AD.[5] Pā'ao was a priest, and the traditions associate him with an origin place named Wawau, possibly Vava'u in the Tonga archipelago, although more likely Porapora Island in the Society group, whose ancient name was Vavau (Henry 1928:102).[6] In yet another instance of sibling rivalry, Pā'ao quarreled with his older brother Lonopele, who accused Pā'ao's son of stealing breadfruit. Pā'ao slit his son's stomach open to prove his innocence, and later killed Lonopele's son in retribution, using the child's body as a roller for launching his voyaging canoe. Pā'ao then departed from Vava'u for Hawai'i, taking with him the high chief Pilika'aiea, a descendant of the 'Ulu branch in the founding Hawaiian genealogies.[7] After arriving at Hawai'i Island, Pā'ao built a temple called 'Aha'ula (later Waha'ula) in Puna, and installed Pilika'aiea as the ruling chief of that island. Traveling to Kohala District in the north, Pā'ao also constructed Mo'okini Heiau. One of the most important lineages of Hawai'i Islands priests, *kahuna*, trace their descent from Pā'ao down to Hewahewanui at the time of Kamehameha I (Fornander 1996:38).

Note that both La'amaikahiki and Pā'ao are credited in the traditions with introducing significant new changes to the religion and ritual practices of Hawai'i. The former brought his idols along with a cylindrical temple drum called a *pahu* (Buck 1957:396–401: Fig. 298; Kaeppler 1993; Tatar 1993). As noted in Chapter 2, drumming of the *pahu* was a key part of *luakini* temple rituals, and it is the case that the Tahitian *pa'u* (with a nearly identical shape) played a similar role in Society Islands *marae* ceremonies. Pā'ao, for his part, is said to have introduced the cult of Kū along with the practice of human sacrifice.

Did Moʻikeha, Kila, Laʻamaikahiki, Pāʻao and others of this time period actually make the round-trip voyages credited to them in the *moʻolelo*? Our heightened understanding of Polynesian double-hulled voyaging canoe capabilities, owed to the experimental voyaging of the *Hokuleʻa* (Finney 1994), make this much more plausible than was thought a few decades ago. Moreover, there is increasing evidence for multiple contacts between Hawaiʻi and the archipelagoes of south-central Polynesia: (1) linguistic evidence of Tahitic borrowings in Hawaiian, which is fundamentally a Marquesic language (Marck 1996b, 2000); (2) mitochondrial DNA lineages of the Polynesian-introduced Pacific rat in Hawaiʻi indicate both Marquesan and Society Islands contacts (Matisoo-Smith et al. 1998); and (3) a stone adz from the Tuamotu Islands has now been directly sourced to basalt from Kahoʻolawe Island in Hawaiʻi, physical evidence for long-distance voyaging (Collerson and Weisler 2007). My own view is that while the *moʻolelo* may have been embellished by later generations, they have a solid core of historical truth, and do accurately refer to a period when the Hawaiian Islands were linked by voyaging to ancestral lands in the south, mostly likely to Tahiti and the other islands of the Society archipelago.

What is perhaps most significant about the voyaging traditions is the way in which they refer to an abrupt end to long-distance, external contacts with "Kahiki." The epic voyages, which Fornander referred to as the "Migratory Period," all take place within a relatively short time span, and are tied to the first five generations of the relative chronology. One of the last voyages referenced in the *moʻolelo* is of a grandson of Moʻikeha, Kahaʻi-a-Hoʻokamaliʻi, who reputedly made a round-trip voyage to Kahiki, returning with the first breadfruit tree to be transplanted to Hawaiʻi.[8] At 20 years per generation, this brackets the voyages to between AD 1310 and 1390, a time period that archaeological work in southeastern Polynesia has demonstrated to have been a period of considerable interarchipelago interaction and exchange (Weisler 1998). If extensive voyaging occurred among the Marquesas, Societies, Australs, Mangareva, and Cooks (as indicated by considerable evidence of interisland transport of stone tools), there is no reason to think that some voyages were not also made to Hawaiʻi during this period. But there is no further mention of such voyages after about AD 1400; thereafter the *moʻolelo* refer exclusively to people and events whose frame of geographic reference is limited to the Hawaiian Islands. This is important, for after the explicitly referenced introductions of the *pahu* drum, human sacrifice, and related temple ritual made by Laʻamaikahiki and Pāʻao, and the breadfruit by Kahaʻi-i-Hoʻokamaliʻi, the indigenous accounts credit all later changes in Hawaiian culture as stemming from the actions of Hawaiian *aliʻi* themselves. In other words, after approximately AD 1400 the further evolution of Hawaiian society, economy, politics, and religion was a strictly endogenous affair. One can thus rule out external contact, influence, trade, or exchange, as causative factors in Hawaiian cultural change after the end of the fourteenth century. And as we see in Chapter 4, the independent archaeological evidence is in strong agreement with the *moʻolelo* in this respect.

POLITICAL DEVELOPMENTS OF THE FIFTEENTH TO MID-SIXTEENTH CENTURIES

With the cessation of long-distance voyaging to Kahiki around the end of the fourteenth century, the genealogies of the ruling lineages of the four major islands of Kauaʻi, Oʻahu, Maui, and Hawaiʻi take on an increasingly firm and frequently cross-linked structure. The period of interest is the nine generations spanning approximately AD 1410 to 1570, during which time Oʻahu was the center of cultural innovation. During a period coincident with the late-sixteenth century, major political upheavals occurred on both Hawaiʻi and Maui Islands, shifting the entire dynamic of change from the westerly islands, especially Oʻahu, to the two large eastern islands. From then on, Maui and Hawaiʻi become the archipelago's nexus of social and political evolution.

I begin with the rich traditions of fifteenth-century Oʻahu *aliʻi*. We saw earlier that Māweke (ca. AD 1310) partitioned the island into three districts: Kona; the ʻEwa, Waiʻanae, and Waialua region; and, the windward Koʻolau region (Fig. 3.1). Following Māweke, the descendants of his first-ranked son, Kumuhonua, held the ʻEwa-Waiʻanae-Waialua region, the offspring of Kalehenui held the Koʻolau District, and those of Moʻikeha occupied the Kona lands. Each of these regions was centered around an important core of irrigation lands, and each also incorporated fisheries and dryland farming areas. None of the individuals in this extended conical clan of Oʻahu *aliʻi* stands out particularly until the rule of Haka, between approximately AD 1470 and 1490, a descendant of the first-ranked Kumuhonua line.

Haka's rise to power may have been a consequence of the first recorded war of interisland aggression, promulgated by the Hawaiʻi Island chief Kalanuiohua (ca. AD 1450) who led a military campaign

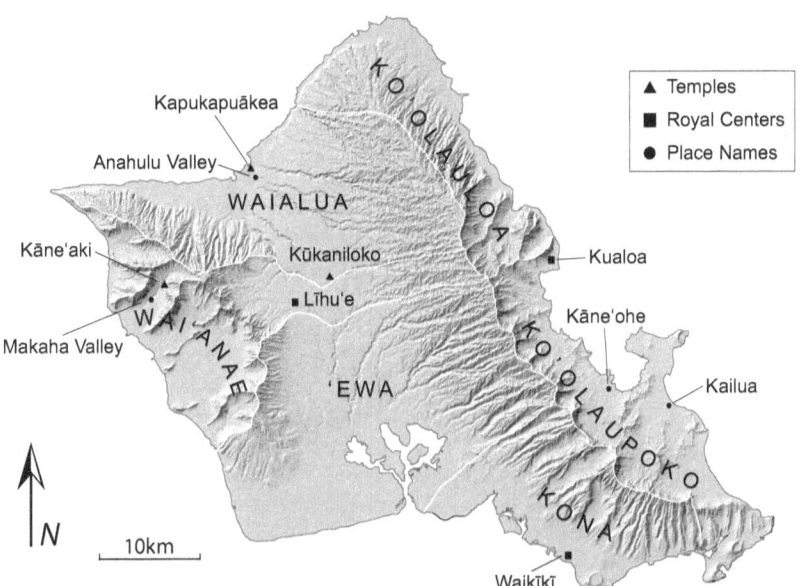

Figure 3.1. Map of Oʻahu Island showing traditional districts and key places mentioned in the text.

westward through the archipelago, routing the Oʻahu warriors under Huapouleilei (Haka's predecessor, and probably his father) at Waiʻanae (Fornander 1996:68). Fear of further aggression may have induced the Oʻahu chiefs to give Haka greater control over the entire island. But the *moʻolelo* state that Haka abused his power, proving to be a "stingy" chief "who did not take care of the chiefs and people" (Kamakau 1991:53–54; Fornander 1996:88). The Oʻahu chiefs rebelled, and Haka was killed in his ridgetop fortress of Waewae, overlooking the chiefly residence of Līhuʻe, betrayed by one of his own warriors who let the rebel forces slip through the defenses while Haka slept (Kamakau 1991:54).

The *ʻaha aliʻi* or council of chiefs then chose Māʻilikūkahi to be the new *aliʻi nui*, or paramount chief of Oʻahu. Māʻilikūkahi traced his line back through the famous voyaging chief Moʻikeha to Māweke, and ultimately back to Nānāʻulu, a prestigious line (Kamakau 1991:76–78). Kamakau emphasizes that Māʻilikūkahi was born at Kūkaniloko, a sacred birthing place of *aliʻi kapu*, sacred chiefs, situated on the interior plateau of Oʻahu (Kirch and Babineau 1996:35). "Chiefs born at Kūkaniloko were the *akua* [gods] of the land" (Kamakau 1991:53). The *moʻolelo* of Māʻilikūkahi reveals that his elevation to the paramountship occurred when he was 29 years old, marked by a ceremony of installation at the sacred Kapukapuākea temple. Two specific rites reserved for the highest-ranked *ali'i*, the cutting of the navel cord and circumcision, were reenacted by the priests (Kamakau 1991:54).

Mā'ilikūkahi moved his primary residence from Līhu'e on O'ahu's interior plateau to Waikīkī in Kona, which thereafter became a royal center of the O'ahu kings. Most significantly, the *mo'olelo* describe how Mā'ilikūkahi administratively organized the island's lands and chiefs. Kamakau's account is worth quoting in full:

> When the kingdom passed to Mā'ilikūkahi, the land divisions were in a state of confusion; the *ahupua'a*, the *kū* ['*ili kūpono*], the '*ili 'āina*, the *mo'o 'āina*, the *pauku 'āina*, and the *kīhāpai* were not clearly defined. Therefore Mā'ilikūkahi ordered the chiefs, *ali'i*, the lesser chiefs, *kaukau ali'i*, and warrior chiefs, *pū'ali ali'i*, and the overseers, *luna* to divide all of O'ahu into *moku* and *ahupua'a*, '*ili kūpono*, '*ili 'āina*, and *mo'o 'āina*. There were six districts, *moku*, and six district chiefs, *ali'i nui 'ai moku*. Chiefs were assigned to the *ahupua'a*—if it was a large *ahupua'a*, a high chief, an *ali'i nui*, was assigned to it. Lesser chiefs, *kaukau ali'i*, were placed over the *kūpono* lands, and warrior chiefs over '*ili 'āina*. Lands were given to the *maka'āinana* all over O'ahu. (Kamakau 1991:54–55)

Kamakau thus credits Mā'ilikūkahi with developing the hierarchical form of land divisions characteristic of later Hawaiian archaic states. Whether or not this was exactly so may be debated (Kamakau may have projected the land system as he knew it back onto Mā'ilikūkahi), but that Mā'ilikūkahi set up some kind of explicit land division and administrative structure seems probable.[9] With Haka, and especially Mā'ilikūkahi, one detects a change in the nature of the O'ahu paramountship, toward an increasingly formal organizational structure that could impose centralized control. Kamakau goes on to emphasize the "prosperity of the kingdom" under Mā'ilikūkahi, how the "land was full of people" (1991:55). "They brought him goods, *waiwai*, and vegetable food, '*ai*, and pigs, dogs, fowl, and fish." Kamakau stresses that these were brought as "gifts, *ho'okupu*, not as tribute," yet one wonders if these are not the roots of the tribute extraction system that was later to be so closely linked with the land hierarchy; the word used for such tribute, after all, continued to be *ho'okupu*.[10]

That O'ahu held a position of central importance at this time is suggested by the decision of the chiefs of Maui and Hawai'i to make war against Mā'ilikūkahi, whose "name became famous from the skies to the earth and from Hawai'i to Kaua'i" (Kamakau 1991:56). The Maui and Hawai'i forces landed at Waikīkī and at Kapua'ikāula in 'Ewa

District but were cut off from the rear and slaughtered at the gulch called Kīpapa, the name evoking the "pavement" of corpses that lined the valley floor at the end of the battle.[11]

A final note in the rich tradition of Māʻilikūkahi concerns his religious practices. This paramount chief was still tied to the Ancestral Polynesian ritual traditions, evidenced not only by his investiture at the temple of Kapukapuākea (see Sahlins 1992:21), but by the fact that "he did not sacrifice men in the *heiau* and *luakini*" (Kamakau 1991:56). This, Kamakau tells us, was the way of the sacred chiefs born at Kūkaniloko, descendants of the Nānāʻulu line. Thus ritual homicide, which was so essential to the validation of the kingship in the contact-era Hawaiian polities, had yet to be instituted.

Although Māʻilikūkahi receives the greatest attention in the *moʻolelo* of this period, two approximate contemporaries deserve mention for similar innovations in administration and development of the economic infrastructures of their islands. On Kauaʻi the chief circa AD 1450, Manokalanipō, is credited "for the energy and wisdom with which he encouraged agriculture and industry, executed long and difficult works of irrigation, and thus brought fields of wilderness under cultivation" (Fornander 1996:93). His island is often memorialized as Kauaʻi-a-Manokalanipō in honor of his deeds. On Maui, the *aliʻi nui* Kakaʻalaneo played a similar role to that of Māʻilikūkahi on Oʻahu.[12] Kamakau credits Kakaʻalaneo with the same imposition of a hierarchical land system "into *ahupuaʻa*, *ʻokana*, and *moku ʻāina*" on Maui. Kakaʻalaneo (who ruled West Maui and Lānaʻi jointly with his brother Kakaʻe) had his chiefly seat at Lahaina, in the center of a vast region also noted for irrigated taro; he is further credited with planting extensive breadfruit groves (Fornander 1996:82). Further evidence of Kakaʻalaneo's development of irrigation is the reference to a famous irrigation canal, or *ʻauwai*, constructed at Lahaina at the instigation of his daughter Wao, and named for her (ʻAuwai-a-Wao; Sterling 1998:39–40).

Finally, on Hawaiʻi Island the key figure in the line of chiefs descended from Pilikaʻaiea (who was brought by Pāʻao from Kahiki) was Kalaunuiohua (Fornander 1996:67; Kamakau 1991:56). The primary *moʻolelo* associated with Kalaunuiohua emphasizes his warlike character, and his raiding westward through the archipelago, as noted earlier.[13] His campaign was successful from Maui through Oʻahu, but he met defeat on Kauaʻi, at the hands of Kūkona (predecessor of Manokalanipō), and reportedly was held prisoner on that island for many years, before being returned to his natal island (Fornander 1996:68).

To sum up, the *moʻolelo* of the fifteenth to mid-sixteenth centuries reveal a consistent pattern of social and political changes following the cessation of contact with Kahiki. Oʻahu, and to a lesser extent Kauaʻi, are the central islands in these traditions. These are the islands of the old, sacred Nānāʻulu line of *aliʻi*, closely linked with the voyaging chiefs from Kahiki. Their religion is of the ancestral style, lacking human sacrifice. The *moʻolelo* of this period emphasize the development and intensification of irrigation, of which these two islands certainly had the greatest natural potential with their valley topography and abundant streams (Ladefoged et al. 2009). With Māʻilikūkahi, a formal system of hierarchical land divisions becomes established, along with the first regularized collection of *hoʻokupu*, tribute. His practices are emulated by the Maui chiefs, and instituted there as well. Hawaiʻi Island remains aloof from these developments, more warlike in its outlook and less focused on agriculture.

USURPATION AND POLITICAL CONSOLIDATION IN THE HAWAIʻI AND MAUI KINGDOMS

A critical juncture in the traditions of chiefly succession for both Hawaiʻi and Maui Islands occurs between AD 1550 and 1590 in the relative chronology of chiefs (Table 3.1). On the large island of Hawaiʻi (Fig. 3.2), the key persons are Hākau and his half brother ʻUmi-a-Līloa, who defeated Hākau in a war of succession and seized control of the entire island for the first time (Kamakau 1961:1–21; Fornander 1917:178–235). On Maui, this period is occupied by Piʻilani, a great *aliʻi nui* who integrated windward and leeward sides of that island, for the first time. Piʻilani also controlled nearby Lānaʻi and Kahoʻolawe islands and at least part of Molokaʻi. In a manner parallel to the events on Hawaiʻi Island, the succession to the Maui kingship after Piʻilani became a heroic struggle between his two sons Lono-a-Piʻilani and Kiha-a-Piʻilani. The *moʻolelo* regarding these individuals are recounted by all of the main sources (Kamakau 1961:1–33; Malo 1951:256–66; Fornander 1916:178–255; Fornander 1996:95–108, 205–7; see also Valeri 1985b), and the rich details offer insights for an "insider," agent-based understanding of Hawaiian political dynamics.[14] I thus consider them in some detail, beginning with the history of ʻUmi-a-Līloa.

The account of ʻUmi properly begins with his father Līloa, an *aliʻi nui* of high (*piʻo*) rank whose genealogy traces back to the ʻUlu line of chiefs through Pilikaʻaiea. Līloa resided in Waipiʻo Valley on the windward

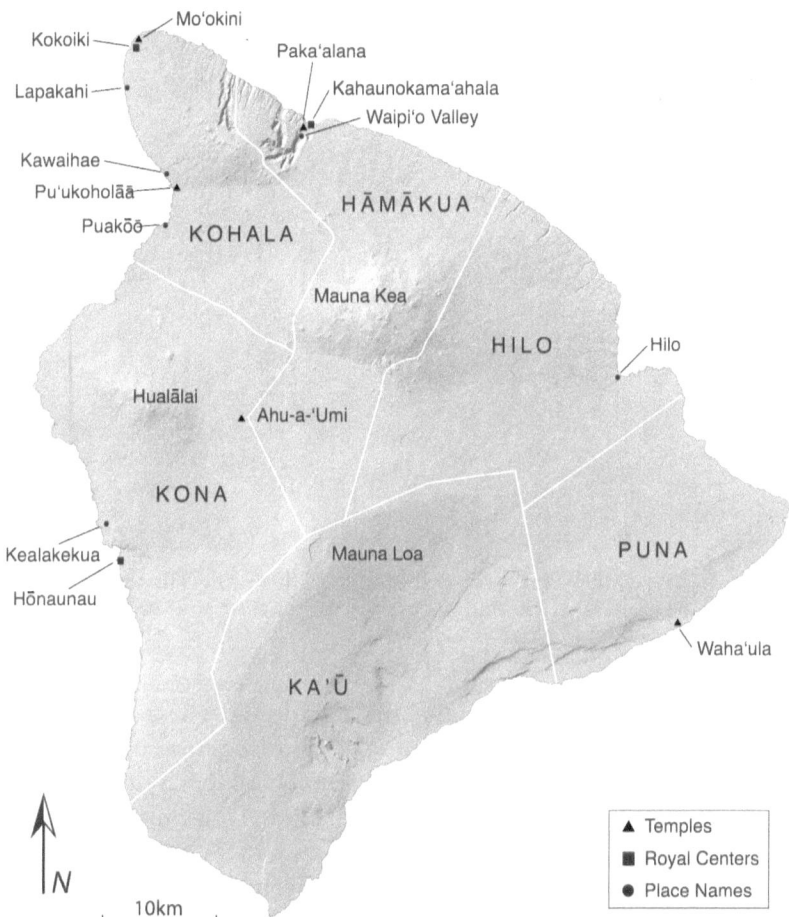

Figure 3.2. Map of Hawai'i Island showing traditional districts and key places mentioned in the text.

coast of Kohala District; the toponym translates as "curved water" but may be an allusion to the *pi'o* chiefs who had made it their home (Fig. 3.3). With the largest expanse of irrigated taro lands on Hawai'i Island, Waipi'o was favored as the seat of the *ali'i nui*. The royal residence, Kahaunokama'ahala, straddled the inland side of a black sand beach ridge, next to the *luakini* temple of Paka'alana; another large *luakini*, Honua'ula, was situated slightly further to the west (Cordy 2000:197–200: Fig. 7-1). These temples were dedicated to a particular manifestation of the war god Kū, associated with the Hawai'i Island chiefly line. This was Kūkā'ilimoku, roughly translated as 'Kū-the-snatcher-of-kingdoms,"

Figure 3.3. View of Waipi'o Valley from the southern rim. The royal center of Līloa was located on the sand dunes north of the river mouth, now covered in trees. (Photo by P. V. Kirch.)

whose manifestation was an anthropomorphic wickerwork head covered in red birds' feathers, with inlaid pearlshell eyes and a flaring mouth rimmed with dog's teeth (Frontispiece). Although the other districts of the island were under the direct control of other high *ali'i*, Līloa exercised some degree of overall authority over the entire island, as evidenced by his travel through Hamakua District to dedicate several *heiau* and to participate in the *pahe'e* or dart pitching games (Kamakau 1961:2; Fornander 1916:178).

While on his Hāmākua journey Līloa became enamored of a beautiful young woman, Akahiakuleana, whom he glimpsed emerging from a stream at Ka'awikiwiki. Akahiakuleana was not regarded as being of true *ali'i* rank, although she possessed a genealogy traceable to Kanipahu, an *ali'i nui* of Hawai'i, and a direct ancestor of Līloa.[15] Līloa could not restrain his lust, and Akahiakuleana consented to his advances. The pair remained together long enough for Akahiakuleana to realize that she was pregnant. Līloa then gave to Akahiakuleana the symbols of his chiefship: "the feather cape, ivory pendant [*lei niho palaoa*], helmet and *kauila* spear" (Kamakau 1961:3), telling her to hide these away safely. Should the child turn out to be a boy, she was to call him 'Umi and raise him until he reached puberty (i.e., the time for the rites of circumcision). Then she was to bestow the chiefly symbols on 'Umi and send him to seek his father in Waipi'o. Līloa left Akahiakuleana to rejoin the other chiefs, wearing only a loin cloth of *kī* leaves and a cape of banana leaves.

'Umi grew up under Akahiakuleana's care, and that of her commoner husband, who sometimes abused the child. One day after 'Umi had come of age, and her husband had beaten him again, Akahiakuleana revealed to 'Umi (and to her shocked and fearful husband) that his real father was Līloa, the sacred chief in Waipi'o. Recovering the royal symbols from their hiding place, she bid 'Umi to go and meet his father. Although only a child, 'Umi had already adopted (*hānai*) another boy named 'Oma'o, who accompanied him on the journey. Along the way two other young men joined them, Pi'i-mai-wa'a and Ko'i. All three became 'Umi's lifelong trusted supporters.

Arriving in Waipi'o, 'Umi instructed his adopted "sons" to wait while he breached the *kapu* barriers marking the royal compound. 'Umi broke a strict *kapu* by entering the side door of the house, reserved for the king, and before the *ilāmuku* (executioners) could stop him, jumped into the lap of his father, another egregious lapse of protocol. Līloa demanded to know whose child this was, and 'Umi answered "Yours! I am 'Umi-a- Līloa" (Kamakau 1961:7). Seeing his own symbols of chiefship left years before with Akahiakuleana, Līloa wailed with joy, and ordered the sacred *pahu* and *ka'eke* drums to be sounded in Paka'alana Heiau. 'Umi was then taken into the *heiau* to be circumcised, transforming him into a proper *ali'i*.[16]

Significantly, Līloa already had a royal heir, Hākau, offspring of his *pi'o* marriage to Pinea, Līloa's own sister. Hākau was probably only a little older than 'Umi, and on hearing the news that his father had taken in this bastard son by a commoner woman, he was furious. Hākau protested to his father, saying "So you have a slave for a son, and he is to call me his brother" (Kamakau 1961:8), but Līloa replied that 'Umi would be a trusted servant to Hākau, "a carrier of your spittoon, tapas and loincloth, a servant who is related by blood (*iwikuamo'o*) to you, the chief." Hākau acquiesced, but periodically berated and beat 'Umi and his adopted sons. Nonetheless, 'Umi became a member of the royal household, learning court etiquette and the arts of war.

When Līloa grew old, nearing death, he gathered his court about him, commanding that his kingdom would be left to his *pi'o* heir, Hākau. But in a perhaps startling gesture, Līloa also "commanded that his son 'Umi-a-Līloa be given the government-snatching god, Kūkā'ilimoku, and said to 'Umi, 'Live humbly'" (Kamakau 1961:9). At first Hākau behaved as a just successor, ensuring that Līloa's bones were enshrined in a special wicker casket of anthropomorphic shape, and placed in a mausoleum in Waipi'o.[17] Soon, however, Hākau resumed his abusive ways, leaving 'Umi to fear for his life. With his three friends 'Umi fled through the forest to Hāmākua District, taking with him the feathered image of Kūkā'ilimoku. He hid the image in a cave, and brought the deity secret offerings. 'Umi took up residence in the *ahupua'a* of Waipunalei, posing as a simple commoner. But being handsome and skilled, 'Umi stood out, and attracted four young women to be his wives. Kaleioku, a local man of chiefly blood,[18] suspected that this was 'Umi, whose absence from the royal court had been "noised abroad," and he used a "chief-sniffing" pig to reveal 'Umi's secret (Kamakau 1961:11).

With Kaleioku's aid, 'Umi began to plot his revenge and the eventual overthrow of Hākau. The details are important from the viewpoint of Hawaiian cultural conceptions of chiefly agency. First, Kaleioku constructed several large eating houses (*halau*) and enjoined passing travelers to partake of 'Umi's hospitality, thus building up the reputation of this generous chief. Second, under Kaleioku's direction the people went "extensively into the raising of animals, and farming" (Fornander 1916:190), in short, intensifying their agricultural production base, necessary to underwrite 'Umi's hospitality, and to support an army. Finally, 'Umi aided by his loyal companions Ko'i, 'Oma'o, and Pi'imaiwa'a (all of whom had become skilled warriors during their years in Waipi'o) began to train the commoners in martial arts, building up the army with which he would seize Waipi'o and the kingdom from Hākau.

While 'Umi was raising up his army in the hinterlands of Hāmākua, two elderly priests, Nunu and Kakohe, who under the late Līloa had been the "custodians of the great god Kaili," were deeply insulted by Hākau, who refused them a request of food, meat, and *'awa* root. Descended from a line of Lono priests, Nunu and Kakohe were related to Kaleioku (they may all have been brothers), and they knew that 'Umi was living with him. The priests secretly left Waipi'o and visited 'Umi, who provided all the hospitality that had been refused them by Hākau. Nunu and Kakohe said to Kaleioku, "We have no gift for your beloved chief except the kingdom. Let your chief have the kingdom and let our chief [Hākau] be put to death." A plot was hatched whereby the old priests would let 'Umi's army down the walls of Waipi'o Valley when most of the chiefs and warriors have gone to the mountains to fetch *'ōhi'a* wood for the *haku'ōhi'a* ceremony, a rite in the annual rededication of the

Native Hawaiian Political History 97

luakini war temple (see Valeri 1985a:262-79). This timing is culturally significant, for Hākau's death was set up precisely at the time that the *hakuʻōhiʻa* rite demands a human sacrifice.

Closely observing the sacred nights of the Hawaiian lunar calendar, ʻUmi's army marched toward Waipiʻo, arriving at the valley's rim on the night of Kāne, 27th in the Hawaiian lunar sequence. The men all took up stones, wrapping them in *kī*-leaf bundles so as to resemble sweet potatoes ready for cooking. The following day, sacred to Lono (patron deity of the sweet potato), the old priests sent the people of Waipiʻo up into the mountains to fetch the *ʻōhiʻa* logs, leaving only Hākau, his personal servant, and the two old priests in residence. ʻUmi, Kaleioku, and their army descended into Waipiʻo. At first Hākau was tricked to believe these were commoners from Hāmākua come with *hoʻokupu* offerings of sweet potatoes, but at the final moment, as the crowd surrounded Hākau and ʻUmi stepped forward, he realized his fate. Hākau was stoned to death.[19] The requisite sacrifice had been secured, but it was the body of the deposed king himself that was offered up on the temple's altar.

Although the slaying of Hākau and seizing of the kingdom by ʻUmi is clearly linked to certain *luakini* rites of the Kū cult (and we should not forget that ʻUmi himself was the keeper of Kūkāʻilimoku), there are consistent references in this sequence of events to the other great god of the Hawaiian pantheon, Lono. Note first that Keleioku, Nunu, and Kakohe are said to be descendants of a great line of Lono priests. Hākau's slaying took place just at the end of the Makahiki festival dedicated to Lono, and specifically on the day named after Lono in the lunar calendar. Moreover, the weapons used to kill Hākau were bundles of *kī*-leaf wrapped stones resembling sweet potatoes, of whom Lono was the patron deity. And in Kamakau's description of the offering up of Hākau's body on the altar of Honuaʻula, he says that "the tongue of the god came down from heaven, without the body being seen. The tongue quivered downward to the altar, accompanied by thunder and lightning, and took away all the sacrifices" (1961:14). Thunder and lightning are distinctly associated with Lono, the god of rain and dryland sweet potato agriculture. The importance of Lono's role in ʻUmi's usurpation of the kingdom is a theme I will return to later. In my view it is intimately linked with the role of dryland agriculture, essential for Hawaiʻi Island's economic base. And, recall that Lono is the god in whose name tribute is collected, and the government supported; he is also the god celebrated by the common people during the annual Makahiki festival. Symbolically, Hākau's defeat and ʻUmi's triumph may be read, culturally, as the ascendance of Lono and all he represents: intensive dryland farming, the commoner base, an organized landscape, government in its peaceful and benevolent form. 'Umi, keeper of the war god, who had respected his father's command to "live humbly" and did so while raising an army of commoner farmers, unites the powers of both Kū and Lono in one. Little wonder his *mo'olelo* is perhaps the most powerful and renowned among the Hawaiian dynastic traditions. In many respects it is the founding *mo'olelo* of Hawaiian divine kingship.

Following 'Umi's installation as the king of Hawai'i (and I now invoke that term intentionally, for I will argue that it is with 'Umi's rise to power that we can mark decisively the transition from chiefship to kingship), he asserted his power by making a division of the lands. Keleioku was made the chief priest and *ali'i-'ai-moku* over Hāmākua District, and the other districts were put under the control of his principal adopted sons and loyal supporters. 'Umi further took his half sister Kapukini-a-Līloa, with an impeccable pedigree, to be his royal mate (but only one of many wives), thus assuring his succession by offspring of *pi'o* rank (Davenport 1994:59). Kapukini-a-Līloa bore 'Umi three offspring: Keli'iokaloa, Kapulani, and Keawe-a-'Umi, two of whom would succeed him as rulers of Hawai'i Island. In Kamakau's words, this incestuous mating was done "to preserve the rank in which there was no mixed blood" (1961:15).

'Umi's division of the kingdom was not accepted by all, especially those chiefs intent on holding on to their hereditary lands. The *mo'olelo* goes into considerable detail, not necessary to recount here, how 'Umi made war against these rebellious chiefs, and eventually secured the entire island, all 10,433 square kilometers, under his unified rule.[20] His unification of this vast island was materially symbolized in a monumental construction, a temple known as the Ahu-a-'Umi, situated at an elevation of 1,585 meters near the center of the island, on a high plateau of lava and volcanic cinder. At the point where all of Hawai'i's six districts come together, its stones are reputed to have been carried from all parts of the island, thus symbolizing 'Umi's great feat of unification.

Having achieved all of this, 'Umi began to court yet another young chiefess of Hilo, but Kaleioku disabused him of this idea, the high priest having other plans for his lord. Kaleioku was aware that Maui Island, across the 'Aleinuihāhā Channel from Waipi'o, had recently been consolidated under the rule of the *ali'i nui* Pi'ilani. Kaleioku proposed that 'Umi should seek a union with Pi'ilani's daughter Pi'ikea, thus joining these two great kingdoms.

Native Hawaiian Political History 99

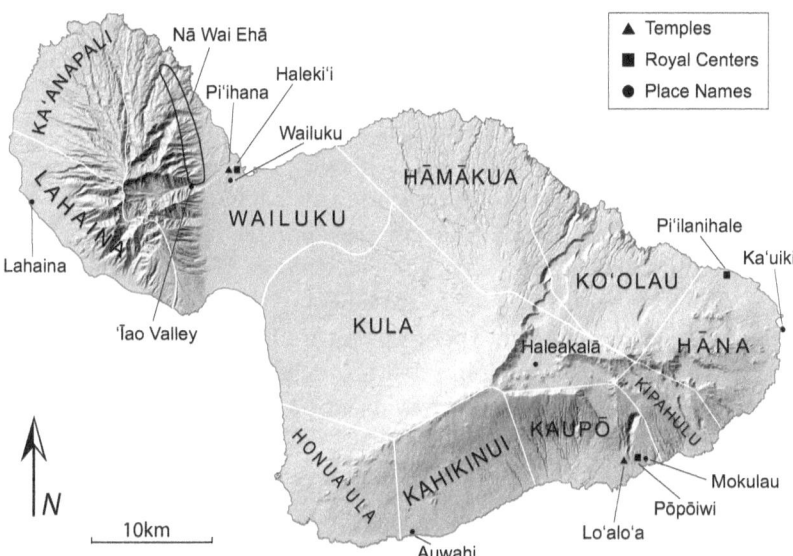

Figure 3.4. Map of Maui Island showing traditional districts and key places mentioned in the text.

Of Pi'ikea's father Pi'ilani, not a great deal is recorded in the *mo'olelo*. Fornander (1996:87) tells us that he succeeded his father Kawaokaohele, whose grandfather Kaka'alaneo had formalized Maui's land system after being influenced by developments on O'ahu. But Kawaokaohele, like his predecessors, was rooted in the lands of western Maui, with its extensive irrigation systems; his line had also controlled Lāna'i Island for some generations. With Pi'ilani, this lineage of western Maui chiefs for the first time asserted its power over eastern Maui, in particular the independent chiefs of fertile Hāna District (Fig. 3.4). Fornander writes that "the Hāna chiefs acknowledged the suzerainty of the Moi of Maui, and Piilani made frequent tours all over his dominions, enforcing order and promoting the industry of the people" (1996:87). He constructed at least the first phase of the massive residential and temple complex in Hāna, Pi'ilanihale ("House of Pi'ilani), about which more is said in Chapter 4.[21]

The real struggle for hegemonic control over a unified Maui kingdom, however, begins not with Pi'ilani's rule, but with his death and a contest for legitimate succession that markedly parallels the struggle between 'Umi and Hākau on Hawai'i Island. Again, a rivalry between junior and senior siblings (and hence a test of inherited privilege versus demonstrated *mana*) is at the core of this *mo'olelo*, recounted in detail by Kamakau (1961:22–33; see also Beckwith 1940:387–89; Fornander

1996:98, 205–6; Fornander 1916:236–55). The two brothers were of equally high rank, differentiated only by birth order, with Lono-a-Piʻilani the senior and hence first in line to inherit the title of *aliʻi nui* from Piʻilani.[22] Perhaps to keep potential sibling rivalry at bay, Kiha-a-Piʻilani had been raised on Oʻahu. With the passing of Piʻilani and ascension of Lono-a-Piʻilani to the paramountship, however, Kiha-a-Piʻilani joined the court of his elder brother, then situated in the rich irrigated taro lands of Nā Wai Ehā on the windward slopes of West Maui. In one version of the *moʻolelo*, a dispute arose between the royal brothers over the size of their respective taro pondfields at Waiheʻe (Kamakau 1961:22). The traditions agree that Lono continually abused and degraded his brother Kiha, in one incident throwing a bowl of fish and octopus into the latter's face. No longer willing to tolerate the abuse, and probably also fearing for his life, Kiha fled into the uplands of Kula, on the leeward slopes of Haleakalā.

That Kiha-a-Piʻilani chose to flee to an area of intensive dryland cultivation, where sweet potatoes were raised in the rain-fed gardens, offers a fascinating parallel with the saga of ʻUmi. Much like the latter, Kiha became proficient at sweet potato cultivation, gaining respect and fame among the *makaʻāinana* farmers for his ability to clear and plant large fields. He did not remain in Kula, however, but proceeded incognito to Hāna, on the far eastern side of Maui. Hāna was at this time under the direct control of Hoʻolaemakua, a district chief loyal to Lono-a-Piʻilani. Kiha, said to possess a "perfect physique" and an accomplished surfer, attracted the attention of Hoʻolaemakua's daughter, Koleamoku, who was betrothed to Lono-a-Piʻilani. Koleamoku wished to take Kiha as her husband, but her father refused, recognizing that this was Kiha-a-Piʻilani. The two young *aliʻi* eloped nonetheless, and Koleamoku bore Kiha-a-Piʻilani a son. Even the sight of his grandson failed to soften Hoʻolaemakua's opposition to Kiha-a-Piʻilani: "He refused utterly and said that he would lend [Kiha-a-Piʻilani] assistance only when he was willing to abide under Lono-a-Piʻilani's rule" (Kamakau 1961:27).

On hearing that his plan to win Hoʻolaemakua over to his side had failed, Kiha-a-Piʻilani became enraged and sailed to Hawaiʻi to enlist the aid of his brother-in-law ʻUmi-a-Līloa, who had married Kiha's sister Piʻikea. Piʻikea entreated her husband, now king of all Hawaiʻi Island, to take up Kiha's cause. A year was spent in preparation, building double-hulled canoes and making war implements. Hearing of the impending attack, which was aimed at Hāna, Hoʻolaemakua directed his forces to prepare the fortress hill of Kaʻuiki, overlooking Hāna Bay.[23] The ensuing invasion and battle is one of the most famous in Hawaiian traditions, for it involved not only Hoʻolaemakua, himself a famous warrior, but also ʻUmi's trio of ʻOmaʻo, Koi, and Piʻimaiwaʻa, who had assisted in the conquest of Hawaiʻi and now came to Kiha-a-Piʻilani's aid. Hoʻolaemakua and his army, holed up in their nearly impregnable fortress, used as a ruse a large dummy of a warrior that they propped up each night at the top of a ladder of *ʻōhiʻa* wood and *ʻieʻie* vines, the only access into the fortress. Piʻimaiwaʻa discovered the trick and led ʻUmi's warriors into the fort where they slaughtered the sleeping Maui defenders. Hoʻolaemakua escaped, but was hunted down at Kapipiwai, tortured, and killed; his hands were brought to Kiha-a-Piʻilani to confirm his death (Kamakau 1961:31).

The traditions differ as to whether Lono-a-Piʻilani, who remained throughout this time at his royal residence in Wailuku (West Maui), died before the actual invasion or shortly thereafter. Kamakau says that the king feared that he would be tortured like his great war leader Hoʻolaemakua, and died (1961:31). By the time that ʻUmi and Kiha arrived in their war canoes at Wailuku, Lono's corpse had been removed by loyal retainers, and the victors were denied their desire to mutilate and offer the body up on the *luakini* temple of Piʻihana at Wailuku.

With the defeat of Maui's forces at Hāna, and the death of Lono-a-Piʻilani, Kiha-a-Piʻilani became the king of this second largest island. ʻUmi-a-Līloa left one of his sons by Piʻikea, ʻAi-hakoko, to remain in the court of Kiha-a-Piʻilani, his mother's brother. Although his father, Piʻilani, purportedly held administrative control over both West and East Maui, Kiha-a-Piʻilani had now united the island by brute force. If one criterion of the archaic state is that it is maintained by the threat—if not indeed the use—of force, then with Kiha-a-Piʻilani's rise to power, as indeed with ʻUmi's on Hawaiʻi, we may mark the reigns of these two kings of the largest easterly islands as signaling a critical juncture in Hawaiian political history.

There are many significant parallels in the *moʻolelo* of ʻUmi-a-Līloa and Kiha-a-Piʻilani, not surprising given how their personal histories were intertwined both through bonds of kinship (the marriage of Kiha's sister Piʻikea to ʻUmi) and mutual assistance. Both were usurping chiefs, who overthrew respectively the legitimate hereditary lords to whom their kingdoms had been entrusted. In both cases the usurpation was considered justifiable, because Hākau and Lono-a-Piʻilani were "evil," oppressive lords who did not display the proper attributes befitting a high chief. But there are other, more subtle similarities between these two insider histories of usurpation and political consolidation. One is the association between ʻUmi and Kiha with the farming population and, in particular, with the dryland cultivation of sweet potatoes. This is especially clear in the many details that relate ʻUmi's rise to power with sweet potato cultivation and the god Lono, but the links are also found in Kiha's stay in the Kula District of Maui (a major dryland cultivation zone) and in his demonstration of great skill in sweet potato cultivation. It would seem that both leaders recognized that political strength was to be found, on their respective islands, not in the more ancient and well established systems of wetland taro cultivation, but in the extensive dryland sectors where growing populations had the potential to radically transform the landscapes into vast productive zones. Both rulers took advantage of these new opportunities for control of the emerging productive dryland landscapes. After unification of their respective islands, both kings moved their royal residences away from the old centers of irrigation (Waipiʻo on Hawaiʻi, Wailuku on Maui) into the core of the sweet potato field systems (Kona on Hawaiʻi, Hāna and Kaupō on Maui). ʻUmi and Kiha-a-Piʻilani were indeed profound individual agents of change, but both also took advantage of emerging systems of production that allowed for new opportunities of exploitation and political control.

The traditions concerning ʻUmi-a-Līloa and Kiha-a-Piʻilani reveal significant details of major political changes sweeping Hawaiʻi and Maui during the late-sixteenth century. Prior to the advent of these powerful rulers, the *aliʻi nui* seem to have occupied roles that were more ceremonial in nature, primarily as ritual leaders. The new generation of *aliʻi nui* on Hawaiʻi and Maui now began to exercise direct control over economic production, through a system of territorial administration. The *moʻolelo* speak to various aspects of the rulers' administrations, such as ʻUmi's institution of labor specialization and enhancement of food production capacity, and the establishment of the *kōʻele* system of chiefly farms yielding tribute. Both ʻUmi and Kiha are associated with the construction of particular temples (*heiau*), and the former is said to have enhanced the priesthood, while the latter built a road network and fishponds.

This period from the close of the sixteenth century to the early decades of the seventeenth century marks a major transition in Hawaiian political history. Power was consolidated in a form previously unknown, as *aliʻi nui* took charge of dominions that encompassed the largest two islands, and in the case of Maui brought nearby islands under its sway.

Lands were redistributed to subchiefs, and the *ahupuaʻa* system of land territories came into full force, along with a tribute system marked by both *kōʻele* fields and by an elaboration of the temple system and the priesthood. As I discuss in Chapter 4, the emerging archaeological record also marks this as a critical time, one of peak population, agricultural intensification, and construction of monumental architecture. There is every reason to point to the period between the late sixteenth and early seventeenth centuries as that when the Ancestral Polynesian sociopolitical system was sundered, and when the first manifestations of an archaic state emerged. And significantly, these developments were centered on the large easterly islands of Maui and Hawaiʻi.

DYNASTIC HISTORIES OF THE SEVENTEENTH
TO EIGHTEENTH CENTURIES

The initial emergence of archaic states out of chiefdoms can most likely be traced to the rise to power of ʻUmi and Kiha-a-Piʻilani. Nonetheless, changes continued to unfold in succeeding centuries, and it is important to review what the *moʻolelo* tell us of patterns of *aliʻi* political strategy in the seventeenth and eighteenth centuries, leading up to the time of first contact with the West. This is the period between AD 1590 and 1730 in the relative chronology. It involves a large number of individuals—kings, royal spouses, district chiefs, war leaders, priests, and others—whose deeds and relationships take up literally hundreds of pages in the traditional narratives. It is beyond my scope to attempt a detailed account of this rich corpus, and I limit myself to a synopsis with a focus on selected individuals who played especially prominent roles, or whose actions exemplify the repeated structural patterns of *aliʻi* agency.

Hawaiʻi Island

I begin with the Hawaiʻi Island kingdom, which, as we have seen, was consolidated by force under ʻUmi-a-Līloa, who also moved the royal seat from its traditional base in Waipiʻo Valley to Kona District on the leeward side. This move marks a shift from the limited areas of irrigation-based production of taro in windward Kohala to the far more extensive leeward, rain-fed production of sweet potato and taro as the economic basis for the kingdom. The Hawaiʻi polity, however, having led the new wave of political transformation through forceful integration of formerly independent district chiefdoms, stands out in failing to maintain that islandwide integration throughout much of the succeeding two centuries. This is in striking contrast with Maui, which once unified by force under Kiha-a-Pi'ilani, remained an integrated and centrally administered polity thereafter. Likewise, although O'ahu had some episodes of internal rebellion, it and Kaua'i also remained largely unified entities up until the contact-era.

Following 'Umi-a-Līloa there was a phase of political fragmentation, followed by a period during which the island was split into two polities, corresponding with the leeward (Kohala, Kona, and Ka'ū districts) and windward (Hāmākua, Hilo, and Puna districts) regions. During this period, the leeward districts were controlled by the Mahi lineage of *ali'i*, based in Kohala, while the windward districts were held by the 'Ī line of *ali'i* originating in Hilo. In the final sequence leading up to contact with the West, a tendency toward islandwide integration and consolidation reasserted itself. The periodic fragmentation of the Hawai'i Island polity, the inability of its kings to hold the entire great island together, may fundamentally reflect its sheer geographical size. At 10,433 km², Hawai'i is larger than all of the other islands combined. Note that it is also significantly larger than the 1,500 km² that Renfrew (1986:2) regards as typical for "early state modules," and indeed is larger than many documented early archaic states (Feinman 1998). Lacking either draft animals or wheeled transport, the Hawaiian rulers had to depend on runners to carry commands and information back and forth. The traditions refer to kings traveling periodically to review their dominions, but holding together a polity of such physical extent was not a simple task for an incipient bureaucracy. In my view, it was the geographic extent and long communication distances (and long distances needed to be traversed by armies) that undermined efforts at islandwide integration on Hawai'i Island. Nonetheless, such integration was periodically achieved, not only by 'Umi but by later kings, especially Alapa'inui, Kalani'ōpu'u, and following European contact, Kamehameha I.

A brief synopsis of dynastic succession following the death of 'Umi-a-Līloa, focusing only on the most prominent individuals, follows: As noted earlier, 'Umi had multiple marriages, but his *pi'o* union with his half sister Kapukini produced two male heirs of the highest rank, Keli'iokaloa-a-'Umi (senior) and Keawenui-a-'Umi (junior) (Kamakau 1961:34; Fornander 1996:103). According to Kamakau, 'Umi divided his kingdom between these two, with Keli'iokaloa taking Kona and the leeward side, while Keawenui was in charge of Hilo and the windward districts.[24] Playing out the now familiar pattern of an oppressive senior sibling (as with Hākau and Lono-a-Pi'ilani), Keli'iokaloa seized "the property of the chiefs and that of the konohiki of the chiefs, the food of the commoners, their pigs, dogs, chickens, and other property" (1961:35). The leeward chiefs appealed to Keawenui in Hilo, who then declared war on his elder brother. A decisive battle was fought on the northern flank of Hualālai Volcano; Keli'iokaloa was killed and Keawenui-a-'Umi became the king of a once again unified island.[25] Keawenui redistributed the island's territories, another theme that emerges repeatedly in the traditional narratives: "He made favorites of his chiefs and made some governors of districts, or large tracts of land (*'okana*) and of *ahupua'a*" (Kamakau 1961:45). After securing his rule, Keawenui voyaged to other islands, especially Maui where he visited in the royal court of the Maui king Kamalālāwalu. He had numerous liaisons, including five unions with high ranking chiefess, such as Ko'ihalawai of Kaua'i and Haokalani of O'ahu (Fornander 1996:113), thus securing ties to the ancient and high-ranking ruling houses of those westerly islands. He also had a *pi'o* union with his half sister Kamolanui-a-'Umi (Davenport 1994:60).

Following the death of Keawenui-a-'Umi, a complex succession occurred involving the granddaughter of Keli'iokaloa, named Kaikilani-Ali'i-Wahine-o-Puna, as a kind of regent and simultaneous co-wife (*punalua*) of two of Keawenui's sons, Kanaloakua'ana and Lonoikama-kahiki. Lonoikamakahiki, who was a child at the time of Keawenui's passing, eventually was elevated to the kingship, and his *mo'olelo*, involving a famous voyage to Moloka'i and O'ahu, is well known (Fornander 1916:256–363; Kamakau 1961:47–63; Beckwith 1940:292–95; Kalākaua 1990:317–31). It was during his reign that Kamalālāwalu, king of Maui, attempted a failed invasion and conquest of Hawai'i (Kamakau 1961:57–61); the Maui forces were repulsed and Kamalālāwalu was killed on the plain of Puakō in South Kohala.[26] Although his invasion was repelled, Kamalālāwalu's aim was territorial conquest, rather than mere raiding, an important distinction.

Next follows the phase of political fragmentation referred to earlier, when the leeward and windward regions came under the control of the Mahi and 'Ī lineages of Kohala and Hilo, respectively. Nominally, following Lonoikamakahiki's death the rule passed to the son of Kaikilani-Ali'i-Wahine-o-Puna with Kanaloakua'ana, named Keakealanikane, but his reign was either ineffectual or simply not recognized by the district chiefs (Fornander 1996:127). Fornander states that "the great houses of *I* in Hilo and of *Mahi* in Kohala, with large territorial possessions, were enabled to assume an attitude little short of independence."

A complex series of successions then followed, involving several female rulers (whose power was evidently limited only to the leeward regions), this occupying roughly the latter half of the seventeenth century. The next major event, probably around AD 1690, following the death of Keakealaniwahine, was the installation of her son Keawe-ʻikekahi-aliʻi-o-ka-moku as king (Fornander 1996:129; Kamakau 1961:64–65). Keawe established some degree of unity over the island, even though the district chiefs retained considerable power.[27] He accomplished this feat, according to the accounts, through marriage (a key union was with Lonomaʻaikanaka, a chiefess of the powerful ʻI line) and "diplomacy" rather than the use of force.

A strong and powerful kingship reasserted itself again after the death of Keawe-ʻikekahi-aliʻi-o-ka-moku with Alapaʻinui, a son of Keawe's half sister Ka-lani-kau-lele-ia-iwi by her union (one of four marriages) with Kauaua-a-Mahi, son of Mahiolole of the powerful Mahi lineage (Fornander 1996:131). Alapaʻinui had close linkages with the ruling house of Maui Island, since his elder half sister Kekuʻiapoiwanui had married another half brother, Kekaulike, then king of Maui. At the time of Keawe's death on Hawaiʻi, Alapaʻinui was residing on Maui, in the court of king Kekaulike. Hearing the news, and knowing well the political vacuum that was likely to ensue, Alapaʻinui left Maui for his ancestral homeland in Kohala, where he quickly assembled a force of warriors loyal to the Mahi line. Alapaʻinui's army defeated an opposing force under one of Keawe's sons, Kalanikeʻeaumoku, who had asserted his claim to the Kona and Kohala lands (Fornander 1996:132–33). Alapaʻinui thus gained control of the leeward districts, but any ambitions he may have then harbored to extend his control over the windward regions was thwarted by the decision of his half sister's husband, Maui king Kekaulike, to invade Hawaiʻi Island. Kekaulike was based in Kaupō District on Maui, where he had lately built or rededicated Loʻaloʻa Heiau, one of the largest *luakini* war temples in the archipelago (see Chapter 4), and assembled a formidable military force (Kamakau 1961:66). Kekaulike's army was repulsed by Alapaʻinui's forces in a naval battle off Kona, but in their retreat the Maui warriors "slaughtered the country people of Kohala." Alapaʻinui felt obliged to avenge his homeland by taking the war to Maui. After assembling a large force and preparing his war canoes, Alapaʻinui's army arrived at Mokulau in Kaupō, Maui, only to hear that Kekaulike had fled to Wailuku, and there had died. Apparently out of affection for his half sister Kekuʻiapoiwanui and her son Kamehamehanui, now proclaimed the new king of Maui, Alapaʻinui ceased hostilities (Kamakau 1961:70; Fornander 1996:136).

Hearing that the forces of Oʻahu Island under Kapiʻiohookalani had invaded Molokaʻi Island, Alapaʻinui now launched his sizeable army in support of the Molokaʻi chiefs, some of whom had connections with Hawaiʻi Island *aliʻi*. Alapaʻinui's army routed the Oʻahuans and killed their young leader Kapiʻiohookalani (Fornander 1996:136–37; Kamakau 1961:71). Emboldened by his success, Alapaʻinui sought next to conquer Oʻahu itself, and took his war fleet there where he engaged the Oʻahu warriors in a series of indecisive skirmishes. With their young king slain on Molokaʻi, the Oʻahu chiefs sent word to the king of Kauaʻi, Peleiʻōhōlani,[28] beseeching him to come to their defense. Peleiʻōhōlani responded, but before the combined Oʻahu and Kauaʻi armies could engage in a major battle with the Hawaiʻi Island forces under Alapaʻinui, a truce was brokered by a councilor named Na-ʻili. Invoking kinship relations between Alapaʻinui and Peleiʻōhōlani, Na-ʻili arranged a meeting of the two "god-kings" at Kāneʻohe on windward Oʻahu; Kamakau dates this to January 1737. Kamakau described the scene as follows:

> The two hosts met, splendidly dressed in cloaks of bird feathers and in helmet-shaped head coverings beautifully decorated with feathers of birds. Red feather cloaks were to be seen on all sides. Both chiefs were attired in a way to inspire admiration and awe, and the day was one of rejoicing for the end of a dreadful conflict. (1961:72)

This was not the end of Alapaʻinui's warlike endeavors, for on his return to Hawaiʻi he discovered that another of Kekaulike's sons had rebelled against his nephew Kamehamehanui, the rightful king of Maui. Alapaʻinui took Kamehamehanui back to Hawaiʻi with him, reequipped his army and naval forces, and reinvaded Maui sometime around 1738 (according to Kamakau). Now Peleiʻōhōlani, king of Oʻahu, came to the aid of the rebellious Maui group, but once again a truce was established between Alapaʻinui and Peleiʻōhōlani (after considerable fighting and loss of life), and Kamehamehanui was returned to his place as king of Maui (Kamakau 1961:74–75; Fornander 1996:140–42).

Alapaʻinui returned permanently to Hawaiʻi where he faced increasing opposition from internal parties. Recall that Alapaʻinui had originally taken control of Hawaiʻi by force following the death of Keawe-ʻikekahi-aliʻi-o-ka-moku. The latter had two grandsons, Kalaniʻōpuʻu and Kalanikepua Keōua, who were in the rightful patrilineal line of descent of Hawaiʻi kings, whereas Alapaʻinui was a usurper from the Mahi line of Kohala. Keawe's grandsons were very young at the time of Alapa'inui's conquest, and he took them into his royal court and trained them as warrior chiefs. They had served the king loyally on his military campaigns but may have harbored resentment toward Alapa'inui. Around AD 1752 according to Kamakau, while Alapa'inui was situated at Hilo, Keōua took ill and died, and it was rumored about court that Alapa'inui was responsible for the death.[29] The death of his half brother seems to have prompted Kalani'ōpu'u to take action against Alapa'inui. A series of skirmishes were fought, then a major battle at Mahinaakaaka, in which Kalani'ōpu'u was almost killed (Kamakau 1961:76). Kalani'ōpu'u gained control of his natal districts of Ka'ū and Puna, while Alapa'inui ruled the rest of the island. The latter shifted his royal seat from Hilo to Waipi'o, and then to the leeward side at Kawaihae. At Kawaihae Alapa'inui became ill, and while lying on his deathbed within the temple of Mailekini, declared that his son Keawe'ōpala would succeed him as ruler.

Keawe'ōpala's reign, beginning about AD 1754, was short. Kamakau says that the new king deprived a number of the chiefs of their lands in the division of territories that took place after the royal succession, and these disaffected war leaders rebelled again him. Kalani'ōpu'u saw his opportunity and moved his forces up the western coast from Ka'ū. Ke'eaumoku, a uterine brother of Alapa'inui (Fornander 1996:145) and prominent war chief, joined forces with Kalani'ōpu'u and together they defeated Keawe'ōpala, who was slain along with his chief priest Ka'akau. Kalani'ōpu'u was now lord of all of Hawai'i Island, and he did not repeat his former opponent's error of slighting his supporters in the division of lands. Moreover, he seems to have devoted considerable attention to administration, appointing various counselors and engaging specialists in canoe building, fishing, and other crafts. But like Alapa'inui before him, Kalani'ōpu'u harbored ambitions of territorial conquest; perhaps his role as a warrior chief in Alapa'inui's army during the campaigns on Maui, Moloka'i, and O'ahu had influenced him. In 1759 in Kamakau's chronology, Kalani'ōpu'u assembled the Hawai'i forces in Kohala, and then led an invasion across the 'Aleinuihāhā channel to Hāna, Maui (Fornander 1996:146–47; Kamakau 1961:79–81). The Maui king Kamehamehanui was taken by surprise, despite the fact that his sister (and at some point *pi'o* mate) Kalola was then married to Kalani'ōpu'u.[30] Kalani'ōpu'u was able to seize Hāna and Kipahulu districts, and he put the famed Hawai'i war leader Puna in charge of those lands, with a base on the fortified hill of Ka'uiki overlooking Hāna Bay. A lengthy period of off-and-on warfare between the Hawai'i and Maui polities, for control of the region from Hāna to Kaupō then ensued, continuing after the death of Kamehamehanui (in 1766) and on into the reign of the new Maui king, Kahekili. This brings us to the point of contact with the West, for when Captain James Cook arrived off the windward coast of Maui in late November of 1778 he was greeted by Kalani'ōpu'u, who was engaged in an effort to keep Kahekili from reconquering eastern Maui.

To summarize, the dynastic history of Hawai'i Island following initial unification under 'Umi-a-Līloa is one of interrupted succession by the line descended from 'Umi, with important usurpations by Keawenui-'a-'Umi and Alapa'inui, and then rebellion by Kalani'ōpu'u who reclaimed the ancestral line. At various periods, especially under such powerful leaders as Alapa'inui and Kalani'ōpu'u, the island was politically consolidated, whereas at other times it fragmented into two or more independent units, often at war with one another. But with these latter two kings, Hawai'i increasingly began to expand its military adventures beyond its shores, especially to Maui. Kalani'ōpu'u, in particular, had aggressive and expansionistic goals of territorial conquest, very much in keeping with his role as the divine leader of an archaic state.

Maui Island

The dynastic history for Maui, and its sequence of kingly succession, are more straightforward than those of Hawai'i. With a land area of 1,884 km^2, or a grand total of 2,363 km^2 when the land masses of the subservient islands of Lāna'i and Kaho'olawe are included, the Maui kingdom was doubtless easier for an incipient bureaucracy to manage. Not that this is a particularly small area; it certainly exceeds Renfrew's estimated extent for early state modules. Kiha-a-Pi'ilani, who forcibly overthrew his older brother Lono-a-Pi'ilani and consolidated power over the island, was succeeded by his son Kamalālāwalu.[31] His reign was long and prosperous, although it ended in a disastrous war against Hawai'i, costing Kamalālāwalu his life (Fornander 1996:207). This war took place while Lonoikamakahiki was king of Hawai'i (see above). Kamalālāwalu sent his son Kauhi-a-Kama (also known as Kauhiokalani) to Hawai'i "to learn the number of people" (i.e., to assess the size of the opposition forces; Fornander 1916:334). Apparently Kauhi-a-Kama traveled only along the shoreline of Kohala, failing to note that the majority of the population resided in the uplands, where the vast dryland field systems were located. He incorrectly reported back to Kamalālāwalu that

"Kohala is depopulated; the people are only at the beach" (1916:336). It was fatally flawed intelligence. Despite warnings from the sorcerer-priest Lanikāula, Kamalālāwalu sailed with his fleet of warriors to Puakō on the lee side of Hawai'i. The details of Kamalālāwalu's doomed campaign are recounted at length in the mo'olelo (Fornander 1916:338 jo). Suffice it to say that the Maui forces were severely routed, Kamalālāwalu killed, and his son Kauhi-a-Kama barely escaped through the assistance of one of Lonoikamakahiki's generals, Hinau.[32]

Having escaped with his life from the disastrous campaign against Hawai'i, Kauhi-a-Kama succeeded to the Maui kingship.[33] His unremarkable reign ended in an attempted military campaign against O'ahu, when he was slain on the beach at Waikīkī and his body offered up as a sacrifice on the temple of 'Āpuakēhau (Fornander 1996:208). Following this second disastrous attempt to extend Maui's power to other islands, there followed a period of three successive rulers who made no further military aggressions. Kauhi-a-Kama was succeeded by his son Kalanikaumakaowakea, who by some accounts was the offspring of a pi'o union between Kauhi-a-Kama and his sister Pi'ilanikapo (Davenport 1994:55).[34] The succession then followed to Lonohonuakini, the son of Kalanikaumakaowakea (Fornander 1996:209). He in turn was succeeded by Ka'ulahea, son of Lonohonuakini by Kalanikauanakinilani (Fornander 1996:209). Ka'ulahea had two wives, a high-ranking chiefess from Hawai'i Island named Kalanikauleleiaiwi,[35] and Papaikaniau. The former bore him a sacred daughter, Kekuiapoiwanui, whereas the latter bore him a son, Kekaulike, who would succeed to the Maui kingship.

The reign of Kekaulike receives much greater attention in the mo'olelo than those of his three predecessors. Kekaulike's succession was contested by some of the Maui chiefs, perhaps because his mother was not of the highest rank. Kamakau (1961:73) speaks of several battles carried out by Kahekili and his son Ka-uhi by which Kekaulike's rule was consolidated. Kekaulike took at least five chiefly wives, one of them his own half sister Keku'iapoiwanui, in a classic pi'o mating (Davenport 1994:55–56) that produced a son, Kamehamehanui (who would succeed his father as Maui king), and a sacred daughter, Kalola (who would become one of the wives of Kalani'ōpu'u of Hawai'i). Fornander (1996:212–13; see also Kamakau 1991:74; Desha 2000:35) discusses these unions in some detail, and they provide an important case study of the strategy of establishing alliances among royal houses. Aside from his pi'o marriage to his sister, Kekaulike married Kahawalu, of a prominent Kaupō District family; Kāne-a-Lae, daughter of one of the then still independent chiefs of eastern Moloka'i; Hōlau, who was descended from Lonoikamakahiki, king of Hawai'i; and, Ha'alo'u, who descended from a brother of Alapa'inui and thus provided a link to the powerful Mahi lineage of Kohala, Hawai'i. Kekaulike established his royal residence at Mokulau, in Kaupō, where he built or rededicated the massive war temple of Lo'alo'a, as well as a vast complex named Pōpōiwi (Kamakau 1961:66; Sterling 1998:172–74). Toward the end of his reign, Kekaulike determined to attack Hawai'i Island, which had come under the rule of his sacred wife Keku'iapoiwanui's half brother Alapa'inui. The raid on Hawai'i was indecisive (Fornander 1996:133), but the treatment of the Kohala populace by Kekaulike's warriors so angered Alapa'inui that the latter retaliated with an attack on Maui. Kekaulike died just prior to the Hawai'i army's landing at Mokulau, declaring that his son Kamehamehanui (offspring of his *pi'o* union with his half sister Keku'iapoiwanui, and hence also the nephew of Alapa'inui) should succeed him. Fornander puts the time of Kekaulike's death sometime between the years 1736 and 1740.

Kamehamehanui's rule was marked by a period of rebellion against him brought about by his half brother Kauhiaimokuakama. As related earlier, Kamehamehanui was forced for a period to flee Maui with his uncle Alapa'inui, who then aided his return to Maui. Kamehamehanui ruled his island peacefully until the abrupt invasion by Kalani'ōpu'u, which Fornander (1996:214) attributes to the year 1759. The outcome of this invasion was the annexation of Hāna and Kaupō by the Hawai'i forces, and Kamehamehanui failed to recapture these East Maui districts. Having lost these key lands, the royal center of the Maui court moved from East Maui back to Wailuku (ancestral home of the Pi'ilani line), where Kamehamehanui died about 1765, according to Kamakau. Kamehamehanui had two wives, a *pi'o* mating with his half sister Namahana (Davenport 1994:56), and a second marriage to Kekukamano whose lineage Fornander says is unknown. Two children born to Namahana died young, and hence at the death of Kamehamehanui there was no direct heir of suitable rank to assume the Maui kingship. Consequently, the rule passed to Kamehamehanui's younger brother, Kahekili, third-born child to Kekaulike's *pi'o* wife Keku'iapoiwanui.

Kahekili was nearly 50 years old when he ascended to the Maui kingship (Fornander 1996:215). He had spent his adult life as a high-ranking warrior chief, loyal to his older brother. Fornander characterizes him as "laborious and persistent, cold, calculating, and cruel" (1996:215). Kamakau describes Kahekili as having a "weak voice," but says that he "was strong in war, an intelligent chief and a thoughtful one who kept watch at night for those who murmured or spoke evil or plotted rebellion against him" (1961:82). Early in his life he had one entire half of his body tattooed solid black, a practice known as *pahupū* ("cut in half"), and his personal bodyguard of warriors were similarly tattooed.[36] Kahekili would prove a formidable enemy to Kaniʻōpuʻu and his successor, Kamehameha I, rulers of Hawaiʻi in the early postcontact era.

Molokaʻi Island

The political history of Molokaʻi, fifth largest island of the main group, is imperfectly known, largely because its hereditary ruling houses were killed off and supplanted during the late seventeenth and eighteenth centuries, when the island came under the domination of Oʻahu and then Maui. McCoy (2006:253–63) has synthesized what can be gleaned of this history (see also Summers [1971]). Molokaʻi was an independent polity under the Kamauaua dynasty that McCoy estimates to have ruled between circa AD 1360 to 1460. This is followed by a long break with no information until circa AD 1700 to 1795, when the Kaiākea dynasty emerges. This later ruling line was weak, however, as evidenced by internal tensions between the Kona (leeward) and Koʻolau (windward) chiefs that led Kualiʻi, king of Oʻahu, to come to the aid of the Kona side; the Koʻolau chiefs and warriors were slaughtered in a battle at Kalaupapa. Around 1760 to 1780, Kualiʻi's son Peleiʻōhōlani invaded Molokaʻi and killed many of the local chiefs, installing Kaiākea as a subservient vassal. Control of Molokaʻi shifted to Maui when Kahekili took possession of Oʻahu in 1783 (see discussion that follows). Thus the later history of Molokaʻi is largely as a possession or tributary polity to either Oʻahu or Maui.

Oʻahu Island

Earlier in this chapter I summarized the key political developments on Oʻahu leading up to the reign of Māʻilikūkahi, who is credited in the indigenous traditions with first establishing the nested hierarchy of land units, and with expanding the island's irrigation systems. By this time (the late-fifteenth century by genealogical estimation), Oʻahu was already unified, and would remain so through most of its successive history, albeit with periods of internal strife or dispute over succession. From Māʻilikūkahi there were four successive rulers of Oʻahu until the sacred female *aliʻi* Kalani-maunia, who had charge over the island during roughly the first two decades of the seventeenth century (Kamakau 1991:57–61). Of Nānāʻulu descent, she was of high rank, being born like her ancestor Māʻilikūkahi at the sacred birthing site of Kūkaniloko. And, like her famous ancestor she is noted for encouraging agricultural production and building a number of fishponds. Internal troubles arose after her death, when she divided the lands among her three sons and one daughter. Once again, the pattern of a greedy and unworthy senior sibling emerges, as her first-born son Kūamanuia abused his authority and attacked his younger brother Kaʻihikapuamanuia. The latter defended himself and with the aid of his brother Haʻo slew Kūamanuia; hence the rule passed to Kaʻihikapuamanuia. Troubles then began between Kaʻihikapuamanuia and Haʻo, and the island seems not to have been completely unified politically until the death of Haʻo (Kamakau 1991:61–67).

After Kaʻihikapuamanuia the rule of Oʻahu passed to his son Kākuhihewa, one of the island's most renowned kings (Kamakau 1991:68–72). He was a sacred *aliʻi*, born at Kūkaniloko; Kamakau says that 48 chiefs witnessed the cutting of his navel cord and the famous *pahu* drums were sounded to announce his birth. When he ascended to the kingship, at age 39, Kākuhihewa made peace with the son of Haʻo, Nāpūlānahumahiki, who had up until then had ruled over Waialua and Koʻolauloa districts as an independent polity. Kākuhihewa married Nāpūlānahumahiki's daughter Kaea-a-Kalona, bringing the entire island of Oʻahu under unified rule. Kākuhihewa's reign, which lasted for 50 years (hence into the late-seventeenth century), is marked in the traditions as one of peace and prosperity, again noted for agricultural developments. Kākuhihewa elaborated the royal court, building a large and sumptuous "palace" at Kailua, named Pāmoa (Kamakau 1991:69; Fornander 1996:274). Kākuhihewa gathered around him various experts in genealogy, chant, "study of the stars," and in the various arts of war. In short, the traditions of Kākuhihewa speak precisely to the elaboration of courtly practices as would be expected with a divine kingship. Kākuhihewa had several wives who gave him alliances to the ruling lines of both Maui and Kauaʻi (Fornander 1996:274).

Following the brilliant reign of Kākuhihewa comes a succession of three undistinguished *aliʻi nui*, all in the same line of descent. During this period, the power of the king lessened and the various district high chiefs began acting more or less independently (Fornander 1996:275–78). All this changed with the rise to power of Kualiʻi, probably around the close of the seventeenth century. Kualiʻi is as famous for Oʻahu as

Lonoikamakahiki or Alapaʻinui are for Hawaiʻi, and his *moʻolelo* runs to many published pages, much of it coded in *mele* or chant (Fornander 1916:364–434; see also Fornander 1996:278–88, 371–99, Appendix V; Beckwith 1940:395–400). There is a curious quality to the Kualiʻi tradition, however, in that unlike most other *moʻolelo* pertaining to ruling chiefs of the seventeenth or eighteenth centuries, which are notable for their apparent factual recitation of the parentage, marriages, and deeds of these individuals, the Kualiʻi story takes on almost mythic tones. Thus Beckwith writes:

> Certain elements in the Kualiʻi tradition give the impression that we have here the legend not of a single chief but of a political movement led in the name of a god, perhaps belonging to the ancient Ku line and directed against the Lono worshipers. The names Kuʻaliʻi, Ku-nui-akea, Ku-i-ke-ala-i-kaua-o-ka-lani (Ku in the stone in battle of the heavenly one) and the repeated assertion of divinity suggest that some symbolic object here is impersonated as a god, like the feather god Kaili. (1940:396)

Fornander, noting that only a single version of the Kualiʻi story was preserved, offers a reason for its unusual character:

> [T]he political destruction of the house of *Kualii* by *Kahekili* of Maui, the spoliation of the territorial resources of its scions by the successful conquerors, and perhaps in no inconsiderable degree the idea set afloat by both the Maui and Hawaii victors that the *Kualiis* were a doomed race, all these co-operative causes first rendered the recital of such legends treasonable, next unfashionable, and lastly forgotten. (1996:279)

In other words, the Kualiʻi *mele* valorizes a king who, although he lived a mere half century prior to European contact, was bestowed with almost super-human qualities by those few who dared to remember him after the devastation of Oʻahu in the late-eighteenth century, first by Kahekili and soon after by Kamehameha I.

To the extent that the various deeds attributed to Kualiʻi can be considered historically valid, the most important were: (1) his subjugation of the independent Oʻahu chiefs who had controlled the ʻEwa and Kona districts, and bringing the entire island back under a single ruler; (2) one and possibly two military raids against the Hilo District of Hawaiʻi Island; (3) a war on Molokaʻi in which Kualiʻi sided with the Kona chiefs of that island against the windward Koʻolau chiefs; and, (4) gaining control over the windward districts of Kauaʻi Island. Exactly how it was that Kualiʻi came to govern half of Kauaʻi is a mystery; no war of conquest is mentioned in the traditions, and Fornander (1996:295) speculates that Kuali'i claimed succession through his grandmother Kawelolauhuki. Certainly the O'ahu and Kaua'i ruling houses had been linked for centuries. Because details of Kuali'i's genealogy were lost (indeed, certainly suppressed after Kahekili's conquest of O'ahu), we do not know much about his marriages, except for one wife, Kalanikahimakeiali'i who is reported by Fornander to have been a daughter of the Maui king Lonohonuakini (1996:282).[37] Nonetheless, we do know that Kuali'i fathered a son Pelei'ōhōlani by a chiefess from Kaua'i, and evidently set Pelei'ōhōlani up to administer his Kaua'i dominions.

After the death of Kuali'i, the O'ahu kingship passed to his son Kapi'iohookalani, like his brother Pelei'ōhōlani an *ali'i kapu* of the highest rank. Kapi'iohookalani led an unsuccessful military campaign against Moloka'i in which Alapa'inui of Hawai'i came to the aid of the Moloka'i chiefs, and Kapi'iohookalani was slain. His infant son, Kanahaokalani, was too young to assume the rule, and hence Pelei'ōhōlani was brought from Kaua'i to assume the O'ahu kingship (Fornander 1996:289). Pelei'ōhōlani expended considerable effort in subjugating the rebellious Moloka'i chiefs. Although he had earlier brought Moloka'i under the hegemony of O'ahu, around 1764 or 1765, according to Fornander, some Moloka'i chiefs killed a daughter of Pelei'ōhōlani named Keelanilonuaiakama. Pelei'ōhōlani descended on Moloka'i with a vengeance, and "the revolted Molokai chiefs, mostly from the Koolau and Manae sides of the island, were either killed and burned or driven out of the island to seek refuge at the courts of Maui and Hawaii" (Fornander 1996:289–90).

Fornander (1996:290) has Pelei'ōhōlani dying about 1770, prior to the arrival of Cook's expedition, but in this he was mistaken. It is clear from the British accounts that Pelei'ōhōlani still ruled over O'ahu and Kaua'i in 1778 to 1779. In his account of political leaders in the archipelago, written in March 1779, Lt. King states: "The two most powerful Chiefs of these Islands are Terreeoboo [Kalani'ōpu'u] of Owhyhee [Hawai'i], & Perree orannee [Pelei'ōhōlani] of Wo'ahoo [O'ahu]" and further notes that "Atou I [Kaua'i] with its adjoining Isles being governd by the Grandsons" of Pelei'ōhōlani (Beaglehole 1967:614). King also usefully informs us that "Perree orannees forces were at Morotoi [Moloka'i] opposing those of the Chief of Mowee [Maui]," i.e., Kahekili.[38] Thus at the time of the Cook expedition, Pelei'ōhōlani and Kahekili were locked in combat on Moloka'i, the old O'ahu king trying to forestall Kahekili's efforts to expand the Maui kingdom by annexing the westerly islands.

Kaua'i Island

The dynastic history of Kaua'i is very incompletely known. In Fornander's words, "the legends are disconnected and the genealogies are few" (1996:291). This no doubt resulted in large part from the ascendancy of Kuali'i and his son Pelei'ōhōlani, to whose genealogists the O'ahu lineages were far more important; and because, following the removal of Kaumuali'i (last independent king of Kaua'i) to O'ahu in 1821 to become a husband of Ka'ahumanu, the Hawai'i Island ruling lines completely dominated the political scene. Fornander offers a brief account of the succession of kingship on Kaua'i, confused as this is (1996:291–98). For our purposes, there is little to note except that until the time of Kuali'i the island retained its status as an independent polity. To be sure, Fornander mentions a number of Kaua'i *ali'i* who became allied with various O'ahu chiefs. In addition, the high-ranking Kaua'i chiefesses were sought out as spouses by the ruling lines of other islands. For the most part, however, Kaua'i functioned as a separate entity, the 116-km-wide, frequently stormy Kaua'i channel separating it from O'ahu serving as a geographic barrier that discouraged frequent interisland communication.

POLITICAL DEVELOPMENTS OF THE CONTACT ERA

We come now to the political situation at the moment of contact with the West, specifically with the arrival of Captain Cook's expedition in 1778 to 1779, and in the decades following with the first Northwest Coast fur traders (Captains Portlock and Dixon in 1786), the Vancouver Expedition (1792–94), and other military and commercial visitors. This was an era of tremendous political upheaval and numerous military campaigns, culminating in the eventual subjugation of the entire archipelago except for Kaua'i and Ni'ihau, by Kamehameha I of Hawai'i in 1804. This history is well known and has been recounted by many historians (e.g., Fornander 1996; Kuykendall 1938; Daws 1968; Sahlins 1992). I limit myself to a brief synopsis of certain events relevant to an understanding of Hawaiian kingship and patterns of political action at the culmination of the indigenous Hawaiian archaic states. Certainly, the later stages of Kamehameha's famous wars of conquest became so enmeshed with Western influence (e.g., the use of Western armament and military advisors) that we cannot really consider them as typical of the *ancien régime* of Hawaiian statecraft.

Immediately preceding Cook's arrival, the archipelago was effectively divided among three polities. In the west, the aged king Pelei'ōhōlani from his base on Oʻahu held Molokaʻi as well, and had at least influence if not total control over Kauaʻi. In the center, Kahekili controlled West Maui along with Lānaʻi and Kahoʻolawe, and had been locked in a continual state of war with Kalaniʻōpuʻu for dominance over East Maui. Kalaniʻōpuʻu, for his part, held Hawaiʻi and a tenuous grip on Hāna and Kaupō districts in East Maui.[39] In short, each of these polities was aggressively pushing its boundaries against its neighbors. Hawaiʻi had since the time of Alapaʻinui become increasingly expansionistic, Maui had made various forays (always unsuccessful) against Hawaiʻi and simultaneously vied with Oʻahu for control of Molokaʻi, while Oʻahu repeatedly subjugated Molokaʻi and now held considerable power over Kauaʻi. One could well argue, though it is sheer conjecture, that had contact with the West been delayed for another century, one of these polities would have won out and gained control over the entire archipelago. In the event, of course, the Hawaiʻi Island polity under Kamehameha I did that within 25 years after Cook's arrival, albeit with the aid of Western armament and military know-how.

When Cook's ships *Resolution* and *Discovery* arrived off the windward coast of Maui in November 1778, one of the individuals they soon encountered was Kalaniʻōpuʻu, although at the time Cook was not aware that this war leader was the king of Hawaiʻi (Beaglehole 1967:476). He would discover that fact later when, after bringing his ships to anchor in Kealakekua Bay, Hawaiʻi, Kalaniʻōpuʻu arrived to greet Cook formally in three large war canoes with carved wooden idols and accompanied by his war chiefs, a scene memorialized by the British artist John Webber (Fig. 3.5). Sahlins (1981, 1995) has analyzed in detail the events that unfolded as Cook, accepting his installation as the returning god Lono, fell into a series of relations that would end tragically, with his attempt to take Kalaniʻōpuʻu hostage and in the ensuing melee, his own death on the lava rocks at Kaʻawaloa.

Following the departure of the British ships, now under the command of Lt. King, several key events occurred in close succession.[40] First, the aged Peleiʻōhōlani died on Oʻahu about 1779, to be succeeded briefly by his son Kūmahana who, proving to be incompetent, was quickly replaced by Kahāhana. Kahāhana was the son of ʻElani, chief of ʻEwa District by the sister of Peleiʻōhōlani, but had been raised in the court of Kahekili of Maui (Fornander 1996:217). Kalaniʻōpuʻu, whose forces had been repulsed once again from East Maui by Kahekili, was now also aged and called together his *ʻaha aliʻi* council in Waipiʻo Valley in 1780. He decreed that his *piʻo* son Kīwalaʻō should succeed him, but

Figure 3.5. King Kalaniʻōpuʻu arriving with his entourage aboard a double-hulled war canoe, to greet Captain Cook at Kealakekua Bay, Hawaiʻi, as depicted by John Webber, artist on Captain Cook's third voyage. (*Source*: Cook and King, 1784, *A Voyage to the Pacific Ocean*, London, Plate 61.)

that the young war chief Kamehameha (Kalaniʻōpuʻu's nephew) would be given charge of the feathered war god, Kūkāʻilimoku. Kalaniʻōpuʻu then left for Kaʻū District to suppress a rebellion by the chief Pakini; the king died at Waioʻahukini near South Point in the early part of 1782.

Although Kahekili had been engaged for a number of years in the continual struggle with Kalaniʻōpuʻu for control of East Maui, the real goal of the Maui king was to dominate Oʻahu. Sahlins writes: "The site of ancient kings of pure descent, and with the reputation besides of great natural fertility, Oʻahu was destined to be a prize object of these hegemonic ambitions" (1992:36). Kahekili tricked Kahāhana into thinking that his high priest and councilor Kaʻopulupulu was subverting him; Kahāhana had the priest slain and sacrificed on his war temple at Waikīkī. His power thus cleverly undermined, Kahāhana then suddenly faced an invasion of Kahekili's army in 1783; the Oʻahu army was routed and Kahāhana fled into the mountains of Oʻahu where he hid for nearly two years, until he was captured and slain by Kahekili's warriors (Fornander 1996:224–25). Kahekili now controlled the entire center of the archipelago, from Maui to Oʻahu, and even had de facto power over Kauaʻi, since this was now controlled by Kahekili's half brother Kaʻeokulani.

The main events now focus back on Hawai'i Island, where a fierce struggle ensued between Kīwala'ō, heir to Kalani'ōpu'u's kingdom, and Kamehameha, keeper of the feared war god Kūkā'ilimoku. After a brief period of mourning for the dead king, and deposition of his bones in the royal burial temple at Hōnaunau, Kīwala'ō and Kamehameha quickly became estranged; by some accounts this had to do with Kamehameha feeling that he was improperly treated in the traditional redistribution of lands. A battle ensued at Moku'ōhai in the summer of 1782, and Kīwala'ō was killed. The Hawai'i kingdom was now in a three-way division between Kamehameha who held the Kohala and Kona districts (his ancestral lands), Keōua[41] who controlled Ka'ū and Puna districts, and Keawemauhili who retained Hilo and Hāmākua. This standoff persisted until about 1790 when Kamehameha reconciled with Keawemauhili. This windward chief contributed to a combined force that then attacked the Maui dominions of Kahekili, by then an old man residing at Waikīkī, on O'ahu. In his absence Maui was being ruled by Kahekili's son Kalanikūpule, whose forces were no match for the Hawai'i army, aided by European arms including small cannon. The Maui forces were badly beaten at 'Īao Valley, and Kalanikūpule barely fled with his life to O'ahu.

After ravaging Maui and Lāna'i, Kamehameha sailed to Moloka'i where he sought out the sacred chiefess Kalola (widow of Kalani'ōpu'u and sister to Kahekili, and also mother of the deposed Kīwala'ō). Kalola, old and dying, had fled to Moloka'i after the disaster at 'Īao. Kamehameha's object was to take control of two young women of the highest possible rank, who were Kalola's charge: Keku'iapoiwa Liliha, the half sister and *pi'o* mate of the deceased Kīwala'ō, and their *pi'o* daughter, Keōpūolani. Keōpūolani was perhaps the highest ranking female in the archipelago at this time, and Kamehameha wanted Kalola's concurrence that he could take her into his court. On her deathbed, Kalola agreed. Kamehameha would afterward mate with Keōpūolani who bore him two sons, to become Kamehameha II and III, as well as a sacred chiefess Nahi'ena'ena.

Although Kamehameha intended to go on to confront Kahekili on O'ahu, he was obliged to return to Hawai'i because Keōua had made war on Keawemauhili and killed him. Returning from Moloka'i with the sacred young women, Kamehameha now focused his efforts on the construction of a massive new war temple, on the hill called Pu'ukoholā (Hill of the Whale) overlooking Kawaihae Bay. While this temple was under construction, Keōua moved his army from Hilo to Ka'ū, via the

Figure 3.6. Kamehameha's war temple at Puʻukoholā, as seen from the south. (Photo by T. Babineau.)

active volcano of Kilauea. A rare explosive eruption of gas and ash wiped out a large part of Keōua's army, and moreover, convinced Keōua that the volcano goddess Pele had taken the side of Kamehameha. While this lessened the threat from the south, Kahekili with Kaʻeo descended on Kamehameha from the west, recapturing Molokaʻi and Maui, and sailing with a large fleet of war canoes toward Hawaiʻi. A famous naval battle ensued off the windward coast of Kohala, called Kepūwahaʻulaʻula ("The Red-mouthed Gun") because Western cannon were employed. The Maui forces were repulsed and Kamehameha returned to the task of building his war temple at Kawaihae (Fig. 3.6).

On completion of the *heiau* of Puʻukoholā, Kamehameha sent emissaries to Keōua inviting him to a meeting at Kawaihae. Keōua fatalistically consented, and with a small retinue of war chiefs sailed up the coast from Kaʻū. Knowing that his own body would be required for the dedication of Kamehameha's temple, Keōua defiled himself at Kekaha, a bay south of Kawaihae, by slicing off the tip of his penis (Kamakau 1961:156), thus depriving Kamehameha of a perfect sacrifice. Landing in his double-hulled war canoe at Kawaihae, Keōua was speared by Keʻeaumoku, his body becoming the dedicatory offering on the altar of the newly constructed Puʻukoholā temple.

In 1795, following the visit of the British expedition under the command of Captain George Vancouver, Kamehameha made his final push to conquer the archipelago. Kahekili had died in 1794, and Kalanikūpule was now ruling over the combined Maui-Molokaʻi-Oʻahu kingdom. Kamehameha's army, by some accounts transported on 5,000 double-hulled war canoes, quickly took Maui and then Molokaʻi. Landing at Waikīkī on Oʻahu, Kamehameha's superior forces pushed the Oʻahu army under Kalanikūpule back into the narrow valley of Nuʻuanu, where many met their deaths by being pushed over the Pali precipice. Kalanikūpule managed to flee into the Koʻolau mountains where he hid out for about a year; eventually he was captured and killed, and his body was offered in sacrifice to Kamehameha's war god, Kūkāʻilimoku.

AGENCY IN HISTORY: *ALIʻI* ROUTES TO POWER

Agency has been a topic of much anthropological interest in recent years, including discussions of the rise of complex societies and the state (e.g., Marcus and Flannery 1996; Spencer 1990; Dobres and Robb 2000; Sahlins 2004). But individuals and their agency do not operate in a vacuum; they are to a significant degree culturally constructed. To point to just one classic example: Kamehameha's usurpation of the kingship from his higher-ranked cousin Kīwalaʻō may certainly be read in terms of the individual agency of this remarkable warrior. But at the same time, historical precedent well known to Kamehameha—a parallel usurpation by his ancestsor ʻUmi-a-Līloa, who like Kamehameha had been handed control over the war god Kūkāʻilimoku—must surely have played some role in the latter's actions. Kamehameha was acting out a role that Hawaiian history had predestined him for.

Several major themes emerge from a close analysis of the Hawaiian *moʻolelo*, and provide critical insights into the problem of how chiefs became kings. Several of these stress the *culturally specific* ways in which Hawaiian elites interacted and the strategies that they pursued in their quest for power and fame. These include: (1) status rivalry and usurpation; (2) elite marriage and royal endogamy; (3) development of the means of production; (4) elaboration of chiefly ritual and human sacrifice; and, (5) the application of force, war, and territorial conquest. I return to these themes in more detail in Chapter 5, when I address the larger problem of historical explanation.

In addition to these major routes to power, the Hawaiian *moʻolelo* offer some further insights into the *longue durée* of Hawaiian sociopolitical history. One of these concerns a distinct trajectory or shift in the geographic locus of historical dynamism over time. During the Voyaging

Period, it is abundantly clear that Kaua'i and O'ahu were the centers of population and of chiefly power. Maui barely figures into the traditions of this period, and on Hawai'i only the large valley of Waipi'o (noted for its taro irrigation) and the Kohala District appear to play any significant role. The geologically older and topographically more developed islands offered a much greater array of resources including streams that could be tapped for irrigation, and far more extensive reefs, lagoons, and marine resources. O'ahu, in particular, seems to have become the center of both economic and sociopolitical developments, during the reign of Mā'ilikūkahi. After his time, however, the geographic focus shifts within the next few generations to Hawai'i and Maui, where the first large-scale political unifications occurred, under 'Umi-a-Līloa and Pi'ilani (and his son Kiha-a-Pi'ilani), respectively. Thereafter, O'ahu and especially Kaua'i recede into the background, no longer centers of social or political innovation, but rather the coveted targets of intended territorial expansion as with Kahekili and Kamehameha. The reasons underlying this west to east shift in the center of historical dynamism will be explored further in the next two chapters.

A further trend more implicit than explicit in the traditions, but with substantial implications, is the gradual increase in the overall size of the *ali'i* class over time. To be sure, the archipelago wide population was also undergoing a considerable expansion, and the empirical evidence for this is explored in Chapter 4. But there is more than a hint in the traditions that the rate of *ali'i* demographic expansion may have been even greater than that of the commoner population, especially in the last two centuries prior to European contact (a time when the *maka'āinana* population may actually have stabilized). There was certainly a strong cultural emphasis on procreation among the chiefly ranks, evidenced by the multiple unions of both male and female chiefs. This proliferation of chiefly offspring is likely to have been one impetus to the highly developed hierarchical gradation of *ali'i* that emerged during the later part of Hawaiian history.

Finally, the Hawaiian traditions offer one additional insight of great importance, which might be impossible to discern had we been left only with the material evidence of archaeology (as with so many other primary archaic states). This concerns the limits to which a Hawaiian archaic state could expand and still hold together. On Kaua'i, O'ahu, and Maui once initial political unification had been achieved, it was only rarely sundered, and then only for brief periods before reconsolidation was again imposed by a new ruler. This was not the case for Hawai'i

Island, which at 10,433 square kilometers has more land area than all of the other islands combined. Hawai'i Island was indeed unified, first by 'Umi-a-Līloa, and again under certain *ali'i nui* after him (most notably in the protohistoric period by Kalani'ōpu'u and then Kamehameha I). But for much of the two centuries prior to Cook's arrival, Hawai'i was divided into two and sometimes more warring factions. On this vast island, the Hawaiian archaic state tested the limits to its ability to govern cohesively. Certain particularly strong rulers were able to subdue their rivals and maintain a pan-island peace, but often as not the island would dissolve into independent factions once again following that leader's death or demise. The reasons for this cyclical pattern may be several, but certainly include the sheer size of the island and difficulties of communication and transport, given that the Hawaiian leaders did not have the benefit of wheels or traction.

In sum, the Hawaiian *mo'olelo* and the genealogies that provide their chronological framework open a marvelous window into the social and political history of the islands, over a period of four to five centuries. Regarded by many Western academics of the twentieth century simply as "myth" (e.g., Beckwith 1940), this rich corpus of traditions has not until recently been tapped for the insights it brings to an understanding of the evolution of Hawaiian culture and society. Regardless of whether every detail of the *mo'olelo* is historically accurate (and certainly there has been embellishment and modification over time, as with all oral traditions [Vansina 1985]), there is good reason to believe that for the most part this body of oral literature is based on a real history, and that it encodes the actions—and agency—of real historical figures. To that end, the Hawaiian *mo'olelo* can only enhance our efforts to understand how Hawaiian chiefs ultimately became kings.

CHAPTER 4

Tracking the Transformations: Population, Intensification, and Monumentality

With the staple food of the country dependent on correct irrigation, it is to be expected that the irrigating systems will be among the finest of the Hawaiian work. . . . The impressive feature of the agricultural terracing is its tremendous extent . . . the maximum of tillable soil was utilized. Even a 10 foot square of soil among a great mass of lava rock will be cultivated.

Bennett (1931:21)

There were many heiaus made famous because of the shine of the grease *(hinu)* of burnt offerings from Hawaii to Kauai; they were offered up by the hundreds and thousands *(he lau, he kini, he lehu)*. The soil became fertile and saturated with slime from the grease of the heavenly chiefs and from the burnt offerings. It is impossible to count the hundreds and thousands of years of sacrificing.

Kamakau (1976:145)

Just as the Hawaiian traditions, the *moʻolelo*, offer an "insider" perspective on historical change, the archaeological record offers a complementary "outsider" perspective. While the traditions offer insights into the cultural logic underlying human actions and therefore reveal something of the force of human agency, so the material record of archaeology privileges larger systemic contexts and long-term processes. Thanks to more than a century of research, the Hawaiian archaeological record and its literature are impressive; they have been bolstered in recent decades by a wave of cultural resource management (CRM) projects (the latter resulting in a formidable "gray" literature as partly documented in Spriggs and Tanaka 1988). I cannot begin to summarize or synthesize all of this rich material (but see Kirch 1985, 1990a; Cordy 2000). Rather, I have selected specific archaeological evidence and examples that I regard as revelatory to the emergence of archaic states in precontact Hawai'i: population and demographic change, the development and intensification of agroecosystems, and the archaeological record of monumental architecture. The material evidence of monumentality, in particular, offers critical evidence regarding the ways in which the Hawaiian elites employed ritual and ideology to increase their control over the political economy, and to legitimate their claims to divine rule.

THE HAWAIIAN CULTURAL SEQUENCE

A culture-historical sequence for Hawai'i, proposed nearly a quarter century ago (Kirch 1985: Fig. 239), was conceived in terms of four temporal periods, beginning with initial Polynesian discovery and settlement of the archipelago as early as AD 300. However, the redating of key early sites both in Hawai'i and elsewhere in Eastern Polynesia (e.g., Kirch and McCoy 2007; Spriggs and Anderson 1993; Tuggle and Spriggs 2000) now makes such an early date for colonization implausible. It seems increasingly likely that all of marginal Eastern Polynesia (which includes New Zealand, the Australs, Marquesas, Mangareva, Easter Island, and Hawai'i) was discovered and settled around AD 800 to 1000.[1] For Hawai'i, the earliest acceptable dates for human arrival derive from anthropogenic charcoal in sediment cores on O'ahu, and from accelerator mass spectrometry ^{14}C dated bones of the Polynesian-introduced rat (*Rattus exulans*) in limestone sinkholes on the 'Ewa Plain (Athens 1997; Athens et al. 2002). These dates can be interpreted as supporting a human presence on O'ahu by AD 800, although the probability of an in-built ("old wood") age factor for the charcoal, as well as possible fractionation or calibration issues with the rat bones could equally be consistent with a slightly later time frame, circa AD 900 to 1000. Only a single well-documented habitation site, with early forms of Eastern Polynesian artifacts (fishhooks, adzes), is arguably dated to this initial phase: the Bellows or O18 dune site at Waimānalo on windward O'ahu (Pearson et al. 1971; Tuggle and Spriggs 2000).[2] In our current state of knowledge, the prudent inference is that Polynesian settlement in Hawai'i had occurred by AD 1000, perhaps a century or two earlier. Resolving the exact timing of initial Polynesian colonization of Hawai'i must await further research.

This significant shortening in the timing of initial settlement requires that the fairly long first two periods (Colonization, AD 300–600; Developmental, AD 600–1100) originally envisioned for the Hawaiian cultural sequence be compressed. McCoy (2005, 2007) and Kirch and McCoy (2007) have proposed replacing these two periods with a combined *Foundation Period* dating from initial Polynesian arrival until AD 1200. A further useful revision is to subdivide the long Expansion Period, originally proposed as spanning AD 1100 until 1650, into an Early Expansion Period (AD 1200–1400) and a Late Expansion Period (AD 1400–1650). The final Protohistoric Period is retained with a temporal span from AD 1650 to 1778 (European contact). The revised Hawaiian cultural sequence, which I use as the basis for temporal analysis in this chapter, is summarized in Table 4.1.

The culture-historical schema outlined in Table 4.1 is a heuristic device enabling discussion of a continuous sequence of historical change in terms of conveniently labeled, discrete blocks of time. It is neither an account of change nor an explanation of change. Nonetheless, the breakpoints between the periods are not entirely arbitrary, and have been chosen because they mark critical junctures. Thus, for example, the beginning of the Early Expansion Period is set at AD 1200 because this date signals the onset of an exponential increase in radiocarbon dated sites, and hence inferred increase in the rate of population growth. Likewise, the transition from Early to Late Expansion Periods is set at AD 1400, the approximate time when all of the major dryland field systems in leeward zones begin to come into existence. The Late Expansion Period, from AD 1400 to 1650, is perhaps the most critical in terms of the arguments advanced in this book, for it was most likely during this 150-year period that the key transformations from chiefship to kingship took place. The major political transformations discussed in Chapter 3, based on genealogical dating of the oral traditions, were completed by the end of the Late Expansion Period. Thus, the Protohistoric Period, representing slightly less than two centuries prior to the arrival of Captain Cook, is the time frame during which divine kingship and archaic states by now had—in my view—come to dominate the sociopolitical landscape of the islands.

TABLE 4.1. A REVISED HAWAIIAN CULTURAL SEQUENCE

Time Span (AD)	Period	Salient Characteristics
(800?) 1000–1200	Foundation	Initial discovery and settlement by Polynesian colonists from central Eastern Polynesia. Small founding population; settlements in a few ecologically favorable locations, primarily on Oʻahu and Kauaʻi Islands.
1200–1400	Early Expansion	The last period with long-distance voyaging contacts with central East Polynesia. Beginning of major phase of exponential increase in population. Adaptation of technology and subsistence economy to local conditions. Development of significant taro irrigation systems on Oʻahu, Kauaʻi, and Molokaʻi islands.
1400–1650	Late Expansion	Population growth peaks and begins to stabilize. Expansion of settlements into leeward and marginal zones, and initial formation of large-scale dryland field systems on Maui and Hawaiʻi islands. Considerable investment in monumental architecture. Archaic states emerge at the end of this period.
1650–1778	Protohistoric	High-density but stable (not expanding) population. Settlements across all ecological zones. Secondary intensification of dryland field systems. Conquest warfare endemic.

POPULATION AND DEMOGRAPHIC TRENDS

Over the course of eight to ten centuries, the Polynesian population of Hawaiʻi grew enormously; this was one of the fundamental changes underlying the historical transformation of Hawaiian society. The first questions to ask about Hawaiian demographic history are the initial starting point, and the size of the population at the time of first contact with Europeans. We know that the initial numbers must have been low, because the colonizing Polynesians in the early first millennium AD came in canoes whose capacities were limited, and because archaeological sites dating to the early part of the Hawaiian sequence are extremely rare. Contact-era double-hulled canoes in Hawai'i and the Society Islands held between 30 and 40 persons, while the largest Tongan double-hulled craft were estimated to hold up to 80 to 100 men (Finney 2006). The 19-meter experimental voyaging canoe *Hokule'a* is typically manned by crews of between 12 and 19 persons (Finney 1994: Appendix). Based on these historical and experimental examples, we can estimate that the double-hulled voyaging canoes that brought the first Polynesian explorers to Hawai'i probably had capacities in the range of 20 to 40 persons, along with substantial cargo including food stores and livestock (pigs, dogs, fowl). Even if two or three such craft were involved, a founding population of fewer than 100 persons is implied.

The size of the Hawaiian population 800 to 1,000 years later, at the moment of European contact, has been a matter of much contention and debate. The 1778 to 1779 Cook expedition was impressed with the large numbers of people they encountered, particularly on Hawai'i Island where they stayed the longest. On entering Kealakekua Bay in January, 1779, Cook wrote that "I have no where in this Sea seen such a number of people assembled at one place" (Beaglehole 1967:490). Lt. King, in his shipboard journal, opined that the archipelago might hold half a million people (Beaglehole 1967:620), but reduced this to a more carefully calculated 400,000 for the official Admiralty account of the voyage. King's figures are given in Table 2.1.

The first census taking, however, did not begin until more than five decades after Cook's visit, at the behest of the newly arrived Protestant missionaries; this followed the devastating effects of Western introduced diseases (Bushnell 1993). A reasonably accurate census in 1832 enumerated 130,393 persons across the main islands (Schmitt 1973). This led twentieth-century historians and demographers to suggest that King's first-contact figure of 400,000 had been inflated, and that the Hawaiian population at contact was only 250,000 to 300,000 (Schmitt 1968:22). More recently, drawing on arguments for virgin soil epidemics and their catastrophic effects in the New World (Dobyns 1983; Ramenofsky 1987), Stannard (1989) reopened the question, arguing that King's estimate was, if anything, too low. He proposed that the Hawaiian population might have exceeded 800,000. Rallu (2007) shows that the effects of epidemics were often devastating in Polynesia, where indigenous populations had no prior exposure to European diseases such as syphilis, smallpox, measles, and even dysentery and respiratory ailments.

Resolving the problem of the size of the Hawaiian population at initial contact will take more refined paleodemographic research. Recent regional-scale estimates for the districts of Kahikinui on Maui and Kohala on Hawai'i are roughly consistent with the overall population level estimated by Lt. King (Kirch 2007b; Ladefoged and Graves 2007).[3] In addition, a recent GIS (geographic information system)-based analysis of irrigated and dryland production capacities for the archipelago (Ladefoged et al. 2009) has suggested that nearly a quarter of a million people were probably directly engaged in agricultural labor, which implies a considerably larger overall population. In this light, my own view is that King's estimate of 400,000 is not overinflated, and might in fact prove to be slightly lower than reality.

Whatever the actual numbers at contact, the conclusion that Hawaiian population grew significantly—to become one of the largest (in fact, *the* largest) of any Polynesian group—is not in question. A founding propagule of perhaps 100 colonizers burgeoned into a population of several hundred thousand some eight centuries later. The simplest model for such population growth, an exponential curve, would require an intrinsic rate (r) of in the range of 0.5 percent (Rallu 2007:19–20), well below potential human reproductive capacities, and considerably lower than the historically documented r of 3.7 percent for the *Bounty* mutineers and their Tahitian wives who colonized remote Pitcairn Island (Terrell 1986:191). But such a simple assumption of a constant growth rate is unwarranted, on both theoretical and empirical grounds (Kirch 1984:101–4; Kirch 2007d:332–36; Puleston and Tuljapurkar 2008; Lee et al. 2009). There is no reason to expect that the conditions affecting fertility and mortality were the same for the initial Polynesian settlers of this vast archipelago as they were for their descendants hundreds of years later, when marginal lands had been occupied and high-density conditions prevailed. Among the particular demographic questions that need to be addressed for Hawai'i, are the following: What was the demographic process underlying this major population expansion? Was growth slow and steady, or were there periods of rapid increase? Was the population still expanding at contact, or had the rate of growth slowed or stabilized? Were population dynamics the same on every island or between districts with varying production regimes and risk factors? What was the range of variation in density levels across different landscapes and agroecosystems?

Models of Hawaiian Population Change[4]

Since past populations cannot be counted directly, answering such questions requires proxy data, usually some form of paleo-census taking (Hassan 1981; Chamberlain 2006). Skeletal series, as exist for a number of large Hawaiian sand dune and cave burials (e.g. Snow 1974; Collins 1986), provide information on life expectancy and survivorship, as well as on health and nutrition, but cannot be used to estimate overall population size or growth rates. To estimate the latter, two methods have been applied in Hawai'i. The first is a form of paleo-census taking, and uses dated house sites as a proxy for population, plotting numbers of houses per unit interval of time and assuming an average number of occupants per household. The second, following Rick's (1987) proposal that the production of anthropogenic charcoal should correlate with population (technology being held constant), uses temporal series of radiocarbon dates as a proxy for demographic rates, but does not estimate actual population size.

Hommon (1976, 1986) attempted to model the role played by population in the rise of Hawaiian "primitive states." He drew on a data set of 51 dated habitation sites from the western side of Hawai'i Island (Hommon 1976:189–224), to generate a set of proxy population growth curves, or what he called "site-population growth sequences." While Hommon's curves vary somewhat, they are consistent in suggesting a *nonlinear* rate of population increase. In all scenarios, population grew relatively rapidly before circa AD 1400, then began to taper off, and in the period from AD 1600 to contact either leveled off or declined (Fig. 4.1). Hommon used these curves to argue that beginning around AD 1400 there was a major phase of "inland expansion," linked with the development of extensive agricultural field systems.

Cordy, in a separate attempt to model population growth on Hawai'i Island, regarded population growth as "the initiating independent input" to change (1974b:97). Cordy's "Hawaiian-specific model" for estimating precontact population counted the archaeological remains of "contemporary sleeping houses" and multiplied this number "by 6 [persons,] to gain an absolute population estimate" (Cordy 1981:91). The mean-per-house figure of six persons was based on Lt. King's 1779's observation, while the contemporaneity of houses was addressed through

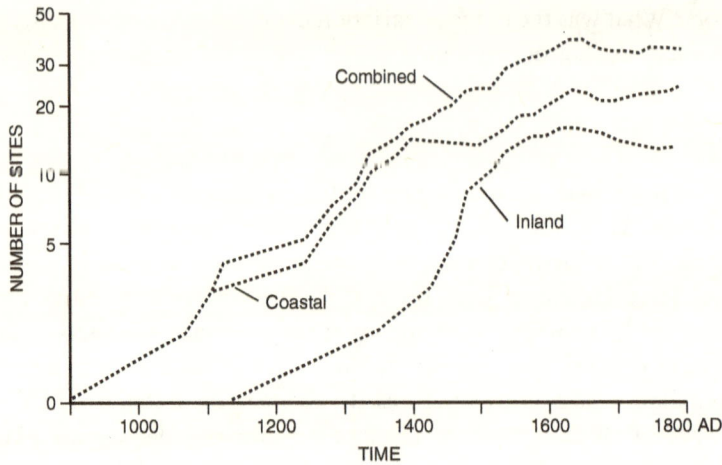

Figure 4.1. Hommon's site population growth curves. (*Source:* Redrawn after Hommon 1976, Fig. 16.)

the use of hydration-rind dating of volcanic glass artifacts. Cordy's North Kona data from eight *ahupua'a* show the regional population beginning with 18 persons at AD 1400 to 1450, rising to a maximum of 240 at AD 1650 to 1700, and falling off slightly to 216 at AD 1750 to 1780 (Cordy 1981: Table 58). Unfortunately, the empirical basis for this chronology was hydration-rind dating of volcanic glass artifacts, a method now regarded as inaccurate.

Like Hommon and Cordy, I favored a key role for "population dynamics" in my initial work on Polynesian and Hawaiian cultural evolution (Kirch 1980:41–43; 1984:104–11; 1985:286–89). Drawing explicitly on a cultural analogue to the r/K selection theory of island biogeography[5] (MacArthur and Wilson 1967), I argued that colonizing populations followed an r-selection pattern—with rapid population growth, generalizing and broad-based subsistence practices, and only weakly developed sociopolitical controls on production. In contrast, later populations with high density levels would be expected to follow K-selection patterns—conscious regulation of population growth, economic specialization, well-developed sociopolitical controls on production, and intense competition.[6] In this view, human population is not a strictly independent or dependent variable in cultural evolution, but a component within a complex biocultural system in which feedback loops can produce significant changes in fertility or mortality patterns over time.

Tracking the Transformations 133

In *The Evolution of the Polynesian Chiefdoms* (Kirch 1984), I devoted an entire chapter to demographic change as one of several key variables underlying Polynesian cultural evolution, drawing on the Hawaiian evidence to test a logistic growth model. I used two data sets: (1) a western Hawai'i Island sample of 113 dated residential sites; and (2) a sample of 655 features from the arid leeward island of Kaho'olawe, dated by the hydration-rind volcanic glass method. Both data sets appeared to confirm a modified logistic curve. These emerging paleodemographic data were critical in outlining the first culture-historical sequence for the archipelago (Kirch 1985). The western Hawai'i Island data showed that "the period from about AD 1250 to 1650 was critical and, in this region at least, may have been a major era of technical, social, and political change in which demography played a significant role" (1985:289). Rapid population growth and concomitant geographic expansion of population into both inland and ecologically-marginal regions were key characteristics of what I called the "Expansion Period" (AD 1100–1650) in my four-period cultural historical sequence (1985:303–4). However, while the Expansion Period as a whole probably witnessed a 10-fold increase in total population, the *rate* of increase changed from early to late phases of this critical period. For the following Protohistoric Period (AD 1650–1795) just prior to European contact, the data suggested that "growth rates had declined substantially and that local populations may have been oscillating around a 'plateau'" (1985:307).[7]

Expanded Regional Data Sets

Since these initial efforts to obtain proxy measures of population numbers and growth rates, much larger data sets have become available, a benefit of large-scale "contract" or CRM archaeology with numerous excavations, which have generated literally hundreds of radiocarbon dates. Dye and Komori exploited this expanded data set to address Hawaiian paleodemography (Dye and Komori 1992; Dye 1994; see also Allen 1992, Williams 1992; Spear 1992). They proposed a method of using cumulative probability distributions of a series of radiocarbon dates as a proxy measure of population. Rather than using radiocarbon dates to temporally order a series of habitation sites, this method takes the dates themselves as a proxy for population numbers. The underlying premise is that "changes in population are reflected in changes in the abundance of wood charcoal recovered from archaeological contexts associated with everyday domestic

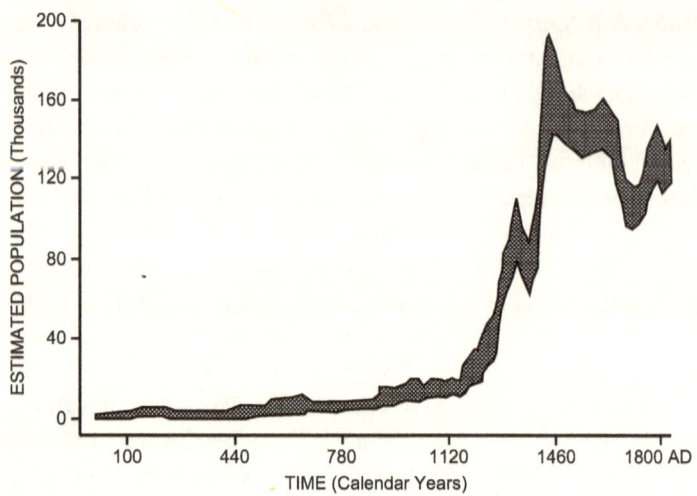

Figure 4.2. The Dye-Komori population curve, based on the cumulative probability distributions of 598 radiocarbon dates from the Hawaiian Islands. (*Source:* Redrawn after Dye and Komori 1992.)

activities of cooking, lighting, and heating" (Dye 1994:2). The Dye-Komori method takes the probability distributions generated by one of the statistical programs (CALIB) for the calibration of radiocarbon years to calendar years, and sums all of the individual probability distributions for a sample of dates into a single cumulative distribution.

Dye and Komori accessed a database of 598 radiocarbon dates. The resulting graph, a version of which is shown in Figure 4.2, was taken by them to be a proxy for actual population numbers over time. Two points are evident from this curve. First, the archipelago-wide population increased dramatically during the Expansion Period, with exponential growth approximating 1.2 percent annually, reaching a peak around AD 1450. Second, growth seems to have stopped rather abruptly in the late 1400s, with population either stable or fluctuating in size after that. The Dye-Komori growth curve is therefore not truly logistic, but rather consists of two distinct sectors: a pre-1450 exponential sector, and a post-1450 stable or fluctuating sector. If the Dye-Komori curve is an accurate reflection of demographic processes, then something happened around the fifteenth century to result in a dramatic demographic shift. Thus, while the Dye-Komori curve reinforces the initial Hawai'i Island data sets, it requires some rethinking of theoretical implications, especially the rapidity of shift in growth rates toward the end of the fifteenth century.[8]

Several additional large-scale data sets have recently become available, for particular islands or regions. Carson (2005, 2006) synthesized 272 radiocarbon dates for Kaua'i Island. This sample shows a steady exponential increase beginning around AD 1000 up to about AD 1500, much like the archipelago-wide curve of Dye and Komori. Carson cautions that "a relative decline in radiocarbon date frequency after AD 1600 does not necessarily indicate an actual population decline" (2006:180). I would agree, but argue that the decline in date frequency does indicate the cessation of exponential growth that had characterized earlier centuries. McCoy (2007) provides a similar compendium of 137 radiocarbon dates from archaeological contexts on Moloka'i Island. Although he does not address the paleodemographic implications of this date series, these data again show a marked exponential rise during the Expansion Period, and a leveling off of growth during the final Protohistoric Period.

Hara (2008) analyzed an even larger sample of 397 radiocarbon dates from Hawai'i Island, mostly in Kohala and Kona districts.[9] Figure 4.3 displays the frequency distribution of these larger radiocarbon data sets by 100-year temporal intervals; note that "conventional" radiocarbon ages (rather than calibrated ages) are plotted.[10] The cumulative distribution shows a strongly exponential growth phase from around the twelfth to sixteenth centuries, followed by a distinct slowing in the rate of radiocarbon date increase, but not a cessation of growth, in the seventeenth and eighteenth centuries.

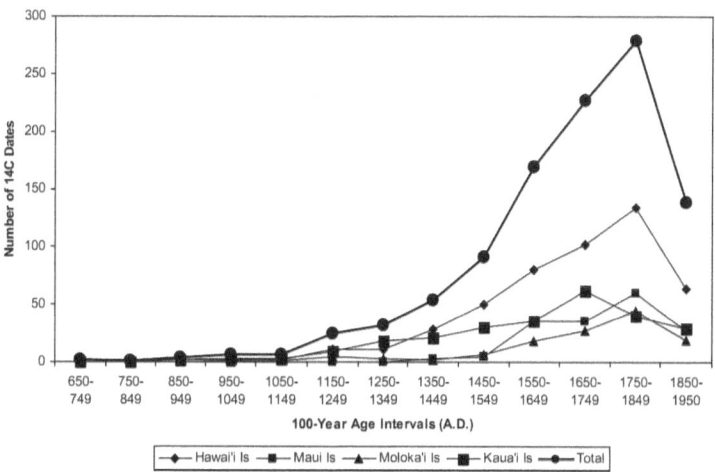

Figure 4.3. Temporal distribution of 1,036 conventional radiocarbon ages from four islands. The Maui series is from Kahikinui District.

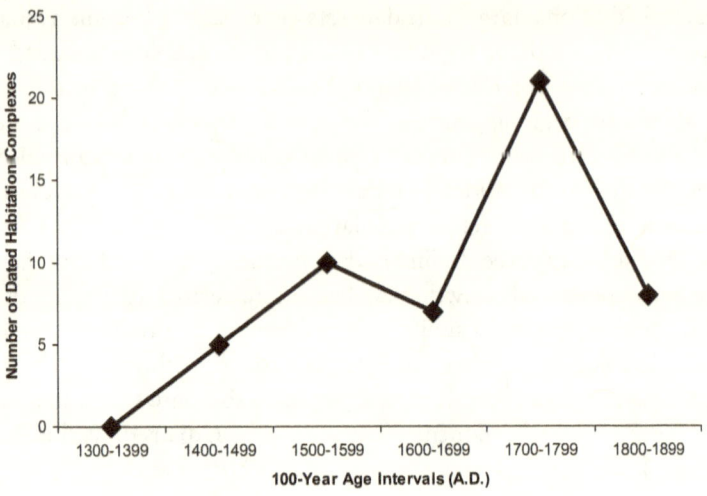

Figure 4.4. Temporal distribution of dated habitation complexes in the Kipapa-Nakaohu area of Kahikinui, Maui (N = 51 sites).

A final paleodemographic data set comes from Kahikinui District on leeward Maui, based on 169 radiocarbon dates (Kirch 2007b); the temporal distribution of these conventional ^{14}C dates is included in Figure 4.3. Kahikinui occupies the leeward slope of Haleakalā Mountain, where arid conditions and seasonal rainfall (with a high degree of temporal variability) make the region marginal for most Polynesian root and tree crops. Intensive archaeological survey over about 12 km² of the Kahikinui District of southeastern Maui, combined with excavation and dating of 51 residential complexes, has allowed us to calculate population sizes over time using a more precise house-count method. Figure 4.4 shows the temporal distribution of these dated residential complexes by century. Settlement in this arid region does not commence until circa AD 1400, three to four centuries later than in the other sequences reviewed above, no doubt reflecting the marginal status of Kahikinui for agricultural production. The number of residential complexes in Kahikinui increases slowly at first, reaches a peak in the eighteenth century, and shows a major decline after European contact. Depending on assumptions concerning the amount of immigration, intrinsic growth rates were somewhere between circa 0.5 and 1 percent per year. Based on these data, population density in Kahikinui increased from around 10 persons/km² in the lowland zone (below about 1,000 m elevation) to close to 60 persons/km² just prior to European contact (Kirch 2007b).

Population Density

Kahikinui, as one of the most arid and marginal zones for agriculture, represents the low end of the Hawaiian population density spectrum. I have estimated that at its peak, the ratio of people to land <900 m elevation in Kahikinui was between 43 and 57 persons (p)/km² (Kirch 2007b). To the east, the Kaupō District with higher average annual rainfall and a highly intensified field system (Kirch et al. in press), had a density in 1831 to 1832 (based on the missionary census; Schmitt 1973:18) of 146 p/km². This was after several decades of contact and depopulation, and it is therefore plausible that the precontact density in Kaupō approached twice this number (ca. 300 p/km²).[11] Based on a detailed study of part of the Kohala Field System on Hawai'i, Ladefoged and Graves (2007:86) estimated that this area of intensive dryland crop production had a density of 139 p/km². These estimates for Kahikinui, Kaupō, and Kohala probably give a reasonably good indication of density levels for areas that were dependent exclusively (or almost exclusively) on intensified dryland cultivation, with sweet potato as the primary crop.

In zones dominated by irrigated taro cultivation, population densities reached considerably higher levels. The Hālawa Valley on windward Moloka'i offers a good example, where the valley floor was covered in about 22 ha of irrigated pondfields and remained a major center for wet taro production well into the nineteenth century (Kirch and Kelly 1975; Anderson 2001). Colluvial slopes between the irrigated fields and the surrounding cliffs provided additional fertile land for nonirrigated cropping of aroids, bananas, and other crops. In 1836, the missionary Hitchcock reported a local population of 506 in Hālawa. A GIS calculation of the total area of arable land below the valley's steep cliffs yields a figure of 1.21 km², and thus a contact-era population density of 418 p/km². The Waialua District on northern O'ahu, with large coastal irrigation complexes, fishponds, and smaller irrigation terraces extending inland up the Anahulu and other gulches (Kirch and Sahlins 1992), supported an even higher density. In 1831, Waialua's population was counted at 2,640 persons (Schmitt 1973:19), and a GIS calculation of the district's core agricultural lands is 3.5 km², yielding a ratio of people to arable land of 754 p/km². Similarly high local densities were achieved in other parts of O'ahu and on Kaua'i Island, reflecting the high productivity of extensive irrigation coupled with large fishponds.

TABLE 4.2. ESTIMATED RATIO OF POPULATION
TO PRIME AGRICULTURAL LAND FOR THE MAIN
HAWAIIAN ISLANDS

Island	Total Area of Prime Agricultural Land in km^2 (% Irrigated)[a]	Estimated Population (Lt. King, 1779)	Density N/km^2 of Prime Agricultural Land
Hawai'i	572 (2.5)	150,000	262
Maui	168 (14.8)	65,400	389
O'ahu	121 (68.5)	76,200	630
Kaua'i	58 (99.6)	64,000	1,103

[a] These estimates derived from geographic information system (GIS) modeling by Ladefoged et al. (2009).

Some idea of the variation in population densities at the archipelago scale can be gained by using the area of prime agricultural lands calculated in a recent GIS geospatial analysis of wet and dryland agricultural potential (Ladefoged et al. 2009), and the population estimates made by Lt. King in 1779. Here prime agricultural lands include those with both "high" and "moderate" potential for irrigation, and "high" potential for intensive dryland farming. The results are shown in Table 4.2. Notice that the lowest overall density is on Hawai'i Island, where only 2.5 percent of the prime agricultural land was suitable for irrigation. The island's density of 262 p/km^2 fits reasonably well with what has been estimated for Kohala or Kaupō, both of which have intensive dryland field systems. Maui's density is slightly higher, boosted by the irrigation lands of geologically older West Maui. O'ahu and Kaua'i have the highest density figures, reflecting the large percentages of prime agricultural land in irrigated taro production on those islands. Although these figures are only order-of-magnitude approximations, their relative quantities are probably reasonably accurate. Among other things, they show clearly the much greater capacity of the geologically older islands of O'ahu and Kaua'i to absorb more people.

Summary of Demographic Trends

The population of the islands first underwent an exponential phase of expansion, between about AD 1100 and 1500, geographically focused on those regions most amenable to agricultural development, first through irrigation and then intensive dryland farming. During this exponential growth phase, the intrinsic rate of increase (r) is likely to have been in a range between 1.2 and 1.8 percent.[12] This was followed by a

Tracking the Transformations 139

period in which the rate of archipelago-wide population growth declined, and may have leveled off, but with continued expansion of settlement in at least some leeward, marginal zones, such as Kahikinui, where local populations continued to grow. This demographic history has enormous implications for sociopolitical change. Over about 350 years (roughly 17 human generations), the population of the islands skyrocketed; doubling-times probably spanned one to two human generations. By the late-fifteenth century, most of the lowland zone had been territorially claimed and demarcated. Quite rapidly, this phase of exponential growth shifted to one with markedly lower growth rates, and probably stabilization of population in some areas.

Such a demographic history, with a transition from exponential growth to slower growth and/or stability after AD 1500, is fraught with larger implications. The rapid drop in the intrinsic rate of growth must have been achieved either through a steep decline in the total fertility rate (TFR), or a significant increase in mortality, or what is more likely, some combination of the two. Either kind of change would have had serious social and economic effects. For example, lowering the TFR could have changed fundamental patterns of daily work and household activity, such as an expansion of women's labor into the agricultural sector, something that is hinted at by Kamakau (1961:239). Similarly, increased mortality of both infants and the elderly could have resulted from pressures on food supply, especially if land was becoming scarce and farmers were expanding into areas previously considered marginal in terms of rainfall (and hence greater risk from drought). The data suggest that this transition was rapid, certainly occurring within the span of a single century, if not slightly less. This would imply that whatever social and economic patterns were linked to the rapid changes in fertility and/or mortality, these changed radically within the time frame of about three to five generations.

The period of major amalgamation of political power, as documented in the Hawaiian oral traditions, occurred just after the peak rate of demographic increase was reached, and as populations were expanding into the leeward, agriculturally more challenging zones such as Kahikinui and Kaupō on Maui, and Kohala and Kona on Hawai'i. This is not to propose that population pressure was a unicausal "prime mover" in the emergence of archaic states in ancient Hawai'i. Indeed, the demographic shift that occurred around AD 1500 was as likely to have been a response to social and economic factors (such as changes in land tenure and in labor patterns), as its cause. Nonetheless, it is difficult to avoid the conclusion that the demographic history traced above was a necessary—if not sufficient—condition to social and political transformation. This is discussed further in Chapter 5.

CONTRASTIVE AGROECOSYSTEMS

As many scholars have pointed out, the Hawaiian economy achieved an apogee of intensified production within Polynesia (Handy 1940; Sahlins 1958; Goldman 1970; Yen 1971; Kirch 1994). This is evident not only in the impressive valley taro irrigation systems (Earle 1980), or the expansive arcs of stone-walled fishponds (Kikuchi 1976), but in the lesser known intensive dryland field systems with short-fallow cropping of taro and sweet potatoes. By the time of European contact, Hawaiian lowland landscapes consisted of a vast canvas of agroecosystems, particularly of two fundamental types, corresponding to two differing temporal trajectories of agricultural intensification (Kirch 1994:251–68). The first consists of irrigated monocropping of taro (*Colocasia esculenta*) in systems of terraced, flooded pondfields watered by canals tapping permanent streams, or in some cases springs. These irrigation systems were constructed on gentler colluvial slopes and on alluvial floodplains, primarily in valleys and to a lesser degree on coastal plains. They fall within what Brookfield (1972; Blaikie and Brookfield 1987) called "landesque capital intensification," in which landscapes are permanently modified by the construction of terraces, canals, and similar infrastructure. Although irrigation systems require substantial labor inputs for their construction, they also produce high yields and do not require lengthy fallow intervals (Kirch 1994). Irrigation systems were found throughout the length of the archipelago, but were principally concentrated on the geologically older, westerly islands, from West Maui to Kaua'i, with their greatest extent on O'ahu and Kaua'i (Handy 1940; Earle 1980). This uneven distribution reflects the dearth of suitable valley landscapes and surface watercourses on the younger islands, especially Hawai'i and East Maui.

Contrasting with the landesque-capital irrigation systems were the dryland field systems, confined mostly to the geologically younger, easterly islands, especially Hawai'i and East Maui (and to the Kalaupapa Peninsula on Moloka'i). The dominant dryland crops were sweet potato (*Ipomoea batatas*) and dryland taro, augmented by secondary cultigens such as yams (*Dioscorea* spp.) and sugarcane. These dryland agroecosystems depended almost exclusively on rainfall (in some localities augmented by fog-drip, or by minor seasonal irrigation), making them susceptible to seasonal variation and risk (Lee et al. 2006). The dryland field systems exemplify a distinct trajectory of intensification, originally defined by Boserup (1965), which I have termed "cropping cycle intensification" (Kirch 1994:19: Fig. 5; Kirch 2006:193). In their final configurations, with a reticulate grid of field boundaries intersected by trails, these systems left permanent traces on the landscape, and in that respect resemble the landesque capital intensive systems. However, in the far greater labor inputs required for their continued maintenance, and in their lower yields coupled with higher risk, the key processes of intensification of the dryland systems were quite distinct from those of the irrigated pondfields. Thus it is conceptually important to distinguish the landesque capital intensification of the irrigation systems from the cropping cycle intensification of the dryland field systems.

The geographical distribution of these two types of agroecosystems strongly mirrors the geological age progression and biogeochemical gradients of the Hawaiian Islands (Vitousek et al. 2004). While minor areas of irrigation were present on Hawai'i and East Maui, the economies of these large islands were primarily dependent on labor intensive rain-fed crop production. In contrast, from West Maui to Kaua'i local populations based their economies largely on the higher yielding, and less risk-prone irrigation. Recent work on soils and agriculture in Hawai'i has shown that "low soil fertility precluded the development of large-scale intensive dryland agricultural systems on stable upland surfaces on the older islands of the archipelago" (Vitousek et al. 2004:1668; Kirch 2010b). The intensive rain-fed dryland agricultural systems of the younger, eastern islands had targeted zones of relatively fertile soils (accompanied by adequate precipitation), where leaching was not sufficient to deprive soils of rock-derived phosphorus and other plant nutrients. On the older islands, similar landscapes (old volcanic shield surfaces) with adequate rainfall have insufficient soil nutrients to sustain intensive agriculture. On these older islands, only in valley topography where mass wasting and streamflow tap unweathered rock and release new nutrient sources, could intensive agriculture be practiced; this, of course, is precisely where the irrigation systems were developed.

The distribution of these contrastive agroecosystems across the Hawaiian archipelago has recently been modeled with the use of a Geographic Information Systems (GIS) approach (Ladefoged et al. 2009), providing a fairly accurate estimate of areas amenable to taro

TABLE 4.3. DISTRIBUTION OF HIGH POTENTIAL
IRRIGATED AND INTENSIVE DRYLAND
AGRICULTURAL LANDS FOR THE
MAIN ISLANDS, IN KM^2

Island	High Potential for Irrigation	High Potential for Intensive Dryland Cultivation	Total Agricultural Land	Total Island Area	% of Island Area with Prime Agricultural Land
Hawai'i	14.3	556.6	570.9	10,433	5.47
Maui	25.7	139.4	165.1	1,884	8.76
Moloka'i	8.7	7.5	16.2	673	2.40
O'ahu	83.3	34.1	117.4	1,546	7.59
Kaua'i	57.6	0	57.6	1,430	4.02

NOTE: Data from Ladefoged et al. (2009).

pondfield irrigation and to intensive dryland cultivation, respectively, for each of the main islands.[13] This considerably improves prior estimations of the differential distribution of agroecosystem types across the archipelago based on ethnohistoric accounts (Kirch 1994: Fig. 101; see also Vitousek et al. 2004: Fig. 1). Such coarse-grained maps can now be replaced with precise geospatial predictions (Ladefoged et al. 2009: Fig. 1). In addition, the actual areas of high and moderate potential irrigation land, and high potential dryland area, can be calculated, as in Table 4.3.

The significance of these results cannot be overestimated. Hawai'i Island has more prime agricultural land than that of all the other main islands combined, yet a mere 2.5 percent of this consists of irrigation lands. Thus while Hawai'i Island was able to support the largest population of any of the contact-era polities, the vast majority of its production had to come from intensive dryland field systems, such as those in Kohala and Kona. These required the highest ratios of labor input to yield and, at the same time, were the most vulnerable to drought. The Maui polity (which at contact included Moloka'i) enjoyed the next largest overall area of prime arable land, with a somewhat more favorable ratio of irrigation to rain-fed lands (15.5% irrigated), owing to the presence of permanent streams and suitable valley topography on West Maui and East Moloka'i. In striking contrast are the geologically older islands of O'ahu and especially Kaua'i, where irrigation lands make up 70.9 and 100 percent, respectively, of these islands' prime arable lands. This corresponds with the higher population densities on these two islands, since the taro pondfield systems were able to produce substantially higher yields per unit area, with lower labor inputs. Moreover, the irrigation systems were far less susceptible to drought.

TEMPORAL PATHWAYS OF INTENSIFICATION

Irrigation and Landesque Capital Intensification

The most extensive data on the temporal development of irrigation on the western islands come from Oʻahu.[14] Yen et al. (1972) were the first to directly date pondfield cultivation layers, in the upland Makaha Valley of the leeward Waiʻanae District. The initial terraces there were constructed in the early-fifteenth century, followed by a rebuilding phase in the mid-seventeenth century. Because the relatively small pondfield system studied in upland Makaha is situated in a leeward valley with limited streamflow, it was probably part of a later phase of expansion of irrigation relating to the exponential increase in population.

In contrast, the Koʻolaupoko District of windward Oʻahu represents the core region of prime irrigation lands on Oʻahu. With numerous perennial streams fed by the high orographic precipitation of the Koʻolau Mountains, the ample slopes and floodplains that form a vast amphitheater of valleys lying inland of Kāneʻohe Bay (including Waiāhole, Kaʻalaea, Waiheʻe, Heʻeia, and Kāneʻohe proper) and extending southeast to Kailua and Maunawili, supported thousands of irrigated pondfields at the time of European contact (Handy and Handy 1972:452–60). Before entering the sea, the fresh waters also fed many large fishponds along the shores of Kāneʻohe and Kailua bays, supporting large populations of milkfish and mullet. J. Allen's (1987; Allen et al. 2002) investigations of several large irrigation systems in the Luluku and Maunawili valleys provide detailed evidence for the temporal development of irrigation on Oʻahu. Excavations in Luluku site G5-85 revealed a complex stratigraphy with multiple episodes of pondfield construction, well dated by radiocarbon samples. In Maunawili Valley, a number of pondfield complexes were similarly excavated and ^{14}C dated (Allen et al. 2002: Fig. 227).

The radiocarbon dates from Luluku reveal that pondfield agriculture in the interior of Kāneʻohe Valley had begun by at least AD 1250; most of the dates for the G5-85 complex "fall between AD 1250 and 1425" (Allen in Allen 1987:230).[15] Continued development and rebuilding of the Luluku terraces is reflected in five or possibly six stratified pondfield layers dating later than AD 1400 (1987:249). From the Luluku evidence, Allen argues that

> increased political control and integration within a socioeconomic system involving an area larger than the local valley are strongly suggested by the evidence for well coordinated construction of large numbers of terraces, effective control over landslides and floods, cooperation in terms of water rights and maintenance of patent [sic] irrigation ditches, and cultivation of taro in quantities large enough to suggest production for a consumer group larger than the local population. (1987:250–51)

In Maunawili Valley, pondfield cultivation had commenced at three localities by AD 1200 (Allen, in Allen et al. 2002:608). The evidence that these agricultural sites had been developed before the post-AD 1600 "period of major sociopolitical change that culminated in the emergence of the Hawaiian state system of government" suggested to Allen that "the control of agricultural production, the coordination of irrigation, and the potential of O'ahu's fields to produce large surpluses contributed significantly to the development of the state on O'ahu" (2002:608–10). These irrigation works were significantly expanded between AD 1400 and 1650, a period also marked by the construction of an important temple site (Kūkapoki Heiau).

Allen (1991, 1992) synthesized the evidence for construction and intensification of the windward O'ahu irrigation systems, noting that the Luluku and Maunawili irrigation systems are "impressive in their own right as hydraulic and architectural—perhaps even monumental—features" (1991:122). The Luluku and Maunawili sequences, both well dated, demonstrate the onset of irrigation system construction by AD 1200 to 1300, with considerable intensification following in the fifteenth and sixteenth centuries. For Allen, "the radiocarbon-dated Hawaiian evidence suggests that irrigation contributed far more importantly to political evolution than did population pressure, which became a factor only late in the transformation process" (1991:121–22). Allen concludes that "supralocal control and institutionalized surplus production for administrative needs appear to have been in place by AD 1400, fully two centuries before the transition to the traditional Hawaiian state" (1991:129).

The eastern half of Moloka'i Island, with four large amphitheater-headed valleys (from west to east, these are Waikolu, Pelekunu, Wailau, and Hālawa) all well supplied with water from permanent streams, was another major region of taro irrigation (Handy 1940:101–3). Riley (1975) studied the extensive Hālawa Valley irrigation systems and reported stratigraphic evidence for a sequence (not radiocarbon dated)

Tracking the Transformations

from earlier side-stream irrigated to main-stream watered pondfields. In Waikolu Valley, the initial phase of a large floodplain irrigation system has been dated to AD 1240 to 1280 (Kirch 2002:46). The most extensive evidence, however, comes from Wailau Valley, where McElroy (2007a, 2007b) has recently mapped, excavated, and dated 19 of the valley's irrigation complexes. With 18 ^{14}C dates from nine complexes, McElroy has convincingly shown that significant irrigation works were under construction in this large windward valley by AD 1200 to 1300 (2007a: Table 6.2). McElroy (2007a:145: Fig. 6.8) divides these dates into three temporal units. The oldest, from about AD 1200 to 1400, included complexes with the best land and water supply, "capable of producing high crop yields" (2007a:247), and included the greatest amount of area. Later intensification efforts (after AD 1400) were directed at less desirable tracts of land. As McElroy writes:

> Farmers first took advantage of any area capable of supporting a high producing *loʻi* system, regardless of risks of flooding or the amount of effort needed to construct a system or transport products to the coast. After these large, high-yielding complexes were established, smaller *loʻi* systems were built, until every cultivable tract of land was under production. (2007a:248–49)

In sum, pondfield irrigation projects on windward Oʻahu and Molokaʻi were established at least as early as AD 1200, and were well developed by AD 1400. To be sure, landesque capital intensification efforts continued after AD 1400, and some pondfield systems were still being built very late, even into the early postcontact period, as in the upper reaches of the Anahulu Valley on Oʻahu (Kirch and Sahlins 1992). But the main conclusion is unmistakable: Irrigation works were developing in lockstep with the exponential rise in population documented by the radiocarbon evidence discussed earlier in this chapter. By the fifteenth to sixteenth centuries, vast irrigation complexes already covered the valley floors and colluvial slopes of windward valleys on both Oʻahu and Molokaʻi, and one presumes on Kauaʻi as well. As we shall see, this record of temporal development of agricultural intensification contrasts markedly with that of the leeward, dryland field systems.

Dryland Field Systems and Cropping Cycle Intensification

The large Maui and Hawaiʻi island polities, situated on geologically young islands lacking extensive areas of topographic relief and streamflow suitable for irrigation, depended heavily on the productions of intensive dryland agriculture (Table 4.3). These intensive zones of rainfed cultivation are marked by field systems in which permanent modifications to the landscape have left a distinctive archaeological signature. The specifics vary, but all known systems include a reticulate gridwork of field walls, terraces, bunds or linear mounds, and trails or territorial boundaries. These features divide the landscape into a rectilinear patchwork of individual garden plots; their orientation varies in different systems. Interspersed among the rectangular fields are residential features (both permanent and temporary), pens or enclosures, and ceremonial structures (*heiau*, shrines). The field systems occur only in certain zones (Vitousek et al. 2004; Kirch et al. 2004; Kirch et al., in press; Ladefoged et al. 2009), where the necessary combination of geological substrate age and rainfall resulted in adequate moisture and soil nutrients sufficient to support intensive cropping of sweet potatoes, dryland taro, and other secondary crops (yams, sugarcane, gourds, paper mulberry and others). On Hawai'i Island, field systems are known for the leeward Kohala mountains, the area around Waimea, the leeward flow slopes of Kona, and in parts of Ka'ū. On Maui, a major zone of intensive field systems extended from Kaupō through Kahikinui to Honua'ula; Hāna evidently had extensive dryland cultivation, although this area has yet to be investigated archaeologically. On Moloka'i, late rejuvenation volcanic flows forming the Kalaupapa Peninsula are young enough to provide the necessary combination of rainfall and nutrient availability to have supported a field system. Everywhere else on Moloka'i the volcanic shield landscapes are otherwise too old and nutrient depleted. Finally, smaller areas on southeast O'ahu, again the result of late-stage volcanic rejuvenation, also offered spatially discrete possibilities for intensive dryland cultivation; as yet we know essentially nothing of these O'ahu areas from archaeology.

The Kohala field system has been the most intensively studied, thanks to a succession of archaeological projects that began in 1968 with research in Lapakahi *ahupua'a* (Newman 1970; Rosendahl 1972, 1994; Tuggle and Griffin 1973), continued with work in the southern part of the field system (Ladefoged and Graves 2008; Ladefoged et al. 1996, 2003), and, most recently, with the multidisciplinary Hawai'i Biocomplexity Project (Kirch et al. 2007; Kirch 2007a; Vitousek et al. 2004). The Kohala field system covers an estimated 60 km^2 on the leeward slopes of the Kohala Mountains, bounded on its lower and upper edges by annual rainfall isohyets of 750 and 1900 mm, respectively. The system extends over geologic substrates of two distinct ages, the Hawi series in the north

Figure 4.5. Dryland field system embankments in the upland area of Kaiholena *ahupua'a*, Kohala District, Hawai'i. (Photo by P. V. Kirch.)

dating to circa 400 kyr, and the Pololu series in the southern part of the system, dating to circa 150 kyr. At least 35 separate *ahupua'a* territories bisect the field system, and their boundaries are marked by trail systems that run up and down slope; the stone walls marking these trails are one of the main archaeological characteristics of the field system (Cordy and Kaschko 1980; Ladefoged and Graves 2006). Running between the trails are thousands of low field divisions, often referred to as "walls," but more correctly described as stone and earth bunds or embankments, typically 1 to 2 m wide and usually 0.5 to .75 m high (Fig. 4.5). These embankments divide the long strips between the stone-lined trails into numerous rectangular field plots. Early postcontact descriptions indicate that the embankments were planted in rows of sugarcane, which served as windbreaks to protect the sweet potato and taro plants from the strong winds that sweep downslope from the Kohala Mountains.

Rosendahl's (1972, 1994) detailed mapping of a section of the Lapakahi uplands provided data on trail wall and field embankment joins and matching patterns. Kirch (1984:185: Fig. 60) used this map to demonstrate a temporal sequence of successive division of originally large fields into increasingly smaller plots. Expanding on this method of relative dating and constructing a set of explicit rules for analysis, Ladefoged et al. (2003) demonstrated similar patterns of spatial intensification in other parts of the Kohala field system. Similarly, the *ahupua'a* territories that subdivide the entire Kohala field system into 35 segments resulted from a pattern of successive subdivision of originally larger units. Thus the original pattern of *ahupua'a* consisted of just nine large territories (Ladefoged and Graves 2006: Fig. 13.9). The relative sequencing of field plots and territorial boundaries reflects an unmistakable progression over time, a pattern of territorial subdivision matched by decreasing garden plot size, that constitute a remarkable record of intensification. This sequence is highly suggestive of Geertz's (1970) process of "agricultural involution," or what Brookfield later characterized as a process "in which smaller and smaller pieces are ever more closely fitted together in a squeezed-down shared poverty" (1972:33).

This relative sequence of territorial subdivision leading to decreased field plot size can be put into an absolute chronological framework through radiocarbon dating. Rosendahl's pioneering work in the Lapakahi uplands included excavations at several residential features within the fields, dated by 10 radiocarbon samples (1972: Table 53). These dates suggested "an overall time estimate of AD 1400 to 1760 . . . for the upland occupation at Lapakahi" (1972:436). A larger sample of 33 AMS radiocarbon dates, obtained as part of the Hawai'i Biocomplexity Project, refines this chronological picture (Ladefoged and Graves 2008).[16] This suite of dates can be divided into three temporal groups: (1) three samples, including a fragment of carbonized sweet potato, dating from cal AD 1270 to 1420, and indicating the earliest land use in this area; (2) 10 samples clustering between cal AD 1420 to 1670; and (3) another group of 10 samples dating from cal AD 1630 into the historic period. An additional seven samples were obtained from residential features within the field system. Integrating these ^{14}C results with the relative chronology of field walls and territorial boundaries, Ladefoged and Graves write:

> The first phase of landesque capital improvements, that is, the construction of walls and trails, probably occurred sometime within the range of AD 1410 to 1630. The relative chronology of territorial units would suggest that some territory boundaries, bracketing larger geographic areas, were in place prior to the construction of the initial set of agricultural walls, but it is unclear how much earlier. Most wall and trail construction in this portion of the LKFS associated with both agricultural expansion and intensification probably occurred after AD 1650. The relative chronology of agricultural development identified at least four phases of construction after this time. There is no evidence of residential occupation before AD 1640, although our sample size is very small. It is tempting to suggest that ca. AD 1650 marks the point when people shifted from seasonal to permanent occupation of the area, but there is as yet limited evidence to confirm this hypothesis. (Ladefoged and Graves 2008:784)

While some low-intensity horticulture (quite likely a form of shifting cultivation) may have commenced on the leeward Kohala slopes as early as the late thirteenth or early-fourteenth century, the construction of physical features such as trails and field embankments that characterize the field system did not begin until after AD 1400. Moreover, a distinct final phase of intensification, marked by subdivision of larger land units into narrow *ahupua'a* and by small individual plot size, took place between AD 1650 and the early postcontact period.

The Hawai'i Biocomplexity Project has studied the geochemical gradients and nutrient status of soils associated with the Kohala field system (Vitousek et al. 2004; Meyer et al. 2007). On a broad landscape scale, by the time of European contact the field system had expanded to incorporate the entire area of leeward Kohala slope with suitable soil conditions. Figure 4.6 depicts a transect across the field system in relation to available phosphorus (P). At its lower limit, the system was being constrained by low P and high aridity, whereas at the inland extent it was low P (and other nutrients) due to leaching from high rainfall that determined the limits to expansion. These data support the hypothesis that the Kohala and other Hawai'i Island field systems had reached their geographic limits of potential expansion (as originally argued by Kirch 1984:187–90). More significantly, analyses of total P and the P:Nb ratio from soil samples taken from paired samples under field embankments and from adjacent fields show a pattern of decreased nutrient availability due to continued cropping.[17] Meyer et al. (2007: Table 1) demonstrate statistically significant differences in P availability between older soils capped by field embankments and the open field soils.

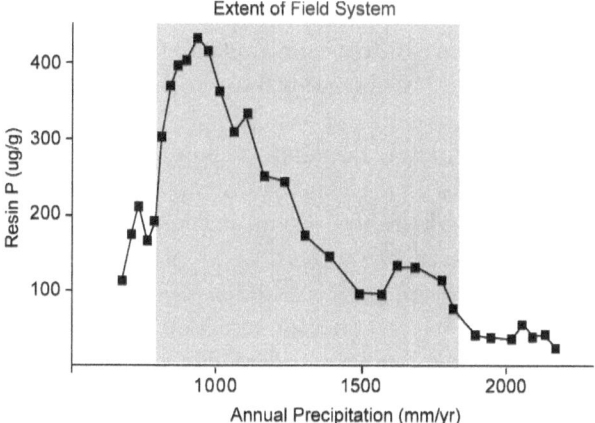

Figure 4.6. An elevation transect taken across the Kohala field system showing the distribution of values of phosphorus (as measured by resin-extractable P). The shaded area indicates the extent of the field system. (*Source:* Redrawn after Vitousek et al. 2004, Fig. 3B.)

They conclude that "over time Hawaiian agriculture decreased levels of P in soils of the Kohala Field System" (2007:352). In short, the long-term consequences of cropping-cycle intensification in the Kohala field system were not restricted to decreasing field size, but also to decreases in nutrient availability, and—one would predict—declining yields.[18]

A second major field system on Hawai'i Island straddles the leeward flanks of Kona District, on relatively young substrates of the Mauna Loa and Hualālai volcanoes. This system was even more extensive than that of Kohala; Allen (in Allen 2001:4) estimates its areal extent at 139 km². As described in Chapter 2, members of the 1779 Cook expedition walked through part of the Kona field system inland of Kealakekua Bay, and wrote admiringly of the high state of cultivation. Like most of the dryland field systems, Kona's fell into decline soon after European contact and depopulation, and much of this area was put into commercial coffee production, or used for cattle ranching, during the twentieth century. The Kona field system was archaeologically "rediscovered" by Soehren and Newman (1968; see also Newman, n.d.), who used aerial photographs to map a portion of the field walls above Kealakekua Bay. In the early 1980s, archaeological study of a 4.9-km long proposed highway corridor running from Kailua into the Kona uplands permitted Schilt (1984) to study variation in agricultural and residential features within the Kona field system, and to obtain a series of radiocarbon dates. A smaller but typical sector within the main upland field system, on the Amy Greenwell Ethnobotanical Garden (AGEG) property, has also been intensively studied by several teams of archaeologists (Allen 2001).

The Kona field system differs from Kohala's in that the principal agricultural features are parallel stone walls or rows running up and down slope, rather than across the slope as in Kohala. Such walls were termed *kuaiwi* in Hawaiian, literally meaning "backbone", and these evidently defined the boundaries of individual garden plots. At the AGEG site, such *kuaiwi* range in width from 2 to 7 m, and in height from 0.2 to 0.8 m, and are regularly spaced between 16 to 20 m apart (Kirch, in Allen 2001:54). Between the *kuaiwi* are found a variety of smaller features, including stone-faced terraces (for soil retention and planting), and numerous stone mounds, as well as residential features.

Based on extensive sampling throughout a long transect in the Kona field system, and supported by 22 radiocarbon dates, Schilt (1984:276–80) proposed three phases of development in the precontact period. A phase of "pioneer settlement" from AD 1050 to 1400 was marked by limited archaeological evidence, suggesting low intensity land use. The second phase, from AD 1400 to 1600/1650, marks the beginnings of the garden complex. It was in the third phase, from AD 1600/1650 up to European contact, that "gardening and seasonal occupation of *kula* slopes... increased dramatically" (1984:278). Both intensive and extensive horticultural features were developed during this time period in every *ahupua'a* unit included within Schilt's transect. This last phase also saw the conversion of two lava tube caves in the study area into refuges for use during times of war. Schilt's temporal sequence is supported by the work at the AGEG site, where 11 radiocarbon samples were dated from a small area in the core of the field system. All but one of these samples dates from after AD 1400 (Allen 2001: Fig. 11.1). Allen notes that stratigraphic evidence suggests that at AGEG the cross-slope terraces may have been constructed first, with the formalized *kuaiwi* being built after AD 1450, and "quite possibly in the mid-1500s to 1600s" (2001:140). In short, the chronology of the Kona field system closely parallels that for Kohala, with initial developments beginning around AD 1400, and a second phase of intensification—including formal field divisions—after AD 1600.

A third Hawai'i Island field system, less studied than those of Kohala or Kona, lies on the upland plateau region in the vicinity of the modern town of Waimea. Agricultural features including earthen embankments similar to those of Kohala were recorded during archaeological survey of a proposed highway corridor by-passing Waimea town (Clark and Kirch 1983), and a more formalized system incorporating intermittent irrigation canals was surveyed at Lālāmilo (Clark MS). Burtchard and Tomonari-Tuggle (2004) studied parts of this Waimea field system and obtained additional radiocarbon dates; they conclude that dryland farming in this area probably began around AD 1400. The addition of irrigation, however, may be quite late, even early postcontact.

A fourth major field system on Hawai'i Island existed in the Ka'ū District in the island's southern region, although it remains to be archaeologically investigated. The potential of this area for intensive dryland cultivation is clear from the GIS analysis of Ladefoged et al. (2009), and physical evidence of a reticulate field-system grid can readily be detected on aerial photographs. Handy (1940:165–66) noted the importance of sweet potato cultivation throughout this region. Archaeological studies of remnant portions of this field season, including dating of its development, would be desirable.

On Maui Island, high potential for intensive dryland farming existed in four zones: (1) a band across the lower eastern slopes of the West

Maui mountains; (2) a strip running inland from Haʻikū to Makawao in Hāmākuapoko District; (3) the area surrounding Hāna; and (4) a zone from Kaupō through Kahikinui to Honuaʻula (Ladefoged et al. 2009). Of these, only the Kaupō-Kahikinui-Honuaʻula zone, which Handy (1940:161) called "the greatest continuous dry planting area in the Hawaiian islands," has been archaeologically studied. A highly developed field system in Kaupō, with regularly spaced field terraces running between longer boundary walls (much like the Kohala field system in configuration), has recently been defined through remote sensing and ground survey (Kirch et al. in press). This system, covering perhaps as much as 15 km^2, is associated with two large temple sites (Loʻaloʻa and Kou), and is known from oral traditions to have been a royal center occupied by Kekaulike, king of Maui in the early-eighteenth century (Kamakau 1961:66).

In Kahikinui, intensive gardening is evidenced by a variety of archaeological features, although most of the area lacks the reticulate field system grid seen in Kaupō or the Hawaiʻi Island systems. Rather, the youthful 'aʻā lava flow topography of Kahikinui lent itself to intensive gardening in swales, some of which were terraced or divided into formal garden plots, and to farming in kīpuka (older lava patches) where the substrate was of ideal age (Dixon et al. 1999; Kirch et al. 2004).[19] Coil and Kirch (2005; see also Coil 2004; Holm 2006) summarize the evidence for dryland farming in Kahikinui, including carbonized sweet potato tubers and various kinds of field evidence. Occupation in the Kahikinui uplands did not commence until around AD 1400. Coil and Kirch argue that two phases of agricultural development can be discerned: an early phase from AD 1400 until about 1640, followed by a phase from AD 1640 to contact, with greater evidence for investment in agricultural facilities. This latter phase correlates with the period of peak population, as estimated by dated house counts (Kirch 2007b).

The Hawaiʻi Biocomplexity Project mapped the relationships between soil nutrients and archaeological evidence for intensive farming on the Kahikinui leeward slopes (Kirch et al. 2004; Hartshorn et al. 2006). As in Kohala, the upland farming zone in Kahikinui corresponds to a "sweet spot" of nutrient availability, defined on the downslope side by aridity and on the upslope side by steeply declining nutrient levels. At the microscale, detailed studies were made in two garden locations where digging stick impressions and other indicators of intensive cultivation were present (Kirch et al. 2005). Comparing cultivated soil from the digging stick depressions with uncultivated parent material,

Tracking the Transformations   153

Hartshorn et al. (2006) estimate significant reduction in soil nutrients, due to uptake from repeated harvesting of sweet potatoes. Thus as in Kohala, continuous and intensive cropping in the Kahikinui uplands led to measurable declines in available plant nutrients over time. A phase of declining yields during the late phase of cultivation seems quite likely.

Proceeding westward from Haleakalā Volcano, the older shield volcanoes making up the archipelago are too old for their land surfaces to have supported intensive dryland cultivation (Vitousek et al. 2004). The shield surfaces from West Maui on to Kaua'i and Ni'ihau have been exposed to rainfall and weathering for too long, and their nutrient status is consequently depleted. However, late stage volcanic rejuvenation on Moloka'i and O'ahu provided limited areas where younger substrates with adequate nutrient supplies were available, and on which field systems were developed. The only one of these to have been archaeologically studied is the Kalaupapa Peninsula, jutting out from the northern side of Moloka'i Island. Much of the peninsula is covered in closely-spaced low stone walls defining sweet potato garden plots (Kirch 2002; McCoy 2006). McCoy (2005, 2006) summarizes the evidence for temporal development of the Kalaupapa field system, based on 13 radiocarbon dates, and concludes that "widespread burning across the Kalaupapa Peninsula indicative of the initiation of the Kalaupapa Field System does not commence until AD 1450 to 1550" (2006:128). More intensive use of the area, however, dates to after AD 1650, when various residential sites and rockshelters within the field system were permanently occupied (Kirch et al. 2004).

To sum up, the chronological development of the Kohala, Kona, Waimea, Kahikinui, and Kalaupapa field systems, spanning three islands, is remarkably congruent. While there was some low intensity land use in Kohala and Kona prior to AD 1400, in all cases the onset of major dryland cultivation began around AD 1400. Following about two centuries of initial development, a final phase of intensification, typically marked by highly formalized garden plots and territorial boundaries, commenced about AD 1600 to 1650, and continued until the early postcontact period. Unlike the irrigation systems, many of which have continued in use throughout the nineteenth and twentieth centuries, the dryland field systems were all rapidly abandoned within a few decades following European contact.

The historical ecology of the intensively farmed dryland zones of Maui and Hawai'i islands, during the seventeenth to eighteenth centuries, provides a well documented instance of what Sahlins once described as "a remarkable tendency to invert by culture the ecology of nature," in which "many of the poorer regions of Polynesian high islands were the more intensively exploited" (1972:141). Across the archipelago-wide spectrum of Hawaiian agroecosystems, with underlying biogeochemical and climate gradients that fundamentally constrained their distribution, it was the easterly islands with their young, nutrient-rich substrates but more risk-prone rain-fed agricultural systems that followed a pathway of labor-demanding, cropping-cycle intensification. Moreover, these same areas were the crucible of dramatic sociopolitical changes, in which the transformation from chiefdom to archaic state first occurred.

MARINE RESOURCES AND AQUACULTURE

The archipelago-wide contrasts in the distribution of wet and dry agricultural systems were mirrored by an equally disjunctive distribution of marine resources and of coastal conditions suitable for aquaculture. Biomass production around tropical shores depends largely on the degree of coral reef development; the more extensive the area of fringing or barrier reef, the more herbivorous fish (such as parrotfish [Scaridae] and wrasses [Labridae]) that can be supported, in turn feeding a trophic pyramid of predators (e.g., jacks [Carangidae], barracudas [Sphyraenidae], sharks). Similarly, coral reefs support a more diverse set of invertebrates (e.g., mollusks, crabs, lobsters) and seaweeds, than do rocky shorelines. Coral reefs develop slowly as the islands' volcanic coastlines submerge and stabilize. Thus on Hawai'i and East Maui, the youthful and geomorphologically dynamic shorelines are dominated by sea cliffs and rocky shores, with sporadic coral growth and no extensive reefs. Significant reef development begins with West Maui and Moloka'i, and is most extensive around the oldest islands of O'ahu and Kaua'i. Since a high proportion of protein in the traditional Hawaiian diet was derived from fish and shellfish, these differentials contributed to the more stressful conditions on Hawai'i and East Maui, where shellfish gathering and fishing were more difficult (in many cases dangerous) and less productive.

In addition, the construction of yet another form of landesque capital intensification—stone walled fishponds for raising mullet (*Mugil cephalus*) and milkfish (*Chanos chanos*) (Summers 1964; Kikuchi 1976)—was limited to older and geomorphologically stable coastlines. Uniquely in Polynesia, the Hawaiians developed true aquaculture, modifying forms of stone fish traps found more widely in the Pacific into enclosed ponds.

Tracking the Transformations   155

The classic morphology of such *loko kuapā* ponds was a semicircular or lunate wall constructed of basalt and/or coral boulders out onto a reef flat. Walls were typically 1 to 2 m wide, and high enough to remain above the high tide level. These were often impressive constructions; the enclosing wall of Heʻeia Fishpond on Oʻahu is 1.52 km long and incorporates more than 2,000 m^3 of stone. Early-twentieth-century estimates of ponds then still in operation indicate annual yields of around 410 kg/ha of fish. Kamakau wrote that "fishponds were things that beautified the land, and a land with many fishponds was called 'fat'" (1976:47). Oʻahu had more fishponds (184) than any other island, and together the ponds of Oʻahu, Kauaʻi, and Molokaʻi made up the majority of pond acreage in the archipelago.

In sum, the western half of the archipelago was doubly fortunate: where irrigation and aquaculture could be intensified the most, there were also the richest and largest stocks of marine resources. The eastern half of the island chain, while comprising more land area overall (12,345 km^2 amounting to 74 percent of the total area of the main islands), got the proverbial short end of the stick: greatly restricted possibilities for irrigation or aquaculture, restricted marine resources, greater labor inputs necessitated by the dryland systems, and the highest levels of risk (due to dependence on stochastically variable rainfall).

Temporal Development of Aquaculture

Being partly submerged and situated in a dynamic marine environment, fishponds are inherently difficult for archaeologists to study. Based on references to construction of particular fishponds and their association with named chiefs in Hawaiian oral traditions, Kikuchi (1976:295) concluded that most ponds had been constructed from the fourteenth through the nineteenth centuries. The probable construction dates for several ponds on Oʻahu, Kauaʻi, and Molokaʻi have now been established by ^{14}C dating of pond sediments (Denham et al. 1999; Athens 2001; Carson 2005b). When fishponds were constructed, the enclosing walls created sediment traps, and the depositional regime within the pond typically changed in a manner that can be detected through physical and biotic changes in the sediment core. Radiocarbon dates from sediments thought to mark the onset of artificial pond conditions are now available from more than 10 ponds (Athens 2001: Table 2). These suggest initial efforts at fishpond construction beginning in the fourteenth century, and continuing into the fifteenth to seventeenth centuries.

MONUMENTALITY AND THE TEMPLE SYSTEM

For archaeologists, archaic states are virtually synonymous with monumentality; indeed, ancient states are usually recognized in part by the presence of monumental constructions, be they temples, palaces, or tombs. Writing comparatively of early civilizations, Trigger notes that "royal tombs, palaces, and temples bore witness to polities that were believed to be legitimated by divine power and inseparable from the cosmic order" (2003:564). Of course, the kinds of vast production systems I have just reviewed—irrigation complexes, fishponds, and reticulate field systems covering tens of square kilometers—were in a landscape sense also monumental. But in addition to these vast infrastructural investments, the Hawaiians, like other early hierarchical and emergent state societies, sank significant time and energy into building other kinds of monuments that must, in a classic Marxian sense, be judged as "superstructure." These monuments consumed labor, material, and supplies, but did not directly contribute to production, although they were certainly an integral part of the emerging ideological system by which production was controlled and surplus extracted.

Flannery argues that while "chiefs could organize corvée labor to build temples and other public buildings, they usually could not have their residences built for them. Kings, on the other hand, could use corvée labor to build their palaces" (1998:21). In precontact Hawai'i, kings and other ranking elites were not often buried in constructed monuments; rather their bodies were secreted away in lava tubes or caves, as was the case with the famous Kamehameha I. However, the royal line of Hawai'i Island descended from 'Umi maintained two special mausoleums, the Hale o Keawe, part of a massive temple and residential complex at Hōnaunau (a detailed description of which follows later in this chapter), and the Hale o Līloa in Waipi'o Valley (Buck 1957:573). Within the special sepulchral house at Hōnaunau were kept the bones of 23 kings and high chiefs, some of them held in special anthropomorphic containers of wickerwork with inset pearlshell eyes (Buck 1957: fig. 347; Rose 1992).

While not investing great labor in the interment of their kings, the Hawaiians did not lack for monumental temple construction. Throughout the archipelago, and well documented archaeologically, may be found the foundations of the functionally varied temples, collectively referred to as *heiau*, which were erected on often monumental platforms and terraces of stacked basalt cobbles and boulders (Kirch 1985:257–65). The origin of these *heiau* can be traced back to Ancestral Polynesian concepts of ritual spaces (see Chapter 1), but in late prehistoric Hawai'i these became highly elaborated and distinctive. In Hawai'i, the early Eastern Polynesian form of temple was retained but then further developed, taking on a new term, *heiau*.[20] By the time of Cook's arrival, the Hawaiian chiefs and the priests conducted the complex temple rituals that validated and legitimated their economic and sociopolitical power in large temples built on massive stone terraces and platforms.

Heiau captured the attention of archaeologists early on, beginning with Stokes's pioneering surveys in 1909 on Hawai'i (Stokes 1991) and Moloka'i islands (Stokes MS). This was followed by islandwide surface surveys of Kaua'i, O'ahu, Maui, Lana'i, and Kaho'olawe islands (Bennett 1931; Emory 1924; McAllister 1933a, 1933b; Walker MS). As stratigraphic archaeology developed after the 1950s in Hawai'i, the focus of archaeologists shifted to habitation sites, especially rockshelters and sand dunes, which tended to yield large arrays of portable artifacts, and *heiau* were neglected. A number of factors have contributed to the reticence of archaeologists to excavate in *heiau*, including the continued significance of them in Native Hawaiian culture, and the fact that many may contain burials or the remains of human sacrifices. The sheer size and daunting task of moving tons of basaltic rock to expose construction sequences have also been off-putting. Thus relatively few *heiau* have been excavated or radiocarbon dated.

On O'ahu Island, one well-excavated temple—Kāne'aki in Makaha Valley—has been traced through six successive architectural phases, beginning with a small set of terraces around AD 1200, to its final rebuilding as a *luakini* or war temple just prior to Cook's arrival, during the Maui-O'ahu wars of conquest (Ladd 1973; see Kirch 1984: Fig. 82). In its final configuration, the temple had two main courts, with the higher court surrounded by walls on three sides, enclosing a stepped altar and foundation for an oracle tower. At 1,010 m² in area Kāne'aki is one of the larger O'ahu temples, though not the largest, which is Kawa'ewa'e at 2,820 m² (Cordy 2002b:34). It is, however, on Maui Island that the most comprehensive evidence for temple development has been forthcoming, and I draw primarily on the Maui evidence to track the course of monumental temple construction.

Development of the Maui Island Temple System

Winslow Walker (MS [1930]; see also Sterling 1998) made the first comprehensive field survey of *heiau* on Maui, recording 228 sites, most of these being pointed out by Native Hawaiian informants, some of whom knew the formal names of these structures, or information about their functions and associations with ruling chiefs. Drawing largely on Walker's pioneering work Kolb (1991) compiled information on 108 surviving *heiau* on the island. He excavated in eight of these, including five major *luakini* or state temples. Kolb reported this research in his dissertation (1991) and in several subsequent articles (Kolb 1992, 1994, 1999, 2006), and his data are important for tracing the development of large-scale monumental architecture on Maui. In the late 1990s, Kolb also mapped and excavated in a number of *heiau* in Kahikinui District, although his results have been summarized only in preliminary form (Kolb and Radewagen 1997; Kolb 2006). Since 1995, I have also studied Kahikinui *heiau* as a part of a long-term project on settlement and human ecodynamics in southeast Maui (Kirch 2004; Kirch 1997b). My database includes detailed plane table and theodolite surveys of 46 *heiau* in Kahikinui and adjacent Kaupō, and excavations in 14 of these. Combining Kolb's and my own data on Kahikinui *heiau*, a regional chronology based on 41 radiocarbon dates can be constructed for temple development.

The extensive data on Kahikinui-Kaupō temples, which includes not only large *heiau* but structures of all sizes and types throughout this substantial region, gives a good picture of variation in late precontact Hawaiian ritual architecture. The size distribution of *heiau* ranges from small shrines of no more than 20 m^2, to midsized agricultural temples of circa 100 to 1,000 m^2, up to the largest state *heiau* such as Loʻaloʻa, which is associated with Maui king Kekaulike (4,160 m^2).[21] The rank-size distribution of Kahikinui and Kaupō *heiau* is shown in Figure 4.7. What is being measured in terms of area (or sometimes cubic meters of fill) is, of course, the stone foundations, which supported a number of perishable superstructures, including thatched houses for keeping images and ritual paraphernalia, for cooking sacrifices, and for sheltering temple drums, barkcloth wrapped oracle towers, offering platforms of wood, and wooden images in a variety of sizes and styles. The stone foundations were dry-laid, using locally available fieldstone—usually subangular or waterworn basalt boulders—or, in areas with young lava flows, *ʻaʻā* cobbles or *pāhoehoe* slabs. Wall and terrace faces were laid with a great deal of skill, large boulders carefully fitted with smaller spacing and chinking cobbles to form near vertical facades 1 to 2 m high. These stone foundations vary in layout and structural detail, and are frequently combinations of such basic forms as enclosures, terraces,

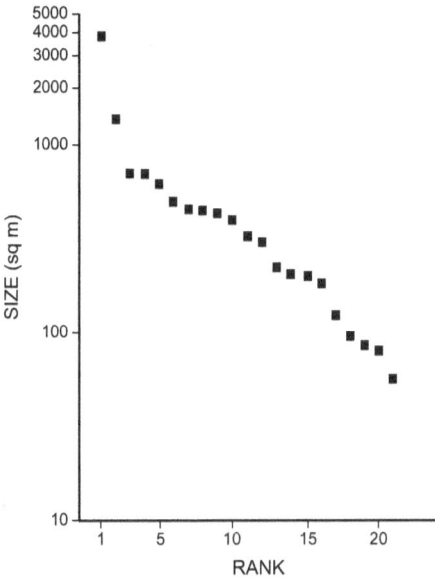

Figure 4.7. The rank-size distribution of temple sites in Kahikinui and Kaupō districts, Maui.

and platforms. A number of morphological types recur, including "notched" enclosures with six sides, double-court enclosures (sometimes with the two courts slightly offset), square enclosures, and terraces. Temples display nonrandom orientation patterns, which I have argued were linked to the hierarchy of deities and cults (Kirch 2004; see also Ruggles 2007).

The spatial distribution of temples shows distinct, nonrandom patterning. Smaller fishing shrines (ko'a) are found along the coastline, but larger temples also occur within a few hundred meters of the shore, and in many cases may mark territorial boundaries, either between ahupua'a or 'ili.[22] Many of these putative boundary temples are oriented to the north, toward the 3,055-m high summit of Haleakalā.[23] A second major zone of temples occurs in the uplands between about 400 and 700 m elevation, in the main residential and agricultural zone. These temples are presumably heiau ho'o'ulu'ai, temples for increasing fertility and crop production, and they include many of the notched forms, along with some enclosures and terraces. The upland temples have preferred orientations of both due east and to the northeast, in the rising position of the star cluster Pleiades (Kirch 2004). Called Makali'i in Hawaiian, the Pleiades were important in the Hawaiian seasonal calendar, as their

Figure 4.8. Aerial photograph of the KIP-1010 temple site in the uplands of Kahikinui, Maui. The buttressed southeastern corner is in the foreground. (Photo by P. V. Kirch.)

acronitic rising determined the onset of the Makahiki season, and was used to recalibrate the lunar horticultural calendar (see Chapter 2). The two largest and most important of these upland temples in Kahikinui were Kohōluapapa (site 50-50-15-186) in Lualaʻilua *ahupuaʻa*, reputed to have been a *luakini*, and site KIP-1010 in Nakaʻaha (Fig. 4.8). Both of these are situated within the core upland dryland farming zone, adjacent to significant tracts of prime garden land. In sum, the Kahikinui *heiau* system provided a means of ideological control and regulation of the district's population and economy, as well as a ritualized network for tribute collection.

The temporal development of this elaborate system is evidenced by 41 radiocarbon dates from 31 temples. This suite of dates, the largest and most systematic for any temple system in the islands, is plotted in Figure 4.9 as a series of probability distributions. Radiocarbon dates falling within the past five centuries are, unfortunately, complicated by oscillations in the atmospheric calibration curve, which yield multiple

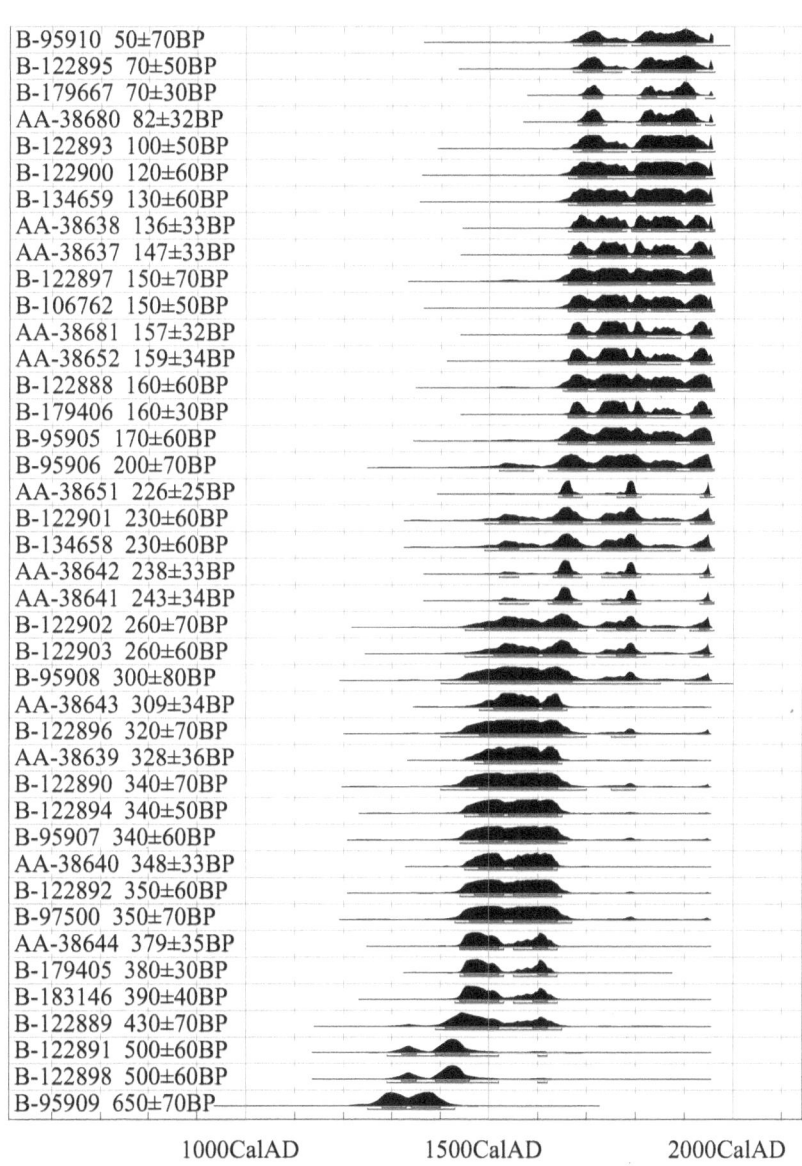

Figure 4.9. Oxcal-generated plot of 41 radiocarbon dates from Kahikinui temples sites.

calibration intercepts and make the dates susceptible to "calibration stochastic distortion" (CSD) (McFadgen et al. 1994). Depending on the slope of the calibration curve, the CSD effect results in systematic increases or decreases in the number of calibrated dates on an absolute calendar scale. Consequently, it is not possible to determine precise calendar ages for most ^{14}C dates in this late time period. This is evident visually in Figure 4.9, where the probability distributions for individual dates are typically bimodal or multimodal. Nonetheless, certain general trends are unmistakable. The three oldest dates, at the bottom of the chart, most likely derive from initial burning of land surfaces, probably for clearance and agricultural use prior to temple construction.[24] The next 16 dates in sequence, moving up the graph, fall into a temporal block between about AD 1450 and 1600, and demonstrate the rapid imposition of the Kahikinui temple system during a period of time that was at the most 150 years long, but may be considerably shorter. Among the temples erected in this first stage were Kohōluapapa and a coastal temple in Auwahi, several upland agricultural temples in the core gardening zone, and a square enclosure and priest's house at Naka'ohu. The remaining 22 dates at the top of the graph indicate continued construction, rebuilding, and use of temples from about AD 1600 until the early postcontact era. A number of these later dates come from secondary phases of the same temples, originally constructed between AD 1450 to 1600. Other dates indicate the late construction of new temples, including at least two of the putative boundary temples.

Kirch and Sharp (2005) applied ^{230}Th dating to branch coral offerings obtained from seven *heiau* in Kahikinui, including two sites that had previously been radiocarbon dated. The dated specimens are branch tips from the species *Pocillopora meandrina*, which had been collected live from the rocky coast and placed as offerings on the temple altars, or incorporated in wall fill during construction. Because the date of death of the corals corresponds closely with the time of their emplacement as offerings (there is no evidence of wear or rounding on the fragile branch tips), one can be confident that the ^{230}Th dates obtained from the outer growth layers give an accurate date of cultural use. The ^{230}Th method is far more precise than radiocarbon, and does not suffer from calibration issues or CSD effects. The dates fall into a tight range, from AD 1569 ± 5 (2 standard deviations) to AD 1629 ± 4. This range is consistent with the older group of 16 radiocarbon dates for the first phase of *heiau* construction plotted in Figure 4.10. However, it suggests that the temple system may have been imposed during an even shorter

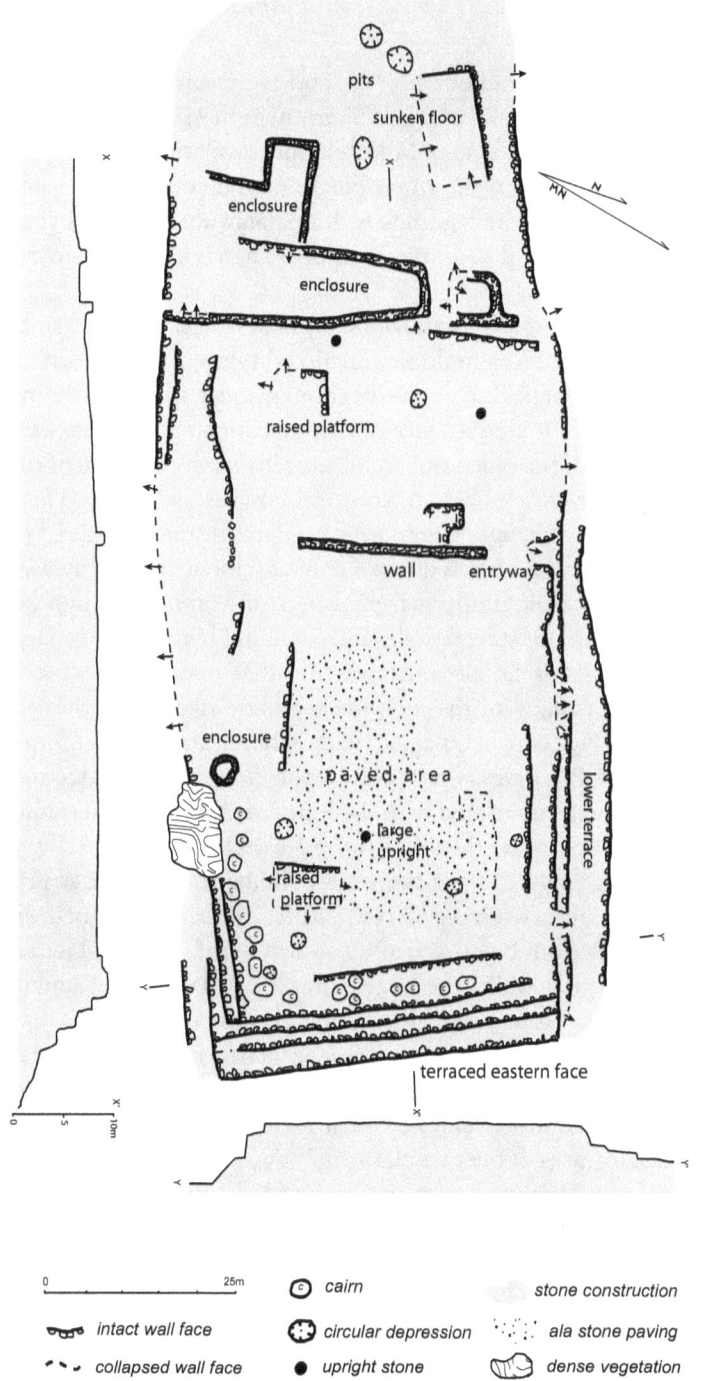

Figure 4.10. Plan and cross-sections of Loʻaloʻa Heiau in Kaupō District, Maui. (Based on plane table map by P. V. Kirch.)

period of time than the radiocarbon method can resolve, within perhaps 60 rather than 150 years. Kirch and Sharp hypothesized that this rapid expansion of the temple system in Kahikinui correlates with the period of Piʻilani's unification of the Maui kingdom and consolidation under his son Kiha-a-Piʻilani and grandson Kamalālāwalu, a period that is dated using genealogical counting to approximately AD 1570 to 1630 (see Table 3.1).

The Kahikinui temple data show the rapid development of a complex temple system—including multiple functional types of *heiau* correlated with the rise of particular cults—beginning most likely in the mid-sixteenth century. Of course, this system did not start *de novo* at this time; it grew out of the older and architecturally simpler system of ritual places that can be traced back to Ancestral Polynesian Society. The key point is that major changes began to take place around the mid-1550s that took the Hawaiian *heiau* down a new developmental pathway.

Situated in an ecologically marginal part of Maui, Kahikinui lacks the uppermost rank of state temples indicated in Figure 4.7. The largest *heiau* on that plot is Loʻaloʻa, a structure that matches in scale and labor investment many of the monuments associated with other early archaic states (Fig. 4.10). Loʻaloʻa, with a basal area of 4,160 m² as determined by GPS survey, was a war temple (*luakini*) dedicated to the god Kū and directly associated with the Maui royal line.[25] Oral tradition links its construction to the Maui king Kekaulike, about AD 1730, although this is likely to have been a rebuilding of an older structure (Kamakau 1961:66; Kolb 1991:168). Kolb radiocarbon dated eight charcoal samples from Loʻaloʻa (Kolb 1991:235–40). These fall into two discrete clusters, much like the larger sample of dates from Kahikinui. The older cluster of four dates suggests initial construction of the temple in the sixteenth century, as a rectangular platform (Kolb 1991:239: Fig. 6.7). A major expansion phase occurred in the eighteenth century (documented by four ^{14}C dates), which included the "addition of the massive rock terraces of the east platform" (1991:239). This latter phase was no doubt undertaken during the reign of Kekaulike, as suggested by the oral traditions.

Three other state or *luakini heiau* on Maui's windward side were investigated by Kolb: Pihana and Halekiʻi, which comprise a linked complex in Wailuku on northwest Maui, and Piʻilanihale in Hāna District. Kolb calculated the basal area of Pihana Heiau at 4,076 m² (1994: Table 1). The temple is situated on a ridge overlooking the Wailuku Stream and its productive taro irrigation systems. Oral tradition

(Sterling 1998:75) credits its initial building to the reign of Kakaʻe (ca. AD 1510 in the chronology), although it certainly was rebuilt and rededicated by later kings, including Kamehameha I after he defeated Kahekili's forces at the battle of ʻĪao Valley. Nearby Halekiʻi Heiau, on the same ridge, may have served as a royal residence. Three dates from Pihana suggest that its initial construction took place between AD 1400 and 1600. The larger set of 12 dates from Halekiʻi indicate some initial activity on the site as early as the 1400s, with the first major phase of construction between AD 1450 and 1600, and a second phase after AD 1600.

Piʻilanihale Heiau in Hāna is the largest stone construction in the islands in terms of the sheer area of its footprint, some 12,126 m². The name means "House of Piʻilani" and it is regarded "as the royal abode of the great Piilani family of Maui chiefs, who flourished in the sixteenth century" (Sterling 1998:123, quoting Walker MS). There are good reasons to believe that the complex, which includes multiple enclosures and features, functioned as a combined royal residence and temple site (a "royal center," discussion follows later in this chapter). The massive central terrace, on which sits a large enclosure (possibly the actual *luakini*), has been faced in six terraced steps on the north side, to a height of 13.4 m (Cordy 1970:4), creating a truly impressive visual effect (Fig. 4.11). East and west wings flank the main terrace, and these probably served as residential wards (Kolb 1999a: Fig. 5). Kolb obtained seven ¹⁴C dates from small excavation units dispersed over this immense structure. The lack of continuous trenches and stratigraphic sections make it difficult to relate these dates to the structural components of this vast complex.[26] Two early dates of between AD 1300 and 1500 demonstrate some cultural activity on the site, but I do not believe they correspond to the major construction phases. The onset of significant building activity more likely began between AD 1500 and 1650, as indicated by the next two dates, and use of the complex continued until the early contact period, as indicated by three final dates.

The extensive evidence from Kahikinui District, when combined with the chronometric evidence from the largest state temples elsewhere on Maui, supports an interpretation of major increases in monumental ritual architecture from the sixteenth to early seventeenth centuries, or Late Expansion Period in the sequence outlined in Table 4.1. This corresponds to what Kolb (1994) called the Unification Period, a time when the formerly independent West and East Maui polities were united under the rule of Piʻilani and his successors (see Chapter 2).[27]

Figure 4.11. View across the massive central courtyard of Pi'ilanihale Heiau, Maui. (Photo by T. Babineau.)

ROYAL CENTERS AND ELITE RESIDENCE PATTERNS

Archaic states are marked not only by monumental temple architecture, but by elite residences that are similarly constructed on a grand scale. Archaeologists working in Hawai'i have not been accustomed to employing the term "palace" as is common in Mesopotamian or Mesoamerican archaeological parlance. Yet it is clear that Hawaiian kings and chiefs resided in residential complexes—often closely associated with temples—that were constructed of special materials, and were significantly larger than ordinary dwellings. The scale of these Hawaiian royal residences certainly is consistent with some of the "palaces" or "royal compounds" in archaic states referred to by Flannery (1998:21–36). Indeed, there is good evidence, especially from Hawai'i and Maui Islands, for the emergence in the Late Expansion and Protohistoric Periods of what may be termed *royal centers*, clusters of temples, houses for the king, his wives and retainers, dwelling compounds of other high-ranking chiefs, storehouses, canoe sheds, and other specialized facilities such as *hōlua* slides.[28] These were not urban centers, because Hawaiian subsistence with its tuber crops defied concentrated storage, and the population was dispersed among the extensive agricultural systems. Indeed, the kings and chiefs were famously peripatetic, moving about regularly to assure administrative control over their territories. Thus, on a vast island such as Hawai'i, more than one royal center was in use by a single king. Several of these royal centers survive, wholly or partially, and have been archaeologically investigated. In addition to the royal centers, there is good archaeological evidence for district (*moku*) level elite centers, and for specialized residences for *ahupua'a*-level chiefs and land managers (*konohiki*). In short, the archaeological evidence supports the interpretation of three levels of hierarchically differentiated residential structures in the late precontact period. A brief review of this evidence follows.

Hawai'i Island Royal Centers

Probably the most famous, and quite likely the earliest, royal center on Hawai'i was situated at the mouth of Waipi'o Valley, the only large valley with a significant expanse of irrigated taro on the island. Waipi'o is referenced in traditions of the early Voyaging Period (see Chapter 3), and by the time of Līloa was firmly established as the ancestral seat of the *ali'i nui* of Hawai'i (Fornander 1996:73). Unfortunately, there has been little direct archaeological investigation of the remains of this center, although Cordy (2000:196–201) synthesizes traditional and ethnohistoric data to describe the main structural elements. In Līloa's time (roughly AD 1550–70) these included a royal residence, named Kahaunokama'ahala, which overlooked a special *lo'i* pondfield whose taro crop was sacred and reserved for the king. Near the king's residence, two major temples surmounted the black sand dunes: Paka'alana and Honua'ula. Both were *luakini* class temples, and Paka'alana was also a *pu'uhonua*, or place of refuge for those who had transgressed against a *kapu*.[29] After the death of Līloa, a mausoleum was constructed to house the deceased king's bones, referred to as the Hale o Līloa ("House of Līloa"); this was apparently attached to or part of Paka'alana Heiau. Large fishponds and a level ground for wrestling and other sports were also part of the Waipi'o royal center (Cordy 2000: Fig. 7.1).

After ʻUmi's unification of the island around AD 1570 to 1590, Waipiʻo lost its primacy, although it continued to be an important location and intermittent seat of the Hawaiʻi kings. ʻUmi moved his court to Kona, and it was probably at this time that the royal center at Hōnaunau first came to prominence. A few kilometers south of Kealakekua Bay, Hōnaunau consists of a small lava peninsula jutting out into the ocean, with a cove permitting sheltered canoe landing on the north side. The extensive complex of walls, platforms, enclosures, and other features has been mapped, studied, and excavated a number of times, beginning with Stokes in 1919, and especially after the complex became a National Historical Park in the 1950s (Bryan and Emory 1986). National Park Service archaeologist Ed Ladd excavated in three of the major temples within the Hōnaunau complex (Āleʻaleʻa, A27 or the "Old Heiau," and the Hale o Keawe), while Soehren and Tuohy excavated structures and deposits within the elite residential areas (Ladd 1969, 1973, 1985, 1986, 1987; Soehren and Tuohy 1987; Stokes 1991:104–7). Cordy (2000:260–77) has again synthesized much of this information.

The royal center of Hōnaunau sprawls over more than 25 hectares; indeed, compounds and residential sites occupied by subsidiary chiefs extend considerably farther to the south. The sacred temple precinct (which also served as a *puʻuhonua* or place of refuge) occupied the low lava promontory, and was defined on the south and east by the Great Wall, an impressive stone construction nearly 4 m high and 5 m thick (Fig. 4.12).

Figure 4.12. The reconstructed sepulchral temple of Hale o Keawe at the royal center of Hōnaunau, Kona. The Great Wall can be seen extending off to the left of the photo. (Photo by T. Babineau.)

Within this sacred space lay 'Āle'ale'a, an elevated platform temple, and the ruins of a larger enclosed temple referred to as site A-27 or the "Old Heiau." The dimensions of both of these structures are impressive: 'Āle'ale'a has an area of 702 m^2 and a volume of about 1,684 m^3, while A-27 has a footprint of around 3,000 m^2. At the northern end of the Great Wall lies the sepulchral temple of Hale o Keawe, which housed the bones of at least 23 high-ranking individuals including those of Keawe-'ikekahiali'iokamoku (see Cordy 2000: Table 9.4). A fourth, smaller temple, the Hale o Papa was situated next to the Great Wall; this was either a temple dedicated to female deities, or the menstruation house of high-ranking chiefesses.

The royal residential compound was located immediately east of the Great Wall, where the king's double-hulled canoe could land in the cove called Keone'ele; this area included several brackish water bathing ponds. Additional elite residential compounds extended southward, housing high chiefs and retainers of the king's court. On the inland slopes overlooking the complex is a large *hōlua* slide, 176 m in length, constructed of basalt stones as a sled way for this chiefly sport. Excavations by Soehren and Tuohy (1987) in parts of this extensive residential zone yielded a wide range of artifacts, including numerous objects of personal adornment such as shell beads, dog tooth pendants, and bracelet plaques carved from pig tusk (1987: Fig. 1.53), all of which suggest the presence of elites. In addition, large quantities of basalt adzes, coral files and abraders, pumice abrading stones, and bone awls and needles indicate that this residential zone housed a substantial number of craft specialists who supported the royal household.

Excavations at Hōnaunau, especially those by Ladd at 'Āle'ale'a, the Hale o Keawe and other structures demonstrate that this royal center developed gradually over a considerable time span. 'Āle'ale'a itself was built in seven construction stages (Ladd (1969); unfortunately, attempts to radiocarbon date materials recovered from the platform were fraught with problems.[30] Ladd (1987:81) believes that the first, small stage of 'Āle'ale'a I may date as early as AD 1250, and following Barrère's (1986) analysis of the oral traditions linked to Hōnaunau, attributes 'Āle'ale'a IV to 'Ehukaimalino, a Kona chief contemporary with Līloa. The substantial 'Āle'ale'a stages V and VI are attributed to 'Umi, and the final 'Āle'ale'a stage VII to Keawekūikekā'ai. This last king is thought by Ladd to have built the enclosing Great Wall, the northern end of which was then later dismantled to build the foundation for the Hale o Keawe, which is linked to Keawe'ikekahiali'iokamoku (approximately

AD 1690–1710). Cordy (2000:265–66) argues that Hōnaunau first became a royal center during the reign of Keakealanikane, between about AD 1660 and 1680 in the relative chronology, and that at this time 'Āle'ale'a III and IV, the Hale o Papa, and the Great Wall were all built using a distinctive masonry style called *pao*.[31] In Cordy's interpretation, Keawe'ikekahiali'iokamoku (dating to approximately AD 1720–40) would have built the final stages of 'Āle'ale'a, as well as the Hale o Keawe. In sum, the Hōnaunau royal center reached its prominence between roughly AD 1630 and 1710 in the relative chronology. Later kings, including Alapa'inui and Kalani'ōpu'u, certainly spent time at Hōnaunau, but established their main seats elsewhere on the island.

Other known important royal centers on Hawai'i included Hilo, Kokoiki, Kailua, Kahalu'u, and Kealakekua-Ka'awaloa. Kokoiki, on the northern tip of the island in Kohala, was an important center during the reign of Alapa'inui, and was used later by the famous Kamehameha, who was born there. As at Hōnaunau, an extensive complex of residences and other structures once surrounded the great enclosed temple of Mo'okini, but only the latter now remains.[32] Mo'okini, with a footprint of 3,002 m^2 and walls up to 4 m high, is one of the largest *luakini* temples on the island (Cordy 2000:284; Stokes 1991:173–78: Fig. 88). The last functioning royal center of the old style, incorporating secular and sacred precincts into a single complex, was Kamakahonu and with the adjacent Ahu'ena temple, situated at one end of Kailua Bay (Barrère 1975; Stokes 1991:43–47). Kamehameha I retired to Kamakahonu after his conquest of the archipelago, and died there in 1819.

Maui Island Royal Centers

Maui also had its royal centers, the best known of which is without doubt Pi'ilanihale in Hāna, which I have already discussed in the context of the Maui temple system. While often referred to as a *heiau*, and undoubtedly incorporating a *luakini*, Kolb (1999) shows that Pi'ilanihale was a combination of temple and royal residence. He believes that the shift from a strictly ritual function to a combined temple and chiefly residence occurred after AD 1400 (1991:308). The name literally means "House of Pi'ilani," and there can be little doubt that it served as the seat of the Pi'ilani lineage. Another Maui royal center is the large complex known variously as Pōpōiwi or Kānemalohemo, situated on a bluff overlooking the bay of Mokulau on the eastern side of Kaupō District, not far from Loʻaloʻa Heiau (Sterling 1998:173-74). This sprawling complex, covering more than 8,000 m², is terraced on the downslope side, and incorporates a number of large and smaller enclosures and pavements (Kolb 1991: Fig. 5.9). Kolb's limited test excavations yielded five radiocarbon dates for this complex, spanning the thirteenth to the seventeenth centuries.[33] Oral tradition links the Pōpōiwi complex with king Kekaulike (Kamakau 1961:66), who also constructed or rebuilt Loʻaloʻa Heiau, and who made Kaupō his seat. Pōpōiwi probably became a royal center during his reign. Finally, the Pihana-Halekiʻi complex also described earlier, located at Wailuku on West Maui, probably also served as a multifunctional ritual and residential center. Kolb's excavations at Halekiʻi (1991:309) yielded faunal assemblages consistent with habitation, and he believes this structure continually served a residential function.

Royal Centers on Other Islands

Oʻahu and Kauaʻi also had their royal centers, although little is known about their development from an archaeological perspective. The sacred site of Kūkaniloko in central Oʻahu was an important early residential center for the Oʻahu elite, but most of the complex was destroyed more than a century ago, only the birthing stones remaining (Kirch and Babineau 1996:34-35). Cordy (2002:34) mentions a number of other royal residential complexes around the island, including Puʻu Kāhea in Waiʻanae District, Kamananui in Waialua District, Waikele in ʻEwa District, and of course the famous Waikīkī in Kona District. Kualoa, in windward Koʻolaupoko District is also noted in traditions as a royal residence, associated with King Kūaliʻi (Fornander 1996:278). On Kauaʻi, a major royal center was located in the central Wailua area, where there are a number of prominent *heiau* (including Poliahu, Kukui, and Malae *heiau*, the latter with a basal area of >8,000 m²), as well as a sacred birthing site (Bennett 1931:125-28: Figs. 37, 39, 40; Kirch and Babineau 1996:16-19).

District Centers and Other Elite Housing

Given the pronounced hierarchical nature of Hawaiian society in the late precontact period (see Chapter 2), a corresponding hierarchy in residential patterns might be anticipated, and is indeed supported by the archaeological record. Here I draw on just a few out of many possible examples to illustrate the variation in elite housing that is indicated by archaeological evidence.

A well preserved example of a district-level center is the complex at Makee in Auwahi *ahupua'a* of Kahikinui District. Auwahi had special significance within the *moku* of Kahikinui, evidenced by the fact that this land section was claimed by the high chiefess Ke'elikōlani during the 1848 division of lands. The best canoe landing bay along the entire Kahikinui coast (notable for its rocky cliffs and lack of a protective reef) is at Makee, and this topographic feature may well have determined the choice of location for this district center. In many respects, this district level center resembles a less elaborate version of a royal center. In the central part of the complex is a temple with a 1.5-m high platform; a high-walled shrine dedicated to the fishing god Kū'ula is nearby, along with a cookhouse for preparing offerings. Radiocarbon and coral dates from these structures indicate that they were in place by the mid-seventeenth century. Several large residential enclosures, with house foundations of fine *'ili'ili* (waterworn pebbles) are situated both seaward and inland of the temple, along with smaller enclosures that probably functioned as store houses or for other specialized purposes. At the top of the complex, situated on a prominent knoll, is an especially well constructed residential platform, faced on the southeast and with a high wall running along the eastern side. Walker (MS) was told by his informants that this was a chief's house, and its residential function was confirmed by our test excavations.

Individual *ahupua'a* also had specialized residential areas either for the *ali'i-'ai-ahupua'a* chief and or the resident *konohiki*. The large *ahupua'a* of Kawela on leeward Moloka'i, which was surveyed extensively by Weisler and Kirch (1985), provides an excellent example of such elite housing. Out of 10 residential complexes mapped and excavated at Kawela, two are prominently located on the west and east promontories overlooking the main alluvial floodplain. These complexes (H and I in Weisler and Kirch 1985: Table 3) are architecturally more elaborate than the others, incorporating formal ritual enclosures (probably household shrines) as well as larger house floors. Both complexes showed evidence of craft specialization, especially in the use of fine-grained lithics, and both contained high status food remains. Radiocarbon dates from Kawela households, as well as a coral date from a small *heiau* at the eastern boundary of Kawela *ahupua'a*, indicate that this settlement pattern with distinct elite residential areas dates to the period from the late-seventeenth century until the early postcontact period.

A similar pattern of elite residences set off from commoner households has recently been investigated in Makiloa *ahupua'a* on Hawai'i Island (Field et al. 2010). As at Kawela, commoner households occupy low ridges overlooking the coast, and are marked by smaller house terraces. In contrast is a large elaborate terrace, site MKI-56, whose plan is shown in Figure 4.13. This site overlooks Kamilo Bay, a protected canoe landing, and the ruins of a canoe shed lie below the main house site. Excavations in this house terrace yielded a rich array of faunal remains, as well as fishhooks and other artifacts suggestive of intensive craft activity. Two radiocarbon dates bracket the occupation span of this elite residence between the late seventeenth and mid-eighteenth centuries, while a branch coral tip from the base of the rear wall was U/Th dated to AD 1623 ± 5. Site MKI-56 provides a good example of an elite residence within a modest-sized *ahupua'a* unit during the Protohistoric Period.

Figure 4.13. Plan of an elite residence (site MKI-56) in Makiloa *ahupua'a*, Kohala, Hawai'i. The main dwelling space is in the center of the structure; the enclosure on the left is a shrine, while the subsidiary enclosure on the right may be a storage area. (Plan based on plane table map by P. V. Kirch.)

WHEN DID THE HAWAIIAN ARCHAIC STATES EMERGE?

All of the archaeological evidence points to the period from the late AD 1400s until around 1650 as the crucial phase during which the Hawaiian archaic states first emerged out of earlier sociopolitical formations of a more classic Polynesian form. By the close of the fifteenth century, Hawaiian population had reached the end of a period of dramatic, exponential population growth that saw virtually all of the agriculturally suitable landscapes across the archipelago now settled and territorially divided. In the succeeding sixteenth and seventeenth centuries, population growth rates declined and in places probably stabilized, although population densities remained high. Intensive development of the archipelago's economic infrastructure began somewhat earlier on O'ahu and Kaua'i, in zones with high potential for wet taro cultivation. Construction of extensive valley irrigation systems proceeded in lockstep with population growth throughout the thirteenth and fourteenth centuries. By AD 1400, major irrigation complexes were already in place on windward O'ahu and in the large windward Moloka'i valleys such as Wailau. Expansion into dryland zones more amenable to intensive sweet potato farming did not begin until the population growth curve was already bending steeply upward, around AD 1400. But throughout the fifteenth century, vast tracts in leeward Hawai'i and Maui islands, and on Kalaupapa Peninsula of Moloka'i, began to be converted into intensive dryland field systems.

Several major transformations followed in the sixteenth and seventeenth centuries. Some of these are encoded in the Native Hawaiian genealogies of chiefly succession and in the *mo'olelo* of wars of conquest and consolidation of kingdoms. Others are evidenced by the megalithic foundations of *heiau* and royal centers that are dated by archaeology to this later time frame. It seems probable that the consolidation of formerly independent political units on Hawai'i and Maui islands was achieved, for the first time, under the respective rules of 'Umi and Pi'ilani. Using the 20-year generation time span, this period dates to approximately AD 1570 to 1590 in the relative chronology (Table 3.1). The latter half of the sixteenth century also accords well with the archaeological evidence for the rapid imposition of a functionally complex temple system in Kahikinui District of Maui (Kirch and Sharp 2005). Political consolidation of O'ahu had actually occurred somewhat earlier (between approximately AD 1490 and 1510), with Mā'ilikūkahi, who by traditional account first devised the *ahupua'a* system of land divisions. This earlier islandwide unification on O'ahu is

Tracking the Transformations

entirely understandable in light of the "jump start" that that island's economy had in the development of its large-scale irrigation works. But I would argue that it was with the consolidation of the Maui and Hawai'i kingdoms, with their vast dryland field systems and significantly larger overall populations, that we see the emergence of divine kingship and archaic states in the Hawaiian Islands.

Of course, the emergence of archaic states in Hawai'i—as surely elsewhere in the world—was a process rather than an event. Thus while we may speak of the polities of 'Umi and Pi'ilani as, for the first time, "kingdoms," no doubt the full trappings of the Hawaiian form of divine kingship witnessed by Cook in 1778 to 1779 continued to develop during the reigns of their successors over the next two centuries. But the archaeological evidence from, for example, the great state temples of Pihana, Haleki'i, Pi'ilanihale, and Lo'alo'a on Maui, speak to the role of monumental architecture and the ritual control that it implies, which was certainly in place by AD 1600 to 1650. Thus to put the question of "when" archaic states emerged in the course of Hawaiian history into the context of the culture-historical framework outlined in Table 4.1 at the beginning of this chapter, they are detectable through their manifestations of monumentality by the close of the Late Expansion Period.

After AD 1650, give or take a decade or two, the world of ancient Hawai'i could no longer be said to conform to the classic structures of Polynesian social and political organization that had been inherited from the Western Polynesian and Lapita homelands two millennia earlier. Everything was different, just as—in the French proverb—everything was the same. People still went about their daily lives in much the same manner, farming their dryland plots and tending their irrigated patches, pulling fish from the sea in nets and with hooks, cooking food in earth ovens. But the ancient *mata-kainanga groups that had controlled valleys and sections of land by virtue of ascent from common ancestors no longer ceased to function as they had in earlier generations. The people at large were now called maka'āinana by the king and chiefs; the word remained yet its meaning had changed radically. The common "people" (nā kanaka) were now expected to offer up a regular portion of their crops and fishing catches to supply the royal and chiefly households (nā li'i), and in exchange were assured their right to work their lands.

The chiefly establishments were growing increasingly large and inclined toward a preindustrial mode of conspicuous consumption. The age-old system of *tapu, whereby the mana of the chief was protected so that his people could enjoy the fruits of the land was becoming increasingly manipulated into the new system of *kapu*, elaborated along the hierarchical dimension of genealogical rank. It was no longer sufficient merely to respect the protocols of deference with respect to the chief's body and especially his head, found throughout all Polynesian societies. Now the highest ranking *ali'i* proclaimed themselves to be *ali'i kapu*, sacred chiefs, and the new category of *pi'o* was invented, as special marriages among the kingly blood lines were arranged to concentrate their *mana*. These *ali'i* could not even be gazed on by the *maka'āinana*. Protected in their royal centers, these *ali'i akua*, literally "god-kings," depended on the newly elaborated state cults of Kū and Lono, supported by specialized cadres of priests who carried out rituals demanding increasingly onerous quantities of sacrificial offerings—pigs, dogs, fish, coconuts in the four hundreds each.

The Protohistoric Period witnessed the further elaboration of this new world of divine kings and their consolidated islandwide polities. Not that everything always went in favor of the ruling elite. On Hawai'i Island in particular, the vast scale of managing a polity encompassing 10,658 km^2 and upward of 150,000 people proved a persistent challenge to an emergent state structure that had neither draft animals nor wheeled transport to effect rapid communication. Throughout the Protohistoric Period, Hawai'i Island cycled through unification and fission, frequently unable to maintain the overarching control first achieved by 'Umi. But elsewhere, consolidation held. The Maui kings began campaigns of aggressive territorial expansion, seizing Moloka'i and O'ahu. Hawai'i, fearing it too might be swallowed up by the expanding Maui kingdom, launched its own wars of aggression against the latter. When Cook arrived in 1779, King Kalani'ōpu'u had taken Hāna District and was locked in a stalemate against his Maui rival Kahekili.

We have arrived, it seems, at a point where Sahlins's "if, how, and when" questions have been answered, if not to complete satisfaction, then at least to the point of defensible argument. To historians or humanists content with a strictly narrative mode of analysis, this may be the end of the road. Note that Sahlins did not include, in the paragraph I have (perhaps unfairly) reified to an epistemological challenge, the simple word "why." On this humble yet formidable "why" rests the distinction between historical description and social science, the issue of whether anything in the past can be said to transcend the particular and the contingent, to inform us more generally about the world as we construct it and as it constrains us. It is to this challenge of explanation, of the generalized "why," that I now turn.

CHAPTER 5

The Challenge of Explanation

As to why in ancient times a certain class of people were ennobled and made into *ali'i*, and another class into subjects *(kanaka)*, why a separation was made between chiefs and commoners, has never been explained. Perhaps in the earliest time all the people were *ali'i* and it was only after the lapse of several generations that a division was made into commoners and chiefs.

Malo (1951:60)

As it is important to the public to be governed only by a single one, it also matters to it that the person performing this function should be so elevated above the others, that no-one can be confused or compared with him.

Louis XIV, King of France (in Elias 1983:118)

In preceding chapters, I have endeavored to show how historical anthropology can address the challenge posed by Marshall Sahlins, that "no one knows, when, how, or if" a radical transformation of Hawaiian society had occurred sometime prior to the arrival of Captain Cook in 1778. Applying a multifaceted triangulation approach, it is possible to demonstrate not only that a fundamental transformation in Hawaiian economic, social, and political structures occurred, but that the timing of these changes was between the late sixteenth and early seventeenth centuries AD. But if historical anthropology also aims to produce a scientific account of cultural change, more than a descriptive historical narrative, then we must address not only how and when Hawai'i was transformed in the course of a few critical centuries, but *why* this particular Polynesian society out of so many others crossed the gulf between kinship and kingship, chiefdom and archaic state.

In this concluding chapter, my aim is to explore the connections between certain long-term, deep-time processes and the short-time, historically contingent events and actions, both of which were essential to the emergence of a uniquely Hawaiian form of archaic state out of a more ancient Polynesian chiefdom structure. As Flannery (1999) has argued, process and agency should be seen as complementary, rather than competing, perspectives. I further argue that any compelling theory of change must attend to both *ultimate* and *proximate* causations, to long-term context and process, and to short-term dynamism and agency. I borrow this essential distinction between ultimate and proximate causation from Ernst Mayr, who offered the following advice with respect to explanatory models in science:

> It is nearly always possible to give both a proximate and an ultimate causation as the explanation for a given biological phenomenon. . . . Many famous controversies in the history of biology came about because one party considered only proximate causations and the other party considered only evolutionary ones. One of the special properties of the living world is that it has these two sets of causations. (Mayr 1997:67)

Mayr's advice is, I believe, equally applicable to the challenges of explaining cultural and social change, such as the transformation of a classic Polynesian chiefdom into an emergent archaic state. For Hawai'i, aspects of long-term, ultimate causation will likely include the demographic transition from a small, density-independent founding population to one that was both large and increasingly density-dependent; the landscape scale biogeographic and biogeochemical gradients that structured and constrained Hawaiian production systems across the archipelago; and the different pathways of agricultural intensification, in wet and dryland systems. It must also take account of deeply ingrained cultural structures, such as the birth rank ordering and status rivalry that pervade Austronesian and Polynesian societies. At the same time, a model that would situate causality exclusively in these ultimate factors will fall short of constituting an adequate theory of change. What happened in Hawai'i in the fifteenth and sixteenth centuries cannot be modeled only as a set of linkages between these long-term constraints and processes. Proximate causation—operating within the larger context just cited—must also have its due, and must be situated in individual historical actors, themselves engaged with manipulating, constructing, and reconstructing their social and political world, as praxis theory insists (Giddens 1979; Bourdieu 1977; Ortner 1984; Sahlins 2004). Fortunately, in the case of Hawai'i, unlike other pristine states that emerged

The Challenge of Explanation 179

and collapsed millennia ago, we have the advantage of a window into this world of agency, of political power, and of proximate causation, through the rich oral histories of the Hawaiian people, and through the ethnohistory of first contact. That leaders such as 'Umi and Pi'ilani changed the course of Hawaiian history through their actions cannot be denied. Yet their generation occupied a critical time and place that was not random, but rather the outcome of a long-term contingent history of which they were the inheritors.

PREVIOUS EXPLANATIONS FOR HAWAIIAN
CULTURAL CHANGE

Several scholars have tackled the problem of how Hawai'i came to be the most socially and politically complex of all Polynesian groups. To be sure, not all of them regarded late Hawaiian polities as archaic states; several consider Hawai'i to have been an exemplar of a "complex chiefdom" stage in political evolution. Regardless of where they would place Hawai'i in a taxonomy of political types, their theories of how and why Hawaiian society and politics changed over time are worth reviewing for the insights they bring to our quest for explanatory understanding. The work of four scholars has been particularly influential: Irving Goldman, Marshall Sahlins, Robert Hommon, and Timothy Earle. Goldman and Sahlins base their analyses largely on the documentary and ethnographic records. Hommon and Earle are archaeologists who have conducted fieldwork in Hawai'i, and have both offered theoretical models of the changes in Hawaiian society.[1]

Irving Goldman: Status Rivalry and Segmentary Organization

Goldman (1955, 1970) applied a classic comparative approach in his study of cultural evolution in Polynesia, including Hawai'i. Working within a mid-twentieth century evolutionary paradigm, Goldman classified the Polynesian societies into three groups, based on the degree of hierarchy and stratification: Traditional, Open, and Stratified (see Kirch 1984: Table 2). The traditional societies had changed the least from a putative ancestral form, Open societies were in various forms of flux or transformation, and the Stratified societies were the most "evolved." Only Tonga, the Society Islands (Tahiti), and Hawai'i were included in the Stratified category, and Goldman regards Hawai'i as having achieved an apogee of political development: "Polynesian social evolution reached its greatest development in the Hawaiian Islands, where all changes in direction or further elaborations of traditional forms under way elsewhere finally came to fruition" (1970:200). Goldman remarks expressly on the character of divine kingship in Hawai'i: "The power of the chief had become equivalent to the power of a god" (1970:218). With this power came a new system of landholding, in which "land tenure was no longer the organic product of pedigree" as it remained in the Traditional and Open societies. Goldman saw this change in the Hawaiian land tenure system as "nothing short of a revolutionary demonstration of personal power" of the god-king (1970:225). Moreover, he recognized that this change in the land system was mirrored in a transformation of "descent group organization" that now "diverged so strongly from the traditional Polynesian type that at first glance Hawaii seems altogether unrelated in this aspect to Polynesia generally" (1970:233).

For Goldman, the driving engine of social and political change in Polynesia was "status rivalry," accompanied by the efforts of chiefs to control the means of production and hence the economy as a whole. "Status rivalry makes its demands upon the economy, upon primary sources of wealth, upon land and upon crop" (1970:484). In Goldman's view, status rivalry "sets political evolution in motion," and this in turn drives the development of the economic forces (1970:486). As the productive apparatus came increasingly under chiefly control, earlier institutions of "first-fruits" offerings to chiefs (given by commoners who were related to the chiefs as kinsfolk) became transformed into compulsory systems of tribute. "What had been a freely given religious offering became a tax" (1970:509); once again, Hawai'i carried this change to the furthest extent, in the institution of the Makahiki (1970:511).

Ultimately, for Goldman, the economic changes set in motion by status rivalry had their most profound implications for the "transformation of the segmentary organization, the main area of enlargement and diversification" (1970:542). By segmentary organization Goldman meant the very kinship structure of ancient Polynesian society, based on the concepts of ascent groups (Proto Polynesian *kainanga and *kaainga, see Chapter 1). Here, echoing Burrows's (1939) earlier arguments about "breed and border" in Polynesia, Goldman remarks on the shift from a biological imagery of segmental unity, to the spatial and explicitly territorial imagery of contact-era Hawai'i (1970:544). It was in this fundamental shift from a segmentary system based on kinship, to one based on territories controlled by chiefs, that Goldman sees Hawai'i pushing Polynesian cultural evolution to its extreme:

> The major change, of course, has been in actual social arrangements. The substitution of a territorial system of subdivision for one of kinship branching has long been regarded as a major divide in human history. Apart from introducing new structural arrangements of great importance, this change has introduced a parallel change in outlook—apart from the specific imagery implied by terminology—from that of a natural to a political order. Kin groups bud, branch, and unfold. Territorial groups are created by chiefs. They express human agency. In this expression, they assert a radically new social idea. (1970:544–45)

In Goldman's analysis, only Hawai'i made this break with the old segmentary order "completely" (1970:546).

Marshall Sahlins: From Energy to Agency

Sahlins's first major contribution to Polynesian studies was a comparative analysis of social stratification (Sahlins 1958; see also Sahlins and Service 1960). Like Goldman, Sahlins classified the Polynesian societies into four groups based on their degree of stratification. Hawai'i (along with Tonga, Tahiti, and Samoa) was part of his Group I, exhibiting the most elaborate indices of hierarchy. Building on the theory of his mentor Leslie White (1949), who linked cultural development to energy capture, Sahlins found a strong positive correlation in the ethnohistoric literature on Hawai'i between productivity and stratification (Sahlins 1958: Table 1). "Within Group I, Hawaii was rated as most stratified, a rating duplicated in productivity" (1958:114). He recognized that "productivity" was a function of both the environment ("diversity of rich environmental zones" [1958:126]) and of available technology, such as irrigation. "Hawaii with its large-scale irrigation techniques and conscious and effective utilization of small ecological niches (such as the use of irrigation banks for secondary crops) stands above the field" (1958:127).

Sahlins realized that it was not just productivity per se, but the *surplus* that could be captured and used by chiefs to advance their own economic and political agendas that provided a key linkage between productivity and stratification. He invoked Polanyi's (1944) concept of *redistribution* to make the case for how Polynesian chiefs manipulated the power of surplus.[2] "The intimate relationship between productivity and stratification is intelligible in Polynesia because of the fact that a redistributive economic system prevailed in these islands" (1958:250). In short, Hawai'i's high degree of stratification was achieved by the power that chiefs acquired through effective redistribution of surplus, the latter made possible by a naturally rich environment exploited through efficient technology.

In the early 1970s, Sahlins bequeathed White's evolutionary paradigm to the archaeologists,[3] and situated himself at the forefront of a new paradigm of cultural theory, structuralist yet incorporating a historical dynamic, Marxist yet not materially deterministic.[4] In *Stone Age Economics* (1972), Sahlins foregrounds Hawai'i in tackling the problem of transformation from a "domestic mode of production" (DMP) to a larger political economy. He argued that "primitive economies" have a natural tendency toward underproduction. "Labor power is underused, technological means are not fully engaged, natural resources are left untapped" (1972:41). Yet time and again in the course of human history, the antisurplus inclination of the DMP is countered by a "grand strategy of economic intensification [that] enlists social structures beyond the family and cultural superstructures beyond the productive practice" (1972:102).

In a key section of *Stone Age Economics* subtitled "the economic intensity of the political order" (1972:130–48), Sahlins uses Polynesian ethnography to illustrate how, in his words,

> [i]n the course of primitive social evolution, main control over the domestic economy seems to pass from the formal solidarity of the kinship structure to its political aspect. As the structure is politicized, especially as it is centralized in ruling chiefs, the household economy is mobilized in a larger social cause. (1972:130)

Echoes of Sahlins's earlier emphasis on surplus and redistribution can be found in this text, as he contrasts the political economy of "big-men" systems with that of chieftainship. Chiefs *inherit* their power, and "the people owe in advance their labor and their products" (1972:139), thus allowing the chief to institute a "public economy greater than the sum of its household parts" (1972:140). But here Sahlins openly refutes his earlier view of a "mechanical" attribution of the "appearance of chieftainship to the production of surplus," arguing that the equation is "rather the other way around." It is the chiefship itself that generates surplus. "The development of rank and chieftainship becomes, *pari passu*, development of the productive forces" (1972:140).

Hawai'i once again occupies a key role, for it takes "the primitive contradiction between the domestic and public economies to an ultimate

The Challenge of Explanation   183

crisis—revealatory [sic] it seems not only of this disconformity but of the economic and political limits of kinship society" (1972:141). Sahlins brings *competition* into the transformational equation, competition between chiefs not only for economic development, but for control over even marginal ecological spaces. Over time, a "bloated political establishment" emerges, funded on the backs of the common people and—lacking a true monopoly of force—maintains its authority "by an awesome display of conspicuous consumption as intimidating to the people as it was glorifying to the chiefs" (1972:145). By now, the heightened demands of the emerging chiefly economy, grating against the inherent antisurplus tendencies of the DMP, inevitably lead to resistance on the part of the people. Talk of rebellion is in the air, always dangerous when junior siblings are ready to pounce on any opportunity to usurp the chiefship. Rather than lessen their demands for surplus, the ruling chiefs attempt to further expand their dominions:

> Conscious, it seems, of the logistic burdens they were obliged to impose, the Hawaiian chiefs conceived several means to relieve the pressure, notably including a career of conquest with a view toward enlarging the tributary base. In the successful event, however, with the realm now stretched over distant and lately subdued hinterlands, the bureaucratic costs of rule apparently rose higher than the increases in revenue, so that the victorious chief merely succeeded in adding enemies abroad to a worse unrest at home. The cycles of centralization and exaction are now at their zenith. (1972:145)

Not remarked in Sahlins's account is that these "cycles of centralization and exaction" are largely confined in protohistory to the vast Hawai'i Island polity, but which in his account becomes generalized to the entire archipelago. The fact that Maui, or O'ahu, had held together as unified polities over many generations is overlooked, a key fact that contradicts Sahlins's interpretation of Hawai'i having reached a threshold that was "the boundary of primitive society itself" (1972:148). Sahlins claims that the Hawaiian chiefs were not kings. "They had not broken structurally with the people at large, so they might dishonor the kinship morality only on pain of a mass disaffection" (1972:148). Left unremarked, however, is abundant evidence that the Hawaiian *ali'i* had in fact already "broken structurally" with the *maka'āinana*, as previous chapters in this book have argued.[5]

In a still unpublished manuscript, which he graciously made available to me on being told that I was writing this book, Sahlins addresses anew the problem of the structural relations between Hawaiian chiefs and the people (Sahlins MS). He begins by observing that the Hawaiians have a distinctly politicized concept of "the people," *nā kanaka*, which stands in opposition to "the chiefs," *nā li'i*, noting that this is unusual for a supposedly "kinship society." Remarking further on the absence of descent groups, the territorial organization of land and society, and on the absence of ancestors (i.e., genealogies) among the people, Sahlins writes:

> To my knowledge, no one has explicitly remarked on this Polynesian invention of "the people"—a development which was approximated in Tonga and Tahiti. Perhaps it has been too obvious to be perceived by Western scholars who live in political societies constituted on the presumption of such an entity. Still the invention of the people would be of no small interest to the study of state formation. (MS:2)

Once again invoking Burrows's notions of "breed and border," Sahlins goes on to observe that the fundamental shift underpinning a distinct concept of "the people" is the movement from kinship to territory, from "clan to class" (MS:9). He writes:

> Kinship to territory seems like a huge social revolution, which in some ways it is, but Hawaiian materials suggest the actual dynamics may be relatively simple. Territoriality does not change: The key move is the break in the genealogical connection between the ruling chiefs and the underlying people. In the political event, extensive relationships of genealogical kinship cum differential rank become characteristic of the chiefs alone—who indeed become an aristocracy of political consciousness and strategic knowledge.... The structure that was then precipitated from this relatively simple move had *evident similarities to class systems and state formations.* (MS: 9-10, emphasis added)

Thus, Sahlins concludes, if the Hawaiians "did not achieve state formation as such ... they did develop a genuine political society" (MS:23).

Robert Hommon: The Limited Land Hypothesis

Robert Hommon has consistently asserted that by the time of first contact with Europeans, Hawaiian polities had already undergone a transformation from chiefdoms to states. Hommon's unpublished 1976 doctoral dissertation, *The Formation of Primitive States in Pre-Contact Hawai'i*, is certainly the most extensive prior treatise on the subject. The work was innovative in its integration of Hawaiian oral traditions with the then newly emerging archaeological data on Hawaiian settlement patterns.[6] A decade later, Hommon (1986) summarized the key elements of his thesis, augmented by more archeological data. Hommon has continued to write about social evolution in Hawai'i (e.g., Hommon 1996, 2001), and recently outlined a research design for testing what he calls the "limited land hypothesis," a pivotal element in his theory of Hawaiian state emergence (Hommon 2008). Hommon's model is framed in terms of a three phase chronological sequence, which I now briefly outline.[7]

Phase I (AD 500–1400). This phase encompassed the initial arrival of Polynesians, probably from the Marquesas Islands, and "the establishment of coastal settlements throughout the island group" (1986:60). Hommon suggests that there was steady population growth throughout Phase I, accompanied by continued exploration and settlement of the coastal zones, with occupation concentrated in "salubrious" core regions. These environmentally favored regions in which population was concentrated became the basis for later territorial districts. "It seems reasonable to suggest that each of these proto-districts was the homeland of an archaic *maka'ainana*" (1986:61). By the term "archaic *maka'āinana*" Hommon implied that at this early stage Hawaiian society was still structured around classic Polynesian ascent groups, which controlled access to land.[8] More specifically, he argues that *ahupua'a* territories, as these are known at the time of European contact, "had not yet formed before the end of the fourteenth century" (1986:61).

Phase II (AD 1400–1600). A key element in Hommon's model of Hawaiian sociopolitical evolution is what he initially termed the "inland expansion" hypothesis. The proximate cause for this expansion was situated in "the need for additional food for a continually growing population" (1986:64).[9] For Hommon, such inland population expansion simultaneously lay the groundwork for the formation of the *ahupua'a* territorial system, and for the "disintegration" of the archaic *maka'āinana* social organization:

> About AD 1400 the coastal population began to expand inland... throughout the fifteenth and sixteenth centuries. With inland expansion, the pattern of economic exploitation, formerly confined in most areas to the coastal zone was extended along a *makai-mauka* (coastal-inland) axis. The establishment of the permanent inland agricultural fields necessitated at least temporary or seasonal residence in the inland zone, which in turn stimulated the development of a distribution system that provided inland produce (including goods from the forest) to the coast and coastal produce to the inland area. Since most of the basic resources were available within the borders of most *ahupua'a*, the *ahupua'a*-pattern of economic self-sufficiency was developed. As economic interests came to be concentrated

within the confines of the developing *ahupua'a*, a strong tendency toward endogamy within its boundaries functioned to integrate the *ahupua'a* community. With increasing *ahupua'a*-endogamy the kinship ties that had once linked one coastal community with another began to disintegrate.

The disintegration of the "archaic *maka'ainana*" was paralleled by a widening gap between chief and commoner as the concept of kinship centered increasingly within the local community. The practice of hypergamy for preservation of rank reinforcing endogamy within the *ali'i* as a social stratum also hastened the formation of socioeconomic classes. (1976:230–31)

By AD 1600, the "cleavage between commoners and chiefs had advanced to such an extent that the control exercised by the chiefs was no longer based on kinship" (1976:231). For Hommon, the developments of Phase II were the necessary precursors to the formation of "primitive states" in the succeeding Phase III.

Phase III (AD 1600–1778). By the beginning of this final phase in his evolutionary sequence, Hommon believes that the population had increased "at least four-fold," and was accompanied by "the development of large, productive agricultural complexes in the salubrious core regions of the districts" (1986:65). In defining the critical developments of this phase, Hommon drew on Hawaiian oral traditions, which he interpreted as including "the earliest examples of expansion of political boundaries through force ... and the first demonstration of the application of superior power to attain the office of *ali'i nui*" (1976:279). He was, of course, referring to the traditions of 'Umi-a-Līloa, Keawenui-a-'Umi, Lonoikamakahiki and other *ali'i* of the seventeenth century. Hommon also speculated that "these early instances of conquest, usurpation, and rebellion may have been precipitated by shortages resulting ultimately from the inland expansion" process (1986:67).

In his most recent work, Hommon (2008) retains the core of his original model, but introduces some new elements. He suggests that the sweet potato, quintessential crop of the dryland agricultural zones (and hence critical to the success of inland expansion in the leeward regions), may not have been introduced into Hawai'i until the thirteenth century (Hommon 2008:69–70).[10] In this, Hommon follows Green's recent arguments regarding sweet potato transfers within Polynesia (Green 2005). Hommon implies that such late arrival of the sweet potato spurred agricultural expansion into leeward regions, especially on Hawai'i and Maui, after AD 1400. While this is plausible, in my view the evidence is as yet too circumstantial to reach a definitive conclusion regarding the date of sweet potato transfer to Hawai'i.

More importantly, Hommon has amended his original "inland expansion" hypothesis, renaming it the "limited land" hypothesis to draw attention to the increasing evidence that by the mid-sixteenth century Hawaiian agriculture had reached the spatial limits to expansion. He states the hypothesis formally as follows: "By AD 1550 ancient Hawaiian agricultural expansion slowed significantly as it approached effective limits on staple production imposed by available technology, sociopolitical factors, and natural variables including rainfall and soil fertility" (2008:4). Some years ago I made essentially the same proposal regarding the dryland field systems based on evidence available by the early 1980s (Kirch 1984:189). Hommon has elaborated this hypothesis, however, laying out a detailed research design by which it may be further tested through ongoing archaeological work in the islands. From the perspective of explanatory theory, Hommon explicitly links the arrival at a point of limited land to (1) a significant slowing in the rate of population growth, and (2) the rise of conquest warfare (2008:23–25). Indeed, war is seen as "a continuation of agricultural expansion by other means" (2008:25). Hommon has also recently suggested that the end of a phase of rapid agricultural expansion (which he calls a "boom" phase), which terminated around AD 1550, was followed by a period of significantly reduced agricultural production (a "bust" phase), precipitating a crisis among the ruling *ali'i* and giving further impetus to conquest warfare (Hommon 2009).

Timothy Earle: The Sources of Chiefly Power

In 1971 to 1972, Earle investigated the archaeological remains of irrigation systems in Halele'a district on Kaua'i Island (Earle 1973, 1978). Although he did not continue his fieldwork in Hawai'i, Earle has repeatedly drawn on Hawaiian data in his research on the comparative evolution of chiefdoms. His earlier writings stress the significance of irrigation as the main source of economic surplus and political power for the chiefs (Earle 1973, 1978, 1980); and the importance of redistribution in the functioning of the Hawaiian political hierarchy (Earle 1977). Firmly situated in the theoretical camp of evolutionary anthropology (see Johnson and Earle 2000), Earle has consistently classified the Hawaiian polities as chiefdoms, while acknowledging that Hawai'i pushes the boundary that divides chiefdoms from states.[11]

For Earle, Hawai'i represents an archetypical staple-finance chiefdom, in which "chiefs created an intensive production system relying on irrigation, dryland terraces, and fishponds" (1997:210).[12] Drawing on theoretical discussions of the role of power in the political process (e.g., Mann 1986), Earle (1997) seeks to explore the sources of power that chiefs exploited in three chiefdom societies: Kaua'i, the Mantaro Valley of Peru, and Thy, Denmark. He identifies three primary kinds of power: economic, military, and ideological, examining each in turn.

Earle's examination of Hawaiian *economic* power (1997:75–89) perpetuates his irrigation-centric perspective. Thus he writes: "The Hawaiian case illustrates how irrigation technology served as a source of economic control in the emergence of complex chiefdoms" (1997:75). To be sure, Earle acknowledges that irrigation was unevenly distributed across the Hawaiian archipelago, and that on Hawai'i Island—where the largest chiefdoms were situated—"irrigation was highly localized and comparatively unimportant" (1997:83). But Earle argues that the intensified dryland systems "had characteristics similar to those of irrigation" because they constituted permanently subdivided and therefore "owned landscapes" (1997:84). In this I agree with Earle that "even for the intensified dryland farming areas, the physical nature of the built landscape created the basis for a land-tenure system not unlike that founded on the irrigation facilities" (1997:85). It is certainly true that a similar territorial hierarchy of *kīhāpai* and *mo'o* plots, nested within an *'ili*, and those in turn nested within *ahupua'a* and *moku*, held for both the wet and dryland landscapes. Yet, Earle's downplaying of the significant differences in the capacity for surplus production in the wet and dry systems paints a monolithic portrait of Hawaiian political economy. And in so doing it masks the critical dynamic tension between those polities fueled primarily by irrigation (O'ahu and Kaua'i) and those dependent on the lower-yielding and more risk-prone dryland systems (Maui and Hawai'i).

Earle's view on the causes underlying intensification of agricultural production in Hawai'i is noteworthy: "It was not a response to population growth" (1997:87). Not that Earle is unaware of the archaeological evidence for significant population increase in Hawaiian prehistory (he cites Dye and Komori [1992] and reproduces their population curve in his Fig. 2.9). But Earle sees intensification as driving population growth: "An increasing dependence on agriculture supported the spread of population through the islands, and, after AD 1200, rapidly expanding populations *required* sustained agricultural intensification" (1997:41, emphasis added). Seeing the Hawaiian case as a prime example of "staple finance," for Earle the intensified production systems were "the very essence of the ordered political economy" (1997:201):

> The origin of the agricultural systems becomes a question of great theoretical significance; they were the ultimate linchpin of the power strategy. The extensive complexes of Hawaiian agriculture were constructed over a relatively brief period. This was not a slow process, gradually solving local problems. It was rapid, a development initiated and overseen by chiefs and their konohiki in the system of staple finance that sustained the evolution of Hawaiian political institutions. (1997:201)

Not that Earle dismisses the two other sources of power—military and ideological—for the Hawaiian chiefs, although for him the Hawaiian power strategy "came eventually to rest firmly on the intensive agricultural facilities" (1997:202). Thus the role that Earle envisions for warfare in ancient Hawai'i was closely tied to agriculture. Conquest warfare "did not seek land primarily, but the improved productive facilities (agricultural fields and fishponds) and commoner labor that produced the 'surplus' that financed the political economy" (1997:132). War was the means of control over the system of staple finance (1997:142).

Earle's discussion of the role of ideology in the Hawaiian political economy builds on concepts from "practice theory" (Bourdieu 1977; Giddens 1979; Ortner 1984; Geertz 1980) and on his own work on "materialization" (DeMarrais et al. 1996), the way that abstract values are translated into and reinforced by material objects. For Earle, the secret of ideology as a power strategy lies in the *public presentation* of the systems of ideas and beliefs, through ceremonies, displays, and other occasions, these being "created and manipulated strategically by . . . the ruling elite, to establish and maintain positions of social power" (1997:149). As DeMarrais et al. argue, it is especially through the manipulation of the built environment, such as public monuments, that ideology is materialized, thus reinforcing "appropriate" values and even dogmas. Earle suggests that materialization operates through three key forms: (1) public ceremonial events; (2) symbolic objects; and (3) cultural landscapes.

Earle argues that ideology and its materialization in Hawaiian power strategies fundamentally reinforced the agricultural base. The major public ceremonies were the annual rituals of the Lono and Kū cults, the first essential to agriculture and the second to war (the means to capture agricultural resources). Hawaiian chiefs used their "elaborate feather cloaks" as material symbols of their god-like status: "The cloak was an ultimate power dress, signifying the sacred and potent persona of its owner" (1997:173). But more than anything else, Earle sees Hawaiian ideology as materialized in its cultural landscapes. *Heiau* were one component of these landscapes, the stone temples that as permanent and impressive monuments provided the stage settings for the chiefs' ritual performances.[13] But Earle does not regard the *heiau* as the most significant materialization of ideology in Hawai'i; this was instead "the building of the agricultural facilities on which the political economy was based" (1997:179). It was this formalized, socially and politically codified, and materially demarcated agricultural landscape that translated ideology into power:

> Property rights became formalized, given permanency, in the constructed, productive facilities—the irrigation systems, the fishponds, and the fenced house lots. Who a person was, how he supported his family, and how he sustained his chiefs were written in the landscape by the construction of the community's facilities. The symbolic order was thus grounded and subsumed within the everyday practice of ritual and subsistence labor in the monuments and fields of the chiefs. (1997:183–84)

Goldman, Sahlins, Hommon, and Earle have all drawn attention to elements of the Hawaiian case that are important in constructing a robust explanatory model of the emergence of archaic states. Goldman emphasizes proximate causation in the form of classic Polynesian status rivalry. Sahlins shows how competition between chiefs worked to counter the antisurplus tendencies of a domestic mode of production, thus creating a true political economy. Hommon situates changes in Hawaiian society in time and space, placing much explanatory weight on the ultimate causal factor of limited land (not unlike Carneiro's well known "circumscription theory [1970]). And Earle looks to the proximate sources of chiefly power, and how these were strategically applied to political ends. These are all significant insights but require further integration, which can be provided by drawing on Mayr's critical distinction between ultimate and proximate causation.

ULTIMATE CAUSATION: POPULATION, INTENSIFICATION, AND SURPLUS

Some causal role for population growth is implicit in the theories of Goldman and Sahlins, and explicit in the writings of Hommon and Earle. But where Hommon sees rapid doubling of population as a "push" factor (2008:2), Earle argues that population increase was a consequence of chiefly investment in agricultural intensification (1997:41). Of course, such debates are unique neither to Hawai'i nor to discussions of social change and political economy in general. Their intellectual roots can be traced back at least to Malthus (1798) and Ricardo (1821), the former known for his observation that whereas human reproduction has the potential to expand exponentially, increases in the food supply are typically arithmetic.[14] Hence the classic notion of periodic "Malthusian" checks on population growth resulting from food shortage, famine, and the like. Boserup (1965) seemed to counter Malthus by arguing that technology and innovation may head off the inevitable Malthusian crunch, and her theory inspired a considerable debate over the processes of agricultural "intensification" (Spooner 1972; Brookfield 1972, 1984; Morrison 1994; Kirch 1994).

Demographers Lee (1986) and Wood (1998) have developed models that to a certain degree reconcile apparent conflicts in the Malthus-Boserup theories. Wood in particular describes a "Malthus-and-Boserup (MaB) ratchet" in which technological advances allow for "a Boserupian escape from the Malthusian trap" (1998:113), although such an escape can only be temporary. I make use of the MaB ratchet concept shortly. Most recently Tuljapurkar and his colleagues (Lee and Tuljapurkar 2008; Puleston and Tuljapurkar 2008; Lee, Puleston, and Tuljapurkar 2009), working within the framework of our Hawai'i Biocomplexity Project, have refined these demographic models so as to formally integrate food supply and vital rates including fertility and mortality. The combined work of all these demographers allows us to move beyond the "chicken and egg" conundrum of whether population drives agricultural intensification or vice versa (as in the contrastive views of Hommon and Earle on Hawai'i). Instead, economic change, well-being (as indexed by the food supply and its effect on vital rates), and population pressure must be seen as linked by a set of feedback loops such that "no single factor is either wholly prior as a cause or wholly posterior as an effect" (Wood 1998:117).

That the Polynesian population of Hawai'i grew enormously from the period of first colonization until its peak at the time of European contact is abundantly evident. In Chapter 4 I reviewed the substantial body of empirical data that not only documents such demographic increase, but also strongly supports an interpretation of a major phase of exponential population growth beginning around AD 1200 and continuing until around the mid-sixteenth century, when the rate of increase certainly declined, and may have stabilized in some areas.

Two demographic factors are critical to our understanding of the emergence of archaic states in Hawai'i: the first is the overall population size as well as density achieved in late precontact times, and the second is the rate of population growth and how this changed over time. It is almost too obvious to point out that the existence of archaic states in Hawai'i depended on a large population base, which certainly numbered several hundred thousand in aggregate. Best current estimates for the sizes of individual polities are in the range between 60,000 and 150,000 persons (see Table 2.1). These large populations provided the labor force required to construct and maintain the vast agroecosystems and to produce the annual tribute in food and other products that supported the nonproducing elites and fueled the political economy. As Chapter 4 showed, local population density levels were high, ranging from an estimated 50 to 150 persons/km^2 in regions with dryland field systems, up to as many as 500 to 750 persons/km^2 in the irrigated valleys of O'ahu and Kaua'i. Such high density levels lend additional support to Hommon's contention that in late precontact times virtually all of the lands suitable to intensive cultivation had been occupied, and that the limits to expansion (if not to intensification) had already been achieved, given the available level of technology.[15] Without such large and dense populations, the Hawaiian elites simply could not have developed the economic base on which to fund their political aspirations. In short, a demographic transition that resulted in such large populations was a *necessary condition* to the emergence of Hawaiian archaic states. By the same token, it was neither a sufficient condition nor an exclusive "prime mover."

The *rates* of population increase are also significant when considering ultimate causality in Hawaiian sociopolitical evolution. The evidence summarized in Chapter 4 speaks to a phase of exponential population increase between about AD 1200 and 1550, during which the intrinsic rate of increase (r) is estimated to have been in the range of 1.2 to 1.8 percent. During this exponential growth phase, the population was doubling every 40 to 60 years, or every two to three generations. Thus for a period of about three and a half centuries, the Hawaiian polities developed in the context of an *expanding, growth economy*. As I shall argue below, this kind of growth economy has huge potential for the extraction of surplus that can be captured and used by the emerging elites. But by the mid-sixteenth century, the rate of population growth fell significantly, and in some areas (especially the leeward zones dominated by dryland field systems) seems to have leveled off.

The Challenge of Explanation 193

Even where population continued to grow, this was at significantly lower rates. A rapid shift in the inflection point of the Hawaiian population curve is thus a second key aspect of the underlying, or ultimate, factors critical to understanding the emergence of archaic state formations. Our models of preindustrial population dynamics indicate that such a change in the rate of population growth must have been accompanied by a significant change in the well-being of these populations, as indexed by the food ratio, as the population neared an equilibrium saturation point (Wood 1998:107).

The critical linkages between population, land, and intensification can be graphically displayed through the use of a *production function* model. Drawing on Sachs (1966) and Friedman (1979), I used such a model to examine intensification in Polynesian, and especially Hawaiian, dryland agriculture (Kirch 1984:161–65, 181–92; see also Kirch 1994:251–68). Renfrew (1982), working in another island setting, likewise used a production function to model the rise of states in the Aegean. Quite independently, Lee (1986) and Wood (1998) applied the production function on a more general scale in their efforts to reconcile Malthus and Boserup. As Wood puts it, the fundamental concept behind the production function is that "gains in productivity resulting from increasing inputs into an otherwise fixed system of production are not linear but decline as the level of input increases" (1998:105). This nonlinear relationship is well known in economics as the principle of declining marginal productivity, and goes back at least to John Stuart Mill's "Law of Diminishing Returns" (Mill 1848). Figure 5.1 displays

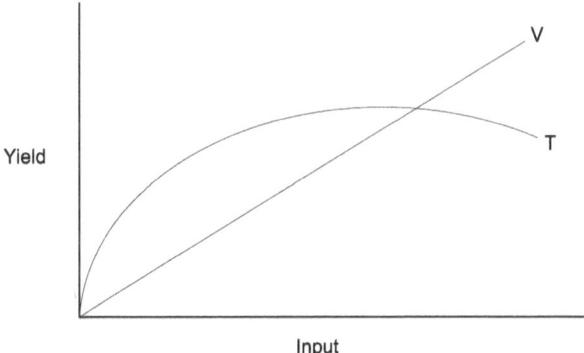

Figure 5.1. The production function T for a given technology shows the relationship between increasing labor inputs and yield, with declining marginal productivity. The line V represents the level of production required for minimal subsistence.

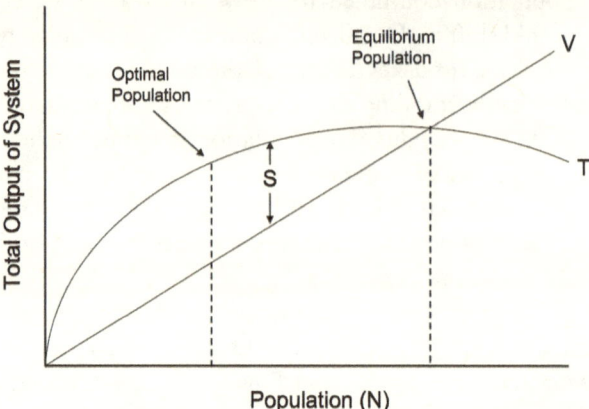

Figure 5.2. The relationship between population and agricultural system output. Surplus (S) is defined as the difference between minimal subsistence production (V) and the production function (T). The optimal population equals the point of maximal surplus production, but this is unstable; equilibrium is reached when T = V.

the basic relationship between output (agricultural yield) and input (in preindustrial societies, typically labor, although this can also refer to capital inputs), with the production function graphed at the curve T. The line V represents the minimal subsistence requirements to maintain the working population.[16] The production function can also be graphed as a relationship between population size (since this is proportional to the labor force) and agricultural system output, as in Figure 5.2. This graph incorporates a definition of surplus (S) as that fraction of output that exceeds the output required for minimal subsistence needs and zero-growth reproduction of the population. Note that there is an optimum population size at which the amount of surplus is maximized. However, for reasons made explicit by both Wood (1998) and Puleston and Tuljapurkar (2008), this optimal population size is not stable, and over time the system will tend toward the only stable equilibrium, which is where T intersects V.[17] This equilibrium point is what Wood calls the "demographic saturation point" of the system, "when the increment in marginal productivity is just enough to allow one more individual to survive and reproduce at levels just sufficient to replace himself or herself exactly" (1998:107). In Puleston and Tuljapurkar's formulation, this is equivalent to the equilibrium food ratio ($\hat{E}$), or "the level of hunger at which vital rates fall to replacement levels" (2008:150).

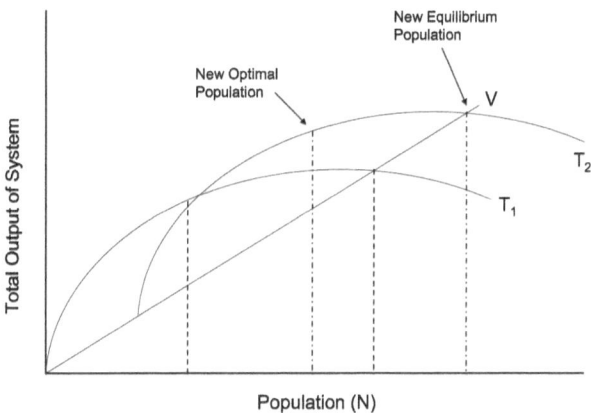

Figure 5.3. The MaB ratchet resulting from intensification of the agricultural system through the application of a new level of technology (T_2).

The closing of the gap between T and V in this model represents the classic Malthusian "scissors," and a population that finds itself at the saturation equilibrium point will be confronted by constant hunger and significant mortality (especially of younger and older cohorts). Here Boserup's (1965) contribution becomes critical, for she demonstrated that innovations such as new crops, new farming technologies, or even changes in labor inputs (such as adding women to a workforce formerly restricted to males) can shift the production function. We can represent such an innovation by the change from T_1 to T_2 in Figure 5.3. With the new technology or other innovation now implemented, the production function shifts to the right, with a new and larger optimal population size (for the same amount of land) and a new equilibrium population. Nonetheless, this shift does not obviate Mill's law of diminishing returns, and in due course the Malthusian scissors will once again begin to clamp down. Thus as Wood points out "over long stretches of time, population and food production may leapfrog over each other, generating ever larger population sizes and more intensive systems of production but never gaining any permanent improvement in well-being" (1998:113).

This periodic "Boserupian escape from the Malthusian trap" is what Wood calls the MaB ratchet. In my view, it is precisely such a periodic turning of this MaB ratchet that is reflected in the archaeological record of agricultural intensification in Hawai'i. On O'ahu and Moloka'i the MaB ratchet is first evident in the landesque capital intensification of the taro irrigation systems, which was underway by AD 1200 and resulted in the construction of extensive valley pondfield systems by

AD 1400 to 1500. On Maui and Hawai'i Islands, the more limited areas for irrigation were probably also developed during this early phase, but it is the later intensification of the vast dryland systems that is so dramatically reflected in the archaeological record. On these large, younger islands, population began expanding out of the limited valley environments by around AD 1400, when cultivation on the leeward slopes is first evidenced. The sequence of agricultural development in leeward Kohala (Ladefoged and Graves 2008) suggests that an initial stage of intensification took place from AD 1400 to 1650, when the geographic limits to the system were probably first reached, followed by a second stage from AD 1650 to contact. During this second stage field plot size was significantly reduced and labor inputs presumably reached their maximum with the use of agronomic strategies such as intensive mulching. Recall as well Kamakau's telling remark that only on the islands of Maui and Hawai'i did women join with men in agricultural field labor (1961:239), something to be anticipated as the MaB ratchet is tightened. In terms of our production function model, such progressive intensification of the major dryland field systems can be seen as sequential turns of the MaB ratchet. These allowed population size to keep expanding, but after each turn of the ratchet the system once again followed the inevitable progression toward marginal returns and an equilibrium saturation point, requiring further adjustments in agronomic methods and/or labor inputs. Indeed, it is questionable whether the MaB ratchet could have been tightened much more in the leeward dryland systems without some exogenous input, such as the introduction of a new crop.

The production function model also allows us to examine the role of surplus, essential to the dynamic political economy within which the Hawaiian archaic states emerged.[18] Anthropologists have long recognized the importance of surplus, that portion of production extending beyond the sphere of the immediate domestic economy (Sahlins's "domestic mode of production" [1972]), which finances the larger political economy and the political aspirations of chiefly elites (Pearson 1957; Polanyi et al. eds., 1957; Dalton 1960; Orans 1966). This is the distinction stressed by Brookfield (1972), in his analysis of agricultural intensification, between "production for use" and "social production." With regard to the latter, Brookfield argues that "inputs may be wildly uneconomic when measured by caloric returns, yet wholly reasonable when measured against social returns" (1972:38). Sahlins recognized that in the inherent tension between the antisurplus tendencies of the domestic mode of production, and the "political pressures that can be mounted

The Challenge of Explanation

on the household economy" lay a key to sociopolitical transformation in chiefdom type societies (1972:82). As the economy is increasingly politicized, household production is more and more co-opted in the service of the elites. Hence, in Sahlins's words, "The development of rank and chieftainship becomes, *pari passu*, development of the productive forces" (1972:130, 140).

Surplus (S), which is output above the level of minimal subsistence and reproduction needs (i.e., the difference between T and V), can be consumed by individual producer households, in which case it will result in an enhanced level of well-being (i.e., less hunger, greater fertility, and decreased mortality). But some portion or even all of S can also be extracted by the nonproducer segment of the population as a tax. Indeed, it was through the formal taxation represented by the Makahiki and other mechanisms of tribute collection that the Hawaiian *ali'i* supported their own elite households and funded their political aspirations. But just as the demographic system is unstable and tends toward equilibrium (at which point S declines to 0), so the level of surplus production is variable over time and will also tend toward the same equilibrium point.

As Friedman (1979:171–74) recognized, we can divide the production function for a particular technology or agricultural regime into a series of regions (shown by the four sectors in Fig. 5.4) that correspond to a hierarchy of additive constraints. Initially, when an agricultural system is first developing and expanding in a new landscape (if land is not yet limiting), as happened on the leeward slopes of Hawai'i and

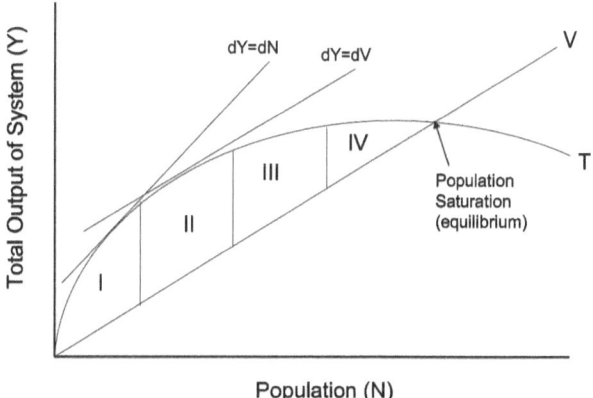

Figure 5.4. The different sectors of surplus production for a particular production function.

Maui in the fifteenth century, surplus can readily be extracted at an *increasing* rate ($d^2S/dY^2 > 0$). Even though they were obligated to turn some of their total production over to the chiefs, the commoner households did not at first suffer, and as the food ratio model predicts, vital rates such as fertility and mortality were not negatively affected. This was the *growth phase* of the political economy, a situation highly favorable to chiefly appropriation of surplus, and to the regularization of surplus extraction as a form of obligatory taxation. The first critical inflection point on the curve was reached when the *rate* of surplus increase relative to labor inputs began to decline ($d^2S/dY^2 < 0$), even though the ratio of surplus to yield remained positive ($dS/dY > 0$). Although the cost of producing a surplus had now increased, and some negative effects both on vital rates and on population well-being began to be felt, the change was presumably subtle and incremental at first, not having too noticeable an impact. The second inflection point was much more critical, for now the real amount of available surplus was declining relative to yield ($dS/dY < 0$), and as the curve trends downward toward $Y = V$, the pressure on farmers became more acute. Elites, who had become accustomed to surplus extraction at a certain level, and who by now had instituted formal structures to ensure such taxation (such as the use of force or punishment in cases where surplus is withheld), would have been resistant to a lowering of their demands. Thus tensions between elites and producers were likely to intensify, especially if the situation was suddenly exacerbated by a crisis, such as a prolonged drought.

When the model shown in Figure 5.4 was first presented some two decades ago (Kirch 1984:162–65: Fig. 50), I argued that the sequence of dryland agricultural intensification for leeward Hawai'i reflected just such a transition from initial high surplus production to an economy in which surplus was beginning to diminish relative to yield. "West Hawai'i may have approached the state where such demand [for surplus] exceeded the ability of the production base to supply it" (Kirch 1984:191). This led me to propose two further hypotheses: (1) that the approaching limits to intensification drove the pattern of "expansionistic warfare and conquest of adjacent political (and economic) territories"; and, (2) that the continued pressures from elites for surplus extraction even in the face of declining yields, helped to explain the "cycle of expansion, rebellion, and contraction of chiefdoms" described in Native Hawaiian political traditions. At the time that these hypotheses were advanced, the best evidence for their support was the emerging archaeological data on

The Challenge of Explanation

progressive subdivision of the Kohala field system into increasingly smaller plot sizes over time (Kirch 1984: Fig. 60), combined with an analysis indicating that the West Hawai'i dryland systems had reached their geographic limits to lateral expansion (i.e., the limits defined by suitable soil and rainfall conditions).

The Hawaiian Biocomplexity Project has now tested this model in new ways that confirm that the late precontact Hawaiian agricultural systems were moving along the trajectory predicted by the model shown in Figure 5.4. It is now evident that the Kohala field system and the dryland cultivation zone in Kahikinui, Maui, had both reached their geographic limits to expansion (Vitousek et al. 2004; Kirch 2010b). They were essentially circumscribed or land limited by the time of European contact. Moreover, comparison of nutrient levels in cultivated and uncultivated soils in Kohala show that the values of calcium (Ca) and phosphorus (P) in the cultivated soils were as much as 30 and 24 percent lower than in the soils under the field walls (Vitousek et al. 2004:1667: Fig. 4B). Similarly, in Kahikinui, there was measurable drawdown in P, Ca, potassium (K), magnesium (Mg) and other key plant nutrients in microscale cultivation features (digging stick impressions) relative to the natural, uncultivated soils (Kirch et al. 2005; Hartshorn et al. 2006). In both areas, the level of harvest off-take of sweet potatoes, dryland taro, and other crops over a 300- to 400-year period seemingly reduced soil fertility by a measurable quantity. Such evidence strongly supports an inference that the *rate* of surplus production in these systems was declining in the late precontact era.

If the late precontact Hawaiian dryland agricultural systems had shifted over the course of three to four centuries from an initial condition of relatively high rates of surplus production (regions I to II in Figure 5.4), to one in which the ability to produce surplus was declining (regions III to IV), this situation was further exacerbated by the degree of *risk* inherent in such dryland farming. Native Hawaiian oral traditions refer more than once to periods of drought, and to resulting famine, social disruption, and warfare. For example, the account of the rise to power of Kiha-a-Pi'ilani on Maui explicitly links this ruler with efforts to enhance dryland agricultural production following a period of famine when the populace had to survive on ferns and other wild plants (Kamakau 1961:23–24; see Chapter 3). Another account, recorded by Fornander (1916:136), relates a time of great drought and famine extending across the length of the archipelago, when "all the wet lands were parched and the crops were dried up on account of the drought."

The lower elevational limits of intensive dryland farming on Hawai'i and Maui were constrained by normal ("average") conditions of low rainfall, but these were also subject to considerable stochastic variation (Giambelluca et al. 1991). In the more marginal zones, periodic drought would have shifted this lower boundary upslope, reducing the area that could yield a crop, and probably reducing yields even on the higher slopes. Consequently, surplus extraction was not only subject to the long-term temporal trends predicted by the production-function model, but almost certainly fluctuated from year to year in response to stochastic variation in precipitation. Immediate and sudden reductions in surplus as a result of drought are likely to have precipitated social and political crises, and may have been a strong impetus to aggression and conquest warfare.

We have now seen that the intertwined linkages between land, population, agriculture, and surplus provide one set of dynamic, long-term causal factors that are essential to explaining the emergence of Hawaiian archaic states. For the first five to seven centuries after colonization (depending on what that date is taken to be), the islands were in a growth economy, with rapidly expanding population and increasing rate of surplus production. Agricultural intensification occurred first in zones optimal for irrigation, mostly on the geologically older islands. By AD 1400, these optimal zones had become filled, and a major phase of expansion into areas amenable to intensive dryland farming commenced. This allowed a first application of the MaB ratchet, with another rapid growth phase that could be exploited by the Maui and Hawai'i Island chiefs to develop their tributary base. It was toward the end of this initial phase of intensification of the dryland field systems that divine kingship and archaic state structures first emerged on both Hawai'i and Maui. It is no coincidence that the *moʻolelo* of 'Umi and Kiha-a-Pi'ilani both stress the importance of dryland farming, for it was on the substantial productions of the vast dryland systems that these rulers built their political economies. But in succeeding generations, as the limits to nonirrigated land that could be intensively farmed were approached, efforts to again turn the MaB ratchet were less rewarding, and the ability to extract surplus became more tenuous. The significant increases in interisland (and on Hawai'i, intra-island) conquest warfare must be considered in this context. Although there is no evidence that the populations of Hawai'i and Maui had reached a final saturation or equilibrium population prior to European contact, all of the evidence strongly suggests that the "Malthusian scissors" were closing down, especially on these two larger, geologically young islands so dependent on dryland system production.

PROXIMATE CAUSATION: STATUS RIVALRY, ALLIANCE, AND CONQUEST

The dynamic linkages between land, population, intensive agriculture, and the food supply provide one axis of "ultimate" conditions critical to the emergence of archaic states in Hawai'i. But these long-term factors only go so far—they define the contexts within which individual actors made their choices, and the constraints that even the strongest chief could not overcome. To complete a model of Hawaiian sociopolitical change we now need to look more closely at the specific strategies used by the political elite to bend the social, economic, and political forces to their will. This is the realm of social power (Mann 1986), especially as manifest through individual actions. But individual action, agency, is mediated by broadly shared cultural structures.

In Chapter 1 I devoted some attention to certain aspects of Ancestral Polynesian societies, including social groups, rank and leadership positions, and the nature of ritual activities. When the first group of Polynesian colonists hauled their canoes ashore on a Hawaiian beach sometime between AD 800 and 1000, they carried with them these ancestral structures, whose ultimate origins can be traced back to early Austronesian societies of island Southeast Asia (Blust 1980; Kirch 1997a). A hallmark of Austronesian social organization is its emphasis on birth order and rank (Bellwood 1996b; Fox 1995), as well as its ancestor-based "house society" structure, and these were well developed in Ancestral Polynesia (Kirch and Green 2001). Thus the earliest Hawaiian societies did not invent *de novo* the fundamental social concepts of rank and segmentation by house groups that would become key building blocks toward a more hierarchical and ultimately class-based social formation. These structures were already deeply ingrained, part of the cultural heritage that was transported to Hawai'i by those first settlers.

The key structures on which later Hawaiian society would build included the following: (1) Early Hawaiian societies were organized as house societies, in which the main social groups were those indexed by the Proto Central Eastern Polynesian (PCEP) terms *mata-kainanga* and *kaainga*. The former was the main landholding or controlling group, which traced ascent back to a founding, often eponymous, ancestor, while the latter were individual residential groups occupying a specific estate with houses and garden land. (As explained in Chapter 1, the PCEP *mata-kainanga and *kaainga became the maka'āinana and 'āina of contact-era Hawaiian society.) These groups were themselves ranked, with seniority dependent on the genealogical relationships of their respective founding ancestors. *Kaainga were ranked within a larger *mata-kainanga, just as *mata-kainanga were ranked relative to each other, providing the basis for "heterarchical" competition between groups. (2) The existence of several well defined leadership positions, including PCEP *ariki as hereditary leader of the *mata-kainanga, *fatu as head of the *kaainga residential group, *tufunga as specialist, and *toa as warrior. The most important category is that of the *ariki, who like the ascent groups they headed, were ranked by birth order, and whose access to the ancestors assured the flow of *mana essential to the well-being of the society as a whole. Competition was always present among the *ariki, for *mana could be equally manifest in demonstrated action, in power, as in hereditary ascent. Junior *ariki knew this well, and it was a strategy that is encoded in Polynesian oral traditions (e.g., the tradition of Pā'ao, see Kamakau 1991:97–100). It seems that in early Eastern Polynesian societies *ariki had already begun to play more of a secular political role than they had in the preceding Ancestral Polynesian homeland. At the same time, the *tufunga in early Eastern Polynesia began to take on some aspects of group ritual that had formerly been the provenance of the *ariki. This shift was a first step toward the emergence of a distinct priestly class in later Hawai'i. (3) By the time Hawai'i was discovered and settled, the Proto Eastern Polynesian language now included the names of four *atua or ancestral deities, *Taangaloa, *Taane, *Tuu, and *Rongo.[19] (These would become the four great Hawaiian deities of Kānaloa, Kāne, Kū, and Lono.) Rituals involving offerings to these deities took place within sacred enclosures, the PCEP *marae (a word that would be lost in later Hawaiian, replaced by heiau), with an elevated altar or *ahu at one end, on which were set up anthropomorphic representations (PCEP *tiki) of the *atua. (4) Chief among the annual rituals in early Eastern Polynesia was the PCEP *mata-fiti, a new year's celebration and first-fruits offering ritual. This was a cultural innovation in the Eastern Polynesian region. The onset of the *mata-fiti was determined by the rising of Pleiades or *mata-liki, and involved first-fruits offerings to the *ariki or leaders of the respective ascent groups (the *mata-kainanga). The PCEP *mata-fiti is, of course, the precursor to the later Hawaiian Makahiki, the ritual apparatus through which the Hawaiian kings both conducted and

The Challenge of Explanation

legitimized their tribute collection. Thus the ritual basis for taxation in the later Hawaiian archaic states was already present structurally in early Eastern Polynesian society.

These four key features of early Eastern Polynesian society—two kinds of ranked social groups, formal leadership positions including hereditary chiefs and priests, a pantheon of four major gods, and an annual first-fruits New Year ceremony—provided the structural basis for later Hawaiian sociopolitical transformation. These were deeply ingrained cultural structures that set the context for individual actions, and that over time would themselves become radically transformed as the cumulative outcome of such actions. To understand how chiefs used these cultural structures to gain increasing power—and in turn redefined them—we need to examine elite strategies as these are revealed through indigenous Hawaiian accounts. In Chapter 3 I identified five power strategies that are well documented in the Hawaiian *moʻolelo*, including: status rivalry and competition between senior and junior ranked lines, marriage alliance, enhancement of economic infrastructure, the use of religion and ritual, and conquest warfare. These are all critical components of "proximate" causation that operated within the long-term "ultimate" factors defined earlier.

A theme resonating strongly throughout the indigenous traditions, from the earliest sagas of the offspring of Māweke in the "Voyaging Period" down through the times of ʻUmi and Kiha-a-Piʻilani, and into the contact-era with Kamehameha is that of rivalry and competition between senior and junior siblings, or senior and junior lines within an ascent group. This is the specifically Hawaiian reflection of the widely evidenced Polynesian, and indeed even Austronesian, emphasis on birth rank order (Fox 1996; Siikala 1996; Valeri 1990). Goldman (1970) in his theory of Polynesian social evolution emphasized the importance of such status rivalry between chiefly lines. Indeed, for Goldman status rivalry within what he called the "status lineage" was the key to Polynesian social evolution. Douglas (1979) further developed the analysis of "interplay" between ascribed and achieved statuses, between "sacred and secular leadership" in particular. This kind of rivalry between senior and junior plays out in Polynesian views of the alternative ways in which *mana* or power is manifest—either through heredity or through demonstrated action (Handy 1927; Shore 1989). Birth precedence privileges access to *mana* from the ancestors, but does not assure it. There is always an ʻUmi, or a Kiha-a-Piʻilani, or a Kamehameha biding his time on the periphery, waiting for the opportunity to demonstrate that the gods favor the junior sibling when the senior line fails to obey the canons of proper chiefship. But even more importantly, such usurpations provided opportunities for ambitious chiefs to build new alliances, to mate with higher-ranking women, and even to restructure key aspects of their social world.

What begins as status rivalry between senior and junior siblings, or between two ranked lineages within an ancestral *mata-kainanga group, ultimately plays out in Hawai'i as the ranked differentiation of a chiefly class (itself highly graded internally) from the commoners. The latter now take on the original word for ascent group ("lineage"), maka'āinana, as their moniker, even as that word now loses all reference to genealogical depth. As Goldman correctly observed: "even after the status lineage has been replaced by a territorial organization in the Stratified societies, it is the commoners whose lineage links have been broken. Royalty continues to regard lineage descent as honorable and as the key to legitimacy" (1970:430). As a consequence of the chiefs reserving for themselves the right to claim ascent from eponymous ancestors, "the status lineage literally cracked" (1970:442). The traditional Polynesian tendency "in the direction of indefinite expansion by branching, so as to incorporate the entire genealogical community," was now replaced by a hyper elaboration of chiefly lineages, while the commoners were dropped entirely from the branches (1970:442–43).

Having created a two-class society in which only the ali'i were allowed to play the power game of status rivalry, the strategies of alliance between lineages became all the more critical. The importance of alliances forged through marriage between ali'i of different lines, and of different islands, is thus a second theme that resonates strongly throughout the corpus of mo'olelo. As Biersack (1996:243) has said of similar patterns of alliance in Tonga, "élite marriage is regulated," and is carefully calculated to fulfill political ambitions, both of the individuals and their larger chiefly kinship groups. Although Hawaiian male ali'i were certainly not above sexual encounters with particularly attractive commoner women (as in the famous case of Līloa and Akahiakuleana), officially sanctioned unions were class endogamous. Moreover, there is a repeated tendency toward hypogamy, of male chiefs of slightly lower status to seek higher-ranked female partners in order to elevate the rank of their offspring. This was, of course, Kamehameha's goal in securing the very sacred ali'i wahine Keōpūolani to be the mother of his intended heir.

Marriages between high-ranked *ali'i* from different, and frequently opposed, polities were a strategy for avoiding or reducing interpolity conflict, and for forming powerful alliances that could be advantageous in times of threat from a third party. The marriage of 'Umi to the Maui chiefess Pi'ikea was just such a strategic alliance, proving critical to the efforts of her brother Kiha-a-Pi'ilani to wrest control of the Maui kingdom from his elder brother. The Maui king Kekaulike had among his several wives Ha'alou, the sister of Alapa'inui of Hawai'i Island, and therefore the uncle of Kekaulike's successor Kamehamehanui (Fornander 1996:213). This kin relationship proved critical when Alapa'inui retaliated against Kekaulike's aborted attempt to conquer Hawai'i. Finding Kekaulike dead and Kamehamehanui in charge of Maui, Alapa'inui ceased his hostilities. Nonetheless, such marriage alliances between dynastic houses did not always result in reduced conflict between their respective polities. A classic case in point is the marriage of Kalola, the high-ranking daughter of Maui king Kekaulike, to Kalani'ōpu'u of Hawai'i. In spite of this marriage, Kalani'ōpu'u was relentless in his attempts to wrest control of parts of Maui from his brother-in-law Kahekili. Following the disastrous defeat of his army on Maui, around the year 1776, Kalani'ōpu'u was obliged to sue for peace, intending first to send Kalola to her brother as an emissary (Fornander 1996:155; Kamakau 1961:88–89). She demurred, telling her husband that they had come on a mission to "deal death." However, a truce was secured when their son Kīwala'ō was sent instead. As a *nī'aupi'o* chief of the highest rank (holding the *kapu moe*), Kīwala'ō was able to pass through the lines of Maui warriors unharmed, where he was greeted by his uncle Kahekili, who agreed to end the conflict.

Precise statistics on the numbers of interpolity marriages are difficult to determine, in part because it is likely that marriages in later generations were more often remembered or recorded in the *mo'olelo*. Certainly, before the time of Mā'ilikūkahi (ca. AD 1490), such marriages were very rare, or at least rarely remarked. One of the earliest is the marriage of O'ahu's 'Olopana to Lu'ukia, the daughter of a chief of Kohala, Hawai'i. Such unions began to become more frequent following the time of 'Umi and Kiha-a-Pi'ilani. By the last three or four generations prior to European contact, such interpolity alliances were a common practice.

Further intensifying the systemic pattern of chiefly endogamy, the Hawaiian *ali'i* developed the practice of royal endogamy, marked by unions between full and half siblings of the highest rank. I have described such *pi'o* marriages in Chapter 2, as one of a number of indicators of divine kingship. Kamakau described the purpose of these *piʻo* matings as follows:

> The mating to a sister or near relative, which was not permitted to lesser chiefs or the relatives of chiefs, was considered desirable between very high chiefs in order to produce children of divine rank who carried the sacred fire (*ahi*) tabu. Such a mating was for the purpose of bearing children, but the two need not become man and wife. (1961:208)

Based on the exhaustive compilation of *piʻo* unions by Davenport (1994), it is evident that this practice was most frequent in the later Maui and especially Hawaiʻi kingdoms, although some *piʻo* unions of Kauaʻi and Oʻahu *aliʻi* are also recorded. Discounting those cases that occur with mythical or cosmogonic individuals (i.e., before Māweke in the chronology), on Maui the first such marriage is of a son of Piʻilani, Nihokela, to his half brother's daughter Kaʻakaupea (Mm2 in Davenport 1994:55). Seven more such unions were consummated in the Maui line, including matings between king Kekaulike with his half sister Kekuʻiapoiwanui and his daughter Kekauhiwamoku, and between king Kamehamehanui with his sister Kalola and his half sister Namahana (Mm5 to 8 and Mh1 in Davenport 1994:55–56, 65). On Hawaiʻi Island, these unions were even more frequent, with at least 28 *piʻo* matings recorded during the period from roughly AD 1550 until European contact (Hm7 to 30, and Hh1 to Hh4 in Davenport 1994:58–67). Among the prominent Hawaiʻi rulers who mated with their sisters or half sisters were Līloa, ʻUmi-a-Līloa, Keawenui-a-ʻUmi (twice), Alapaʻinui, KalaninuiʻIamamao (twice), Kīwalaʻō, and Kamehameha I (twice). Note that the practice of royal endogamy is closely correlated in time with the period of consolidation of the Maui and Hawaiʻi Island kingdoms (the seventeenth and eighteenth centuries), when it becomes increasingly prevalent on those islands.

A third chiefly power strategy referred to repeatedly in the *moʻolelo* is the enhancement of the polity's economic infrastructure. On the older, westerly islands, the construction of fishponds and the development of valley irrigation systems were favored projects directed under chiefly aegis. On the younger islands, the chiefs of Maui and Hawaiʻi emphasized the expansion and intensification of the vast dryland field systems. Some of the earliest accounts of this genre date to the Voyaging Period, with Olopana's and Moʻikeha's development of the irrigation works in Waipiʻo Valley on Hawaiʻi, and Kahaʻi's bringing of the first breadfruit seedlings to the archipelago. The reign of Māʻilikūkahi on Oʻahu is especially notable for his expansion of that island's irrigation systems, as well as his imposition of a hierarchical system of land divisions. With 'Umi-a-Līloa on Hawai'i and Kiha-a-Pi'ilani on Maui (both around the close of the sixteenth century), however, we see what I take to be the history-changing association between these rulers and the intensification of dryland agriculture, in the vast leeward field systems of these two islands. These linkages are salient, for it was the expansion and intensification of dryland field systems beginning in the fifteenth century and continuing thereafter, that provided the economic basis for both the Maui and Hawai'i kingdoms. The practice of Hawaiian kings to encourage economic development does not end with 'Umi and Kiha-a-Pi'ilani, of course, but continues as a theme into the early contact period. Kamehameha I was highly regarded by the people for his willingness to lead by example, even in the manual labor of clearing and planting fields (Ī'ī 1959:68), and in the work of fishing and repairing fishing gear (Kamakau 1961:176).[20]

A fourth power strategy involved the manipulation and elaboration of religion and ritual practice. In Chapter 1, I summarized the evidence for Ancestral Polynesian ritual practices, and when these are compared with the nature of Hawaiian state cults at the contact period (see Chapter 2), it is obvious that major transformations in religion and ritual practice had occurred in Hawai'i. The Hawaiian *mo'olelo* themselves speak to some of these changes. Some early changes in ritual practice are ascribed to events of the Voyaging Period, such as the introduction of *pahu* temple drums from Kahiki. The priest Pā'ao is also credited with introducing changes in temple architecture, the worship of Tū/Kū, and human sacrifice. However, the tradition of the O'ahu king Mā'ilikūkahi is quite specific in stating that human sacrifice was not yet practiced during his reign (Kamakau 1991:56). Indeed, the westerly islands of O'ahu and Kaua'i may have continued to emphasize the cults of Kāne and Kanaloa until quite late in protohistory, as Valeri (1985a:185) has suggested.

Pā'ao is associated primarily with Hawai'i Island, and it is plausible that his introduction of a Kū cult may have been confined to that island, at least in earlier centuries. He is credited with bringing the chief Pilika'aiea, of the 'Ulu line, and installing him on Hawai'i. Pā'ao also constructed the famous *luakini* temples of Waha'ula in Puna and Mo'okini in Kohala (Kamakau 1991:100). Thus, the traditions associate the rise of the formal Kū and Lono cults, and the practice of human sacrifice, with Hawai'i Island. The war god Kūkā'ilimoku is traced in the traditions back to Pā'ao (Kamakau 1991:3), and was a major personal god of the Hawai'i Island *ali'i nui* by the time of Līloa, who entrusted the care of this deity to 'Umi. Human sacrifice is explicitly referenced with 'Umi's offering up of Hākau's body on the *heiau* in Waipi'o. I have also drawn attention, however, to 'Umi's many associations with Lono, patron deity of the sweet potato and dryland agriculture. The rise of the cults of Kū and Lono, inseparably linked in the seasonal cycle of state rituals, may well have become formalized around the time of 'Umi's unification of Hawai'i. With the close linkages between the Hawai'i and Maui ruling lines, they were probably also adopted on Maui at this time. The *mo'olelo* that follow the period of 'Umi and Pi'ilani leave no doubt that human sacrifice had become a central part of elite temple ritual by this time.

This oral tradition evidence for elaboration of ritual and the formalization of the Kū and Lono cults on Hawai'i and Maui around the time of 'Umi and Kiha-a-Pi'ilani has resonances in the archaeological record of monumental temple construction, especially that for Maui Island. The radiocarbon and coral dating sequences from Kahikinui and elsewhere on Maui suggest that the temple system was radically transformed around the end of the sixteenth or beginning of the seventeenth centuries. In Kahikinui, it looks as though an organized system of local temples (probably *heiau ho'oulu 'ai* or agricultural temples) was emplaced on the landscape within a relatively short time span. As I have suggested (Kirch and Sharp 2005), this is likely to be the material reflection of a ritual "control hierarchy" by which both agricultural production and the extraction of surplus (as ritualized tribute) was organized by the political elites. Indeed, it may have been at this same time that the ancestral Eastern Polynesian *mata-fiti* New Year's celebration was transformed into the classically Hawaiian Makahiki harvest and tribute collection period of four months. Many of the Kahikinui temples display orientations associated with either Pleiades rising positions, or solstice positions, suggesting that they were integrated with such an annual ritual (Kirch 2004; Ruggles 2007). The first unambiguous reference to a royal Makahiki circuit is that of 'Umi's journey around Hawai'i after his unification of the island (Fornander 1916:210).

A fifth major power strategy was warfare, especially conquest warfare. War is deeply rooted in Polynesian societies; a word for warrior, *toa*, can be reconstructed to the Proto Polynesian language (Kirch and Green 2001:222, 225). But the particular ways in which aggression and warfare developed varied considerably in different Polynesian islands (Kirch 1984:204–16), and here the Hawaiian *mo'olelo*, with their frequently detailed accounts of wars and battles (including motivations), are especially valuable. Traditions of aggression—whether of simple raiding or of outright war—occur from quite early in the sequence of *moʻolelo*. A theme that begins with early traditions and continues right up until contact, is fighting between close siblings (brothers or cousins) who are rivals for succession to hereditary titles and land. We have, for example, the early instance of ʻOlopana and Moʻikeha fighting against Kumuhonua for control of Oʻahu. Sometimes such struggles are attributed to the oppressive rule of the senior sibling, as in the case of the war against Haka, or even more classically, in ʻUmi's usurpation of the chiefship from Hākau. Most of these earlier conflicts, however, occurred within the confines of a single polity, and warfare that extended to another island seems to have been a rare occurrence before the time of ʻUmi (ca. AD 1570–1590, in the relative chronology). The only significant example of this would be the great raiding expedition of Kalaunuiohua. After ʻUmi, the frequency of warfare began to increase significantly. Although there are peaceful intervals, wars between the Hawaiʻi and Maui island polities became commonplace during this later period. Examples include Kamalālāwalu's attempt to conquer Hawaiʻi, Kekaulike's and Alapaʻinui's respective invasions of each other's islands, and Kalaniʻōpuʻu's numerous efforts to gain control over the Maui dominions of Kahekili. But such interisland wars also began, in the late period, to extend beyond Maui and Hawaiʻi, especially over control of Molokaʻi, which became something of a contested ground between the Maui and Oʻahu polities. Indeed, Molokaʻi during this period lost its independence (its own indigenous chiefly line dying out), turning into a vassal island of either Oʻahu or Maui. But after the end of the sixteenth century, warfare was not only interpolity but intrapolity as well. This was most notably the case for Hawaiʻi Island, which, as I have speculated, had difficulty holding together as a cohesive unit because of its vast size. Hawaiʻi repeatedly divided into two or sometimes more internal divisions (often along a roughly north-south and windward-leeward set of axes), these being continually at war with each other.

Although difficult to quantify, there seems to have been a shift in the nature of aggression after circa AD 1570. The earlier conflicts appear to have been more in the manner of raiding expeditions, rather than attempts at territorial conquest and annexation. For many (although admittedly not all) of the later wars, conquest was clearly the objective, especially for those wars being promulgated in the last few generations prior to and at the time of European contact. Motivations for war certainly varied, and in some cases simply involved the urge for vengeance.

Disputes over territorial control, particularly the grievances of some chiefs who felt that they had been slighted in the division of lands following the accession of a new *ali'i nui*, were sometimes the immediate cause (or at least, the excuse) for war (e.g., Kamakau 1961:78). Such was the case with Kamehameha after the division of lands by Kīwala'ō (Kamakau 1961:118–19). The desire to take over lands and resources that were more bountiful and productive is certainly indexed as a motive.[21] And, there can be little doubt that many of the later wars, especially those promulgated by the Maui and Hawai'i rulers, were intended for the conquest and annexation of territory. Kamakau, for example, describes how the Maui king Kahekili "coveted Oahu and Molokai for their rich lands, many walled fishponds, springs, and water taro patches" (1961:132). Moreover, the "ultimate" factors of limited land and the inevitable Malthusian scissors that began to reduce the ability of kings and chiefs to extract surplus from the dryland field systems, strongly encouraged such tendencies toward conquest warfare on the part of the Maui and Hawai'i Island leaders.[22]

WHY DID ARCHAIC STATES EMERGE FIRST ON HAWAI'I AND MAUI?

The indigenous Hawaiian political traditions and the material evidence of archaeology both point to O'ahu Island as an early center of social and economic developments. From the end of the Voyaging Period until the late-fifteenth century, the *mo'olelo* speak of the progressive development and intensification of O'ahu's irrigation systems, culminating in the reign of Mā'ilikūkahi, who famously established the *ahupua'a* system of hierarchically nested land units. Archaeology confirms that O'ahu was an early center of irrigation, with extensive pondfield systems and canals in place by the fifteenth century. But then the locus of sociopolitical dynamism appears to have shifted eastward, to the much larger and geologically younger islands of Maui and especially Hawai'i. It was on these two islands, in the late-sixteenth century and early seventeenth centuries, that the critical transformations in social structure, including the sundering of the old system of "archaic *mata-kainanga*," and the emergence of a new form of divine kingship with its attendant state cults of Kū and Lono apparently took place. The traditions link these changes to the powerful 'Umi and Pi'ilani ruling lines; archaeologically their emergent power is evident in the monumental temples and royal centers that they built.

That divine kingship, conquest warfare, and an archaic state structure first arose on Maui and Hawai'i is also strongly suggested by differences in the political and religious structures of the eastern and western polities, differences that have typically been glossed over or ignored in the standard works on Hawaiian ethnography (see Kirch 1990b). In particular, the complex Makahiki or wet-season harvest ritual, along with the emphasis accorded the cult of the war-god Kū and its attendant *luakini* temple ritual, were most elaborately developed on Hawai'i and Maui, less so on the westerly islands of O'ahu and Kaua'i (Valeri 1985a:184–85). This is reflected, for example, in the distinctive iconographic style of temple images, referred to by Cox and Davenport (1974) as the "Kona style," reflecting a particular emphasis in the Hawai'i Island kingdom on the Kū cult and conquest warfare. Lono was the key deity in the annual Makahiki harvest festivals as practiced in the Kona and Kohala districts of Hawai'i, and apparently also on Maui. As the god of rain-fed cultivation and patron deity of the sweet potato, Lono was associated with "clouds bearing rain," thunder, the rise of Pleiades, and the rainy season (Valeri 1985a:15: Table 1).

Thus the classic Kū-Lono cycle so celebrated in Hawaiian ethnohistory, and so central to the Hawaiian archaic states, is inextricably linked to the political economies of the large eastern islands, with their economies based on intensified dryland cultivation. On O'ahu and Kaua'i, religious practice continued to emphasize Kāne until late in the precontact period (see Valeri 1985a:184–85). This emphasis on Kāne, who was the deity of running water, springs, fishponds, male procreative powers, and irrigation, speaks to the dominance of wetland taro cultivation on the older western islands.[23] Kāne's close relation to taro is made clear in a taro-planting prayer recorded by Kamakau:

Pause and receive thanks, O god,
O Kane, O Kane-of-life-giving-water;
Here is *lu'au*, the first leaves of our taro;
Turn back and eat, O god. (1976:35)

In *Islands of History*, Sahlins explicitly remarked on the dynamic tension that divided the eastern and western sectors of the Hawaiian Islands:

As a general rule, the oldest and most senior lines are in the western islands, Kaua'i and O'ahu, whence originate also the highest tabus. But then, the historical dynamism of the system is in the east, among Maui and

Hawai'i chiefs, who are able to differentiate themselves from local competitors, or even from their own dynastic predecessors, by appropriating ancestry from the ancient western sources of legitimacy. (1985a:20)

The historical primacy of O'ahu and Kaua'i thus continued to be recognized in the genealogies of their kings, but by the late-sixteenth century, these islands were no longer the center of political action.

Based on their work in the Kohala district of Hawai'i, Tuggle and Tomonari-Tuggle argued that "agricultural growth had reached its limits in the Kohala-Hamakua region, under the constraints of a simple irrigation technology and probably a comparable level of dry-field technology" (1980:311). These scholars further pointed to a key link between the limits to intensification and political developments on Hawai'i Island:

> There is some evidence that Hawai'i was politically unified at an earlier date than the other islands and that it may have had a somewhat more complex political hierarchy. If so, it can be argued that demand for agricultural land, particularly irrigation land, increased competition among polities, thus acting as a variable in the process of political elaboration. (1980:311)

Hommon (1986) rightly pointed out that the leeward Hawai'i Island systems were also those most susceptible to environmental perturbations and to depletion of soil nutrients:

> With the expansion of population into marginal regions came an increase in the frequency and intensity of the adverse socio-political effects of crop failure and famine resulting from drought.... Irregular and unpredictable oscillations in the amount of goods available to chiefs increased in magnitude with the increase of agricultural lands that were susceptible to drought, soil exhaustion resulting from insufficient fallow periods, increased soil erosion, the effects of deforestation, and other factors that reduced the capacity of the land to produce. (1986:66)

Hommon relates these agroecological conditions to the cyclical political history of Hawai'i Island, suggesting that the rivalry between leeward and windward chiefs was rooted in two disparate economic histories (1986:67). In particular, this rivalry may have involved competition between an alliance of windward polities whose wealth and power were founded on a long-established stable productive economy supported in part by valley irrigation (in the Kohala and Hāmākua areas) and the upstart *nouveaux riches* leeward districts with their rapidly growing but somewhat unstable economies based on the dryland field complexes.

Schilt (1984), in her intensive study of the Kona district of Hawai'i, pointed to direct archaeological evidence for overt competition and

The Challenge of Explanation

warfare in the final centuries prior to European contact, in the form of caves modified for refuge and defense. The conversion of these caves to refuges, between about AD 1500 and 1600, coincides with the traditional accounts of late precontact political rivalry in Kona and with the contemporaneous intensification of leeward field systems (Schilt 1984:294). Schilt opines that because Hawai'i Island "presented less total, sustainable production potential than the older [western] islands, where irrigation was the characteristic mode of taro production," it was also "possibly the first place where a disjunction between an expanding population and the limits of agricultural development, within a politically competitive cultural system, was realized" (Schilt 1984:292).

Was it merely an accident of history that the dynamics of sociopolitical transformation shifted from O'ahu to Maui and Hawai'i during the course of the sixteenth century? The evidence suggests not, and a further examination of the critical differences in the archipelago's environmental canvas, the biogeochemical gradients that were so critical to support the agroecosystems, may sharpen our understanding of why Maui and Hawai'i were the focus of archaic state emergence.

In Chapters 2 and 4 I documented the striking contrast between the older western islands with their extensive irrigation systems, highly productive fishponds, and generally richer marine resources, and the younger (but much larger) eastern islands in which the intensified dryland field systems dominated and irrigated lands constituted only a relatively small fraction of the total arable lands, and where marine resources were limited (see Table 4.3). But this contrast between eastern and western islands is not simply a matter of the ratio of wetland to dryland cultivation; we also need to take into account the significant differences in total agricultural output, and the implications of such output for the political economy. The hallmark of taro irrigation is its remarkable propensity to produce high yields (ca. 25 metric tons per hectare, or even more) with relatively low labor inputs (Kirch 1994:175; Spriggs 1981, 1984). In contrast, the Hawaiian dryland field systems at peak production probably did not yield more than 10 tons/ha, and required far greater labor inputs in weeding and mulching (Kirch 1994: Table 10; Massal and Barrau 1956). Thus while O'ahu had only about one-fifth the area of prime arable land as Hawai'i, the irrigated systems of O'ahu were capable of yielding a proportionally much higher harvest than the more extensive dryland fields of Hawai'i (ca. 242,350 metric tons for O'ahu compared to ca. 560,175 tons for the Hawai'i field systems). Figure 5.5, which shows the estimated agricultural yields from both

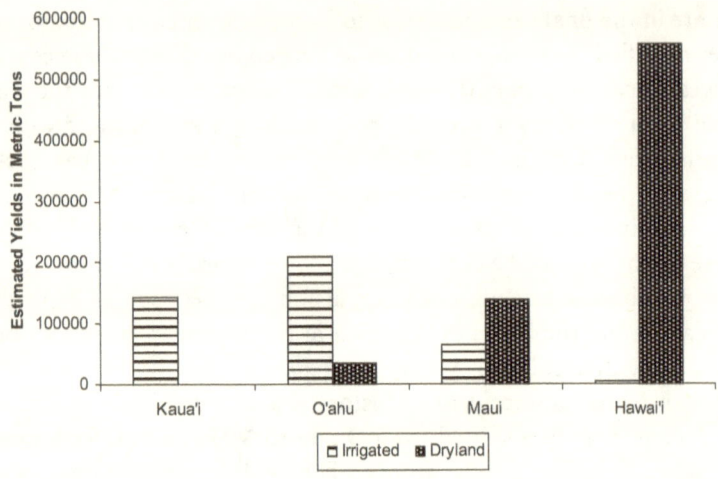

Figure 5.5. Estimated yields of the irrigated and dryland agricultural sectors of the four major islands. Irrigated yields are based on 25 mt/ha and dryland yields are based on 5 mt/ha.

irrigated and intensive dryland cultivation areas on the four major islands, highlights two points: (1) the dominance of irrigation on the western islands; and (2) the overall higher productive capacity of Hawai'i Island. Maui, interestingly, had the best balance of wet and dryland production, although this was unevenly divided between the western (largely irrigated) and eastern (largely dryland) parts of the island.

These contrasts in agroecosystems become more interesting when we factor in labor requirements. Taro irrigation not only produces higher yields than intensive dryland fields, but achieves those yields with considerably lower labor inputs (Kirch 1994). Ethnographic evidence from traditional subsistence regimes in Oceania suggests that labor inputs in the dryland systems were probably double those in the irrigated lands.[24] Figure 5.6 shows the estimated labor inputs required to cultivate the combined wet and dryland agricultural systems on the four major islands. Comparing this graph to Figure 5.5, it is evident that while Hawai'i Island had the greatest potential yield (owing to its vast areas amenable to intensive dryland cultivation), this would have to have been achieved with a far greater labor input. These estimates of agricultural labor can also be converted into per capita figures, as shown in Figure 5.7, by dividing the total labor by the approximate populations of each island as estimated by Lt. King in 1779 (see Table 1.2). Seen in this light, the huge differential between agricultural output (yield) and

The Challenge of Explanation

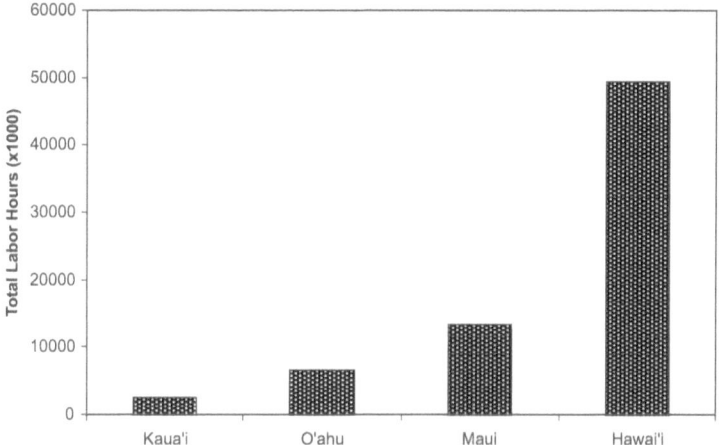

Figure 5.6. Estimated agricultural labor requirements (in work days/person) for the major islands. These estimates are based on the differential labor requirements of the irrigated and dryland agricultural systems.

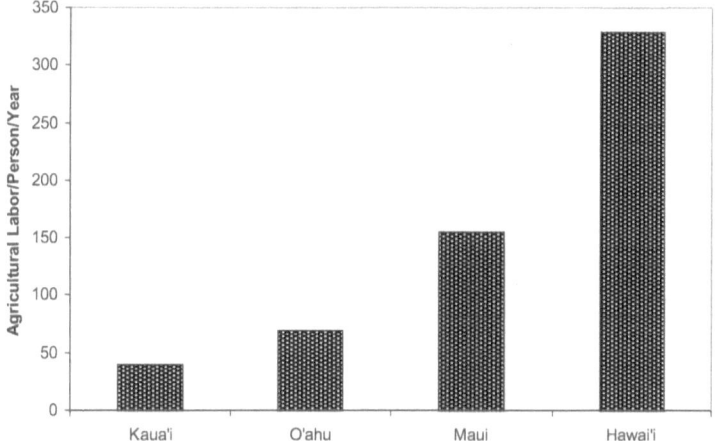

Figure 5.7. Estimated per capita agricultural labor requirements for the four major islands, based on island population sizes estimated by Lt. James King in 1779.

input (labor) across the archipelago is striking. Maui and especially Hawai'i had the potential to support the largest populations, but only through the greatest labor costs.

One can now understand why O'ahu, with its highly favorable mix of wet and dry arable lands, augmented by especially rich marine resources, was favored by the chiefly elite in the first few centuries following Polynesian colonization. An early intensification of irrigation on Oʻahu provided the basis for Māʻilikūkahi and succeeding rulers to build up their political economy. But the real transformation from a complex chiefship to an archaic state took place not on Oʻahu, but on Hawaiʻi, with the opening up of the vast potential of the leeward dryland systems. ʻUmi certainly recognized this potential, moving his royal seat from Waipiʻo (the major irrigation valley on Hawaiʻi) to Kona, location of the largest dryland field system. During the first two centuries of expansion and intensification of the dryland field systems (ca. AD 1400–1600) the Hawaiʻi Island economy experienced a remarkable phase of growth, both in sheer population and in the surplus production that could be extracted by means of the increasingly ritualized Makahiki system. However, the critical inflection points on the production function curve outlined earlier, when the boom phase passes and the ability to extract surplus declines, would have been reached earlier on Hawaiʻi and Maui, given their substantially greater dependence on intensive dryland production.

The political configurations and distinctive cycles of territorial expansion and conquest characteristic of late Hawaiian society display a pattern of geographic distribution that mirrors these fundamental differences in agricultural base. The aggressive, expansionist, Kū-cult centered polities of Maui and Hawaiʻi were precisely those most dependent on intensified dryland field cultivation. In Hawaiʻi and Maui, and especially in their leeward regions that constituted the ancestral seat of the most powerful and aggressive kings, the limits of increased productivity even with significant labor inputs (including the addition of female labor in field cultivation) had probably been reached by the end of the seventeenth century. And, the increasingly frequent objects of their aggression became the western islands of Molokaʻi, Oʻahu, and Kauaʻi, rich in irrigated pondfields and fishponds. The production-function model is again informative. By the late 1600s, the leeward Hawaiian field systems had arguably entered that sector of the production curve (Fig. 5.4, regions III–IV) in which surplus was diminishing relative to yield. The late precontact rulers of Hawaiʻi and Maui would have increasingly found that their demands for tribute were straining or even exceeding the capacity of the *makaʻāinana* to meet them. This would have been politically intolerable, for the king and chiefs were accelerating demands on a total surplus that was now in absolute decline. The only obvious escape from these Malthusian scissors was conquest warfare that, as the oral traditions show, increased significantly during this late period.

The Challenge of Explanation 217

The historical dynamism of Maui and Hawai'i thus owes much to the particulars of its agricultural production base. The pathway of labor-intensive, short-fallow, dryland field agricultural development followed in most of Hawai'i and East Maui had dramatic social and political consequences, as Sahlins (1972) rightly detected. But even as we acknowledge that the contrastive pathways of agricultural intensification across the archipelago helped to determine the respective sociopolitical structures of these polities, this does not require adherence to a strict environmental determinism. The particular cultural, symbolic structures that emerged in the eastern and western sectors of the archipelago, such as the elaborated Kū and Lono cult cycle of Hawai'i Island, were not specifically "determined" by their agroecosystems. In each region, chiefs and their followers seized such opportunities for development and enhancement of the production apparatus as were at hand; at the same time they were constrained in their abilities to make alternative choices. Whereas the Kaua'i and O'ahu elites benefited from a landscape favoring valley pondfield irrigation and fishpond aquaculture, the Hawai'i and Maui *ali'i* operated under severe limits to irrigation or aquacultural expansion. The dryland agricultural regimes of these eastern islands—as they became increasingly intensified through shorter-fallow and labor-intensive methods in late prehistory—put increasing pressure on the political elite for territorial expansion. It is an accident of history that Kamehameha I found himself in a position to use the "structure of the conjuncture" (Sahlins 1985a) between Hawai'i and the expanding World System of the late-eighteenth century in order to extend his hegemony over the entire archipelago. That he should have harbored such ambitions, that his greatest desire was the conquest and subjugation of the irrigation-based western polities, however, is bound up in a contingent history that can be traced at least as far back in time as 'Umi-a-Līloa.

HAWAI'I AND ARCHAIC STATE EMERGENCE

As the most isolated archipelago on Earth, not discovered or settled by humans until Europe was entering its early Middle Ages, is Hawai'i simply a footnote on the larger saga of world history? Or, does its unique position in time and space lend Hawai'i a special significance for the comparative understanding of human societies? I have suggested that Hawai'i offers a "model system" for understanding the emergence of primary archaic states and the divine kingship that separates these from simpler ranked societies. Using a Sapirian historical anthropology that draws on the independent evidence of ethnography and ethnohistory, oral tradition, and archaeology, I have tackled Marshall Sahlins's challenge: When and how in the course of Hawaiian history was a kinship society originally organized by classic Polynesian structures of lineage and chiefship transformed into a political society headed by god-kings? I have also endeavored to go beyond a strictly narrative account, offering in this final chapter elements of a theory of why this particular Polynesian society crossed over the structural divide separating ranked societies from archaic states. But if Hawai'i is a model system for the emergence of archaic states, then the historical processes I have identified should be more generally applicable.

If archaeologists have learned anything from their collective efforts to unravel the historical sequences of archaic state emergence in various parts of the world, and to isolate and define the processes responsible for these major transformations in human sociopolitical organization, it is that there is no single "smoking gun," no universal "prime mover" or causal agent. Hawaiian history underscores this conclusion and, as I have argued, an adequate theoretical account of state emergence in the islands requires the invocation of both ultimate and proximate causation. Put another way, the transition from chiefdom to state was an outcome of the contingent interaction between certain environmental contexts and long-term processes with the particular motivations and strategies of individual human actors. Process and agency—both are essential to our understanding of how kingship, class stratification, and states arose out of ranked societies.

Yet to assert that the emergence of divine kingship and archaic states was a multicausal and complex phenomenon is not to deny the role of common and recurrent themes in the specific histories of state formation in different times and places. A number of such themes recur with sufficient frequency that we can identify them as necessary components to a more general model of archaic state emergence. This is surely the case for *circumscription*, a fundamental environmental (and social) context for the transformation of chiefdoms to states, as Carneiro (1970) rightly pointed out. For Hawai'i, the circumscription of this remote archipelago is obvious, yet more importantly it was the delimited and restricted nature of the main zones amenable to intensive production that were so critical to socioeconomic change. This was especially the case for the rain-fed dryland cropping systems of Maui and Hawai'i, which formed the economic backbone of their emergent kingdoms, in a manner not dissimilar to the circumscribed agricultural zones of the Peruvian coastal valleys invoked by Carneiro (1970:734–35; see also Stanish 2001:57).

Another recurring theme in the history of primary state emergence is *expansion*, typically the predatory expansion by one polity into the territories of its neighbors, thus significantly increasing its geographic range but also ramping up the size of its tributary base. Examples of expansion in the rise of early states range from Uruk in Mesopotamia (Algaze 1993) to Monte Albán in Mesoamerica (Spencer and Redmond 2004). Indeed, Spencer (1998:17) regards "interpolity expansion combined with tributary extraction" as a key element in a general model of primary state formation. The Hawaiian data are again consistent with this proposition. I have argued that it was with the consolidation of the Hawai'i and Maui Island kingdoms, around AD 1600, that true kingship and the beginnings of archaic state structure first arose in the islands. In both cases, this involved the expansion of one chiefdom to incorporate other, formerly independent polities, creating new levels of spatial and economic integration.

Isolated from other land masses by thousands of kilometers of ocean, the Hawaiian polities developed their sociopolitical structures through an entirely endogenous history, not influenced by other states or civilizations either in Asia or the Americas. But the Hawaiian polities—each consolidating on a naturally circumscribed island—interacted with and significantly influenced each other, through the process that Renfrew (1982, 1986) labeled *peer polity interaction*. It is not surprising that Renfrew's theory of peer polity interaction emerged from his study of another set of islands, the Cyclades of the Aegean. Hawaiian history exhibits critical interactions among several island polities, most particularly between Maui and Hawai'i (recall the frequent alliances as well as aggressions between their dynastic houses), but also with the western islands of O'ahu and Kaua'i. Such interactions included both aggressive conflict and peaceful alliances, but more importantly allowed for "competitive emulation" of elite strategies and for the sharing of innovations (Renfrew 1986:8).

A fourth theme of undoubted importance in the emergence of archaic states is *intensification*, whether of agricultural production (in the so-called "staple economies") or of material crafts and durable goods (in "wealth economies"). Here the Hawaiian case may be of unusual interest, for it shows how the transformation from chiefship to kingship was linked to a rapid growth phase in the political economy in which elites were able to take advantage of expanding rates of surplus production. This was also the period of initial expansion and consolidation of the emerging state structures. Indeed, it is an interesting question whether state emergence ever occurred in the absence of a robust growth economy. But Hawaiʻi also shows what happened when the limits to economic growth were approached, if not absolutely reached, and the ability of kings and their elite cadres to extract surplus from the now socially distanced commoners became more difficult and at times oppressive. This is the phase in which conquest warfare took on its prominence, and was apparently the situation in which the Hawaiʻi and Maui kings found themselves in the decades immediately prior to Cook's arrival.

Yet chiefs did not become kings solely through increasing their extraction of surplus, or by taking direct control over land allocation. The very social contract had to be rewritten, requiring the manipulation of *ideology*, notably through daily practice and *materialization* (Miller and Tilley 1984; DeMarrais et al. 1996). In Hawaiʻi, as elsewhere, elites built on preexisting power relations, which in Polynesia included birth-order ranking and its inherent relationship to *mana* and the ancestral sources of fertility, to elaborate new structures of authority and command. A major arena for these restructurings was in the rituals of first-fruits and of sacrifice. These had always been the prerogative of the senior ranks, but were now transformed into state cults of tribute collection and of war (the cults of Lono and Kū, respectively). On Maui, the rapid imposition of a temple system in the late sixteenth and early seventeenth centuries can be seen as one material reflection of the transformation of ritual in the service of a new political structure. Redmond and Spencer (2008:263) have pointed to a parallel development of standardized temples and sacrifice "to legitimize the rulers' authority" in the Monte Albán state of Mesoamerica. And in Hawaiʻi, as in many other early states, the nature of sacrifice itself was transformed, with the king claiming the ultimate prerogative to offer up other human beings on the altar of Kū.

As the chiefly class increasingly differentiated and distanced itself from the commoners—with whom they no longer shared common bonds of kinship, the classic Polynesian lineage structure having been sundered—their new power and authority (and the potential fear these engendered) had to be materially symbolized (Marcus 2007:98). Many of the symbolic elements themselves were old and hence deeply imbued with meaning, such as the association between red feathers and deified ancestors. But by literally cloaking themselves in thousands of these feathers, the highest chiefs and kings displayed their connections to the ancestors, their divinity, for all to see and wonder at. Religion and secular power were intertwined in these new material symbols. And as competition among the ranks of the elite grew and was elaborated through formal distinctions of grade, an elite wealth economy was superimposed on the underlying staple economy. Hommon (2009) has gone so far as to suggest that the protohistoric rise in interisland aggression evidenced by the Hawaiian traditions may have been linked as much to a developing shortage in red and gold birds' feathers, as in the need for increased food supply.

How did chiefs become kings? As in all human history, there is no simple answer, for the course of human affairs is by its very nature both complex and contingent. But through close analysis of the material record of early state emergence, archaeologists have come a long way toward isolating key processes that were widely shared and seem to have been consistently influential in effecting sociopolitical transformation. The history of Hawai'i adds yet another case to this body of evidence. Yet Hawai'i stands out in one critical aspect, for having witnessed the rise of divine kings and archaic states so late on the stage of world history, the emergent Hawaiian polities came face to face with the expanding European world system in AD 1778 to 1779. And this has left us a legacy rich both in the ethnographic observations of those Enlightenment voyagers, and in the oral traditions of the Hawaiians themselves, who retained a vivid and nuanced historical memory of how their chiefs had become kings.

Notes

CHAPTER ONE

1. The genetic comparative method of historical linguistics is essentially the same in its fundamental principles as the modern method of cladistics in biology. Both depend on the identification of shared innovations ("synapomorphies" in cladistic terminology) to establish subgroups.

2. On phylogenetic models and methods in historical anthropology, see Bellwood (1996a), Shennan (2002), and Mace and Pagel (1994).

3. On the theory and method of the phylogenetic model, see Kirch and Green (2001).

4. On semantic history hypotheses, see Dyen and Aberle (1974) and Kirch and Green (2001:44–46). On Proto Polynesian reconstructions in general, see Biggs et al. (1970).

5. Both PPN *kainanga and *kaainga are extensively represented by cognate reflexes in extant Polynesian languages, allowing the reconstruction of both the root forms and the extended semantic values in Proto Polynesian (see Kirch and Green 2001: Tables 8.3 and 8.4).

6. Whereas anthropologists have tended to speak of kin groups in terms of "descent" from a common ancestor, in the Austronesian-speaking world the pervasive metaphor is one of "ascent" from such ancestors (Fox 1995; Kirch and Green 2001:224). Polynesians typically use a botanical metaphor of growth (*tupu*) from ancestors who occupy the trunk of a branching family tree, in which the contemporary generation occupies the branching tips.

7. PPN *mata is a complex, polysemous word, with a primary referent of "face." In Ancestral Polynesia it may also have had a secondary meaning of "society," prior to its being prefixed to *kainanga as an innovation at the Proto Central-Eastern Polynesian language interstage (Kirch and Green 2001:218).

8. The Hawaiian reflexes of these four deities are Kanaloa, Kāne, Kū, and Lono.

9. The Hawaiian word *ahu*, "altar," derives from PPN *qafu, the low foundation mound of the sacred house in Ancestral Polynesia.

CHAPTER TWO

1. A critical review of ethnohistoric and ethnographic sources for traditional Hawai'i is offered by Valeri (1985a:xvii–xxviii).
2. The two words *moʻolelo* and *moʻoʻōlelo* are synonymous.
3. For biographies of D. Malo and S. Kamakau, see Chun (1993).
4. Valeri (1972:36) comments on the formation of a class-based society in Hawai'i as follows: "C'est la tendance de la société hawaiienne, qui n'a pu se manifester pleinement qu'avec le processus d'étatisation mené a bien par Kamehameha et l'élimination de la notion de parenté commune entre chefs et peuple. Ce processus conduisait à la formation d'une stratification en classes."
5. Kepelino's use of *noa* for commoners is interesting since *noa* means "free from taboo (*kapu*)." As I discuss later, the elites (*aliʻi*) are defined in terms of their relation to *kapu*; thus the absence of *kapu* is the sine qua non of the commoner class.
6. The numbers and role of *kauwā* in late Hawaiian society remain matters of considerable ambiguity. Kepelino (Beckwith 1932:142–47) implies that they were not numerous and stresses that because they were the antithesis of chiefs, *kauwā* were likewise *kapu*. This *kapu* status correlates with their suitability for human sacrifice.
7. Kirch and Sahlins (1992) provide many examples of such land claims from the Anahulu Valley, Oʻahu; see also Kirch (2002) for examples from the Kalaupapa Peninsula, Molokaʻi. In many cases, commoner claimants reference "inheritance" of land parcels from parents (*makua*), but this is always validated by reference to continued approval of the *konohiki* and by regular payment of *hoʻokupu*.
8. Kamakau (1961:211–12) describes how at the time of his death, Kamehameha was carried back and forth between the several houses of the royal compound, "to prevent his dying in the eating house" and thus defiling it. "Such defilement must be avoided lest the whole race perish in consequence" (1961:212).
9. The prostrating *kapu* was described many times in the journals of Cook's expedition in 1778 to 1779. Captain Clerke writes, "The respect they pay the King and two or three of their principal Chiefs [presumably *nīʻaupiʻo* and *piʻo* ranked chiefs] here is, whenever they see one of them coming they fall down flat on their faces scarcely daring to look up, and in this position they continue till he is twenty or thirty yards past them" (Beaglehole 1967:596).
10. According to Kamakau (1961:88), a battle between the forces of Hawaiʻi and Maui was temporarily halted when the sacred *nīʻaupiʻo* chief Kīwalʻō appeared, requiring that the warriors of both sides perform the *kapu moe*.
11. The compound term derives from *ʻahu*, the general word for garment, and *ʻula*, meaning red. Buck (1957:216) speculates that the original Hawaiian capes were probably made "mostly or entirely of red feathers." The transition to yellow feathers as the more valuable was a later development, in Buck's scenario, "owing to the difficulty of obtaining a sufficient supply."

12. In postcontact times, *kāhili* or feathered standards were greatly elaborated, and were well known symbols of the Hawaiian monarchy (Kamehiro 2009:41–42). Small wands or fly-whisks tipped with feathers were in use at the time of first contact by elites and their attendants, and four of these were collected by Cook's expedition (Kaeppler 1978:77–78).

13. Hawaiians also had a highly developed tradition of performance arts, particularly dance (*hula*). Formalized dance entertainments for the king and chiefs were accompanied by beating the *pahu* drums (Kaeppler 1993:5–6). Tatar (1993:19) states that "the primary function of the *pahu* was to signal major events in the rituals of the *heiau* and the lives of the *ali'i*, such as the sacrifice of a human being or the birth of an *ali'i*." Malo (1951:231) writes that the *hula* was a "means of conferring distinction upon the ali'i," and is probably referring to the dances in honor of the genitals and generative powers of the elite, known as *mele ma'i* (Kaeppler 1993:222). *Hula* performances were staged on special stone platforms, the most famous being at Kē'ē on Kaua'i Island (Barrère et al. 1980).

14. The term *mō'ī* is problematic; Stokes (1932) thought the word to be a nineteenth-century innovation, although it appears in the first Hawaiian dictionary compiled by Lorrin Andrews (1865). Malo (1951:162, 173) says that the principal *haku-'ōhi'a* idol in the *luakini heiau*, which was clothed with a special loincloth during the *haku-'ōhi'a* rites, was called the *mō'ī*, or "lord of all the idols." That this term may also have been applied to the king would not be surprising.

15. The word is derived from *kālai*, "to divide, as land," "to plan, formulate, budget," and *moku*, "island" (Pukui and Elbert 1986:121). Kepelino (Beckwith 1932:132, 146) uses the alternative term *kuhina* for the "office of counselor." There was probably just a single *kālaimoku*, with other trusted advisors of the king being called *kuhina*.

16. Kepelino begins the section of his *mo'o'ōlelo* dealing with "food and farming" with an account of "government" and of tribute collection (Beckwith 1932:146 passim). In essence, Hawaiian government was the management of food production and regular collection of tribute up through the system of land hierarchy.

17. Titcomb (1969) summarizes the ethnohistoric references to domestic dogs in Hawai'i.

18. Demands for pigs as tribute from the estates of the great *ali'i* continued well into the contact period, as demonstrated by the letters sent by Paulo Kānoa, secretary to the ruling chiefess Kīna'u, to the *konohiki* of Anahulu Valley in the 1830s (Sahlins 1992:144).

19. As Valeri (1985a:184–85) points out, Kāne may have played a much greater role on O'ahu and Kaua'i than on Hawai'i Island. Most of the *luakini* temples of Kaua'i Island were dedicated to Kāne and sometimes to Kanaloa.

20. See Emerson's notes, in Malo (1951:126, 132–33), regarding the *heiau* within the *mua*. In archaeological excavations of structures interpreted as *mua*, in Kahikinui District, Maui, I have found simple niche shrines in the northeast corner, sometimes containing waterworn beach pebbles (Kirch 1997b).

21. Kamakau (1961:149–58) gives an account of the prophecy, the *heiau* construction, and the events surrounding Keōua's surrender to Kamehameha at Kawaihae, Hawai'i.

22. The observation of either the acronical or heliacal rising or setting of Pleiades to establish the new year is widespread throughout Polynesia and can be traced back to Ancestral Polynesian times (Kirch and Green 2001:261–65).

23. That Captain Cook was taken to be Lono returning from Kahiki has much to do with the timing of his two visits to the islands, in the early part of the Makahiki season (see Sahlins 1981, 1985a, 1989, 1995; cf. Obeyesekere 1992).

24. The *kapu* put on gardens at this time may also be interpreted as the fields being taken over by the god for fertilization. Maunupau (1998:152–53) describes rituals attending sweet potato planting in Kaupō district on East Maui, including prayers offered to the pig god Kamapua'a, whose excrement was symbolically compared to the gnarled sweet potato tubers.

25. The word *ho'okupu* has a literal meaning of "to cause to grow," suggesting that the origins of the term lie in an earlier form of first-fruits rite, probably with offerings to Lono intended to ensure fertility.

26. Kepelino (Beckwith 1932:148–51) describes the rendering of *ho'okupu* or offerings.

27. *Ka'upu* is the Hawaiian name for the Laysan Albatross (*Diomedea immutabilis*), a seabird with a pure white pelt and black back (Berger 1972:43). The birds lay their eggs around mid- to late November (Berger 1972:44; Harrison 1990:115), the time of Pleiades rising, and this aspect of their biology (along with their white color) probably led the Hawaiians to associate them with Lono.

28. This rite of feeding Lono was called the *hānaipū* and was what Captain Cook was induced to participate in on January 17, 1779, on the main platform of Hikiau Heiau at Kealakekua (Beaglehole 1967:505–6).

29. Far less is known about the circuit of the *akua poko* or "short god" than about the circuit of the long god associated with the main *ho'okupu* tribute collection. 'Ī'ī (1959:75–76) remarks that during the Makahiki on O'ahu after Kamehameha's conquest, Kailua and Kāne'ohe were among the lands "designated for its visit." Because these were Kamehameha's personal lands, Sahlins (1981:19, 73n; see also Sahlins 1995:29, n16) inferred that the tour of the *akua poko* was specifically to the "ruling chief's own lands."

30. Kamakau was describing the Makahiki circuit in the time of Kamehameha I, hence this reference to iron, which would have been a highly valued trade item, subject to tribute collection.

31. The spelling—and implied etymology—of this term vary. Valeri uses Kahōāli'i, whereas Desha (2000:343) uses Kaho'āli'i. The latter spelling is presumably based on *ho'āli'i*, "to make a chief" (Pukui and Elbert 1986:20). However, an alternative etymology would drive from *hoa-li'i* meaning "friend or companion of the chief" (*hoa*, "companion"; *li'i*, "chief," short for *ali'i* [Pukui and Elbert 1986:205]).

32. Valeri (1985a:325) interprets the act of eating the victim's eye as one of acquiring divine "sight" or superior knowledge, part of the transformation of the king into a divine being.

33. Valeri (1985b:83–93) offers an interesting comparison between Hawai'i and European feudalism, in particular the *seigneurie*.

34. This multiple layering of chiefly rights is evidenced in early-nineteenth-century records from the Anahulu Valley. Emerson, who was resident in the valley, observed that "every land has been regarded as having some owner, and many lands have six or eight owners at the same time" (quoted in Sahlins 1992:143). Waialua, he noted, "has seven lords, one above the other."

35. A further recent study of Mahele land claims focuses on the large Kahana Valley on windward Oʻahu (Stauffer 2004).

36. Hālawa, an important *ahupuaʻa* with large irrigated tracts, went to the high chiefess Victoria Kamāmalu in the Mahele division (Barrère 1994:225; Commissioner of Public Lands 1929:4).

37. Desha (2000:400) writes of Kamehameha's war fleet for the invasion of Oʻahu in 1795 that "this was a genuinely great expedition, and the sea was reddened by the great numbers of the fleets going to make war on Kalanikūpule."

38. In a comparison of Hawaiʻi with New Zealand Maori, Sahlins writes of "a complementary relation between cannibalism and human sacrifice" (1985b:215). The Maori practiced cannibalism but spoke of sacrifice only in myth, whereas the Hawaiians practiced human sacrifice but told "mythic tales of cannibal exploits." This systematic relationship "predicts a complementary distribution of cannibalism and human sacrifice, in correlation with the transformation to divine kingship" (Sahlins 1985b:216).

39. Marcus and Flannery (1996:156–58) associate the transition from chiefdom to state in Hawaiʻi with Kamehameha's rise to power and military consolidation of the archipelago following European contact. While I agree that "states arise when one member of a group of chiefdoms begins to take over its neighbors," I believe that the evidence shows that this happened considerably earlier in Hawaiʻi than with Kamehameha, and was an endogenous phenomenon.

CHAPTER THREE

1. According to Thrum's preface in Fornander (1916–19), these Native Hawaiian assistants include S. M. Kamakau, J. Kepelino, and S. N. Haleole.

2. Beckwith's work is important, but in keeping with early-twentieth-century anthropological views, she tended to regard the Hawaiian traditions as myth or legend, rather than as historical accounts.

3. ʻUlu and Nānāʻulu, sons of Kiʻi, are two significant ancestors in the chiefly lineages of Hawaiʻi. The latter is said to have voyaged to Hawaiʻi from Kahiki, whereas ʻUlu remained in Kahiki but later descendants of his appear as early ruling chiefs of Maui (e.g., Paumakua a Huanuiikalālaʻilaʻi).

4. Various versions of this saga, which includes the voyaging feats of ʻOlopana, Moʻikeha, Kila, and Laʻamaikahiki, are found in Kamakau (1991:76–79), Fornander (1996:46–58), Kalākaua (1990:117–35), and Beckwith (1940:352–62). These accounts vary slightly, but all follow the same essential narrative line.

5. Individual accounts of Pāʻao include Kamakau (1991:97–100), Fornander (1996:33–38), and Beckwith (1940:363–75).

6. The name Porapora appears in Hawaiʻi as Polapola, a land area (*ʻili*) on Kalaupapa Peninsula of Molokaʻi Island (Kirch 2002:22).

7. Most chiefs trace their ascent from either ʻUlu or Nānāʻulu, both of whom were sons of Kiʻi (Tiki) in the Hawaiian genealogies.

8. Kaha'i-a-Ho'okamali'i was a contemporary of the O'ahu ruling chief Kahōkūpohākano, around AD 1390.

9. Sahlins (1992:21–26) discusses Mā'ilikūkahi in relation to the "remembered landscape" of Waialua district.

10. *Ho'okupu* is a compound term derived from the causative prefix *ho'o*, and *kupu*, "growth." Hence, "to cause to grow" with an obvious reference to the products of the land.

11. Both the earlier war led by Kalanuiohua of Hawai'i, and this aggression by the combined Maui and Hawai'i island forces seem to have been raiding expeditions, rather than intended conquests.

12. Kaka'alaneo is not known to have visited O'ahu. However, Kaka'alaneo's father, Ka'ulahea did make a visit to O'ahu, where he was the only Maui king to enter Kūkaniloko (Kamakau 1991:38).

13. Malo (1951:251–54) provides a detailed version of this *mo'olelo*, in which Kalaunuiohua derives his military prowess from a prophetess named Wa'ahia.

14. While all of the sources agree in the major outlines of the history of Līloa, 'Umi, and Hākau, there are minor differences, some of which are significant. Here I take Kamakau's account (1961:1–21) as the primary text, supplemented by the equally detailed version in *Fornander's Collection of Hawaiian Antiquities* (Fornander 1916:178–235).

15. This genealogy is given in Fornander (1916:180) and also by Kamakau (1961:4).

16. Līloa elevated 'Umi's commoner adopted sons to minor chiefly status, giving them lands in Hāmākua, and he made Akahiakuleana the chiefess over the *ahupua'a* of Kealahaka (Kamakau 1961:8).

17. The wicker casket was one of two famous *kā'ai*, shaped in the form of a limbless human torso with a head displaying an open mouth and pearl-shell eyes (Buck 1957:575–76, Fig. 347; see also Rose 1992). The other *kā'ai* was said to contain the bones of Lonoikamakahiki.

18. From Kamakau's account, it would appear that Kaleioku was from a line of Lono priests, as later he is said to be a "younger brother" of the two old priests Nunu and Kakohe (1961:12).

19. There is some variation in the two versions of Kamakau (1961) and Fornander (1916–20) as to the particulars of Hākau's slaying. The latter account has only Hākau, his servant, and the two priests present, whereas Kamakau indicates that other warriors and members of Hākau's court were also slain, their bodies all offered up in Honua'ula *heiau*.

20. A detail in Fornander's version (1916:210) refers to a trip that 'Umi made to Kawaihae, in Kohala district. 'Umi intended to proceed in a westerly direction, but his priest Kaleioku advised him: "The proper thing for you to do is to travel toward the east first, this being your first journey around your kingdom [*aupuni*]." Kaleioku was thus recommending a clockwise circuit of the island, which is precisely the course taken by the *akua loa*, or "long god" of Lono during the Makahiki procession (see Chapter 2). Here again is another cultural association of 'Umi with Lono.

21. It is also possible that this major royal center was built, or at least expanded, by Piʻilani's son Kiha-a-Piʻilani, after the latter's defeat of his brother Lono-a-Piʻilani.

22. The chiefess Laʻielohelohe was the mother of both Lono-a-Piʻilani and of Kiha-a-Piʻilani, as well as of their sister Piʻikea, who married ʻUmi-a-Līloa (McKinzie 1986: Vol. 2, 12). Laʻielohelohe's genealogy traces back to Muliʻelealiʻi of the Nānāʻulu line on Oʻahu (McKinzie 1986: Vol. 2, 26). This would not only have conferred high rank but may explain why Kiha-a-Piʻilani was reared on Oʻahu, with maternal kinfolk.

23. Kaʻuiki is a cinder cone on the south side of Hāna Bay, whose steep sides offer a natural fortification. The hillfort is well known in Hawaiian traditions (Sterling 1998:131, 135–36).

24. Fornander (1996:106) has Keliʻiokaloa ruling the entire island after ʻUmi but dying soon thereafter, either from illness or assassination.

25. Fornander (1996:111) says that Keawenui's succession to the kingship was not without opposition, that various district chiefs refused to acknowledge his rule, and that war followed, with Keawenui defeating and killing several district chiefs, keeping their bones wrapped in bundles as trophies.

26. Lonoikamakahiki's older half brother Kanaloakuaʻana played a notorious part in this war, serving under the Maui king Kamalālāwalu against his own kinsmen. After Kanaloakuaʻana was captured by the Hawaiʻi forces, he was tortured by having "his eyelids turned inside out and tattooed" (Kamakau 1961:58; Fornander 1996:123).

27. Kamakau (1961:64) states that Keawe ruled "only over Kohala, Kona, and Ka-ʻu" but it is clear that he had some influence over the windward chiefs as well.

28. The spelling of the name of this king of Kauaʻi and Oʻahu differs among scholarly authorities. Here I follow the version in the Bishop Museum edition of Kamakau (1991) translated by Mary Kawena Pukui.

29. The probable cause would have been by "praying to death" or *kahuna ʻanāʻanā*, or by poisoning (Fornander 1996:142–43).

30. The kinship relations here are complex, for Kalola, the daughter of Kekaulike and Kekuʻiapoiawanui (hence, offspring herself of a *piʻo* union) was the full sister of Kamehamehanui as well as the latter's wife, a *piʻo* mating (Davenport 1994:56). But Kalola also married Kalaniʻōpuʻu, by whom she bore Kīwalaʻō, later to succeed Kalaniʻōpuʻu briefly as king of Hawaiʻi, and his sister Kekuʻiapoiwa Liliha. Kīwalaʻō and Kekuʻiapoiwa Liliha themselves engaged in a full sibling *piʻo* union, to produce the sacred female child Keōpūolani, who was sought after and eventually married by Kamehameha I (Davenport 1994:56–57) to produce his royal heir, Liholiho.

31. Kamalālāwalu's mother was Kumaka, a chiefess from a prominent Hāna line, hence in his genealogy Kamalālāwalu further integrated West and East Maui.

32. Lonoikamakahiki was furious when he discovered that Hinau had helped Kauhi-a-Kama to escape, and he ordered a plot whereby Hinau was tricked to return to Hawaiʻi from Maui, where he was living in the court of

Kauhi-a-Kama; in the middle of the 'Alenuihāhā channel Lonoikamakahiki's men cut Hinau in two and tossed the parts of his body into the sea (Fornander 1916:350).

33. Kauhi-a-Kama was the son of Kamalālāwalu by Pi'ilani-Wahine, a granddaughter of Lono-a-Pi'ilani, who thus carried the high-ranking line descended from Pi'ilani.

34. The traditions are inconsistent on this point, with some (e.g., Fornander 1996:209; Kamakau 1991:74) insisting that Kauhi-a-Kama was married only to Kapukini, who traced her descent from Keli'iokaloa of Hawai'i Island.

35. Kalanikauleleiaiwi was the daughter of Keakealani, a female ruler of Hawai'i and half sister of Keawe-'ikekahiali'iokamoku who succeeded to the kingship of that island (Fornander 1996:210). Ka'ulahea's marriage to her was thus an important link between the ruling houses of Hawai'i and Maui.

36. Dening (1988:95) describes the fearful *pahupū* warriors who killed William Gooch and two of his companions of Vancouver's supply ship *Daedalus*, behind the beach in Waimea Valley, O'ahu, in 1792.

37. Slightly later, Fornander (1996:284) contradicts himself and says that she was the daughter of Kaulahea.

38. Slightly later, King adds the following information: "We only know in regard to Perree orannee that he is an Airee taboo [*ali'i kapu*] & Moee [*moe*], that he is actually making an attack on Taheterrees possessions, & that his Grandsons command to leeward [i.e., Kaua'i]" (Beaglehole 1967:616). This information confirms Pelei'ōhōlani's status as an *ali'i* of the highest rank, subject to the *kapu moe* or prostrating *kapu*.

39. In about 1775, Kahekili repulsed the Hawai'i forces at Hāna, retaking the fortress hill of Ka'uiki, forcing Kalani'ōpu'u to retreat to Hawai'i. Kalani'ōpu'u then reassembled and reorganized his army (Fornander 1996:151 describes its organization in six named brigades) and in 1776 attacked central Maui. A massive battle ensued, with heavy losses on both sides. The *pi'o* son of Kalani'ōpu'u, Kīwala'ō (whose mother Kalola was sister to Kahekili) was sent to negotiate a truce. Kalani'ōpu'u withdrew but was back again the next year, raiding Lāna'i and around West Maui into the Hāmākua district, where he met up with Cook's ships in late 1778.

40. In this account, I follow closely the analysis of Kuykendall (1938:29-70).

41. This was Keōuakuahu'ula, a younger son of Kalani'ōpu'u and half brother of the slain Kīwala'ō, and not to be confused with Keōua Kupuapāikalaninui, Kamehameha's father.

CHAPTER FOUR

1. A major lacuna in our knowledge of Eastern Polynesian settlement remains the Society Islands, the largest archipelago in the central tropical core of East Polynesia. Sites such as Maupiti and Vaito'otia-Fa'ahia, once thought to have dated to the initial colonization period, have recently been shown to date to a later time, in the thirteenth century (Anderson et al. 1999; Anderson and Sinoto 2002).

2. The Bellows dune site (O18) has been the subject of much controversy with respect to its dating and age. Recent redating of materials originally excavated by

Pearson et al. (1971) has resulted in an estimation of the age of initial occupation of the O18 site as circa AD 1040–1219 (Dye and Pantaleo 2010).

3. For example, Kirch (2007b:102) uses archaeological house count data to estimate a maximum population of Kahikinui of between 3,074 and 4,096 persons. Kahikinui's population was the smallest of any district on Maui, and other districts such as Kaupō or Wailuku had populations up to double this number. This suggests that King's islandwide estimate for Maui of 65,400 is, if anything, on the low side.

4. This section draws in part on Kirch (2007c).

5. The terms r and K stand, respectively, for the intrinsic rate of population increase and for carrying capacity.

6. MacArthur and Wilson (1967) initially applied the concept of r/K selection in island biogeography. See Pianka (1978:122 passim) and especially Hutchinson (1978:1–40) for further discussion of r and K in population ecology.

7. Clark (1988) offered a critique of these initial efforts at Hawaiian paleodemography.

8. Dye and Komori's model is affected by certain peculiarities of radiocarbon dating (see Kirch 2007c:63–64), such as the nonlinear relationship between radiocarbon years and calendar years, due to temporal variation in the production of ^{14}C in the atmosphere (Taylor 1987:24). As a smoothed curve, the Dye-Komori model strongly validates a phase of rapid growth in the Hawaiian population beginning around AD 1100 and peaking around AD 1400 to 1500. However, it would be an overinterpretation to take the "waves" in the recent, right-hand portion of the curve as direct reflections of population trends in the late precontact period, because these undulations are responding to peculiarities in the way that ^{14}C dates are calibrated.

9. The emphasis on Kona and Kohala means that this sample derives almost exclusively from the leeward side of the island, with little representation of the windward zones.

10. Unfortunately, the calibration of ^{14}C ages that fall within the last two centuries of the precontact era in Hawai'i results in a strongly bimodal distribution, itself an artifact of the calibration curve, what McFadgen et al. (1994) refer to as the "calibration stochastic distortion (CSD) effect."

11. The 1831 to 1832 census gave the population of Kaupō as 3,220, and that for all of Maui Island as 35,062 (Schmitt 1973:18). This island total is a little more than half of King's estimate for the island in 1779. If we assume that the population of Kaupō was reduced in roughly the same proportion as the entire island, then a precontact population for Kaupō of about 6,440 would yield a density of 292 persons/km².

12. The rate of intrinsic growth, r, is determined by the formula $r = \ln (N_2/N_1)/t$ where N_1 and N_2 are the founding and ending population sizes and t is the elapsed time (Hassan 1981:139). N_1 is likely to have been in the range of 50 to 100 persons, and N_2 was likely to have been around 400 to 500,000 persons. Depending on the date of initial settlement (sometime between AD 800 and 1000), with population peaking at roughly AD 1500, t varies between 500 and 700 years. Various combinations of these parameters thus give us the range in likely r values from 1.2 to 1.8 percent.

13. This GIS model does not include areas of colluvial soil in valley regions on the older islands that were also well suited to dryland cultivation, but on higher slopes than Hawaiians typically used for irrigation. Because these colluvial soils benefit from nutrient inputs due to mass-wasting on their higher slopes (Vitousek et al., 2003), they do not suffer from the nutrient depletion on older and wetter substrates on the old volcanic shield surfaces. Including such areas in a GIS model would increase the areas of potentially prime dryland cultivation on the older islands, especially Oʻahu and Kauaʻi.

14. With the greatest extent of irrigated lands anywhere in the archipelago, Kauaʻi Island would be the ideal location to study the course of this mode of landesque capital intensification. The extensive alluvial floodplain pondfields of Hanalei Valley were studied by Schilt (1980) and Athens (1983), who obtained dates suggesting a major phase of pondfield development beginning around the thirteenth to fifteenth centuries.

15. A few substantially earlier ^{14}C dates were also obtained, which Allen thought might indicate cultivation as early as AD 440. These dates must be discounted in light of new chronological evidence for Hawaiian colonization; they most likely reflect the persistent problem of old wood.

16. Many of these dated samples were obtained by trenching through the field embankments. Embankment construction often sealed in pockets of intact pre-embankment soil containing charcoal resulting from anthropogenic burning of the landscape prior to cultivation. All samples were identified to botanical taxon, and whenever possible short-lived species were selected for dating, to avoid the "old wood" problem of in-built age.

17. When a field embankment was constructed, it capped the area of soil under the embankment, which was then no longer subject to nutrient uptake, in contrast to the soil in the adjacent open field areas. Thus comparing samples from under embankments with those from adjacent open fields provides a relative measure of nutrient loss due to cropping between the time when the embankment was constructed and field use was abandoned.

18. Our biocomplexity research has modeled the coupled effects of stochastic rainfall variation on soil organic matter dynamics, and how this influenced harvest output in the dryland agricultural systems (Lee et al., 2006). Using a modified version of the CENTURY model (Parton et al., 1987), Lee et al. demonstrate that a combination of low nutrient availability, nutrient-poor plant tissue, high water-holding capacity soils, and the seasonal climatic variation present in leeward Hawaiʻi "results in nonlinear dynamics that substantially increase yield variation in some areas." Simulations for the Kohala field system area demonstrate that the lower-elevation areas would have been especially vulnerable to stochastic climate variations, encouraging a bet-hedging strategy in which any given social unit (a household or group of such households) maintained farming sites at different elevations in order to minimize the degree of risk. Allen (2004) has similarly pointed to such bet-hedging agronomic strategies within the Kona field system on Hawaiʻi Island.

19. Geological substrates in the western part of Kahikinui range from as young as 8 kyr to around 75 kyr, while those in the eastern part of the district are considerably older, ca. 225 kyr or greater.

20. The word *heiau* is thought to be derived from the term *hai*, meaning "to sacrifice" (Valeri 1985:173).

21. Loʻaloʻa is not the largest temple on the island. This distinction goes to Piʻilanihale Heiau in Hāna, with a surface area of 12,126 m² (Kolb 1991).

22. Weisler and Kirch (1985) identified a pattern of small temples situated near the eastern borders of *ahupuaʻa* along the southern coastline of Molokaʻi, and they interpreted these as Hale o Lono temples associated with the annual Makahiki tribute collection. Recent fieldwork along the Kohala coastline, in Makiloa and Kālala *ahupuaʻa* (Kirch, unpublished data) also shows a pattern of temples located near, and marking, territorial boundaries. Also in Kohala, Mulrooney and Ladefoged (2005) trace the development of upland *heiau* along *ahupuaʻa* boundaries.

23. The war god Kū is associated with high mountains and forested regions; the orientation of these temples toward the Haleakalā summit may be one indication of their association with the Kū cult.

24. The three oldest dates were obtained by Kolb (2006) and all have contexts noted by him as "basal." As original landscape-burning events, these may have incorporated old wood from long-lived dryland forest trees, thus creating an in-build age effect.

25. Kolb (1991:173) gives the area of Loʻaloʻa as 5,115 m². I believe that the figure of 4,160 m², based on recent high-precision GPS survey, is more accurate.

26. I question Kolb's estimation of the size of the initial construction phase at Piʻilanihale, which he puts at 9,363 m² (Kolb 1999, Table 1). This is effectively the size of the entire main terrace at the site. However, Kolb's limited excavations (mostly 1 and 2 m² test pits) were not sufficient to reveal the stratigraphy across this immense structure. His two earliest dates (Beta-40360 and -40635) come from two test units each of 2 m² penetrating, respectively, 0.46 and 0.85 cm into the terrace (Kolb 1991, table B-7). No stratigraphic sections of these units are provided in Kolb's dissertation or articles, and they cannot be linked in a convincing manner to the full extent of the central terrace. Most likely, these two dates derive from cultural activity on top of the relatively level lava flow that was later expanded into the massive terrace forming the central part of the site. It is more likely that the central terrace, including the impressive six-stepped retaining face, was formally defined during the second construction phase, which based on Kolb's dates probably took place in the sixteenth century.

27. Kolb (1991, 1994) interpreted the data from his eight temple excavations around Maui Island in terms of a four-phase sequence: Formation (AD 1200–1400), Consolidation (AD 1400–1500), Unification (AD 1500–1650), and Annexation (AD 1650–1820). His conclusion that the Consolidation Period saw the greatest labor investment in East Maui, however, rests on assigning the entire massive central terrace at Piʻilanihale to the site's first construction phase. Phase Piʻilanihale I, which Kolb estimates required 84,012 labor days to build, is assigned by him to his Consolidation Period (1994a: Table 2). Of the overall total of 117,933 labor days that Kolb estimates for all of the Consolidation Period constructions at his eight dated *heiau*, Piʻilanihale I thus accounts for 71 percent. This swamping of the labor-estimate values for the Consolidation phase by including the Piʻilanihale I figure contributes to the apparent

early spike in temple construction investment for the East Maui polities, as plotted by Kolb (1994a: Fig. 6). If, however, the main terrace dates instead to the sixteenth century (Kolb's Unification Period), as my reading of the evidence suggests, then the patterns for both East and West Maui temples become consistent. This would make the period of greatest investment in temple construction Kolb's Unification Period, an interpretation I believe to be more consistent with the radiocarbon evidence.

28. *Hōlua* was a competitive sport of the Hawaiian *ali'i* that involved riding a specially constructed narrow sled with two parallel runners down a steep hillside (Malo 1951:224). *Hōlua* slides were constructed of stone and earth, and topped with dry grass to make the sleds run faster (Buck 1957:383, Fig. 252).

29. Many of the royal centers share the quality of having a *pu'uhonua* as a part of the complex.

30. Ladd (1969, appendix) reports several ^{14}C dates, all but one of which gave results of "modern." The single nonmodern date has an age of 320 ± 90, but this seems not to have been corrected for δ^{13}C and thus cannot be calibrated.

31. The *pao* technique involves using large rectilinear slabs of lava in a kind of post and lintel construction, leaving chambers within the wall.

32. Fowke (1922:187) described numerous enclosures and walls extending "for nearly a mile south of the heiau." Unfortunately, these subsidiary structures were mostly destroyed by the sugar plantation in the twentieth century.

33. Kolb (1991:235–40) believes that much of the massive terrace base of Pōpōiwi was constructed between AD 1300 to 1465, but this interpretation depends on just two radiocarbon dates from small test pits (Kolb's excavations at the site constitute a mere 0.2 percent sample). As in the case of Pi'ilanihale (see note 26), no continuous stratigraphic trenches were excavated, precluding accurate interpretation of construction sequences.

CHAPTER FIVE

1. One could extend this discussion to include the writings of several others, including Burrows's early work on "breed and border" in Polynesia (Burrows 1939), as well as the writings of archaeologists such as Allen (1991, 1992), Cordy (1974a, 1974b, 1981), Ladefoged and Graves (2006, 2007, 2008), Saxe (1977), and Spriggs (1988). Friedman's (1981, 1982) models of social evolution in Oceania, in which he refers to Hawai'i as representing an unstable "quasi-state" formation, are also relevant here.

2. Sahlins's invocation of Polanyi's notion of redistribution was taken up by many anthropological archaeologists, who saw this as a key factor in the development of chiefdoms (e.g., Peebles and Kus 1977; Earle 1977).

3. Sahlins as evolutionist correlates with his period at the University of Michigan, which in the early 1970s emerged as a center for anthropological archaeology based on "neoevolutionary" theory, much of it originally propounded by Sahlins and Service (1960).

4. Sahlins spent 1967 to 1969 as a visitor in the Laboratoire d'Anthropologie of Claude Lévi-Strauss, and his Paris sojourn influenced his theoretical turn, not just in his adoption of structuralist principles, but in his melding of these with the French *Annales* school of history as practiced by Fernand Braudel and others.

5. Sahlins (1992) broke ground with previous accounts of Hawaiian post-contact history in recognizing that the Hawaiian *ali'i* were (at least partial) authors of their own history. "Hawaiians too were authors of their history and not merely its victims. While capitalism (in all its cultural manifold) was imposing itself on them, and precisely as it could not be denied, Hawaiians synthesized the experience in their own cultural terms. Specifically Polynesian and local, these terms gave a specific historic turn to Western capitalism; indeed they gave capitalism powers and forces unparalleled even in other Pacific societies, including societies exposed to a Western 'impact' of similar degree" (1992:215–16).

6. Roger Green introduced the settlement pattern approach to Hawai'i in the late 1960s, and the first major applications were in the Makaha Valley, Hālawa Valley, and Lapakahi projects (Green 1980; Kirch and Kelly 1975; Tuggle and Griffin 1973). The data provided by these projects were crucial in providing Hommon with evidence to support his "inland expansion" hypothesis.

7. There are some differences between the original 1976 dissertation and Hommon's 1986 synopsis, such as in the phase sequences he outlines: four phases in the original work, reduced to three in the published version. Since the published version presumably represents his more considered views, I use his three-phase sequence in this discussion.

8. Hommon defines the "archaic *maka'ainana*" as follows: "All members of the 'archaic *maka'ainana*' were conceived of as related by bonds of kinship and the chiefs were considered senior relatives whose authority was based to a great extent on institutionalized generosity" (1976:230).

9. Hommon rejected a simplistic, unicausal role for "population pressure" and went to some lengths to point out why this was untenable (1976:249–58). Hommon's model contrasts with that of Cordy (1974b:98), who regarded population pressure as "an initiating independent variable" driving social change in Hawai'i.

10. Carbonized sweet potato tubers or tuber fragments (parenchyma) have been recovered from a number of archaeological contexts in Hawai'i, and radiocarbon dated. The earliest of these, reported by Ladefoged et al. (2005) from the Kohala field system, has a direct AMS ^{14}C determination on the tuber of 580 ± 40, which gives a calibrated age range of AD 1290 to 1430 at two standard deviations. Thus sweet potatoes were unequivocally present in Hawai'i by the beginning of the fifteenth century, when the dryland field systems began to be developed.

11. In their comparative evolutionary study of human societies, Johnson and Earle (2000:284–94) use Hawai'i as an example of a "complex chiefdom" that was positioned at "the threshold of state society." Earle uses similar language throughout his book on chiefdom political economy, for example: the Hawaiian chiefdom was the "most complex ... of any chiefdoms known elsewhere in the world" (1997:34); "Hawaiian warfare was successful in expanding the polities to the brink of statehood" (1997:141); the Hawaiian chiefdoms "verged on state societies" (1997:200); "Hawaiian chiefdoms would, eventually, have reinvented themselves as states" (1997:202); and "the strengthening of institutional control that took [Hawai'i] to the very edge of state society" (1996:210).

12. Earle overemphasizes the extent to which Hawai'i was dependent on staple finance, overlooking the considerable wealth finance in feathers and

feathered objects, fine barkcloth, mats, cordage, and other material goods that also helped to fuel the Hawaiian political economy.

13. In his discussion of the Hawaiian *heiau*, Earle draws on the work of his former student Kolb (1991, 1994) and uses Kolb's phase sequence. He accepts Kolb's conclusion that the period of greatest investment in temple construction was during Kolb's "Consolidation Period" (AD 1400–1500) and that after that "Hawaiian chiefdoms turned away from monumental construction" (Earle 1997:179). However, Kolb's model depends unduly on a limited data set from a single site (Piʻilanihale) on East Maui. Kolb's conclusion that the peak of *heiau* construction occurred during the sixteenth century is questionable. More likely, *heiau* building was at its greatest extent somewhat later in time, during the seventeenth to early eighteenth centuries, although it may well have declined prior to European contact (see Chapter 4).

14. Hatcher and Bailey (2001:21 passim) offer a useful review of Malthusian theory, as this relates to modeling long-term economic development in Medieval England.

15. The caveat on level of technology is not trivial. For all its intensity, Hawaiian land use depended exclusively on a "Neolithic" technology in which the main agricultural tools were digging sticks and stone adzes for forest clearance. Lacking metal, as well as draft animals, there were limits to the Hawaiian farmers' abilities to modify the landscape. With the introduction of metal tools in the postcontact era, these limits did begin to be surpassed. For example, in the Waikolu Valley of windward Molokaʻi, taro irrigation systems were extended farther up steeper slopes by cutting and filling terraces (Kirch 2002:40–41), presumably using metal tools such as picks and spades.

16. In Wood's model, this is the "level of average well-being, call it θ, at which population replacement is just possible" (1998:109).

17. Puleston and Tuljapurkar write that "we find that given space limitation a population in the neighborhood of its equilibrium is drawn to a population size at which the balance between production and consumption results in a population growth rate of zero" (2008:156).

18. The following paragraphs on the "production function" are drawn in part from Kirch (2007a).

19. On the origin of this Eastern Polynesian pantheon (for only *Taangaloa is found in Western Polynesia), see Marck (1996a). These deities may well have originated in the names of eponymous ancestors of Central Eastern Polynesian ascent groups. This was the view of Buck, who wrote, "I believe that the major gods—Tane, Rongo, Tu, Tangaroa—and the other older gods were navigating ancestors who guided their voyaging ships through the later part of the eastward movement through Micronesia into the Society Islands. . . . There was ample time for them to be deified and then to become enshrouded with the mists of antiquity" (Buck 1939:36).

20. Kamakau (1961:154–55) describes how, during the construction of the war temple of Puʻukoholā at Kawaihae, Kamehameha set an example by carrying heavy stones up the hill. However, he refused to let his younger brother Kealiʻimaikaʻi participate in this work, saying, "You must preserve our tabu."

21. Kamakau (1961:46) relates the story of Kanaloa-kua'ana whose priests and counselors came and urinated in his presence to demonstrate that their urine was like water, a sign that they lacked sufficient 'awa to drink and rich foods to eat (which would have turned their urine yellow).

22. Hawaiian conquest warfare may well have been driven by other incentives than just a desire to acquire agriculturally productive lands. Hommon has argued that "the fact that wars of conquest begin to appear in the traditional histories about AD 1600, soon after the apparent end of significant expansion, is consistent with the view that a major goal of Hawaiian warfare was the acquisition by warrior chiefs of scarce goods such as pigs and yellow feathers" (2009).

23. Handy and Pukui describe the mythic associations between Kāne and taro, noting that "the family bowl of *poi* (starch staple made from taro) in the household was sacred to Haloa, who is Kane" (1972:34; see also Handy and Handy 1972:76, 79–83).

24. Spriggs (1984) provides data on pondfield labor inputs, suggesting about 437 work days/ha/yr, whereas the intensive dryland agricultural system observed by Yen (1973) on Anuta required an estimated labor input of 875 work days/ha/yr.

Glossary of Hawaiian Terms

'aha ali'i A council of chiefs.
ahupua'a A territorial land unit, under the control of a subchief (the ali'i 'ai ahupua'a). Such units typically ran from the mountains to the sea.
'āina Land.
akua God, spirit, deity.
ali'i Elite, member of the chiefly class.
ali'i akua Literally, "god-king." An expression reserved for the highest ranking ali'i, especially those of pi'o rank.
ali'i nui Literally, "great chief." The highest ranked chief within a polity; king.
'aumakua Ancestral deities; literally "collective parents."
'awa Kava, *Piper methysticum*, the root of which was used to prepare a psychoactive (but nonalcoholic) beverage consumed in substantial quantity by the elites.
haku'āina A landlord, typically a konohiki or ahupua'a-level chief.
haku'ōhi'a The main 'ōhi'a wood image in a temple; rites for the consecration of the image.
hale naua The house in which genealogical specialists gathered to question chiefs regarding their pedigrees, and to ascertain whether they would be allowed to join the royal household.
hale o Lono Temple dedicated to the god Lono (literally, "house of Lono").
heiau The general term for a Hawaiian ritual place, where sacrifices of any kind were offered to the gods or to ancestral spirits.
heiau ho'oulu 'ai Agricultural temple (literally, "temple to increase food").
hoa'āina A cultivator who worked a land section directly under the control of the konohiki (a tenant); literally "friend of the land."

hōlua A competitive sport of the elites, involving riding a narrow two-runner sled down a specially prepared course.

ho'okupu Tribute (literally, "to cause to grow or increase").

hula Various forms of traditional dance.

'ie'ie An indigenous climbing shrub of the Pandanus family (*Freycinetia arborea*), the tough fibers of which were used to weave the foundations for feathered garments.

ilāmuku Executive officer, adjutant; these individuals were responsible for maintaining the *kapu* associated with the household of a high chief or king.

'ili A land unit, smaller in size than an *ahupu'a*.

'ili kūpono A special kind of *'ili* segment within an *ahupua'a*, under the direct control of the king, rather than the *ahupua'a* chief, and whose tribute was reserved for the king.

kahuna Priest.

kahuna nui High priest, usually of the Kū cult, who officiated at ceremonies in the king's temple.

kahuna pule Priests who officiated in formal temple ceremonies, especially of the Kū, Lono, and Kāne cults.

kālaimoku Counselor to the king; sometimes translated as "prime minister."

kama'āina Someone born to a particular locale; literally "child of the land".

Kanaloa One of the four major gods of the Hawaiian pantheon.

Kāne A principal god of the Hawaiian pantheon; the creator god, also deity of flowing waters and irrigation, to whom taro (*kalo*) was sacred.

kapa Barkcloth.

kapu Sacred; prohibited; forbidden.

kapu moe The prostrating taboo, obligatory for the highest ranked chiefs.

kaukau ali'i Lesser grades of chiefs.

kāula A prophet or seer, one who has the ability to transmit oracles.

kauwā (or kauā) Member of the lowest social class, sometimes referred to as "outcasts" or "slaves." *Kauwā* were suitable for offerings of human sacrifice at the *luakini* temples.

Kī The ti plant, *Cordyline fruticosum*.

ko'a A fishing shrine, dedicated to the god Kū'ula.

kō'ele An area of pondfields or a garden segment worked by the common people on behalf of the *konohiki* and the chief; the production of the *kō'ele* was reserved for the use of the *konohiki* and *ali'i*.

konohiki Land manager for an *ahupua'a* land unit, representing the *ali'i 'ai ahupua'a* chief.

Kū One of the four principal gods of the Hawaiian pantheon; god of war.

kuaiwi Literally, "backbone." A stone wall or alignment running up and down the slope, demarking divisions within a dryland field system, as in the Kona Field System.

kū'auhau A specialist within the royal court, responsible for memorizing the genealogies and oral traditions of the *ali'i*.

kula Dryland cultivation areas; in Mahele land claims *kula* lands are typically distinguished from irrigated taro lands (*lo'i*).

Glossary of Hawaiian Terms

lei niho palaoa A special neck ornament worn by chiefs, consisting of a tongue-shaped pendant suspended by braids of human hair.
lele The sacrificial altar on a temple.
lua A pit, such as the pit for disposing of sacrificial offerings on a temple.
luakini A state temple dedicated to the god Kū, at which human sacrifice was performed.
loʻi An irrigated pondfield for the cultivation of taro (*Colocasia esculenta*).
loko kuapā A fishpond formed by constructing a stone wall out onto the reef flat.
Lono One of the four principal gods of the Hawaiian pantheon; god of dryland agriculture, to whom the sweet potato (*ʻuala*) was sacred.
maika A game in which a special bowling stone was rolled along a pitch with two upright sticks at the end.
makaʻāinana Commoner.
Makahiki A four-month period which commenced with the first visibility of Pleiades in November; this was the period of tribute collection, sacred to Lono, when war was forbidden.
mana Supernatural or divine power, efficacy.
mele Song or chant.
moku A political district.
mokupuni Island.
moʻo A land unit, smaller in size than an *ʻili*.
moʻokūʻauhau Genealogy or pedigree.
moʻolelo (or moʻoʻōlelo) Oral tradition, history.
mua The men's eating house. The *mua* of a king was where he would hold court with other high-ranking males and advisors.
naha One of the high ranks of chiefs.
nīʻaupiʻo Offspring of a royal incestuous marriage between half brother and sister, or full brother and sister (literally, "recurved coconut midrib").
noa Free, without *kapu*, the opposite of *kapu*.
ʻokana A district or subdistrict, usually incorporating several *ahupuaʻa*.
pahu Particular kind of cylindrical drum, with a tympanum of shark's skin, used during *luakini* temple ceremonies.
pahupū Cut in half; the name was given to a special cadre of Maui warriors, fiercely loyal to Kahekili, who were tattooed completely black on one-half of their bodies.
piʻo Marriage between a brother and sister, or between half siblings; the term also denotes the offspring of such a union. *Piʻo* unions were the exclusive privilege of the highest ranked *aliʻi*.
pūloʻuloʻu A barkcloth covered ball on a shaft, either carried before the king or set up in front of his residence, as a mark of taboo.
punalua Spouses sharing a spouse, as in two brothers sharing a wife.
waiwai Wealth, goods, property (literally, "water" reduplicated).
wohi A rank of chief which was exempt from the prostrating *kapu*.

References

Adams, R. McC. 1966. *The Evolution of Urban Society.* Chicago: Aldine.
Algaze, G. 1993. *The Uruk World System: The Dynamics of Expansion of Early Mesopotamian Civilization.* Chicago: University of Chicago Press.
Allen, J., ed. 1987. *Five Upland 'Ili: Archaeological and Historical Investigations in the Kaneʻohe Interchange, Interstate Highway H-3, Island of Oʻahu.* Anthropology Department Report 87-1. Honolulu: Bishop Museum.
Allen, J. 1991. The role of agriculture in the evolution of the pre-contact Hawaiian state. *Asian Perspectives* 30:117–32.
———. 1992. Farming in Hawaiʻi from colonization to contact: Radiocarbon chronology and implications for cultural change. *New Zealand Journal of Archaeology* 14:45–66.
Allen, J., M. R. Riford, P. Brennan, D. Chaffee, L. S. Cummings, C. Kawachi, L. Liu, and G. Murakami. 2002. *Kula and Kahawai: Geoarchaeological and Historical Investigations in Middle Maunawili Valley, Kailua, Koʻolau Poko, Oʻahu.* Report prepared for HRT, Ltd. Honolulu: AMEC Earth and Environmental.
Allen, M. S., ed. 2001. *Gardens of Lono: Archaeological Investigations at the Amy B. H. Greenwell Ethnobotanical Garden, Kealakekua, Hawaiʻi.* Honolulu: Bishop Museum Press.
Anderson, A., E. Conte, G. Clark, Y. Sinoto, and F. Petchy. 1999. Renewed excavations at Motu Paeao, Maupiti Island, French Polynesia. *New Zealand Journal of Archaeology* 21:47–66.
Anderson, A., and Y. Sinoto. 2002. New radiocarbon ages of colonization sites in East Polynesia. *Asian Perspectives* 41:242–57.
Anderson, P-K. 2001. Houses of the *Kamaʻaina*: Historical anthropology in a rural Hawaiian valley. PhD diss., University of California, Berkeley.

Andrews, L. 1865. *A Dictionary of the Hawaiian Language*. Honolulu: Whitney.
Anonymous. 1838. *Ka Mooolelo Hawaii [The History of Hawai'i]*. Lahainaluna, Maui: Lahainaluna Seminary Press. Facsimile reprint 2005. Honolulu: Hawaiian Historical Society.
Athens, J. S. 1983. Prehistoric pondfield agriculture in Hawai'i: Archaeological investigations at the Hanalei National Wildlife Refuge, Kaua'i. Unpublished report. Honolulu: Bernice P. Bishop Museum Library.
———. 1997. Hawaiian native lowland vegetation in prehistory. In P. V. Kirch and T. L. Hunt, eds., *Historical Ecology in the Pacific Islands: Prehistoric Environmental and Landscape Change*, 248–70. New Haven: Yale University Press.
———. 2001. Identification of fishpond sediments, Loko Pa'au'au, Pearl City Peninsula, O'ahu, Hawai'i. Manuscript report prepared for IT Corporation. Honolulu: International Archaeological Research Institute, Inc.
Athens, J. S., H. D. Tuggle, J. V. Ward, and D. J. Welch. 2002. Avifaunal extinctions, vegetation change, and Polynesian impacts in prehistoric Hawai'i. *Archaeology in Oceania* 37:57–78.
Baker, P. T., and W. T. Sanders. 1972. Demographic studies in anthropology. *Annual Review of Anthropology* 1:151–78.
Barrau, J. 1965. L'humide et le sec: An essay on ethnobiological adaptation to contrastive environments in the Indo-Pacific area. *Journal of the Polynesian Society* 74:329–46.
Barrère, D. B. 1975. *Kamehameha in Kona: Two Documentary Studies*. Pacific Anthropological Records 23. Honolulu: Bishop Museum.
———. 1986. A reconstruction of the history and function of the *pu'uhonua* and the Hale o Keawe at Hōnaunau. In E. H. Bryan and K. P. Emory, eds., *The Natural and Cultural History of Hōnaunau, Kona, Hawai'i*, 117–36. Department of Anthropology Report Series 86-2. Honolulu: Bishop Museum.
———. 1994. *The King's Mahele: The Awardees and their Lands*. Unpublished Xerox manuscript (566 pp.). Copy in author's possession.
Barrère, D. B., M. K. Pukui, and M. Kelly. 1980. *Hula: Historical Perspectives*. Pacific Anthropological Records 30. Honolulu: Bishop Museum.
Beaglehole, J. C., ed. 1967. *The Journals of Captain James Cook. The Voyage of the Resolution and Discovery, 1776–1780*. 2 vols. Cambridge: Hakluyt Society.
Beckwith, M. W., ed. 1932. *Kepelino's Traditions of Hawaii*. Bernice P. Bishop Museum Bulletin 95. Honolulu: Bishop Museum Press.
———. 1940. *Hawaiian Mythology*. Honolulu: University Press of Hawai'i.
Bellwood, P. 1996a. Phylogeny *vs* reticulation in prehistory. *Antiquity* 70:881–90.
———. 1996b. Hierarchy, founder ideology and Austronesian expansion. In J. J. Fox and C. Sather, eds., *Origins, Ancestry and Alliance: Explorations in Austronesian Ethnography*, 18–40. Canberra: Australian National University.
Bennett, W. C. 1931. *Archaeology of Kauai*. Bernice P. Bishop Museum Bulletin 80. Honolulu: Bishop Museum Press.
Berger, A. J. 1972. *Hawaiian Birdlife*. Honolulu: University of Hawai'i Press.
Biggs, B. 1967. The past twenty years in Polynesian linguistics. In G. A. Highland, R. W. Force, A. Howard, M. Kelly, and Y. H. Sinoto, eds., *Polynesian*

References

Culture History: Essays in Honor of Kenneth P. Emory, 303–22. Bernice P. Bishop Museum Special Publication 56. Honolulu: Bishop Museum Press.
———. 1971. The languages of Polynesia. In T. A. Sebeok, ed., *Current Trends in Linguistics*, vol. 8, part 1, *Linguistics in Oceania*, 466–505. Mouton: The Hague.
———. 1998. POLLEX: Proto Polynesian Lexicon. Computer file maintained at the Department of Maori Studies, University of Auckland, New Zealand.
Biggs, B., D. S. Walsh, and J. J. Waqa. 1970. *Proto-Polynesian Reconstructions with English to Proto-Polynesian Finder List*. Working Papers in Linguistics. Auckland: Department of Anthropology, University of Auckland.
Biersack, A. 1996. Rivals and wives: Affinal politics and the Tongan ramage. In J. J. Fox and C. Sather, eds., *Origins, Ancestry and Alliance*, 237–79. Canberra: Department of Anthropology, Australian National University.
Blaikie, P., and H. C. Brookfield, eds. 1987. *Land Degradation and Society*. London: Methuen.
Bloch, M. 1953. *The Historian's Craft*. Trans. P. Putnam. New York: Vintage Books.
Blust, R. 1980. Early Austronesian social organization: The evidence of language. *Current Anthropology* 21:205–26.
Boserup, E. 1965. *The Conditions of Agricultural Growth: The Economics of Agrarian Change under Population Pressure*. Chicago: Aldine.
Bourdieu, P. 1977. *Outline of a Theory of Practice*. Trans. R. Nice. Cambridge: Cambridge University Press.
Braudel, F. 1980. *On History*. Trans. S. Matthews. Chicago: University of Chicago Press.
Brigham, W. T. 1899. *Hawaiian Featherwork*. Bernice P. Bishop Museum Memoir Vol. I, Part 1. Honolulu: Bishop Museum Press.
Bryan, E. H., Jr., and K. P. Emory, eds. 1986. *The Natural and Cultural History of Hōnaunau, Kona, Hawai'i*. Anthropology Department Report 86-2. Honolulu: Bishop Museum.
Brookfield, H. C. 1972. Intensification and disintensification in Pacific agriculture: A theoretical approach. *Pacific Viewpoint* 13:30–48.
———. 1984. Intensification revisited. *Pacific Viewpoint* 25:15–44.
Brumfiel, E. M., and T. K. Earle. 1987. Specialization, exchange and complex societies: An introduction. In E. M. Brumfiel and T. K. Earle, eds., *Specialization, Exchange, and Complex Societies*, 1–9. Cambridge: Cambridge University Press.
Buck, P. H. (Te Rangi Hiroa). 1938. *Vikings of the Sunrise*. New York: Frederick Stokes Co.
———. 1939. *Anthropology and Religion*. New Haven: Yale University Press.
———. 1957. *Arts and Crafts of Hawaii*. Bernice P. Bishop Museum Special Publication 45. Honolulu: Bishop Museum Press.
Burrows, E. G. 1938. Western Polynesia: A study in cultural differentiation. *Etnologiska Studier* 7:1-192. Goteborg.
———. 1939. Breed and border in Polynesia. *American Anthropologist* 41:1–21.
Burtchard, G. C., and M. J. Tomonari-Tuggle. 2004. Agriculture on leeward Hawai'i Island: The Waimea agricultural system reconsidered. *Hawaiian Archaeology* 9:50–73.

Bushnell, O. A. 1993. *The Gifts of Civilization: Germs and Genocide in Hawai'i.* Honolulu: University of Hawai'i Press.

Cachola-Abad, C. K. 1993. Evaluating the orthodox dual settlement model for the Hawaiian Islands: An analysis of artefact distribution and Hawaiian oral traditons. In M. W. Graves and R. C. Green, eds., *The Evolution and Organization of Prehistoric Society in Polynesia,* 13–32. New Zealand Archaeological Association Monograph 19. Auckland.

Carneiro, R. L. 1970. A theory of the origin of the state. *Science* 169:733–38.

———. 1981. The chiefdom: Precursor of the state. In G. D. Jones and R. R. Kautz, eds., *The Transition to Statehood in the New World,* 37–79. Cambridge: Cambridge University Press.

Carson, M. T. 2005a. A radiocarbon dating synthesis for Kaua'i. In M. T. Carson and M. W. Graves, ed., *Na Mea Kahiko o Kaua'i: Archaeological Studies in Kaua'i,* 11–32. Society for Hawaiian Archaeology Special Publication No. 2. Honolulu.

———. 2005b. 'Alekoko fishpond. In M. T. Carson and M. W. Graves, ed., *Na Mea Kahiko o Kaua'i: Archaeological Studies in Kaua'i,* 66–71. Society for Hawaiian Archaeology Special Publication No. 2. Honolulu.

———. 2006. Chronology in Kaua'i: Colonisation, land use, demography. *Journal of the Polynesian Society* 115:173–86.

Carsten, J., and S. Hugh-Jones, eds. 1995. *About the House: Lévi-Strauss and Beyond.* Cambridge: Cambridge University Press.

Cartwright, B. 1929. Notes on Hawaiian genealogies. *Hawaiian Historical Society 38th Annual Report,* 45–47. Honolulu.

———. 1933. Some aliis of the migratory period. *Bernice P. Bishop Museum Occasional Papers* 10(7):1–11.

Chamberlain, A. T. 2006. *Demography in Archaeology.* Cambridge: Cambridge University Press.

Childe, V. G. 1936. *Man Makes Himself.* New York: New American Library.

———. 1942. *What Happened in History.* Harmondsworth: Penguin Books.

Chinen, J. J. 1958. *The Great Mahele: Hawaii's Land Division of 1848.* Honolulu: University of Hawai'i Press.

Chun, M. N. 1993. *Nā Kukui Pio 'Ole: The Inextinguishable Torches.* Honolulu: First People's Productions.

Claessen, H. J. M. 1978. The early state in Tahiti. In H. J. M. Claessen and P. Skalnik, eds., *The Early State,* 441–67. The Hague: Mouton Publishers.

———. 1991. State and economy in Polynesia. In H. J. M. Claessen and P. van de Velde, eds., *Early State Economics,* 291–325. New Brunswick: Transaction Publishers.

Clark, J. T. MS [1981]. *Archaeological Survey of the Proposed Lālāmilo Agricultural Park, South Kohala, Island of Hawai'i.* Unpublished manuscript. Honolulu: Bernice P. Bishop Museum Library.

———. 1988. Paleodemography in leeward Hawaii. *Archaeology in Oceania* 23:22–30.

Clark, J. and P. V. Kirch, eds. 1983. *Archaeological Investigations in the Mudlane-Waimea-Kawaihae Road Corridor, Island of Hawaii: An Interdisciplinary Study of an Environmental Transect.* Department of Anthropology Report No. 83-1. Honolulu: Bishop Museum.

References 247

Cohen, R. 1978. Introduction. In R. Cohen and E. R. Service, eds., *Origins of the State: The Anthropology of Political Evolution*, 1–20. Philadelphia: Institute for the Study of Human Issues.
Cohen, R., and E. R. Service, eds. 1978. *Origins of the State: The Anthropology of Political Evolution.* Philadelphia: Institute for the Study of Human Issues.
Coil, J. H. 2004. "The Beauty That Was": Archaeological investigations of ancient Hawaiian agriculture and environmental change in Kahikinui, Maui. PhD diss., University of California, Berkeley.
Coil, J., and P. V. Kirch. 2005. An Ipomoean landscape: Archaeology and the sweet potato in Kahikinui, Maui, Hawaiian Islands. In C. Ballard, P. Brown, R. M. Bourke, and T. Harwood, eds., *The Sweet Potato in Oceania: A Reappraisal*, 71–84. Oceania Monograph No. 56. Sydney: University of Sydney.
Collerson, K. D., and M. I. Weisler. 2007. Stone adze compositions and the extent of ancient Polynesian voyaging and trade. *Science* 317:1907–11.
Collins, S. L. 1986. Osteological studies of human skeletal remains from the Keopu burial site. In T. L. Han, S. L. Collins, S. D. Clark, and A. Garland, *Moe Kau a Hoʻoilo: Hawaiian Mortuary Practices at Keopu, Kona, Hawaiʻi*, 165–250. Department of Anthropology Report 86-1. Honolulu: Bishop Museum.
Commissioner of Public Lands, Territory of Hawaii. 1929. *Indices of Awards Made by The Board of Commissioners to Quiet Land Titles in the Hawaiian Islands.* Honolulu: Office of the Commissioner of Public Lands.
Cordy, R. 1970. *Piilanihale Heiau Project: Phase I Site Report.* Department of Anthropology Department Report 70-9. Honolulu: Bishop Museum.
———. 1974a. Cultural adaptation and evolution in Hawaii: A suggested new sequence. *Journal of the Polynesian Society* 83:180–91.
———. 1974b. Complex rank cultural systems in the Hawaiian Islands: Suggested explanations for their origin. *Archaeology and Physical Anthropology in Oceania* 9:89–109.
———. 1974c. The Tahitian migration to Hawaii ca. 1100–1300 AD: An argument against its occurrence. *New Zealand Archaeological Association Newsletter* 17:65–76.
———. 1981. *A Study of Prehistoric Social Change: The Development of Complex Societies in the Hawaiian Islands.* New York: Academic Press.
———. 2000. *Exalted Sits the Chief: The Ancient History of Hawaiʻi Island.* Honolulu: Mutual Publishing.
———. 2002a. *The Rise and Fall of the Oʻahu Kingdom.* Honolulu: Mutual Publishing.
———. 2002b. *An Ancient History of Waiʻanae.* Honolulu: Mutual Publishing.
Cordy, R., and M. W. Kaschko. 1980. Prehistoric archaeology in the Hawaiian Islands: Land units associated with social groups. *Journal of Field Archaeology* 7:403–16.
Cox, J. H., and W. H. Davenport. 1974. *Hawaiian Sculpture.* Honolulu: University of Hawaiʻi Press.
Crumley, C. L. 1987. A dialectical critique of hierarchy. In T. C. Patterson and C. W. Gailey, eds., *Power Relations and State Formation*, 155–69. Washington, DC: American Anthropological Association.

Culbert, T. P., ed. 1991. *Classic Maya Political History: Hieroglyphic and Archaeological Evidence*. Cambridge: Cambridge University Press.
Dalton, G. 1960. A note of clarification on economic surplus. *American Anthropologist* 62:483–90.
D'Altroy, T., and T. K. Earle. 1985. State finance, wealth finance, and storage in the Inka political economy. *Current Anthropology* 26:187–206.
Davenport, W. H. 1994. *Pi'o. An Enquiry into the Marriage of Brothers and Sisters and other Close Relatives in Old Hawai'i*. New York: University Press of America.
Davis, E. H. 1979. *Abraham Fornander: A Biography*. Honolulu: University of Hawai'i Press.
Daws, G. 1968. *Shoal of Time: A History of the Hawaiian Islands*. New York: MacMillan.
DeMarrais, E., L. J. Castillo, and T. Earle. 1996. Ideology, materialization and power strategies. *Current Anthropology* 37:15–31.
Denham, T., F. J. Eble, B. Winsborough, and J. V. Ward. 1999. Paleoenvironmental and archaeological investigations at 'Ōhi'apilo Pond, leeward coast of Moloka'i, Hawai'i. *Hawaiian Archaeology* 7:35–60.
Dening, G. 1988. *History's Anthropology: The Death of William Gooch*. New York: University Press of America.
Desha, S. L. 2000. *Kamehameha and his Warrior Kekūhaupi'o*. Trans. F. N. Frazier. Honolulu: Kamehameha Schools Press.
Dixon, B., P. J. Conte, V. Nagahara, and W. K. Hodgins. 1999. Risk minimization and the traditional *ahupua'a* in Kahikinui, Island of Maui, Hawai'i. *Asian Perspectives* 38:229–55.
Dobres, M-A., and J. E. Robb, eds. 2000. *Agency in Archaeology*. London: Routledge.
Dobyns, H. F. 1983. *Their Number Become Thinned: Native American Population Dynamics in Eastern North America*. Knoxville: University of Tennessee Press.
Douglas, B. 1979. Rank, power, authority: A reassessment of traditional leadership in South Pacific societies. *Journal of Pacific History* 14:2–27.
Dye, T. S. 1994. Population trends in Hawai'i before 1778. *Hawaiian Journal of History* 28:1–20.
Dye, T. S., and E. Komori. 1992. A pre-censal population history of Hawaii. *New Zealand Journal of Archaeology* 14:113–28.
Dye, T. S., and J. Pantaleo. 2010. Age of the O18 site. Paper presented at the Annual Meeting of the Society for Hawaiian Archaeology. Honolulu.
Dyen, I., and D. F. Aberle. 1974. *Lexical Reconstruction: The Case of the Proto-Athabascan Kinship System*. Cambridge: Cambridge University Press.
Earle, T. 1973. Control hierarchies in the traditional irrigation economy of Halelea District, Kauai, Hawaii. PhD diss., University of Michigan, Ann Arbor.
———. 1977. A reappraisal of redistribution: Complex Hawaiian chiefdoms. In T. Earle and J. Ericson, eds., *Exchange Systems in Prehistory*, 213–32. New York: Academic Press.
———. 1978. *Economic and Social Organization of a Complex Chiefdom: The Halele'a District, Kaua'i, Hawai'i*, Anthropological Papers of the Museum of Anthropology, University of Michigan, No. 63. Ann Arbor.

———. 1980. Prehistoric irrigation in the Hawaiian Islands: An evaluation of evolutionary significance. *Archaeology and Physical Anthropology in Oceania* 15:1–28.
———. 1997. *How Chiefs Come to Power: The Political Economy in Prehistory*. Stanford: Stanford University Press.
Ehrenreich, R. M., C. L. Crumley, and J. E. Levy, eds. 1995. *Heterarchy and the Analysis of Complex Societies*. Archeological Papers of the American Anthropological Association No. 6. Arlington: American Anthropological Association.
Elias, N. 1983. *The Court Society*. Trans. E. Jephcott. New York: Pantheon Books.
———. 1994. *The Civilizing Process*. Trans. E. Jephcott. Oxford: Blackwell.
Emerson, N. B. 1909. *Unwritten Literature of Hawaii: The Sacred Songs of the Hula*. Bureau of American Ethnology Bulletin 38. Washington DC: Smithsonian Institution.
Emory, K. P. 1924. *The Island of Lanai: A Survey of Native Culture*. Bernice P. Bishop Museum Bulletin 12. Honolulu: Bishop Museum Press.
———. 1965. Warfare. In E. S. Handy, K. P. Emory, E. H. Bryan, P. H. Buck, and J. H. Wise, *Ancient Hawaiian Civilization*, 233–40. Rutland, VT: Charles E. Tuttle Company.
Feinman, G. M. 1998. Scale and social organization: Perspectives on the archaic state. In G. M. Feinman and J. Marcus, eds., *Archaic States*, 95–134. Santa Fe: School of American Research.
Feinman, G. M., and J. Marcus, eds. 1998. *Archaic States*. Santa Fe: School of American Research.
Field, J., P. V. Kirch, K. Kawelu, and T. Ladefoged. 2010. Households and hierarchy: Domestic modes of production in leeward Kohala, Hawai'i Island. *Journal of Island and Coastal Archaeology* 5:52–85.
Finney, B. R. 1994. *Voyage of Rediscovery: A Cultural Odyssey Through Polynesia*. Berkeley: University of California Press.
———. 2006. Ocean sailing canoes. In K. R. Howe, ed., *Vaka Moana: Voyages of the Ancestors*, 100–153. Auckland: David Bateman.
Flannery, K. V. 1972. The cultural evolution of civilizations. *Annual Review of Ecology and Systematics* 3:399–426.
———. 1995. Prehistoric social evolution. In C. Ember and M. Ember, eds., *Research Frontiers in Anthropology*, 1–26. Englewood Cliffs, NJ: Prentice Hall.
———. 1998. The ground plans of archaic states. In G. M. Feinman and J. Marcus, eds., *Archaic States*, 15–58. Santa Fe: School of American Research.
———. 1999. Process and agency in early state formation. *Cambridge Archaeological Journal* 9:3–21.
Flannery, K. V., and J. Marcus, eds. 1983. *The Cloud People: Divergent Evolution of the Zapotec and Mixtec Civilizations*. New York: Academic Press.
Fornander, A. 1916–20. *Fornander Collection of Hawaiian Antiquities and Folk-Lore*. Edited by T. G. Thrum. Bernice P. Bishop Museum Memoirs, Volumes IV, V, and VI. Honolulu: Bishop Museum Press.
———. 1996. *Ancient History of the Hawaiian People to the Times of Kamehameha I*. [Reprint of Vol. II of *An Account of the Polynesian Race*, first published 1878–85]. Honolulu: Mutual Publishing.

Fowke, G. 1922. *Archaeological Investigations*. Bureau of American Ethnology Bulletin 76. Washington DC: Government Printer.

Fox, J. J. 1993a. Comparative perspectives on Austronesian houses: An introductory essay. In J. J. Fox, ed., *Inside Austronesian Houses: Perspectives on Domestic Designs for Living*, 1–29. Canberra: Australian National University.

———., ed. 1993b. *Inside Austronesian Houses: Perspectives on Domestic Designs for Living*. Canberra: Australian National University.

———. 1995. Origin structures and systems of precedence in the comparative study of Austronesian societies. In P. J. Li, C-H. Tsang, Y-K. Huang, D-A. Ho, and C-Y. Tseng, eds., *Austronesian Studies Relating to Taiwan*, 27–58. Symposium Series of the Institute of History and Philology, Academia Sinica No. 3. Taipei: Academia Sinica.

———. 1996. Introduction. In J. J. Fox and C. Sather, eds., *Origins, Ancestry and Alliance*, 1–17. Canberra: Department of Anthropology, Australian National University.

Fried, M. H. 1967. *The Evolution of Political Society: An Essay in Political Anthropology*. New York: Random House.

Friedman, J. 1979. *System, Structure, and Contradiction in the Evolution of "Asiatic" Social Formations*. Social Studies in Oceania and South East Asia 2. Copenhagen: National Museum of Denmark.

———. 1981. Notes on structure and history in Oceania. *Folk* 23:275–95.

———. 1982. Catastrophe and continuity in social evolution. In C. Renfrew, M. J. Rowlands, and B. A. Segraves, eds., *Theory and Explanation in Archaeology*, 175–96. New York: Academic Press.

Geertz, C. 1970. *Agricultural Involution: The Processes of Ecological Change in Indonesia*. Berkeley: University of California Press.

———. 1980. *Negara: The Theatre State in Nineteenth-Century Bali*. Princeton: Princeton University Press.

Giambelluca, T. W., M. A. Nullet, M. A. Ridgley, P. R. Eyre, J. E. T. Moncur, and S. Price. 1991. *Drought in Hawai'i*. Report R88, Commission on Water Resource Management. Honolulu: Department of Land and Natural Resources, State of Hawai'i.

Giddens, A. 1979. *Central Problems in Social Theory: Action, Structure, and Contradiction in Social Analysis*. Berkeley: University of California Press.

Gifford, E. W. 1929. *Tongan Society*. Bernice P. Bishop Museum Bulletin 61. Honolulu: Bishop Museum Press.

Goldman, I. 1955. Status rivalry and cultural evolution in Polynesia. *American Anthropologist* 57:680–97.

———. 1970. *Ancient Polynesian Society*. Chicago: University of Chicago Press.

Goodenough, W. H. 1955. A problem in Malayo-Polynesian social organization. *American Anthropologist* 57:71–83.

———. 1957. Oceania and the problem of controls in the study of cultural and human evolution. *Journal of the Polynesian Society* 66:146–55.

———. 1961. *Property, Kin, and Community on Truk*. Yale University Publications in Anthropology 46. New Haven.

———. 1997. Phylogenetically related cultural traditions. *Cross-Cultural Research* 31:16–26.

References

Green, R. C. 1979. Lapita. In J. D. Jennings, ed., *The Prehistory of Polynesia*, 27–60. Cambridge: Harvard University Press.
———. 1980. *Makaha Before 1880 AD* Pacific Anthropological Records 31. Honolulu: Bishop Museum.
———. 1997 [1995]. Linguistic, biological, and cultural origins of the initial inhabitants of Remote Oceania. *New Zealand Journal of Archaeology* 17:5–27.
———. 1998. From Proto-Oceanic **rumaq* to Proto-Polynesian **fale*: A significant reorganisation in Austronesian housing. *Archaeology in New Zealand* 41:253–72.
———. 2005. Sweet potato transfers in Polynesian prehistory. In C. Ballard, P. Brown, R. M. Bourke, and T. Harwood, eds., *The Sweet Potato in Oceania: A Reappraisal*, 43–62. Oceania Monograph 56. Sydney: University of Sydney.
Green, R. C., and P. V. Kirch. 1997. Lapita exchange systems and their Polynesian transformations: Seeking explanatory models. In M. I. Weisler, ed., *Prehistoric Long-distance Interaction in Oceania: An Interdisciplinary Approach*, 19–37. New Zealand Archaeological Association Monograph 21. Auckland.
Haas, J. 1982. *The Evolution of the Prehistoric State*. New York: Columbia University Press.
Haddon, A. C., and J. Hornell. 1936. *Canoes of Oceania. Volume I, The Canoes of Polynesia, Fiji, and Micronesia*. Bernice P. Bishop Museum Special Publication 27. Honolulu: Bishop Museum Press.
Handy, E. S. C. 1923. *Native Culture in the Marquesas*. Bernice P. Bishop Museum Bulletin 9. Honolulu: Bishop Museum Press.
———. 1927. *Polynesian Religion*. Bernice P. Bishop Museum Bulletin 34. Honolulu: Bishop Museum Press.
———. 1930. *History and Culture in the Society Islands*. Bernice P. Bishop Museum Bulletin 79. Honolulu: Bishop Museum Press.
———. 1940. *The Hawaiian Planter*, Vol. 1. Bernice P. Bishop Museum Bulletin 161. Honolulu: Bishop Museum Press.
Handy, E. S. C., and E. G. Handy. 1972. *Native Planters in Old Hawai'i: Their Life, Lore, and Environment*. Bernice P. Bishop Museum Bulletin 233. Honolulu: Bishop Museum Press.
Handy, E. S. C., and M. K. Pukui. 1958. *The Polynesian Family System in Ka-'u, Hawai'i*. Wellington, NZ: The Polynesian Society.
Hara, K. 2008. From Dates to Rates: Emergent Demographic Trends Through the Analysis of Radiocarbon Data from Hawai'i Island. Unpublished Senior Honors Thesis, Department of Anthropology, University of California, Berkeley.
Harrison, C. S. 1990. *Seabirds of Hawaii: Natural History and Conservation*. Ithaca: Cornell University Press.
Hartshorn, A. S., O. A. Chadwick, P. M. Vitousek, and P. V. Kirch. 2006. Prehistoric agricultural depletion of soil nutrients in Hawaii. *Proceedings of the National Academy of Sciences* 103:11092–97.
Hassan, F. 1981. *Demographic Archaeology*. New York: Academic Press.
Hatcher, J., and M. Bailey. 2001. *Modeling the Middle Ages: The History and Theory of England's Economic Development*. Oxford: Oxford University Press.

Henry, T. 1928. *Ancient Tahiti*. Bernice P. Bishop Museum Bulletin 48. Honolulu: Bishop Museum Press.

Holm, L. A. 2006. The archaeology and the 'aina of Mahamenui and Manawainui, Kahikinui, Maui Island. PhD diss., University of California, Berkeley.

Hommon, R. J. 1976. The formation of primitive states in pre-contact Hawaii. PhD diss., University of Arizona.

———. 1986. Social evolution in ancient Hawai'i. In P. V. Kirch, ed., *Island Societies: Archaeological Approaches to Evolution and Transformation*, 55–68. Cambridge: Cambridge University Press.

———. 1996. Social complex adaptive systems: Some Hawaiian examples. In J. M. Davidson, G. Irwin, B. F. Leach, A. K. Pawley, and D. Brown, eds., *Oceanic Culture History: Essays in Honour of Roger Green*, 579–90. Special Publication, New Zealand Journal of Archaeology. Dunedin, NZ.

———. 2001. The emergence of large-scale society in Hawai'i. In C. M. Stevenson, G. Lee, and F. J. Morin, eds., *Pacific 2000: Proceedings of the Fifth International Conference on Easter Island and the Pacific*, 141–49. Los Osos, CA: Bearsville Press.

———. 2008. Watershed: Testing the Limited Land Hypothesis. In T. Dye, ed., *Research Designs for Hawaiian Archaeology*, 1–92. Honolulu: Society for Hawaiian Archaeology.

———. 2009. The emergence of primary states in ancient Hawaii. Paper presented at the Theoretical Archaeology Group conference, Stanford University, Palo Alto, May 2, 2009.

Hutchinson, G. E. 1978. *An Introduction to Population Ecology*. New Haven: Yale University Press.

'Ī'ī J. P. 1959. *Fragments of Hawaiian History*. Trans. M. K. Pukui. Honolulu: Bishop Museum Press.

Johnson, A. W., and T. Earle. 2000. *The Evolution of Human Societies*, 2nd ed. Stanford: Stanford University Press.

Joppien, R., and B. Smith. 1988. *The Art of Captain Cook's Voyages*. Vols. 3 and 4: *The Voyage of the Resolution and Discovery 1776–1780*. New Haven: Yale University Press.

Kaeppler, A. 1978. *"Artificial Curiosities": An Exposition of Native Manufactures Collected on the Three Voyages of Captain James Cook, R.N.* Bernice P. Bishop Museum Special Publication 65. Honolulu: Bishop Museum Press.

———. 1985. Hawaiian art and society: Traditions and transformations. In A. Hooper and J. Huntsman, eds., *Transformations of Polynesian Culture*, 105–31. Auckland: The Polynesian Society.

———. 1993. *Hula Pahu: Hawaiian Drum Dances. Volume I, Ha'a and Hula Pahu, Sacred Movements*. Bishop Museum Bulletin in Anthropology 3. Honolulu: Bishop Museum Press.

———. 1997. Polynesia and Micronesia. In A. L. Kaeppler, C. Kaufmann, and D. Newton, *Oceanic Art*, 21–155. New York: Harry N. Abrams, Inc.

———. 1998. Hawai'i—Ritual Encounters. In B. Hauser-Schaublin and G. Kruger, eds., *James Cook: Gifts and Treasures from the South Seas*, 234–48. Munich: Prestel.

Kahn, J., and P. V. Kirch. 2004. Ethnographie préhistorique d'une « société à maisons » dans la vallée de 'Opunohu (Moʻorea, îles de la Société). *Journal de la Société des Océanistes* 119:229–56.
Kalākaua, D. 1990. *The Legends and Myths of Hawaii*. Honolulu: Mutual Publishing. [Reprint of 1888 edition published by Charles L. Webster and Co., New York]
Kamakau, S. 1961. *Ruling Chiefs of Hawaii*. Honolulu: Kamehameha Schools Press.
———. 1964. *Ka Poʻe Kahiko: The People of Old*. Trans. M. K. Pukui. Bernice P. Bishop Museum Special Publication 51. Honolulu: Bishop Museum Press.
———. 1976. *The Works of the People of Old: Na Hāna o ka Poʻe Kahiko*. Bernice P. Bishop Museum Special Publication 61. Honolulu: Bishop Museum Press.
———. 1991. *Tales and Traditions of the People of Old. Nā Moʻolelo a ka Poʻe Kahiko*. Trans. M. K. Pukui, and edited by D. B. Barrère. Honolulu: Bishop Museum Press.
Kameʻeleihiwa, L. 1992. *Native Land and Foreign Desires*. Honolulu: Bishop Museum Press.
Kamehiro, S. T. 2009. *The Arts of Kingship: Hawaiian Art and National Culture of the Kalākaua Era*. Honolulu: University of Hawaiʻi Press.
Kikuchi, W. K. 1976. Prehistoric Hawaiian fishponds. *Science* 193:295–99.
Kirch, P. V. 1980. Polynesian prehistory: Cultural adaptation in island ecosystems. *American Scientist* 68:39–48.
———. 1984. *The Evolution of the Polynesian Chiefdoms*. Cambridge: Cambridge University Press.
———. 1985. *Feathered Gods and Fishhooks: An Introduction to Hawaiian Archaeology and Prehistory*. Honolulu: University of Hawaiʻi Press.
———. 1990a. The evolution of socio-political complexity in prehistoric Hawaii: An assessment of the archaeological evidence. *Journal of World Prehistory* 4:311–45.
———. 1990b. Monumental architecture and power in Polynesian chiefdoms: A comparison of Tonga and Hawaii. *World Archaeology* 22:206–22.
———. 1994. *The Wet and the Dry: Irrigation and Agricultural Intensification in Polynesia*. Chicago: University of Chicago Press.
———. 1996. Tikopia social space revisited. In J. Davidson, G. Irwin, F. Leach, A. Pawley, and D. Brown, eds., *Oceanic Culture History: Essays in Honour of Roger Green*, 257–74. Dunedin: New Zealand Journal of Archaeology Special Publication.
———. 1997a. *The Lapita Peoples: Ancestors of the Oceanic World*. Oxford: Blackwell Publishers.
———, ed. 1997b. *Nā Mea Kahiko O Kahikinui: Studies in the Archaeology of Kahikinui, Maui*. Oceanic Archaeology Laboratory, Special Publication No. 1. Berkeley: Archaeological Research Facility, University of California.
———. 2000. *On the Road of the Winds: An Archaeological History of the Pacific Islands Before European Contact*. Berkeley: University of California Press.
———. ed. 2002. *From the "Cliffs of Keolewa" to the "Sea of Papaloa": An Archaeological Reconnaissance of Portions of the Kalaupapa National*

Historical Park, Molokaʻi, Hawaiian Islands. Oceanic Archaeology Laboratory, Special Publication No. 2. Berkeley: Archaeological Research Facility, University of California.

———. 2004. Temple sites in Kahikinui, Maui, Hawaiian Islands: Their orientations decoded. *Antiquity* 78:102–14.

———. 2005. *From Chiefdom to Archaic State: Social Evolution in Hawaii.* Grace Elizabeth Shallit Memorial Lecture Series. Provo: Department of Anthropology, Brigham Young University.

———. 2006. Agricultural intensification: A Polynesian perspective. In J. Marcus and C. Stanish, eds., *Agricultural Strategies,* 191–220. Los Angeles: Cotsen Institute of Archaeology, UCLA.

———. 2007a. Hawaii as a model system for human ecodynamics. *American Anthropologist* 109:8–26.

———. 2007b. Paleodemography in Kahikinui, Maui: An archaeological approach. In P. V. Kirch and J.-L. Rallu, eds., *The Growth and Collapse of Pacific Island Societies: Archaeological and Demographic Perspectives,* 90–107. Honolulu: University of Hawaiʻi Press.

———. 2007c. "Like shoals of fish": Archaeology and population in pre-contact Hawaiʻi. In P. V. Kirch and J.-L. Rallu, eds., *The Growth and Collapse of Pacific Island Societies: Archaeological and Demographic Perspectives,* 52–69. Honolulu: University of Hawaiʻi Press.

———. 2007d. Concluding remarks: Methods, measures, and models in Pacific paleodemography. In P. V. Kirch and J.-L. Rallu, eds., *The Growth and Collapse of Pacific Island Societies: Archaeological and Demographic Perspectives,* 326–38. Honolulu: University of Hawaiʻi Press.

———. 2010a. Controlled comparison and Polynesian cultural evolution. In J. Diamond and J. Robinson, eds., *Natural Experiments of History,* 1–52. Cambridge: Harvard University Press.

———. ed. 2010b. *Roots of Conflict: Soils, Agriculture, and Sociopolitical Complexity in Ancient Hawaiʻi.* Santa Fe: School of Advanced Research Press.

Kirch, P. V., and T. I. Babineau. 1996. *Legacy of the Landscape: An Illustrated Guide to Hawaiian Archaeological Sites.* Honolulu: University of Hawaiʻi Press.

Kirch, P. V., O. A. Chadwick, S. Tuljapurkar, T. Ladefoged, M. Graves, S. Hotchkiss, and P. Vitousek. 2007. Human ecodynamics in the Hawaiian ecosystem, 1200–200 BP. In T. A. Kohler and S. E. van der Leeuw, eds., *The Model-Based Archaeology of Socionatural Systems,* 121–39. Santa Fe: School for Advanced Research Press.

Kirch, P. V., J. Coil, A. S. Hartshorn, M. Jeraj, P. M. Vitousek, and O. A. Chadwick. 2005. Intensive dryland farming on the leeward slopes of Haleakala, Maui, Hawaiian Islands: Archaeological, archaeobotanical, and geochemical perspectives. *World Archaeology* 37:239–57.

Kirch, P. V., and R. C. Green. 1987. History, phylogeny, and evolution in Polynesia. *Current Anthropology* 28:431–43, 452–56.

———. 2001. *Hawaiki, Ancestral Polynesia: An Essay in Historical Anthropology.* Cambridge: Cambridge University Press.

Kirch, P. V., A. S. Hartshorn, O. A. Chadwick, P. M. Vitousek, D. R. Sherrod, J. Coil, L. Holm, and W. D. Sharp. 2004. Environment, agriculture, and settlement patterns in a marginal Polynesian landscape. *Proceedings of the National Academy of Sciences (USA)* 101:9936–41.

Kirch, P. V., J. Holson, and A. Baer, in press. Intensive dryland agriculture in Kaupō, Maui, Hawaiian Islands. *Asian Perspectives.*

Kirch, P. V., and M. Kelly, eds. 1975. *Prehistory and Ecology in a Windward Hawaiian Valley: Halawa Valley, Molokai.* Pacific Anthropological Records 24. Honolulu: Bishop Museum.

Kirch, P. V., and M. McCoy. 2007. Reconfiguring the Hawaiian cultural sequence: Results of re-dating the Halawa dune site (MO-A1-3), Molokaʻi Island. *Journal of the Polynesian Society* 116:385–406.

Kirch, P. V., S. O'Day, J. Coil, M. Morgenstein, K. Kawelu, and S. Millerstrom. 2004. The Kaupikiawa Rockshelter, Kalaupapa Peninsula, Molokaʻi: New investigations and reinterpretation of its significance for Hawaiian prehistory. *People and Culture in Oceania* 19:1–27.

Kirch, P. V., and J.-L. Rallu, eds. 2007. *The Growth and Collapse of Pacific Island Societies: Archaeological and Demographic Perspectives.* Honolulu: University of Hawaiʻi Press.

Kirch, P. V., and M. Sahlins. 1992. *Anahulu: The Anthropology of History in the Kingdom of Hawaii.* 2 vols. Chicago: University of Chicago Press.

Kirch, P. V., and W. D. Sharp. 2005. Coral ^{230}Th dating of the imposition of a ritual control hierarchy in precontact Hawaii. *Science* 307:102–4.

Kirchhoff, P. 1955. The principles of clanship in human society. *Davidson Anthropological Society Journal* 1:1–11.

Kolb, M. J. 1991. Social power, chiefly authority, and ceremonial architecture in an island polity, Maui, Hawaii. PhD diss., Los Angeles: University of California.

———. 1992. Diachronic design changes in *heiau* temple architecture on the island of Maui, Hawaiʻi. *Asian Perspectives* 31:9–38.

———. 1994. Monumentality and the rise of religious authority in precontact Hawaiʻi. *Current Anthropology* 35:521–48.

———. 1999. Monumental grandeur and political florescence in pre-contact Hawaiʻi: Excavations at Piʻilanihale Heiau, Maui. *Archaeology in Oceania* 34(2):73–82.

———. 2006. The origins of monumental architecture in ancient Hawaiʻi. *Current Anthropology* 47:657–65.

Kolb, M. J., and B. Dixon. 2002. Landscapes of war: Rules and conventions of conflict in ancient Hawaiʻi (and elsewhere). *American Antiquity* 67:514–34.

Kolb, M. J., and E. Radewagen. 1997. Nā heiau o Kahikinui: The temples of Kahikinui. In P. V. Kirch, ed., *Nā Mea Kahiko o Kahikinui: Studies in the Archaeology of Kahikinui, Maui,* 61–77. Oceanic Archaeology Laboratory Special Publication No. 1. Berkeley: University of California.

Kooijman, S. 1972. *Tapa in Polynesia.* Bernice P. Bishop Museum Bulletin 234. Honolulu: Bishop Museum Press.

Koskinen, A. 1960. Ariki *the First Born: An Analysis of a Polynesian Chieftain Title.* Folklore Fellows Communications No. 181. (Second printing 1972) Helsinki: Academia Scientiarum Fennica.

Krebs, H. A. 1975. The August Krogh principle: "For many problems there is an animal on which it can most conveniently be studied." *Journal of Experimental Zoology* 194:221–26.
Krogh, A. 1929. Progress of physiology. *American Journal of Physiology* 90:243–51.
Kuykendall, R. 1938. *The Hawaiian Kingdom. Volume I.* 1778–1854, *Foundation and Transformation*. Honolulu: The University Press of Hawai'i.
Ladd, E. J. 1969. 'Alealea temple site, Honaunau: Salvage report. In R. Pearson, ed., *Archaeology on the Island of Hawaii*, 95–132. Asian and Pacific Archaeology Series No. 3. Honolulu: Social Science Research Institute, University of Hawai'i.
———. 1973. Kaneaki temple site—an excavation report. In E. Ladd, ed., *Makaha Valley Historical Project: Interim Report No. 4*, 1–30. Pacific Anthropological Records 19. Honolulu: Bishop Museum.
———. 1985. *Hale-o-Keawe Archaeological Report*. Western Archaeological and Conservation Center, Publications in Anthropology No. 33. Honolulu: National Park Service.
———. 1986. *Test Excavations at Sites B-105, B-107, and B-108*. Western Archaeological and Conservation Center, Publications in Anthropology No. 34. Honolulu: National Park Service.
———. 1987. *Excavations at Site A-27*. Western Archaeological and Conservation Center, Publications in Anthropology No. 43. Honolulu: National Park Service.
Ladefoged, T. N., and M. W. Graves. 2006. The formation of Hawaiian territories. In I. Lilley, ed., *Archaeology of Oceania: Australia and the Pacific Islands*, 259–83. Oxford: Blackwell.
———. 2007. Modeling agricultural development and demography in Kohala, Hawai'i Island. In P. V. Kirch and J.-L. Rallu, eds., *The Growth and Collapse of Pacific Island Societies: Archaeological and Demographic Perspectives*, 70–89. Honolulu: University of Hawai'i Press.
———. 2008. Variable development of dryland agriculture in Hawai'i: A fine-grained chronology from the Kohala Field System, Hawai'i Island. *Current Anthropology* 49:771–802.
Ladefoged, T. N., M. W. Graves, and J. H. Coil. 2005. The introduction of sweet potato in Polynesia: Early remains in Hawai'i. *Journal of the Polynesian Society* 114:359–74.
Ladefoged, T. N., M. W. Graves, and R. P. Jennings. 1996. Dryland agricultural expansion and intensification in Kohala, Hawai'i island. *Antiquity* 70 (270):861–80.
Ladefoged, T. N., M. W. Graves, and M. D. McCoy. 2003. Archaeological evidence for agricultural development in Kohala, Island of Hawai'i. *Journal of Archaeological Science* 30:923–40.
Ladefoged, T. N., P. V. Kirch, S. M. Gon III, O. A. Chadwick, A. S. Hartshorn, and P. M. Vitousek. 2009. Opportunities and constraints for intensive agriculture in the Hawaiian archipelago prior to European contact. *Journal of Archaeological Science* 36:2374–83.
Ledyard, J. 1963. *John Ledyard's Journal of Captain Cook's Last Voyage*. J. K. Munford, ed. Corvallis, OR: Oregon State University Press.

Lee, C. T., C. O. Puleston, and S. Tuljapurkar. 2009. Population and prehistory III: Food-dependent population dynamics in variable environments. *Theoretical Population Biology* 76:179–88.
Lee, C. T., and S. Tuljapurkar. 2008. Population and prehistory I: Food-dependent population growth in constant environments. *Theoretical Population Biology* 73:473–82.
Lee, C. T., S. Tuljapurkar, and P. M. Vitousek. 2006. Risky business: Temporal and spatial variation in preindustrial dryland agriculture. *Human Ecology* 34:739–63.
Lee, R. D. 1986. Malthus and Boserup: A dynamic synthesis. In D. Coleman and R. S. Schofield, eds., *The State of Population Theory: Forward from Malthus*, 96–103. Oxford: Basil Blackwell.
Lévi-Strauss, C. 1979. Nobles sauvages. In R. Aron, ed., *Culture, Science et Développement : Contribution à une Histoire de l'Homme*, 41–55. Paris: Edouard Privat.
———. 1982. *The Way of the Masks*. Trans. Sylvia Modelski. Seattle: University of Washington Press.
Linnekin, J. 1990. *Sacred Queens and Women of Consequence: Rank, Gender, and Colonialism in the Hawaiian Islands*. Ann Arbor: University of Michigan Press.
MacArthur, R., and E. Wilson. 1967. *The Theory of Island Biogeography*. Monographs in Population Biology 1. Princeton: Princeton University Press.
Mace, R., and M. Pagel. 1994. The comparative method in anthropology. *Current Anthropology* 35:549–64.
Makemson, M. W. 1941. *The Morning Star Rises: An Account of Polynesian Astronomy*. New Haven: Yale University Press.
Malo, D. 1951. *Hawaiian Antiquities*. Bernice P. Bishop Museum Special Publication 2. Honolulu: Bishop Museum Press.
Malthus, T. R. 1798. *An Essay on the Principle of Population*. London: J. Johnson.
Mann, M. 1986. *The Sources of Social Power*. Cambridge: Cambridge University Press.
Marck, J. 1996a. The first-order anthropomorphic gods of Polynesia. *Journal of the Polynesian Society* 105:217–58.
———. 1996b. Eastern Polynesian subgrouping today. In J. Davidson, G. Irwin, F. Leach, A. Pawley, and D. Brown, eds., *Oceanic Culture History: Essays in Honour of Roger Green*, 491–511. Dunedin: New Zealand Journal of Archaeology Special Publication.
———. 1996c. Was there an early Polynesian 'Sky Father'? *Journal of Pacific History* 31:8–26.
———. 2000. *Topics in Polynesian Language and Culture History*. Pacific Linguistics. Canberra: Australian National University.
Marcus, J. 2007. Great art styles and the rise of complex societies. In J. A. Sabloff and W. L. Fash, eds., *Gordon R. Willey and American Archaeology: Contemporary Perspectives*, 72–104. Norman: University of Oklahoma Press.
Marcus, J., and G. M. Feinman. 1998. Introduction. In G. M. Feinman and J. Marcus, eds., *Archaic States*, 3–13. Santa Fe: School of American Research Press.

Marcus, J., and K. V. Flannery. 1996. *Zapotec Civilization: How Urban Society Evolved in Mexico's Oaxaca Valley*. London: Thames and Hudson.

Massal, E., and J. Barrau. 1956. *Food Plants of the South Sea Islands*. Technical Paper No. 94. Noumea: South Pacific Commission.

Matisoo-Smith, E., R. M. Roberts, G. J. Irwin, J. S. Allen, D. Penny, and D. M. Lambert. 1998. Patterns of prehistoric rat mobility in Polynesia indicated by mtDNA from the Pacific rat. *Proceedings of the National Academy of Sciences, USA* 95:15145–50.

Maunupau, T. K. 1998. *Huakai Makaikai a Kaupo, Maui: A Visit to Kaupō, Maui*. N. N. C. Losch, ed. Honolulu: Bishop Museum Press.

Mayr, E. 1997. *This is Biology: The Science of the Living World*. Cambridge: Harvard University Press.

McAllister, J. G. 1933a. *Archaeology of Oahu*. Bernice P. Bishop Museum Bulletin 104. Honolulu: Bishop Museum Press.

———. 1933b. *Archaeology of Kahoolawe*. Bernice P. Bishop Museum Bulletin 115. Honolulu: Bishop Museum Press.

McCoy, M. D. 2005. The development of the Kalaupapa field system, Moloka'i Island, Hawai'i. *Journal of the Polynesian Society* 114:339–58.

———. 2006. Landscape, social memory, and society: An ethnohistoric-archaeological study of three Hawaiian communities. PhD diss., University of California, Berkeley.

———. 2007. A revised late Holocene culture history for Moloka'i Island, Hawai'i. *Radiocarbon* 49:1273–1322.

McElroy, W. K. 2007a. The development of irrigated agriculture in Wailau Valley, Moloka'i Island, Hawai'i. PhD diss., University of Hawai'i.

———. 2007b. Wailau Archaeological Research Project 2005 and 2006 Results: Wailau and Halawa Ahupua'a, Ko'olau District, Moloka'i, Hawai'i. Xerox report. Honolulu: Department of Anthropology, University of Hawai'i, Manoa.

McFadgen, B. G., F. B. Knox, and T. R. L. Cole. 1994. Radiocarbon calibration curve variations and their implications for the interpretation of New Zealand prehistory. *Radiocarbon* 36:221–36.

McKinnon, S. 1991. *From a Shattered Sun: Hierarchy, Gender, and Alliance in the Tanimbar Islands*. Madison: University of Wisconsin Press.

———. 1995. Houses and hierarchy: The view from a South Moluccan society. In J. Carsten and S. Hugh-Jones, eds., *About the House: Lévi-Strauss and Beyond*, 170–88. Cambridge: Cambridge University Press.

McKinzie, E. K. 1983. 1986. *Hawaiian Genealogies Extracted from Hawaiian Language Newspapers*. 2 vols. Laie, Hawai'i: Institute for Polynesian Studies.

Menzies, A. 1920. *Hawaii Nei 128 Years Ago*. Honolulu: W. F. Wilson.

Meyer, M., T. N. Ladefoged, and P. M. Vitousek. 2007. Soil phosphorus and agricultural development in the leeward Kohala field system, Island of Hawai'i. *Pacific Science* 61:347–53.

Mill, J. S. 1848. *Principles of Political Economy, with Some of Their Application to Social Philosophy*. London: Routledge.

Miller, D., and C. Tilley, eds. 1984. *Ideology, Power and Prehistory*. Cambridge: Cambridge University Press.

Morgan, L. H. 1877. *Ancient Society: Or, Researches in the Lines of Human Progress from Savagery, Through Barbarism to Civilization.* New York: Henry Holt and Company.
Morrison, K. D. 1994. The intensification of production: Archaeological approaches. *Journal of Archaeological Method and Theory* 1:111–60.
Mulrooney, M. A., and T. Ladefoged. 2005. Hawaiian *heiau* and agricultural production in the Kohala dryland field system. *Journal of the Polynesian Society* 114:45–67.
Newman, T. S. n.d. [1970]. *Hawaiian Fishing and Farming on the Island of Hawaii in AD 1778.* Honolulu: Department of Land and Natural Resources, State of Hawai'i.
Obeyesekere, G. 1992. *The Apotheosis of Captain Cook: European Mythmaking in the Pacific.* Princeton: Princeton University Press.
Ohnuki-Tierney, E. 1990. *Culture Through Time: Anthropological Approaches.* Stanford: Stanford University Press.
Oliver, D. L. 1974. *Ancient Tahitian Society.* 3 vols. Honolulu: University of Hawai'i Press.
Orans, M. 1966. Surplus. *Human Organization* 25:24–32.
Ortner, S. 1984. Theory in anthropology since the sixties. *Comparative Studies in Society and History* 26:126–66.
Paglinawan, R. K., M. Eli, M. E. Kalauokalani, and J. Walker. 2006. *Lua: Art of the Hawaiian Warrior.* Honolulu: Bishop Museum Press.
Parsons, J. R. 1974. The development of a prehistoric complex society: A regional perspective from the Valley of Mexico. *Journal of Field Archaeology* 1:81–108.
Pauketat, T. R. 2001. Practice and history in archaeology. *Anthropological Theory* 1:73–98.
Pawley, A. 1966. Polynesian languages: A subgrouping based on shared innovations in morphology. *Journal of the Polynesian Society* 75:39–64.
———. 1967. The relationships of Polynesian Outlier languages. *Journal of the Polynesian Society* 76:259–96.
Pearson, H. 1957. The economy has no surplus: Critique of a theory of development. In K. Polanyi, C. Arensberg, and H. Pearson, eds., *Trade and Market in the Early Empires*, 320–41. Chicago: Henry Regnery Co.
Pearson, R. J., P. V. Kirch, and M. Pietrusewsky. 1971. An early prehistoric site at Bellows Beach, Waimanalo, Oahu, Hawaiian Islands. *Archaeology and Physical Anthropology in Oceania* 6:204–34.
Peebles, C. S., and S. M. Kus. 1977. Some archaeological correlates of ranked societies. *American Antiquity* 42:421–48.
Pianka, E. R. 1978. *Evolutionary Ecology.* New York: Harper & Row.
Polanyi, K. 1944. *The Great Transformation.* New York: Farrar and Rinehart.
Polanyi, K., C. M. Arensberg, and H. W. Pearson, eds. 1957. *Trade and Market in the Early Empires: Economies in History and Theory.* Glencoe, IL: Free Press.
Possehl, G. L. 1998. Sociocultural complexity without the state: The Indus civilization. In G. M. Feinman and J. Marcus, eds., *Archaic States*, 261–92. Santa Fe: School of American Research Press.

Puleston, C. O., and S. Tuljapurkar. 2008. Population and prehistory II: Space-limited human populations in constant environments. *Theoretical Population Biology* 74:147–60.
Pukui, M. K. 1983. *'Ōlelo No'eau: Hawaiian Proverbs and Poetical Sayings.* Bernice P. Bishop Museum Special Publication 71. Honolulu: Bishop Museum Press.
Pukui, M. K., and S. H. Elbert. 1986. *Hawaiian Dictionary.* Revised and enlarged edition. Honolulu: University of Hawai'i Press.
Rallu, J.-L. 2007. Pre- and post-contact population in island Polynesia. In P. V. Kirch and J.-L. Rallu, eds., *The Growth and Collapse of Pacific Island Societies: Archaeological and Demographic Perspectives,* 15–34. Honolulu: University of Hawai'i Press.
Ramenofsky, A. F. 1987. *Vectors of Death: The Archaeology of European Contact.* Albuquerque: University of New Mexico Press.
Rathje, W. L. 1972. Praise the gods and pass the metates: A hypothesis of the development of lowland rainforest civilizations in Mesoamerica. In M. P. Leone, ed., *Contemporary Archaeology,* 365–92. Carbondale: Southern Illinois University Press.
Redmond, E. M. 1994. *Tribal and Chiefly Warfare in South America.* Memoirs of the Museum of Anthropology, University of Michigan, No. 28. Ann Arbor.
Redmond, E. M., and C. S. Spencer. 2008. Rituals of sanctification and the development of standardized temples in Oaxaca, Mexico. *Cambridge Archaeological Journal* 18:239–66.
Remy, J. 1859. *Récits d'un Vieux Sauvage pour Servir a l'Histoire Ancienne de Hawaii.* Châlons-sur-Marne: Laurent.
Renfrew, C. 1982. Polity and power: Interaction, intensification and exploitation. In C. Renfrew and M. Wagstaff, eds., *An Island Polity: The Archaeology of Exploitation in Melos,* 264–90. Cambridge: Cambridge University Press.
———. 1986. Introduction: Peer polity interaction and socio-political change. In C. Renfrew and J. Cherry, eds., *Peer Polity Interaction and Socio-Political Change,* 1–18. Cambridge: Cambridge University Press.
Ricardo, D. 1821. *On the Principles of Political Economy and Taxation.* 3rd ed. London: John Murray.
Rick, J. W. 1987. Dates as data: An examination of the Peruvian preceramic radiocarbon record. *American Antiquity* 52:55–73.
Riley, T. 1975. Survey and excavation of the aboriginal agricultural system. In P. V. Kirch and M. Kelly, eds., *Prehistory and Human Ecology in a Windward Hawaiian Valley: Halawa Valley, Molokai,* 79–115. Pacific Anthropological Records 24. Honolulu: Bishop Museum.
Romney, A. K. 1957. The genetic model and Uto-Aztecan time perspective. *Davidson Journal of Anthropology* 3:35–41.
Rose, R. G. 1992. *Reconciling the Past: Two Basketry Kā'ai and the Legendary Līloa and Lonoikamakahiki.* Bishop Museum Bulletin in Anthropology 5. Honolulu: Bishop Museum Press.
Rosendahl, P. H. 1972. Aboriginal agriculture and domestic residence patterns in Upland Lapakahi, Island of Hawai'i. PhD diss., University of Hawai'i.

———. 1994. Aboriginal Hawaiian structural remains and settlement patterns in the Upland Agricultural Zone at Lapakahi, Island of Hawai'i. *Hawaiian Archaeology* 3:14–70.
Ruggles, C. 2007. Cosmology, calendar, and temple orientations in ancient Hawai'i. In C. Ruggles and G. Urton, eds., *Skywatching in the Ancient World: New Perspectives in Cultural Astronomy*, 287–329. Boulder: University Press of Colorado.
Sachs, I. 1966. La notion de surplus et son application aux économies primitives. *L'Homme* 6:5–18.
Sahlins, M. 1958. *Social Stratification in Polynesia*. Seattle: American Ethnological Society.
———. 1972. *Stone Age Economics*. Chicago: Aldine-Atherton.
———. 1981. *Historical Metaphors and Mythical Realities: Structure in the Early History of the Sandwich Islands Kingdom*. Ann Arbor: University of Michigan Press.
———. 1985a. *Islands of History*. Chicago: University of Chicago Press.
———. 1985b. Hierarchy and humanity in Polynesia. In A. Hooper and J. Huntsman, eds., *Transformations of Polynesian Culture*, 195–217. Auckland: The Polynesian Society.
———. 1989. Captain Cook at Hawaii. *Journal of the Polynesian Society* 98:371–423.
———. 1990. The political economy of grandeur in Hawaii from 1810 to 1830. In E. Ohnuki-Tierney, ed., *Culture Through Time*, 26–56. Stanford: Stanford University Press.
———. 1992. Historical Ethnography. In P. V. Kirch and M. Sahlins, *Anahulu: The Anthropology of History in the Kingdom of Hawai'i*, vol 2. Chicago: University of Chicago Press.
———. 1995. *How "Natives" Think: About Captain Cook, for Example*. Chicago: University of Chicago Press.
———. MS [1999]. From totemic differences to political society in Polynesia: The Hawaiians invent "The People." Unpublished paper presented at the Valerio Valeri memorial symposium, University of Chicago.
———. 2004. *Apologies to Thucydides: Understanding History as Culture and Vice Versa*. Chicago: University of Chicago Press.
Sahlins, M. D., and E. R. Service. 1960. *Evolution and Culture*. Ann Arbor: University of Michigan Press.
Sanders, W. T. 1974. Chiefdom to state: Political evolution at Kaminaljuyu, Guatemala. In C. Moore, ed., *Reconstructing Complex Societies*, 97–121. Supplement to the Bulletin of the American Schools of Oriental Research. Cambridge M.A.
Sanders, W. T., and B. J. Price. 1968. *Mesoamerica: The Evolution of a Civilization*. New York: Random House.
Sapir, E. 1916. *Time Perspective in Aboriginal American Culture: A Study in Method*. Department of Mines, Geological Survey Memoir 90. Anthropological Series No. 13. Ottawa: Government Printing Bureau.
Saxe, A. 1977. On the origin of evolutionary processes: State formation in the Sandwich Islands. In J. N. Hill, ed., *Explanation of Prehistoric Change*, 105–51. Albuquerque: University of New Mexico Press.

Schele, L., and M. E. Miller. 1986. *The Blood of Kings: Dynasty and Ritual in Maya Art*. Fort Worth: Kimbell Art Museum.
Schilt, A. R. 1980. Archaeological investigations in specified areas of the Hanalei Wildlife Refuge, Hanalei Valley, Kaua'i. Unpublished report. Honolulu: Bernice P. Bishop Museum Library.
———. 1984. *Subsistence and Conflict in Kona, Hawai'i*. Department of Anthropology Report 84-1. Honolulu: Bishop Museum.
Schmitt, R. C. 1968. *Demographic Statistics of Hawaii, 1778–1965*. Honolulu: University of Hawai'i Press.
———. 1973. *The Missionary Censuses of Hawaii*. Pacific Anthropological Records No. 20. Honolulu: Bishop Museum.
Schütz, A. J. 1994. *The Voices of Eden: A History of Hawaiian Language Studies*. Honolulu: University of Hawai'i Press.
Seaton, S. L. 1978. The early state in Hawaii. In H. J. M. Claessen and P. Skalnik, eds., *The Early State*, 269–88. The Hague: Mouton.
Service, E. 1967. *Primitive Social Organization: An Evolutionary Perspective*. New York: Random House.
———. 1975. *Origins of the State and Civilization*. New York: Norton.
Shennan, S. 2002. *Genes, Memes and Human History*. London: Thames and Hudson.
Shore, B. 1989. Mana and tapu. In A. Howard and R. Borofsky, eds., *Developments in Polynesian Ethnology*, 137–74. Honolulu: University of Hawai'i Press.
Siikala, J. 1996. The elder and the younger—foreign and autochthonous origin and hierarchy in the Cook Islands. In J. J. Fox and C. Sather, eds., *Origins, Ancestry and Alliance*, 41–54. Canberra: Department of Anthropology, Australian National University.
Snow, C. 1974. *Early Hawaiians: An Initial Study of Skeletal Remains from Mokapu, Oahu*. Lexington: University of Kentucky Press.
Soehren, L. J., and T. S. Newman. 1968. *The Archaeology of Kealakekua*. Special publication of the Departments of Anthropology, University of Hawai'i and Bishop Museum. Honolulu.
Soehren, L. J., and D. P. Tuohy. 1987. *Archaeological Excavations at Pu'uhonua o Hōnaunau National Historical Park, Hōnaunau, Kona, Hawai'i*. Anthropology Department Report 87-2. Honolulu: Bishop Museum.
Spear, R. L. 1992. Settlement and expansion in a Hawaiian valley: The archaeological record from North Halawa, O'ahu. *New Zealand Journal of Archaeology* 14:79–88.
Spencer, C. 1987. Rethinking the chiefdom. In R. Drennan and C. Uribe, eds., *Chiefdoms in the Americas*, 369–89. Boston: University Press of America.
———. 1990. On the tempo and mode of state formation: Neoevolutionism reconsidered. *Journal of Anthropological Archaeology* 9:1–30.
———. 1998. A mathematical model of primary state formation. *Cultural Dynamics* 10:5–20.
Spencer, C., and E. Redmond. 2001. Multilevel selection and political evolution in the Valley of Oaxaca, 500–100 BC. *Journal of Anthropological Archaeology* 20:195–229.
———. 2004. Primary state formation in Mesoamerica. *Annual Review of Anthropology* 33:173–99.

References

Spooner, B., ed. 1972. *Population Growth: Anthropological Implications.* Cambridge: MIT Press.
Spriggs, M. 1981. Vegetable kingdoms: Taro irrigation and Pacific prehistory. PhD diss., Australian National University, Canberra.
———. 1984. Taro irrigation techniques in the Pacific. In S. Chandra, ed., *Edible Aroids,* 123–35. Oxford: Clarendon Press.
———. 1988. The Hawaiian transformation of Ancestral Polynesian Society: Conceptualizing chiefly states. In J. Gledhill, B. Bender, and M. T. Larsen, eds., *State and Society: The Emergence and Development of Social Hierarchy and Political Centralization,* 57–72. London: Routledge.
Spriggs, M., and A. Anderson. 1993. Late colonization of East Polynesia. *Antiquity* 67:200–27.
Spriggs, M., and P. L. Tanaka. 1988. *Nā Mea 'Imi I Ka Wā Kahiko: An Annotated Bibliography of Hawaiian Archaeology.* Asian and Pacific Archaeology Series No. 11. Honolulu: Social Science Research Institute, University of Hawai'i.
Stanish, C. 2001. The origin of state societies in South America. *Annual Review of Anthropology* 30:41–64.
Stannard, D. 1989. *Before the Horror: The Population of Hawai'i on the Eve of Western Contact.* Honolulu: Social Science Research Institute, University of Hawai'i.
Stauffer, R. H. 2004. *Kahana: How the Land Was Lost.* Honolulu: University of Hawai'i Press.
Steadman, D. W. 1997. Extinctions of Polynesian birds: Reciprocal impacts of birds and people. In P. V. Kirch and T. L. Hunt, eds., *Historical Ecology in the Pacific Islands: Prehistoric Environmental and Landscape Change,* 51–79. New Haven: Yale University Press.
Sterling, E. P. 1998. *Sites of Maui.* Honolulu: Bishop Museum Press.
Stokes, J. F. G. 1932. *The Hawaiian King.* Hawaiian Historical Society Papers No. 19. Honolulu: Hawaiian Historical Society.
———. 1933. New bases for Hawaiian chronology. *Hawaiian Historical Society 41st Annual Report,* 23–65. Honolulu: Hawaiian Historical Society.
———. (Dye, T., ed.) 1991. *Heiau of the Island of Hawai'i: A Historic Survey of Native Hawaiian Temple Sites.* Bishop Museum Bulletin in Anthropology 2. Honolulu: Bishop Museum Press.
———. MS [1909]. *Heiau of Molokai.* Unpublished manuscript in Library, Bernice P. Bishop Museum. Honolulu.
Summers, C. C. 1964. *Hawaiian Archaeology: Hawaiian Fishponds.* Bernice P. Bishop Museum Special Publication 52. Honolulu: Bishop Museum Press.
———. 1971. *Molokai: A Site Survey.* Pacific Anthropological Records 14. Honolulu: Bishop Museum.
Sutton, D. G. 1990. Organization and ontology: The origins of the northern Maori chiefdom, New Zealand. *Man* (n. s.) 25:667–92.
Tatar, E. 1993. Hula Pahu: *Hawaiian Drum Dances. Volume II, The* Pahu, *Sounds of Power.* Bishop Museum Bulletin in Anthropology 3. Honolulu: Bishop Museum Press.
Terrell, J. 1986. *Prehistory in the Pacific Islands.* Cambridge: Cambridge University Press.

Thomas, N. 1995. *Oceanic Art*. London: Thames and Hudson.
Titcomb, M. 1969. *Dog and Man in the Ancient Pacific*. Bernice P. Bishop Museum Special Publication 59. Honolulu: Bishop Museum Press.
Trigger, B. G. 2003. *Understanding Early Civilizations: A Comparative Study*. Cambridge: Cambridge University Press.
Tuggle, H. D., and P. B. Griffin, eds. 1973. *Lapakahi, Hawai'i: Archaeological Studies*. Asian and Pacific Archaeology Series 5. Honolulu: Social Science Research Institute, University of Hawai'i.
Tuggle, H. D., and M. J. Spriggs. 2000. The age of the Bellows Dune Site O18, O'ahu, Hawai'i and the antiquity of Hawaiian colonization. *Asian Perspectives* 39:165–88.
Tuggle, H. D., and M. Tomonari-Tuggle. 1980. Prehistoric agriculture in Kohala, Hawai'i. *Journal of Field Archaeology* 7:297–312.
Upham, S. 1987. A theoretical consideration of middle range societies. In R. D. Drennan and C. A. Uribe, eds., *Chiefdoms in the Americas*, 345–68. Lanham, MD: University Press of America.
Valeri, V. 1972. Le fonctionnement du système des rangs a Hawaii. *L'Homme* 12:29–66.
———. 1985a. *Kingship and Sacrifice: Ritual and Society in Ancient Hawaii*. Chicago: University of Chicago Press.
———. 1985b. The conqueror becomes king: A political analysis of the Hawaiian legend of 'Umi. In A. Hooper and J. Huntsman, eds., *Transformations of Polynesian Culture*, 79–104. Auckland: The Polynesian Society.
———. 1990. Diarchy and history in Hawaii and Tonga. In J. Siikala, ed., *Culture and History in the Pacific*, 45–79. Helsinki: The Finnish Anthropological Society.
van Bakel, M. 1991. The political economy of an early state: Hawaii and Samoa compared. In H. J. M. Claessen and P. van de Velde, eds., *Early State Economics*, 265–90. New Brunswick: Transaction Publishers.
———. 1996. Ideological perspectives on the development of kingship in the early states of Hawaii. In H. J. M. Claessen and J. G. Oosten, eds., *Ideology and the Formation of Early States*, 321–38. Leiden: E. J. Brill.
Vansina, J. 1985. *Oral Tradition as History*. Madison: University of Wisconsin Press.
Vitousek, P. 2004. *Nutrient Cycling and Limitation: Hawai'i as a Model System*. Princeton: Princeton University Press.
Vitousek, P. M., O. A. Chadwick, P. A. Matson, S. Allison, L. A. Derry, L. Kettley, A. Luers, E. Mecking, V. Monastra, and S. Porder. 2003. Erosion and the rejuvenation of weathering-derived nutrient supply in an old tropical landscape. *Ecosystems* 6:762–72.
Vitousek, P., T. Ladefoged, A. Hartshorn, P. V. Kirch, M. Graves, S. Hotchkiss, S. Tuljapurkar, and O. Chadwick. 2004. Soils, agriculture, and society in precontact Hawai'i. *Science* 304:1665–69.
Vogt, E. Z. 1964. The genetic model and Maya cultural development. In E. Z. Vogt and A. Ruz L., eds., *Desarrollo Cultural de los Mayas*, 9–48. Mexico, D. F.: Universidad Nacional Autónoma de México.

———. 1994. On the application of the phylogenetic model to the Maya. In R. J. DeMallie and A. Ortiz, eds., *North American Indian Anthropology: Essays on Society and Culture*, 377–414. Norman: University of Oklahoma Press.
Walker, W. M. MS [1930]. *Archaeology of Maui*. Unpublished manuscript. Honolulu: Bernice P. Bishop Museum Library.
Waterson, R. 1990. *The Living House: An Anthropology of Architecture in South-East Asia*. Singapore: Oxford University Press.
Webster, D. 1975. Warfare and the evolution of the state: A reconsideration. *American Antiquity* 40:464–70.
Weisler, M. I. 1998. Hard evidence for prehistoric interaction in Polynesia. *Current Anthropology* 39:521–32.
Weisler, M. I., and P. V. Kirch. 1985. The structure of settlement space in a Polynesian chiefdom: Kawela, Moloka'i, Hawaiian Islands. *New Zealand Journal of Archaeology* 7:129–58.
White, L. 1949. *The Science of Culture*. New York: Farrar, Straus and Giroux.
Williams, S. 1992. Early inland settlement expansion and the effect of geomorphological change on the archaeological record in Kane'ohe, O'ahu. *New Zealand Journal of Archaeology* 14:67–78.
Wittfogel, K. A. 1957. *Oriental Despotism*. New Haven: Yale University Press.
Wood, J. W. 1998. A theory of preindustrial population dynamics: Demography, economy, and well-being in Malthusian systems. *Current Anthropology* 39:99–135.
Wright, H. T. 1977. Recent research on the origin of the state. *Annual Review of Anthropology* 6:379–97.
Wright, H. T., and G. A. Johnson. 1975. Population, exchange, and early state formation in southwestern Iran. *American Anthropologist* 77:267–89.
Yen, D. E. 1971. The development of agriculture in Oceania. In R. C. Green and M. Kelly, eds., *Studies in Oceanic Culture History*, vol. 2, 1–12. Pacific Anthropological Records 12. Honolulu: Bishop Museum.
———. 1973. Agriculture in Anutan subsistence. In D. E. Yen and J. Gordon, eds., *Anuta: A Polynesian Outlier in the Solomon Islands*, 112–49. Pacific Anthropological Records 21. Honolulu: Bishop Museum.
Yen, D. E., P. V. Kirch, P. Rosendahl, and T. Riley. 1972. Prehistoric agriculture in the upper Makaha Valley, Oahu. In E. Ladd and D. E. Yen, eds., *Makaha Valley Historical Project: Interim Report No. 3*, 59–94. Pacific Anthropological Records 18. Honolulu: Bishop Museum.
Yoffee, N. 2005. *Myths of the Archaic State: Evolution of the Earliest Cities, States, and Civilizations*. Cambridge: Cambridge University Press.

Index

Special abbreviations following page numbers indicate the following: (f) figure, (t) table, (n) notes, and the note number.

agency, 8, 10, 78, 121–123, 178
aggression, see warfare
agriculture, see agroecosystems
agroecosystems
  distribution of, 141, 142t
  Hawaiian, 51–55; 140–143
  intensification of, 212–217
  soils and, 141, 142t, 149–150, 152–153
  yields of, 213–215
  see also dryland agriculture, intensification, irrigation
Ahu-a-'Umi, 93f, 98
ahupua'a
  etymology of, 24
  origin of, 90, 91, 210
  organization of, 47–48, 67–68, 103, 185–186
  size of, 47
  temporal segmentation of, 147–148
Akahiakuleana, 94–95, 204, 228n16
Alapa'inui, 83t, 104, 106–108, 111, 115, 170, 206
'Āle'ale'a Heiau, 168–170
ali'i
  agency and, 78
  categories of, 36t, 48
  class of, 26, 34
  demographic expansion of, 122
  elite art and, 41–47

  female, 65
  genealogies of, 79–80
  peripatetic movements of, 50, 75
  royal courts of, 39–40
ali'i nui, 48–49
Allen, Jane, 3, 143–144
alliance, 204–206; see also marriage
Anahulu Valley, O'ahu Island, 48, 67–68, 89f, 137, 145, 224n7, 225n18, 227n34
ancestors, 21–22
Ancestral Polynesia, 9, 15
  cultural differentiation in, 16
  heterarchy in, 18
  society, 16–24
  rank in, 19–21
  ritual in, 22–24
  see also Proto Polynesian
aquaculture, see fishponds
archaic states, 1, 2, 4–6, 9, 15, 74
  administrative hierarchies in, 47
  characteristics of, 6
  emergence of, 174–176, 210–221
  monumentality and, 27
  population sizes of, 6
  religion and, 55–56
  territorial scale of, 32–33, 104, 122–123
  war and, 69
art, elite, 41–46

267

ascent groups, 33, 73, 223n6
  and land, 12, 66
  in Ancestral Polynesia, 17–19
  transformation of, 24
'aumakua, 56–57
Auwahi, Maui Island, 172
'awa, 62, 96, 237n21

barkcloth, 45–46, 53, 63, 65, 68, 73
Beckwith, Martha, 81, 114, 227n2
birds, use of feathers, 43–44
Bishop Museum, 43, 81
Boserup, Esther, 141, 191, 193, 195–196
breadfruit, 87, 206
Brookfield, Harold, 196
Buck, Peter H. (Te Rangi Hiroa), 42, 44, 70, 84

calendar
  Ancestral Polynesian, 23
  Hawaiian, 60–61
canoes, 46
  for war, 70, 106, 120, 121, 227n37
capes, feathered, 43f, 47; see also cloaks, featherwork
Carneiro, Robert, 7, 190, 219
causation, 11, 178–179, 190, 218
chiefdoms, 2, 4, 7, 9, 187
  territorial size of, 32
  war and, 69
chiefship, in Ancestral Polynesia, 19–20
circumscription, theory of, 7, 190, 218
classes,
  endogamous, x, 204
  formation of, 224n4
  stratification of, 33–35, 204
  see also stratification
cloaks, feathered, 42–45, 47; see also featherwork
colonization, of Hawai'i, 126–127
conical clan, ix, 33
conquest, territorial, 121, 186–187, 189, 208–210, 211, 216–217, 219–220; see also warfare
controlled comparison, 8, 11, 29
Cook, Captain James, 30, 42, 46, 62, 75, 109, 116–117, 118f, 127, 129, 176, 226n23
Cordy, Ross, 81–82, 84, 131–132
court, royal, 39–40, 50, 79; see also royal centers
craft specialization, 42–47, 169; see also barkcloth, featherwork

deity, see gods
demography, Hawaiian, 128–140, 192–193; see also population

descent groups, see ascent groups
direct historical approach, x
divine kingship, ix, 5, 21, 38, 74
  emergence of, 209, 210, 211
  Hawaiian, 37, 39–41, 180, 200
  in Tonga, 28
  state cults and, 60
dogs, 51, 62, 225n17
domestic mode of production, 182–183, 196
drought, 54, 199–200, 212
dryland agriculture, 51–55, 61, 98, 100, 102, 140, 145–154, 188, 199–200, 206–208, 212–214; see also field systems, sweet potato
Dye, Thomas, 133–135, 231n8

Earle, Timothy, 3, 46, 72, 187–190, 235n11–12, 236n13
Egypt, 1, 37, 74
endogamy, royal, 37, 121, 205–206; see also pi'o
expansion, of primary states, 218–219

famine, 54, 199, 212
feathers
  iconography of, 44–45, 64
  supply of, 220–221, 237n22
  as tribute, 46–47, 63, 73
featherwork, 41–45, 189, 220; see also cloaks
Feinman, Gary, 5–6, 32, 74
field systems, dryland, 51–55, 61, 140–141, 142t, 145–154, 212–214
fishponds, 54, 55t, 56, 71, 113, 137, 140, 143, 154–155, 206, 210, 211, 216
Flannery, Kent, 8, 14, 156, 166, 178, 227n39
Fornander, Abraham, 80–81, 99, 105, 114, 116
fortifications, 70, 89, 100–101; see also Ka'uiki
Friedman, Jonathan, 193, 197

genealogies, 35, 57, 72–73, 79–82, 204
  dating of, 82, 127
god-kings, ix, 40–41, 45, 176, 217–218; see also divine kingship
gods
  in Ancestral Polynesia, 21–22
  Hawaiian, 56
  see also 'aumakua, Kanaloa, Kāne, Kū, Lono
Goldman, Irving, 8, 27, 179–181, 203–204
Goodenough, Ward, 18

Index

Haas, Jonathan, 6, 7
Haka, 83t, 88–90
Hākau, 83t, 92, 95–97, 208, 228n19
Hālawa Valley, Moloka'i Island, 60, 67, 137, 144–145, 227n36
Hale o Keawe, 156, 168f, 168–169
Hale o Lono, 50, 58–59, 60, 63–64; see also temples
Hāmākua District, Hawai'i Island, 94, 96, 98
Hāna District, Maui Island, 99f, 100–101, 108–109, 117, 146, 164, 176, 230n39
Handy, Edward S. C., 31, 38, 51, 61
Hawai'i
 administrative hierarchy in, 47–49
 agricultural systems of, 51–55
 aquaculture in, 54
 archaeological record of, 125–126
 art in, 41–46
 contact-era sources for, 30–31
 cultural sequence for, 126–128
 demographic trends in, 128–131, 138–140
 divine kingship in, 38–41
 economic system, 46–47, 51–55
 initial settlement of, 126–127
 land hierarchy in, 48–51
 lunar calendar of, 60–61
 population at contact, 32–33, 129–130
 population density, 137–138
 population dynamics, 131–136
 settlement pattern, 50–51
 size of polities, 31–33
 social stratification in, 33–35
 warfare in, 69–72, 208–211
Hawai'i Biocomplexity Project, xi, 9, 146, 149, 152, 191, 199
Hawai'i Island, 32, 33t, 44, 50, 55t, 60, 81, 85, 88, 92–98, 93f, 103–109, 167–170, 210–217
heiau, see temples
helmets, feathered, 44, 47, 94
heterarchy, 18, 202
historical anthropology, 13
Hommon, Robert, 3, 81, 131, 132f, 184–187, 212, 221, 235n7–9
homology, 11, 15
Hōnaunau, Hawai'i Island, 50, 156, 168–170
Honua'ula Heiau, 97, 167
ho'okupu, see tribute
Ho'olaemakua, 100–101
houses
 eating, 39, 96
 elite, 171–173

 of the king, 50, 113
 see also royal centers
house society, in Ancestral Polynesia, 17–19, 201–202
hula, 225n13

ideology
 and power, 189
 and state emergence, 220
'Ī'ī, John Papa, 30, 40, 50, 61, 64, 66, 69
'ili, 48, 49; see also *ahupua'a*
images
 feathered, 44–45, 62
 Kona style, 211
 of Kū, 44, 64, 94
 see also Kūkā'ilimoku
incest, royal, 37, 205–206
inland expansion, 131, 187; see also limited land hypothesis
intensification
 cropping cycle, 141, 145–154, 212–213
 of dryland field systems, 212–217
 landesque capital, 53, 140, 143–145
 as power strategy, 206–207
 production function and, 193–201
 and state emergence, 219–220
 see also irrigation, field systems
irrigation, 7, 51, 52f, 55t, 56, 71, 91, 102, 122, 137, 140, 143–145, 164, 174, 181, 188, 200, 210, 212–217

Kaeppler, Adrienne, 44–45
Kahāhana, 117–118
Kahekili, 71, 74, 83t, 109, 111–112, 114–115, 117–121, 122, 176, 210, 230n39
Kahiki, 61, 82, 85–87, 207, 226n23, 227n3; see also voyaging
Kahikinui District, Maui, 32, 52, 86, 130, 136, 137, 139, 146, 152–153, 158–164, 172, 174, 208, 225n20
kāhili, 44, 47, 225n12; see also featherwork
Kaho'olawe Island, 86, 87, 92, 109
kahuna, 26, 49–50, 57–58; see also priests
kahuna nui, 57
Kaka'alaneo, 91
Kākuhihewa, 113
kālaimoku, 50, 225n15
Kalākaua, King David, 81
Kalanikūpule, 83t, 119, 121
Kalani'ōpu'u, 74, 83t, 104, 107–109, 112, 117–118, 170, 176, 229n30
Kalaunuiohua, 88, 91, 228n11, 228n13

Kalaupapa Peninsula, Moloka'i Island, 53, 112, 140, 153, 174, 224n7
Kaleioku, 96–98, 228n18
Kalola, 108, 110, 119, 206, 229n30
kama'āina, 68
Kamakau, Kēlou, 30–31, 62
Kamakau, Samuel M., 30–31, 34, 37, 61, 63, 64, 71, 79–80, 90, 107, 139, 155, 210, 228n14
Kamalālāwalu, 83t, 105, 109–110, 164, 229n26, 229n31, 230n33
Kame'eleihiwa, Lilikalā, 31, 39
Kamehameha I, x, 30, 39, 48, 50, 54, 58, 59, 69, 71, 75, 83t, 104, 112, 114, 118–121, 122, 170, 204, 210, 224n8
Kamehamehanui, 83t, 107, 108, 111, 206
Kanaloa, 56, 207
Kāne, 41, 56, 207, 211, 225n19, 237n23
Kāne'aki Heiau, 59f, 157
Kāne'ohe, O'ahu Island, 143, 226n29
kapa, see barkcloth
kapu, 30, 36t, 38–39, 69, 175–176
kapu moe, 40–41, 224n9, 224n10
Kapukapuākea, 89f, 90, 91
Ka'ū District, Hawai'i Island, 52, 108, 118, 119, 120, 146, 151
Kaua'i Island, 32, 33t, 52f, 53, 54, 55t, 85–86, 91, 116, 122, 135, 171, 216, 232n14
Ka'uiki, Maui Island, 70, 99f, 100–101, 108, 230n39
Kaumuali'i, 116
Kaupō District, Maui Island, 52, 106, 109, 111, 117, 137, 146, 152, 163f, 226n24, 231n11
kauwā, 34, 69, 224n6
kava, 22; see also 'awa
Kawela, Moloka'i Island, 172–173
Kealakekua Bay, Hawai'i Island, 62, 129, 150, 168
Kekaulike, 83t, 106, 110–111, 152, 164, 206
Keōpūolani, 119, 204, 229n30
Keōua, 58, 71, 107–108, 119–120, 225n21
Kepelino, 31, 34, 39, 40, 50
Kiha-a-Pi'ilani, 83t, 92, 100–102, 122, 164, 199, 200, 205–208
Kila, 86, 87, 227n4
kingship, and gods, 5; see also divine kingship
kinship
  in chiefdoms, 33
  Hawaiian, 12, 184
  see also marriage
Kīwala'ō, 71, 83t, 117, 119, 206, 210, 224n10, 229n30

kō'ele fields, 67, 102–103; see also tribute
Kohala District, Hawai'i, 32, 52, 86, 105, 106, 109–110, 122, 130, 137, 146, 196
Kohala field system, 137, 146–150
Kolb, Michael, 69, 158, 164, 165, 170–171, 233n25–27, 234n33
Komori, Eric, 133–135
Kona District, Hawai'i Island, 52, 150
Kona field system, 150–151
konohiki, 35, 49, 50, 63, 67–68, 73
Kū
  cult of, 30, 41, 50, 57, 64–65, 74, 86, 97, 189, 207–208, 210–211, 217, 220; functions of, 56, 233n23
  images of, 44
  temples of, 93
  see also sacrifice, human
Kūali'i, 83t, 112, 113–115, 171
Kūkā'ilimoku, 59, 62, 93–96, 118–119, 121, 207
Kūkaniloko, 89, 91, 113, 171
Kūmahana, 117
Kumuhonua, 83t, 88

La'amaikahiki, 86, 87, 227n4
labor
  agricultural, 53, 67, 141–142, 154, 193–198, 213–215, 214f, 215f
  female, 53, 139
Lāna'i Island, 32, 91, 92, 99, 109, 230n39
land tenure, 24, 34, 66–68, 90, 92, 103, 180, 201; see also konohiki, Mahele
Lanikāula, 110
Lapakahi, Hawai'i Island, 146–148
Lapita Cultural Complex, 15
lei niho palaoa, 45, 62, 94
Liholiho (Kamehameha II), 30, 39, 40
Lili'uokalani, x
Līloa, 83t, 92–96, 167, 204, 206, 207
limited land hypothesis, 185–187
lineage, see ascent groups
Lo'alo'a Heiau, 99f, 106, 111, 152, 158, 163f, 164, 171, 233n21, 233n25
Lono, 41, 46, 50, 56, 57, 60, 62, 65, 66, 74, 97, 189, 207–208, 210–211, 217, 220
  and Makahiki, 61–66
Lono-a-Pi'ilani, 92, 100–101
Lonoikamakahiki, 83t, 105, 111, 228n17, 229n32
luakini, 41, 58–59, 60, 64–65, 74, 86, 91, 93, 97, 106, 157, 170, 207, 211, 225n19; see also temples
Luluku, O'ahu Island, 143–144

Index

Mahele, 31, 35, 66–68
Mahi line of chiefs, 104, 111
Māʻilikūkahi, 83t, 89–91, 92, 112, 122, 174, 207, 210, 215, 228n9
makaʻāinana, 24, 26, 34, 39, 72, 175, 185, 202, 216
   labor obligations, 67–68
   land rights of, 66–68
   origins of, 204
   rituals of, 56–57
Makaha Valley, Oʻahu Island, 143, 157
Makahiki, 23, 46, 56, 60–65, 67, 70, 97, 180, 197, 202–203, 208, 211, 216, 226n23, 226n29, 226n30, 228n20; see also surplus, tribute
Malo, David, 30–31, 34, 35, 39, 49, 61, 64, 70, 73, 80
Malthus, Thomas, 191, 193, 195–196
mana
   in Ancestral Polynesia, 21
   in Hawaiʻi, 38, 41
   and status rivalry, 203
Manokalanipō, 91
Marcus, Joyce, 5, 8, 14, 74, 227n39
marine resources, 54, 154–155; see also fishponds
marriage, royal, 35, 55, 98, 204–206; see also piʻo
martial arts, 70
materialization, 189–190, 220
Maui Island, 32, 33t, 54, 55t, 69, 88, 91, 99f, 99–102, 109–112, 122, 151–153, 210–217
Maunawili Valley, Oʻahu Island, 143–144
Māweke, 83t, 84, 88, 89, 203
Mayr, Ernst, 178
McCoy, Mark, 153
McElroy, Windy, 145
Menzies, Archibald, 53
Mesoamerica, 14, 78–79, 166, 219, 220
Mesopotamia, 1, 166, 217
model systems, 4, 8–11, 217–218
mōʻī, 48, 225n14
Moʻikeha, 85–86, 87, 206, 227n4
Molokaʻi Island, 32, 53, 54, 55t, 60, 67, 80, 92, 107, 112, 114, 115, 120, 135, 144–145, 216
monumentality, 27, 74, 126, 156, 175, 190; see also temples
Moʻokini Heiau, 86, 207
moʻolelo, see oral traditions
Muliʻelealiʻi, 83t, 84–85, 229n22

Nānāʻulu, 84, 91, 92, 113, 227n3, 227n7, 229n22
Nā Wai Ehā, 99f, 100

nīʻaupiʻo, 37, 40; see also endogamy, incest, piʻo
Niʻihau Island, 32

Oʻahu Island, 32, 33t, 49, 53, 54, 55t, 68, 69, 81, 85, 88–91, 89f, 107, 112–115, 118, 122, 171, 210, 215, 216
ʻOlopana, 85, 206, 227n4
oral traditions, 3, 9, 10, 76, 77–82, 123, 221

Pāʻao, 31, 86–87, 202, 207, 227n5
pahu drums, 86–87, 95, 207
Pakaʻalana Heiau, 93, 95, 167
palaces, 6, 156, 166; see also royal centers
peer-polity interaction, 7, 219
Peleiʻōhōlani, 83t, 107, 115–116, 117, 230n38
phylogenetic model, 10, 13–16, 29, 223n2
pigs, 51, 63, 68, 225n18, 237n22
Pihana Heiau, 164–165, 171
Piʻikea, 98–99, 100, 205
Piʻilani, 83t, 92, 98–100, 122, 164
Piʻilanihale Heiau, 99f, 164–165, 166f, 170, 233n21, 233n26, 233n27
Pilikaʻaiea, 83t, 86, 91, 92, 207
piʻo, 36t, 37, 92, 93, 95, 104, 108, 110, 111, 119, 176, 205–206, 229n30; see also incest, royal
Pleiades, 23, 56, 61, 159–160, 202, 208, 226n22
Pōhaku o Kāne, 58
political economy, 46–47, 182–184, 189, 197–199; see also wealth finance
political society, 184
Polynesia
   cultural evolution in, 13–16
   as cultural region, 11
pondfields, 51, 140, 143–145, 167, 210; see also irrigation
Pōpōiwi Heiau, 170–171, 234n33
population
   of chiefdoms, 6
   growth rates, 130, 174
   Hawaiian, 32–33, 128–131, 188–189, 192–193
   irrigation and, 145
   post-contact decline in, 129–130
   pressure, 7, 139, 188–189, 191
   ratio to prime agricultural land, 138t
   size at contact, 129;
Possehl, Gregory, 5
power
   strategies, 203–210
   theories of, 188–190, 201
practice theory, 8, 178, 189

priests
  in Ancestral Polynesia, 20
  Hawaiian, 43, 49, 57–58, 86
  see also *kahuna*
primary states, formation of, 6–8, 72, 218–220
prime movers, 7, 11, 218
Primordial Pair, 21–22
production function model, 193–201, 216
Proto Polynesian
  dialect chain, 16
  language, 15
  vocabulary, 17
Pukui, Mary Kawena, 31, 50, 56, 80
pūlo'ulo'u, 40–41; see also *kapu*
pu'uhonua, 167, 168
Pu'ukoholā Heiau, 58–59, 64, 119–120, 120f, 236n20

r/K selection theory, 132, 231n5, 231n6
rank
  in Ancestral Polynesia, 19–21
  of Hawaiian chiefs, 36t
ranked societies, 4–5
rats, Pacific (*Rattus exulans*), 15, 126
redistribution, 46, 181–182
religion, 207–208; see also temples
Renfrew, Colin, 33, 104, 109, 193, 219
ritual spaces, in Ancestral Polynesia, 22–23
Rosendahl, Paul, 147, 148
royal centers, 165, 166–171, 176

sacrifice
  human, 30, 34, 41, 55, 56, 64–65, 71, 74, 86, 91, 97, 120, 121, 207–208, 227n38
  of pigs, 51, 64–65, 176
Sahlins, Marshall, 8, 11–13, 27, 31, 118, 153–154, 176, 177, 181–184, 197, 217, 218, 234n2–4, 235n5
Sapir, Edward, x, 13
Schilt, Arline, 150–151, 212–213
Service, Elman, 4, 7, 69
settlement pattern, Hawaiian, 50–51
sharks, 57
  chiefs as, 41, 50, 75
social classes, in ancient Hawai'i, 34–35
Society Islands, 27, 42, 85, 86, 179, 230n1; see also Kahiki
sociopolitical structure, Hawaiian, 13
soils

and agriculture, 141, 146, 149–150, 212
nutrient depletion in, 149–150, 152–153, 199
sorcery, 57; see also *kahuna*
Spencer, Charles S., 8, 219
sports, of chiefs, 40, 94
Spriggs, Matthew, 3, 237n24
Stannard, David, 129
staple finance, 46–47, 51, 63, 219
states, primary, 2, 4; secondary, 2, 4
status rivalry, 121, 180–181, 203–204
stratification, social, 34–35, 72, 181; see also classes
sugarcane, 140, 147
surplus, 65, 68, 144, 181–182, 188, 193–201, 216, 220
sweet potato (*Ipomoea batatas*), 51, 52, 56, 68, 97, 100, 102, 140, 147, 148, 152, 186, 226n24, 235n10

Tahiti, 27, 85, 179, 181; see also Society Islands
tapu, 21; see also *kapu*
taro (*Colocasia esculenta*), 51, 68, 140, 213; see also irrigation
temples
  archaeological investigation of, 157
  coral dating of, 162–164
  distribution of, 60, 159–160
  in Eastern Polynesia, 23
  fishing, 58
  Hawaiian, 57, 58–60, 74, 97, 102–103, 156–157, 175
  ideology and, 190
  Maui system of, 157–166, 208, 220
  radiocarbon dating of, 160–162, 161f, 208
  size range of, 158, 159f
  war, 58, 61, 64–65
  see also Hale o Lono, *luakini*
Tonga, 27–28, 179, 181, 204
tribute, 33, 35, 46, 61–63, 73–74, 90, 92, 102, 180, 197, 225n18; see also Makahiki, surplus
Tuljapurkar, Shripad, 191, 194

'Umi a Līloa, 83t, 92, 94–98, 100–101, 102, 122, 200, 205, 206, 207
urbanism, lack of, 75, 167
usurpation, 48, 121, 204

Valeri, Valerio, 31, 41, 44–45, 58, 59, 61
Vancouver, Captain George, 120

Index

voyaging
  Polynesian, 16
  period, 81, 84–88
Waikīkī, 84, 89f, 90, 110, 118, 121, 171
Waikolu Valley, Moloka'i Island, 145, 236n15
Wailau Valley, Moloka'i Island, 145, 174
Waimānalo, O'ahu Island, 126
Waimea field system, 151
Waipi'o Valley, Hawai'i Island, 50, 85, 92–93, 93f, 94f, 103, 117, 122, 156, 167, 206, 207, 216
warfare, 7, 45, 69–72, 100–101, 105, 108–111, 187, 189, 198, 199, 208–210, 219–220
war god, see Kū
wealth finance, 46–47, 51, 53, 63, 73, 219; see also staple finance
weapons, 70
Wood, J. W., 191, 193–194
Wittfogel, Karl, 7
writing systems, 75
yams (*Dioscorea*), 140

Composition: Michael Bass Associates
Text: 10/13 Sabon
Display: Sabon

www.ingramcontent.com/pod-product-compliance
Lightning Source LLC
Chambersburg PA
CBHW030530230426
43665CB00010B/825